gratefulness

"We look for happiness in all the wrong places. Susan Muto shows that it's to be found in a grateful heart. Gratitude is the antidote to negativity. It's the key to understanding reality—the only key that fits. Thanks to Susan Muto for giving us this very simple, very practical, very needed book."

**Mike Aquilina**
Author of *A History of the Church in 100 Objects*

"Susan Muto's book gently offers insights and practical guidance on living a grateful life through the mountain tops, valleys, and flatlands of life's journey, along with distinctive counsel from 'a great cloud of witnesses' spanning the ages of Christian history. Come and read and join a company of grateful souls."

**Rebecca S. Letterman**
Associate Professor of Spiritual Formation
Northeastern Seminary

"Susan Muto's reflections on the challenges of the Christian life together with insights gleaned from the saints help the reader understand the practical aspects of a life of holiness. *Gratefulness* is a blessing for all of us who seek to follow Christ in the midst of our everyday lives."

**Rev. Gregory Jensen**
Chaplain at University of Wisconsin–Madison

"In this reflective work on gratitude, renowned spiritual author Susan Muto offers God's people a critical word for today. She provides a vibrant explication on fulfilling the apostolic command to 'give thanks in all circumstances.' Even as much of the world sinks into the darkness of depreciation and offense, Muto shines the joyful light of Christ upon the path of those yearning for something more than seeing only what is wrong with life."

**Stephen L. Martyn**
Asbury Theological Seminary

# gratefulness

## The Habit of a Grace-Filled Life

Susan Muto

AVE MARIA PRESS   AVE   Notre Dame, Indiana

_____

© 2018 by Susan Muto

Founded in 1865, Ave Maria Press is a ministry of the United States Province of Holy Cross.

www.avemariapress.com

Paperback: ISBN-13 978-1-59471-785-7

E-book: ISBN-13 978-1-59471-786-4

Cover image © Adobe Stock.

Cover and text design by Brianna Dombo.

Printed and bound in the United States of America.

*Library of Congress Cataloging-in-Publication Data*
Names: Muto, Susan, 1942- author.
Title: Gratefulness : the habit of a grace-filled life / Susan Muto.
Description: Notre Dame, Indiana : Ave Maria Press, [2018] | Includes bibliographical references.
Identifiers: LCCN 2017043758 (print) | LCCN 2017050878 (ebook) | ISBN 9781594717864 (ebook) | ISBN 9781594717857 (pbk.)
Subjects: LCSH: Gratitude--Religious aspects--Christianity. | Spiritual life--Catholic Church. | Catholic Church--Doctrines.
Classification: LCC BV4647.G8 (ebook) | LCC BV4647.G8 M88 2018 (print) | DDC 241/.4--dc23
LC record available at https://lccn.loc.gov/2017043758

I dedicate this book
to the most appreciative person
I have ever known:
Adrian van Kaam, C.S.Sp., PhD
(1920–2007)

So be grateful for every little gift and you will be worthy to receive greater ones. Consider the least gift as great and the most common as something special. If you consider the dignity of the giver, no gift will seem small or unimportant. Nothing given by the most high God is insignificant. And if he should send you pain and sorrow, you ought to be thankful, too, for whatever he permits he does for our own good. The person who wishes to keep God's grace should be thankful when it is given, and he should be patient when it is taken away. Pray for its return, then be cautious and humble lest it be lost.

—*Thomas à Kempis*

We grow in love when we grow in gratefulness. And we grow in gratefulness when we grow in love.

—*Br. David Steindl-Rast*

Joy springs from a grateful heart . . . [and from] remembrance of the amazement which our encounter with Jesus Christ awakens in our hearts. . . . Let us seek the grace of remembrance so as to grow in the spirit of gratitude. Let us ask ourselves: are we good at counting our blessings, or have we forgotten them?

—*Pope Francis*

# CONTENTS

# INTRODUCTION

I grew up a cradle Catholic in an Italian American family of immigrants forever grateful for having had the chance to pursue the American dream and attain citizenship in this great country of ours.

At the turn of the century, my grandfather left Calabria in southern Italy for a job as a barber in Pittsburgh, Pennsylvania. It would allow him later to bring his wife here and start a family of his own. Despite the prejudices against newcomers to this country that he and his fellow immigrants had to endure, he conveyed his gratitude for coming to these sacred shores to every customer, friend, and family member who took the time to listen to his story.

My mother was a first-generation Italian American, while my father was born in Italy and only came to America at the age of six. So I am a first-generation child on his side. Around the dinner table, my father often told of his parents' struggle to learn a new language, to adjust to Anglo-American ways, and to pursue a work ethic they passed on to their children and grandchildren.

What stayed with me as a lasting legacy, and what I intend to share in this book, is the gift given to me by my maternal grandmother, Elizabeth. It was her thank-you prayer. I knew that she had to go through many traumatic events, not the least of which was an arranged marriage at the age of sixteen, the death of five of her eleven children in infancy, and the final agony of severe stomach cancer. And yet this prayer never left her lips. This illiterate peasant woman, this pillar of the Catholic faith, taught me most of what I know about finding the balance between hardship and happiness, between the best of times and the worst of times.

Instead of complaining about everything—which she had every right to do—she chose to see that proverbial silver lining in every cloud. She never missed playing the most hysterical practical jokes on us on April Fool's Day and laughed until she cried. How often I watched her fold her hands, raise her eyes to heaven, and thank God that her family had a roof over their heads and good food on the table. She thanked God when she opened her eyes in the morning and when she fell asleep at night. This simple lesson, like a pebble dropped in a still pond, has sent ripples of gratitude throughout my entire life. Among the many grateful moments I want to share with you, this one provides a good starting point.

One morning after Mass, as I was rushing off to work, I noticed tucked into the corner of my pew a holy card that had to have been placed there just for me. On the front was a sketch of the Family of Nazareth, and on the back was a prayer—one that I now say every morning: "Thank you, Lord, for a truly perfect day. Grant that my whole being, no matter how tiny, may be an embodiment of your eternal, infinite love for souls."

What was it about this prayer that resonated so deeply with me? Perhaps it was the emphasis on gratitude not *after* something good happens to us but *before* the day even begins. It assumes that no matter what the day holds, we can find in it reasons to be thankful. I love the holistic orientation the prayer connotes. Yes, my mortal being is tiny, no bigger than a grain of sand on a beach, and yet it is an embodiment of God's love eternally bestowed.

Who among us has not scanned the shelves of our favorite bookstores and found on them titles referring to "positive thinking" and to the importance of adopting an optimistic rather than a pessimistic outlook? Written on the labels of my favorite bottled water are slogans such as "U-R-A-MAZE-ING" and "SMILE, IT'S CONTAGIOUS."

Why, then, have I found it necessary to write a book on how the grace of gratefulness can change our lives? It would be naïve to think that this move toward being more positive would exonerate us automatically from the downswings of depression, cynicism, disbelief, and outright distrust of God. To reverse these negative outlooks is the task of a lifetime. The apostle Paul expresses this Christian ideal in 1 Thessalonians 5:18, advising us to "give thanks in all circumstances." We must trust that this is not an impossible imperative to fulfill. Only when we commit ourselves to practice the art and discipline of grateful living can we benefit from it and all of the other imperatives we find in 1 Thessalonians 5:12–22. Allow me to paraphrase them in service of helping us grow from the start of this book in the joy of grateful living. To do so we must

1. respect those who labor among us and have charge of us in the Lord and admonish us;
2. esteem them very highly in love because of their work;
3. be at peace among ourselves;
4. admonish the idlers;
5. encourage the faint-hearted;
6. help the weak and be patient with all of them;
7. see that none of us repays evil for evil;
8. always seek to do good to one another and to all;
9. rejoice always;
10. pray without ceasing;
11. give thanks in all circumstances;
12. not quench the Spirit;
13. not despise the words of the prophets;
14. test everything;
15. hold fast to what is good; and
16. abstain from every form of evil.

In this brief passage, St. Paul gives us sixteen directives that detail the human and spiritual benefits of growing day after day in gratitude. I witnessed these benefits firsthand in the life of my teacher, spiritual guide, mentor, and colleague, Fr. Adrian van Kaam, C.S.Sp., PhD (1920–2007), to whom I have dedicated this book. He exemplified all sixteen of these signs of gratefulness. His respect for each person's unique communal life call was one of his most admired traits. Anyone who sought his counsel felt like the only person in the room with him at that moment. Fr. Adrian appreciated his collaborators and showed equal respect for those in authority over him in the university and in his religious community. He taught his students to see in every criticism a grain of truth. Anyone deserving of praise for a job well done received the warmest of heartfelt compliments. Although Fr. Adrian exuded the peace of Christ, he also had the courage to correct unjust actions and unkind behavior. It was one of his most beloved customs to tell the faint of heart to keep courage, no matter the hardships they had to undergo.

As a counselor, professor, and shepherd of souls, he never hesitated to help the weak and to show patience with anyone who tried to excel in academic or other work despite repeated failures. His first reaction was to treat people kindly. There was not a malicious nor judgmental bone in his body. Fr. Adrian prayed for us, guided us toward the best course of action, and trusted totally in Divine Providence. He was a gentle, joyful man whose "ministry of the smile" brightened every room. We could sense that, in all circumstances, his contemplative core prompted him to give thanks to God and never to quench the Spirit under whose inspiration one could discern the best course of action. And because he held fast to what was good, he did all in his power to guard his heart against the Evil One.

Gratitude is not a luxury for believers only; it is an absolute necessity in today's world. Ponder what happens when we fail to thank God for the benevolent love bestowed upon all people. We reverse these sixteen scriptural commands and, as a result, create around us a poisonous climate of ingratitude and thankless living characterized by

1. disrespecting those with whom we live and work, resenting legitimate authority, and responding defensively to any admonishment;

2. envying originality instead of esteeming everyone's gifts;

3. expressing ill will and lack of peace among us;

4. condoning sloth rather than admonishing laziness, lack of follow-through, and indifference to the plight of the poor;

5. blaming the faint of heart for their predicament and refusing to encourage the efforts they do make to be stronger people;

6. making fun of the weak and being impatient with their mistakes;

7. harboring a vengeful spirit that insists on an eye for an eye and a tooth for a tooth;

8. seeing as a rule of thumb "What's in it for me?" rather than giving priority to the good of others;

9. being a killjoy as often as possible;

10. praying perhaps only once in a while and in a merely routine way;

11. complaining about everything and being unthankful most of the time;

12. quenching the inspirations of the Holy Spirit and pursuing our own agendas instead;

13. resisting the writings of the spiritual masters rather than resonating with them;

14. discerning mainly what advances our own self-centered quests for more power, pleasure, and possessions;

15. holding on to what is good for us, no matter how much it may hurt others; and

16. indulging in hidden and overt acts of evil that make us ready targets for the Evil One.

How to counteract such blatant expressions of ingratitude—so contrary to our Christian faith and formation tradition—will be one of the central aims of this book. I will draw upon holy scripture and the writings of the spiritual masters to exemplify ways and means to be thankful under all circumstances. More inspiration from these companions in grateful living will guide the reflective questions and prayerful meditations at the end of each chapter. It is my hope that this book, and especially its counsels on the grace of gratefulness in the appendix, will reveal why we need to practice grateful living and to pass this gift on to generations of Catholic and Christian faithful now and for years to come.

Needless to say, I owe an enormous debt of gratitude to the staff and students of the Epiphany Academy of Formative Spirituality—notably to my publication manager, Mary Lou Perez—and to my publishers, without whose help this work would not have come to fruition. They know as well as I how hard it is to remain thankful to God for all the good we have been given. Only in faith can we see that in every end there is a new beginning and that with the saints we, too, can say: "Thanks be to God for his indescribable gift!" (2 Cor 9:15).

# ONE

# BEING GRATEFUL DESPITE THE CIRCUMSTANCES

Trust in the L ORD with all your heart,
and do not rely on your own insight.
In all your ways acknowledge him,
and he will make straight your paths.
—*Proverbs 3:5–6*

Anyone who has read Charles Dickens's famous novel *A Tale of Two Cities* probably remembers its opening phrase: "It was the best of times, it was the worst of times." Who of us has not had a moment when we felt, or longed to feel, that life could not get any better than this? Those "best of times" are captured in our memory banks: the birth of a child; their Baptism, First Communion, or Confirmation; a bridal shower, a honeymoon, a fiftieth wedding anniversary; the trip of a lifetime, a family reunion, one's first car or house . . . the best, to be sure.

How we long to repeat that first kiss or that chance meeting with the person meant for us or that perfect breakfast with the

1

sun rising over the shore or that job we loved so much that we couldn't believe we were being paid to do it.

Commingled with these good times, and perhaps always lurking in the shadows, are the "worst of times"—sudden infant death syndrome; the official visit or letter declaring the death of a beloved daughter or son in a war zone; the diagnosis of a terminal disease; a pink slip firing the family breadwinner; the loss of a spouse who happened also to be one's best friend. We want nothing more than to forget that infant's funeral or the devastation of hearing that our brave soldier is missing in action or severely wounded or the look in the eyes of our dearest friend when the routine visit to the doctor ended with tragic news. How is it possible to keep a steady stream of gratitude flowing when boulders of bad news tumble into it?

When my friend and mentor Fr. Adrian van Kaam wrote his bestselling book *Spirituality and the Gentle Life*, he recalled the day when his typist was about to quit. She asked him, "How can you write so eloquently about gentleness and devote most of the chapters of your book to the themes of anger and aggression?" Dismayed as he was about her leaving, he told her why he had done so, and his reply to her was one I'll never forget. He said that an author writes not so much about what he has attained as about what he is still striving to gain. He admitted that he had to work through what angered him and what evoked aggressive feelings, because unless he faced them, he could never succeed in practicing a gentle lifestyle. That lesson applies here. We have to face the abyss of ingratitude in our souls if we are to be released from its grip and see the grateful side of every experience. The death of someone we love can pull us further from the other people we love and further still from gratitude. The choice is ours. We can, as the familiar saying goes, see the glass half-empty or half-full. The latter option is the one toward which we ought to aim.

Like you, I want to improve my life on every level. Socially, I hope to enjoy satisfying and trustworthy friendships. Physically, I try to follow wise advice regarding nutrition and exercise. Functionally, I seek to use the skills God gives me to serve others in family life, church, and society. Spiritually, I strive to be a woman of prayer living in the awareness that without God's grace, I am and can do nothing. Daily I seek to experience more harmony between body and spirit, thought and action, head and heart.

Even at my worst moments, new depths of meaning may emerge. Because the word of God is "living and active" (Heb 4:12), I cannot predict where God will lead me. For every answer I receive, another question may be forthcoming. As I read in Psalm 86:5–7, "For you, O Lord, are good and forgiving, abounding in steadfast love to all who call on you. Give ear, O LORD, to my prayer; listen to my cry of supplication. In the day of my trouble I call on you, for you will answer me."

God addresses us as much in felt absence as in faith-filled presence. The generosity embedded in a grateful heart is what stands behind acts as simple as washing the dinner dishes or as profound as a busy parent stopping to listen to a tearful child. Rather than performing chores to prove how clever or productive we are, we try to see all that we do from a divine perspective. Life is not a ledger sheet on which God adds or subtracts graces based on performance models. Both paupers and princes are pleasing in God's sight. The benefits we receive, deserved or undeserved, are God's way of showing us how much we are loved.

Contemporary research has evidence to prove that a grateful outlook on life can boost our immune systems, decrease low-grade depression, and enhance our energy quotients. By contrast, ingratitude may prompt us to blame others for our problems or to feel as if life is empty of meaning. Ingratitude, with its litany of endless complaints, results in sorrow, not joy. We may be driven to tackle projects at a fevered pace, only to find that we remain strangely ineffective.

Required of us is not mere behavioral modification. To begin anew calls for internal examination of our penchant for living in thankless, distrustful ways. What follows must be the willingness to convert our hearts and the readiness to choose to act in a more thankful manner.

I don't think it is possible to say thanks despite the circumstances in which we find ourselves until we are willing to learn from our mistakes. Let's face it: no matter how sincere our efforts to turn to thankfulness, we relapse to ingratitude all too often. I confess that my heart is a veritable battlefield between positivity and negativity. One minute I thank a coworker, the next I am tempted to judge her unkindly. The analytical "me" leads to self-talk that goes something like, "In the grand scheme of things, does it really matter whether I am grateful or not? Who really knows or cares anyway?"

Another odious intention that can smother a grateful outlook is the need to look good in the eyes of everyone around us. Appearances can become more important to us than examining our motives for acting in a certain way. If anyone dares to question what drives us, do we immediately go on the defensive? Can't they see that our aim is to function more efficiently than anyone else in the office? Don't they understand that the pressure to perform perfectly is more important to us than taking time for self-examination?

To correct these morose ways of reasoning, I need to hold on to at least these two thoughts: there is a blessing in every burden, and the mystery embracing us is ultimately benevolent.

What happened to my aging mother offers a vivid example of what I mean. Dizzy spells of an unknown origin forced her to go to the hospital for observation. One test followed another as our family anxiously awaited the outcome. I remember holding Mother's trembling hand when a nurse named Lizzy came into her room to take her vital signs. She and my mother struck up a conversation. They chatted about this and that, and then Lizzy asked if there was any more she could do for her: "Helen, how about it? Let me bring you a glass of orange juice and a cookie to go with it." Her demeanor was patient, and Mother responded with gratitude. When Lizzy left the room, she said, "That nurse knows my name and cares about how I feel." Lizzy was a skillful caregiver, but more than that, she had an uncanny ability to make a frail woman feel better.

I notice, as I'm sure you do, that when I am feeling stressed, fatigued, and perhaps caught in a nasty set of circumstances, I tend to lose the graciousness Lizzy displayed that so blessed us. Consider how my neighbor Daniel felt when he was handed a pink slip without warning. What happened to the promotion he had been promised before the company downsized? His temper flared up like a firecracker and tore through his intentions to assess the situation more rationally. Despite his best efforts to be an exemplary employee, he felt undervalued and ill-treated, especially after he was fired. In a calmer moment, he began to reassess these circumstances in a more thankful manner. Working with the staff in human resources, he discovered that he was eligible for an opening in another branch of the business. It meant moving, but he and his family agreed that this was a minor hassle since he would still have a job. Difficult as it was, he found lots of reasons to be thankful.

As Daniel later shared with me, opting for gratitude prevented him from chiding himself when he first thought he would be without work and blamed himself, thinking, "*I* should have known better. *I* ought not to have done that. *I* am shocked that *my* best efforts produced such paltry results." He went from wallowing in self-pity, blame, and anger to praying with humble confidence, "God, come to my assistance. Lord, make haste to help me."[1]

After hearing Daniel's story and thanking God for its good outcome, I found myself meditating on the first mystery of joy that the Blessed Mother experienced, the Annunciation. Despite the circumstances of Mary's tender age and purity, the angel of the Lord invited her to accept the call to be the mother of God's own Son. The narration of this story culminates with

Mary's consent. When we have heart-rending choices to make, we can count on her help.

Much later, her son made a similar appeal to his disciples. In his farewell discourse in the Gospel of John, Jesus asks them in so many words what the Spirit asked of Mary. How he longed for them to be with him, as his mother was, so that their *yes* to God in circumstances that would test their faith by fire would flow from pure and grateful hearts.

As we heed the call of grace to live a more committed, Christ-formed life, the invitation to say thanks may be given to us when we least expect it. In shy but stirring whispers, the breath of the Spirit begins to break through the stubborn fortifications of ingratitude that have trapped us. We notice a diminishment of such stressors as excessive time urgency, task avoidance, and useless worry because others with whom we work seldom take time to listen to us. We may have displayed hostile feelings toward them because we concluded that they only wanted to advance their crass ambitions. The Spirit softens such harsh outlooks on life and challenges us to initiate more compassionate encounters, allowing the love of God to appeal to others through us.

In this state of grace, the Prince of Peace enters into our daily existence and sheds light on its meaning. Jesus opens us to "the wisdom from above [that] is first pure, then peaceable, gentle, willing to yield, full of mercy and good fruits, without a trace of partiality or hypocrisy. And a harvest of righteousness is sown in peace for those who make peace" (Jas 3:17–18).

No earthly power can match the joy we feel in Christ's presence. It sweeps away all traces of fear and unforgiveness. His light begins to shine through our entire being as the halo effect that sacred art so touchingly depicts. We find our peace not in passing pleasures but in the love of God that "has been poured into our hearts through the Holy Spirit that has been given to us" (Rom 5:5).

Formation in gratitude despite the circumstances in which we find ourselves begins to be habitual when we look at ordinary events in a way that enables us to behold their extraordinary potential. Examples abound. "Yes, it's a cold, damp morning, but think of how much better this cup of hot coffee tastes. The timer I set on the new coffee maker last night is a marvel of modern technology. The old percolator made even the best brews taste bitter." In a media-oriented world, the focus is on the spectacular, but we must not miss the richness of the ordinary that unrolls at our feet.

Once I had the privilege of serving with a mission team among newly converted Zulu people in South Africa. I reminded myself to ponder how fortunate I was to have a ballpoint pen in my purse, when in these primitive schoolrooms a stubby lead pencil was a treasure. I noticed that the Range Rover transporting us from village to village was so sturdy that we hardly felt the ruts in the road. What must it be like to traverse them on a bicycle with tires so worn one practically peddles on the rim? The scraps from our dinner table would have made a full meal for the hungry children we met. We had blankets to pull under our chins while they did not even have beds. What had we done to deserve these gifts? How could we not be grateful for them?

Helpful sayings in this regard might be these:

"I do believe God's plan is always better than my own."

"This may not be the position I wanted, but at least I have a job when so many of my peers are unemployed."

"Maybe my parents weren't perfect, but whose are? Life might have been unimaginably more difficult had I been an orphan."

Ceasing to obsess over what has to happen for us to be happy is the key to celebrating the giftedness of each day we are alive.

This counsel is incredibly countercultural since reliance on our own resources has been made into a sacrosanct virtue. What child has not been taught to pull up her bootstraps, stop asking God or anyone else for help, and get on with life? The goal being taught to reach is not dependence on the initiative of grace but rather individualistic independence.

In a functionalistic culture like our own, this do-it-yourself mentality prevails. Its corollary is to turn us into producers of useful goods and services, worker bees more valued for what we do than for who we are. Self-help books tend to obscure the truth that our own efforts to save ourselves always fall short of the mark.

The great Evangelical preacher Corrie ten Boom confesses in her autobiography, *The Hiding Place*, that she who had spoken so eloquently of the healing power of Christ's forgiveness could not shake the hand of a Gestapo guard she recognized in her church. Though the war was over, the remembrance of what the guard had done to her and her sister Betsie paralyzed her power to forgive. Only when Corrie prayed to the Lord to enter her heart and soften it did she feel a warm flood of grace move from her shoulder through her arm to the hand that reached out to grasp his. God initiated in Corrie the grace to practice what she preached. The moment she surrendered to it, she was able to do what Jesus asked and turn the other cheek. The same may happen to us when we stand before a mountain of negativity and ask God to move it. We do not have the power to move it, but God does.

Even in the flea-bitten, filthy bunkers of the Nazi prisoner-of-war camp in Ravensbrück, Betsie ten Boom reminded her then-doubtful sister Corrie that there is no pit so deep that the Lord is not there. For Betsie, there were only God moments, whether saying grace over a bowl of watery soup and a crust of stale bread or rising from the ground after receiving a cruel beating. Every time she practiced appreciation in these deplorable circumstances, a light radiated from her being that inspired the other women in the barracks not to lose hope. With few words, she became a saintly teacher who gave God free rein over her life and her death.

Once, while doing the work of a beast of burden, Betsie in her frailty prayed softly, nonstop, to Jesus, begging him to show her that he was near. Suddenly another prisoner rushed to her side, risking being beaten by the guards, and pressed into her hand a gnarled crucifix she had been carrying. She said to Betsie, "Here, you take him. You love him more than anyone

I know." The tears streamed down Betsie's face. Between her filthy fingers, she held the sign for which she had prayed, and she proclaimed without words the supernatural beauty of this precious gift.

Growth in grateful living changes our hearts and restores our compassion for others. When more battered women were pushed into the already overcrowded barracks where Betsie and Corrie were imprisoned, they were the first to make room in their bunks to house them. Because every life was precious to them, they did what they could to help these women crushed by grief and on the verge of despair. Betsie taught Corrie to temper her initial, often prejudicial, assessment of new arrivals and to see behind their grim appearances souls terrified of their captors and begging for some sign of humane treatment.

When a woman full of hate challenged Betsie's claims that "God is love," she resisted the temptation to engage in a theological debate and devoted herself instead to showing as much kindness to her as she possibly could. In a situation as unreasonable as Ravensbrück, what good would it do to try to reason one's way to the truth of God's word? Betsie simply chose to live what she believed, and her witness softened the hardest of hearts. She showed everyone that God is with us in the gains and pains of daily life. That was the secret of her capacity to give thanks always. That was why the guards who assumed they had control over her had no authority at all. Even the most demeaning task had a dignity about it that her faithful heart could readily grasp. Betsie taught her little congregation the art of appreciation. She directed their tired eyes upward to the cloudless sky and invited them to savor the freedom God had in store for them, whether they were alive on earth or on their way to heaven.

Stubborn pride had replaced Corrie's service to the Lord. Inspired by her sister's example, though, Corrie began to relinquish the hatred she felt for her captors and to live in the loving embrace of Jesus for herself and her fellow sufferers. She repented for the times she had missed the chance to give glory to God and, under all circumstances, began to humble herself and seek forgiveness. Betsie taught her to be his handmaiden and pray for help. Forgetfulness of God's fidelity to her and everyone he created was her greatest fault. Bonded anew to grace, she would have the strength to persevere in the belief that God would set both of them free. Betsie's end would be heaven-bound and Corrie's to do the ministry of evangelism here on earth.

Every event in life—from the birth of a child to the death of a parent, from a passing meeting with a friend to an exchange of marriage vows—shapes our sense of meaning and purpose. Every experience, from dressing for work in the morning to cooking in the evening, is a chapter in the unfolding story of God's guidance of our lives.

Were we asked in advance how pieces of the puzzle fall into place, we would be hard-pressed to find an answer. Rather than trying to analyze every detail of our emerging life's call, it is best to trust the divine light we receive. We need to stop what we are doing and discern its meaning. Daily happenings become the windows through which we behold, beyond threats and fears, paths not anticipated that turn out to be the ones most in tune with who we are and hope to become.

In my experience, the pledge to remain thankful under all circumstances benefits from the following six practices. Once we may have deemed them impossible; with practice they are woven into the fabric of our everyday lives and worthy of being passed on to all those entrusted to our care:

1. Let the invitation to gratitude alert us to the fact that ingratitude can impair, if not destroy, our physical, emotional, and spiritual energy, rendering our lives ultimately unfulfilling.

2. Let the will to be grateful heighten our consciousness to symptoms that signify our willingness to listen to this call, including stress, anxiety, and discontent. We need to question why even worthwhile projects do not give us much joy. Think of how it feels to celebrate the goodness of life rather than giving way to a faultfinding mentality. Is there not a direct correlation between crabbiness and irritability and our becoming short-tempered and impatient with everyone?

3. Let the spiritual exercise of thank-you prayers encourage us to investigate the causes of thanklessness as we read books that teach us how to see the blessings hidden in every burden. We can mindfully avoid the urge to change others and work on transforming ourselves.

4. Let the joy of grateful living encourage us to assess our moods and redirect them before frustration,

disillusionment, suspicion, and neglect of prayer get the best of us.

5.  Let the goal of being full of thanks widen our vision of God's ongoing revelation in the wonders of the world around us. Lost as we may feel on occasion, we trust that God has our best interests at heart and that our misery attracts God's mercy.

6.  Let the practice of appreciation remind us that we do not need to know the reason for everything that happens to us. We take it in stride and walk with childlike faith hand in hand with God.

It goes without saying that when life flows in smooth channels and the crosses we have to carry are few, we slip more easily into an attitude of appreciation for the grace of gratefulness. The test is what happens when these waters turn rough—raging with white caps and full of jagged rocks. Suddenly, life lifts us beyond our comfort zones and challenges us to remain upbeat even when cloudbursts soak us to the skin and shelter is nowhere to be found. The raft we counted on to carry us to shore springs a leak—but we must keep paddling until we are dockside. Surprising as this turn of events may be, it proves again that God's fidelity to us is much greater than our fidelity to God.

Whenever we feel sorry for ourselves, we need to compare our momentary suffering to what Christ underwent for the sake of our salvation. Were you or I the only person on earth, he would have made the same sacrifice. The light shining on us from the risen Lord illumines the midnight moments of our lives. With naked faith comes unrelenting hope and self-giving charity. The obstacles that stood in the way of grace now become the gateways to living more thankfully in union with the Lord. To embrace his cross is the best way to dispel forecasts of gloom and awaken to forgiveness. No pit of despair is so deep that we cannot climb out of it with the Lord's help. Every end marks a new beginning; every step toward the Gospel increases our longing to be more faithful disciples, and so we pray:

*Lord,* in the face of every human flaw, of powers unleashed by nature that are beyond our control, give us the grace to see your holy will in everything—not with a sense of fatalistic surrender but with a yielding in faith to a mystery beyond our reckoning. Help us to cling amid the swirling waters of uncertainty to the sturdy raft of your Word. Let us know in love that you are there with us from our first to our last breath. What matters is the truth that we need not make this journey on our own. You are at our side, encouraging us every time we fall to rise up and start over again. Amen.

## QUESTIONS FOR REFLECTION

1. What makes distrust and discouragement such treacherous obstacles to reaching the goal of being thankful in all circumstances?

2. What reforms must occur in our inner and outer lives before we can begin to show more gratitude for people, events, and things?

3. Can we recall a time when the grace of gratefulness helped us to say *yes* to God's guidance in the unforeseen circumstances that confronted us?

## COMPANIONS IN GRATEFUL LIVING

### JULIAN OF NORWICH

What is impossible to you is not impossible to me.
I shall preserve my word in everything, and I shall
make everything well.
—*Julian of Norwich (1342–1373)*

This extraordinarily gifted fourteenth-century English mystic and solitary anchoress lived simply yet comfortably in a cell attached to the Church of St. Julian in Norwich, England. She was about thirty years old and in the throes of a near fatal illness when she experienced a series of sixteen revelations, or "showings," which included visions of Mary and Jesus and even the devil. Until the day she died, Julian pondered the meaning of these visions. Though little is known of her life, one thing is certain: she wrote her famous *Showings*, or *Revelations of Divine Love*, in a turbulent era, riddled with catastrophic events such as the Black Plague, the Hundred Years' War, religious persecution, and a papal schism. Women were largely unrecognized in intellectual circles, but Julian's contributions were taken seriously as the cloistered life gave her a voice commanding respect. Her incredible optimism has contributed to her reputation as one of the holiest and wisest of the English spiritual writers. Her work is lauded not only by scholars but also by the common folk she loved and guided. Like us, they were people who questioned the meaning of life and their own approaching deaths. No wonder Julian's most-quoted sentence has touched hearts over the ages: "All shall be well and all manner of things shall be well."

Despite the chaotic times in which Julian lived and wrote, she never failed to see the presence of God everywhere, even in something no bigger than a hazelnut. When she held this tiny bit of creation in the palm of her hand, Julian saw something of the nature of God, who made it, loves it, and preserves it as he does each of us, his children.

Julian's authentic visions included the recollection of Christ's Passion in vivid, even frightening detail. From what she saw she was better able to interpret the meaning of suffering and bodily sickness, beheld in the light of God's fatherly and motherly goodness. She also caught sight of three wounds that imprinted the Passion of Christ on our souls, these being contrition, compassion, and the longing for God.

Julian contrasts the horror of sin with the happiness that is ours as recipients of divine mercy. With the certitude of one who has seen the Christ who redeemed us, she knew of his desire to be united with us. She also introduced the notion of Jesus as our true Mother. In celebrating the tenderness of Christ's humanity and the saving grace of his divinity, Julian was convinced that love, not sin, is the ultimate determinant of our existence. In her book, she affirms the goodness of creation, the friendship of Christ, and the sweet solicitude of the Blessed Trinity.

Julian of Norwich confirms the truth emerging from grateful living that there are no coincidences, only providences. Instead of asking why something happened, we wait upon the Lord to reveal its deepest meaning in our unfolding story. Sooner or later shadows of despair begin to be dispelled along with the negativity that spreads around them.

When a jarring crisis like the loss of a job hits us, we may be able with lightning speed to move *from* the negating circumstances that led to this downsizing *through* the rush of emotions we feel, ranging from anger at the boss to condemnation of ourselves, *to* the conviction that all shall be well. We may choose, even in the face of injustice, to make the effort to respond with forgiveness rather than to react with revenge. The latter stance harms us most of all. Reinforcing the spirit of gratitude lets us refrain from castigating ourselves for a less-than-perfect performance and leaves room for God to grace us with the gift of appreciation as we pray with the psalmist: "Why are you cast down, O my soul, and why are you disquieted within me? Hope in God; for I shall again praise him, my help and my God" (Ps 42:11).

Hope widens our vision of what can be; hopelessness narrows it. The first perspective leads to possibility thinking; the second to the conclusion that there is no exit from this pain. Attention to the richness of the ordinary changes our perception of time from *chronos* (clock-bound) to *kairos* (the inbreaking of the Eternal). Trusting surrender, as Julian experienced, stills the disquiet of a distracted mind. We take time to listen to the language of the heart, allowing God's word to change our lives. We relish the countless blessings bestowed on us by the Lord. Where once we saw only reasons to lose courage, now we see the beneficial results of relying on a love that knows no limits. No longer do we take for granted revelatory moments of care and concern. Instead we thank God for giving us another chance to be thankful despite the situations that surround us.

Julian's conviction that "all shall be well" proves that there is ample evidence in the treasury of our faith and formation traditions that, in her words, "Mercy works, protecting, enduring, vivifying and healing, and it is all the tenderness of love; and grace works with mercy, raising, rewarding, endlessly exceeding what our love and labor deserve, distributing and displaying the vast plenty and generosity of God's royal dominion in his wonderful courtesy."[2]

## LET US PRAY

*Lord,* widen our range of vision so that we can follow you on a road whose destination you alone can see. Give us a disposition of receptivity, responsive to where your call intends to lead us. Protect us from passive postures lacking the courage to take the path your providence discloses. Dispel the shadows of depreciation that distract us so that we can hear and heed whatever you ask of us. Amen.

## BROTHER LAWRENCE OF THE RESURRECTION

There is no mode of life in the world more pleasing
and more full of delight than continual conversation with God.
—*Brother Lawrence of the Resurrection (1611–1691)*

Born in the Lorraine region of France, Nicholas Herman served
in the army and worked as a household employee before decid-
ing in middle age to enter the Discalced Carmelite Order. There
he assumed his new name, Brother Lawrence, but remained a
humble worker, enjoying his kitchen duties and cobbler tasks
for the next forty years and learning the wisdom that comes
with unceasing prayer.

Abbé Joseph de Beaufort, who had often visited the monk
before his death, published a memoir in Brother Lawrence's
name based on their conversations as well as sixteen of Brother
Lawrence's letters and some of his spiritual maxims. *The Practice of the Presence of God* would become a Christian classic. In
it we learn that faith in the midst of everyday events brings us
to a high degree of perfection, whether or not special feelings
accompany our quest for holiness.

Brother Lawrence's way of spiritual childhood was so simple anyone could follow it, with or without the help of a spiritual director. His "shortcut to God" consisted not of traditional
methods of prayer and ascetic practices but of the continual
commitment to do everything for the Beloved with humility
and reverence. *Forget about the past. Do not worry about the*

*future,* he counseled others. *Live in the present and count on God to give you whatever you need when you need it.*

Brother Lawrence's approach to prayer was simple yet profound. Do everything for God's sake, and don't get discouraged when small tests come your way. Adhere to God in labor and leisure, and cultivate the sense of his presence. In due course, prayer will become as natural to you as breath. As he wrote to a priest, "I keep myself in his presence by simple attentiveness and a general loving awareness of God that I call 'actual presence of God' or better, a quiet and secret conversation of the soul with God that is lasting."[3] Recognized as a spiritual guide by religious and laity alike, Brother Lawrence lived an exemplary life and died a holy death at the age of eighty.

From his wisdom gathered amid the pots and pans, we learn to welcome that voice crying out in the wilderness and to reject that void empty of meaning. We discover the love of God, who knows us better than we know ourselves, who never retires to a distant galaxy beyond our reach but meets us where we are in the give-and-take of true friendship. Between God and us, there ought to be a steady stream of pleasing conversation that symbolizes the staying power of our bond of love, which nothing the world has to offer can replace. God has chosen to be Emmanuel, God with us. Our Lord embraces our wounded condition through every phase of living and dying.

Brother Lawrence encouraged candid conversation with the One who loves us and wills our good. He wants us to converse with the Divine about the details of our daily lives, saying, for example, "Lord, I wish I had more to bring before you than this load of dirty laundry, but I might as well make the best of it, thanking you for my family and not feeling as if I have been taken for granted." This humble Carmelite cobbler and cook shows us that fully awake and falling asleep, driving the car and searching for a parking space—in these and myriad other instances of everydayness—the way to be grateful can be found along the path on which we now trod.

## LET US PRAY

*Lord,* how foolish we are to treat you as if you are a distant deity unconcerned about the details of day-to-day life. Help us to overcome that deception by the grace of continual conversation with you, the One who loves us. With simple, trustful talk, we enjoy the privilege of walking in your company, of becoming one with that great cloud of witnesses, thanking you endlessly and praising your glory. Amen.

# TWO
# BENEFITS OF POSITIVITY

O give thanks to the Lord, for he is good; for his
steadfast love endures forever.
—*Psalm 107:1*

Please don't accuse anyone trying to be more positive of being
Pollyannaish, because nothing could be further from the truth.
Times when I've been so accused have really been hurtful and
have tempted me to go on the defensive. It is not possible to
reason a person into positivity. It takes practice, and it must
start with a change of heart. People, by nature, are quick to
critique and slow to compliment.

I recall having a teacher in high school who must have
believed that the worse she made us feel about our performance
in class, the more likely we were to improve. How wrong she
was. We all began to hate her class and to find any reason
we could not to incur her look of disgust, her sharp-tongued
reprimands, her constant statements that she was correcting
us for our own good. She was like that chronically impossi-
ble-to-please parent whose child none of us want to be.

By contrast, we could not wait to be in class with the teacher whose heart warmed to us the minute we walked in the room. She pointed to what she liked in our papers and offered creative suggestions about how this or that section or paragraph could be improved. She even asked if we agreed with what she said, as if she had missed our points! Her humility was amazing, and it produced positive results. She kept her authority as our teacher. She did not try to be our best buddy. She taught us the meaning of self-respect and respect for others.

The center stone around which all her decisions and actions gravitated was positivity, not negativity. The benefits of this positive outlook have stayed with me from that day to this. Positivity taught me the importance of cooperating with the grace of gratefulness in times of consolation as well as desolation. Doing so is an ongoing challenge. With the least provocation, I can lose my footing and fall into the quicksand of negativity, so I must be on guard.

Positivity corrects my course the moment I am tempted to blame others for my ill fortune and wager that the bad day I am having will never end. Positivity overcomes the fear that if one shoe falls, the other will surely drop. It prevents me from worrying about situations over which I have no control; it alerts me to what triggers a negative response and challenges me to put a stop to it before it consumes my good mood. Being a killjoy or a sourpuss hurts me as much as it deflates the upbeat feelings of those around me.

A positive outlook on life calms our defenses and allows us to accept in humility the grain of truth in every criticism leveled against us. Our negative arguments come to a full stop, and we begin to assess situations from the perspective of the good that may come from them: "True," we say, "It's pouring rain and we're off to a family picnic, but the weather cannot dampen the fun of our being together. We'll head for the shelter, light a fire, and wait until the downpour subsides. There's plenty of food to eat, and it's cozy enough to enjoy conversations we'd miss on the playing field."

What if the promotion I wanted goes to another partner in the company? I can see this decision as a sign of disapproval or detect in it a hidden opportunity. Perhaps it is an invitation to improve the way I treat the customers and to put my hat in the ring for the next promotion.

Even if we relapse once in a while into a litany of negativity, the struggle to become more positive gains ground every time we try to reconfigure the miserable moods triggered by worry and anxiety. Positivity is the best way to acknowledge that, when all is said and done, life is meaningful. This response prevents us from living in the illusion that we can operate independently from a power greater than we are.

The challenge posed by our option to trust in the help of the Lord and be thankful reflects the conviction that good prevails over evil. Once we accept the truth that God is in charge, we can approach whatever happens with a joyful heart. At times questions avalanche us and we find ourselves questioning God's plan, but we do so in as positive a way as possible. We thank God in advance for the benefits we know in our heart we will receive. We trust in the mercy that responds to human misery with miracles of grace. Every disappointment becomes an incentive to pray harder, to resist the demon of doubt, and to focus on simple favors that might otherwise have passed us by.

Positivity enables us to modify the disaster scenarios that can propel us from normal stress to abnormal, even chronic, distress. It encourages us to relativize what might otherwise paralyze our creativity: "I might as well put that memory to rest. The past is behind me. Tomorrow will be a better day." We can say, as Job did, that the Lord gives and the Lord takes away; blessed be the name of the Lord.

Positivity is like a deep clean of the soul; it wipes away the dust of whatever disappoints us. There go failed relationships, promises broken, expected phone calls that never come, prayers that at the moment do not appear to be heard, and trips that end in disaster.

Major or minor disappointments may recur here and there, but we cease to be bent out of shape by them. We believe that our trust in the Lord will never be disappointed, that no prayer goes unanswered, and that the gifts bestowed by God bear lasting fruit in the long run. Though we may drift away at times from the hope that never disappoints, we know that God never breaks the promise not to leave us or anyone orphaned (see John 14:18), for Jesus says, "I am with you always, to the end of the age" (Mt 28:20).

Not surprisingly, one sure sign of advancement in positivity is the ability to laugh at ourselves and not to take occasional setbacks too seriously. It is wise to pay attention to the inner tensions we feel. For example, is excessive fatigue (not appreciating our own organic limits) eroding our effectiveness? Would the world come crashing to a halt if we had the courage to say no for the sake of saying yes to a greater good (like maintaining Sabbath rest)?

The spark of positivity rekindles itself like one of those birthday candles we cannot blow out. Others may see changes in our character, even though we view ourselves as still weaker than we would like to be. The slightest sign of appreciation, such as a smile instead of a frown, is an advancement not to be discounted. What carry us forward are not dramatic changes but words of gratitude that confirm the goodness we see around us. Our whole existence becomes a hymn of praise and thanksgiving to God. We try to move from condemnation of failings to forgiveness of self and others. Seven advancements in positivity assure us that our vigilance has been worth it:

1. We focus less on our imperfections and more on God's loving us as we are.
2. We remember with humility that in the order of grace, we can do nothing without God's help.
3. Deep thanks accompanies the humble admission of our dependence on God, without whose sustaining and fortifying grace no lasting conversion of heart is possible.
4. While we continue to assess the long-range effects of grateful living, we can testify already that it makes us much happier than the unhealthy adoption of plummeting moods.

5.  Instead of chafing against the setbacks we incur, we try to see them as invitations to trust wholly in the guidance of God and reset our courses.

6.  We realize that each improvement in a thankful outlook on life, however slight it may be, gives us another reason not to be discouraged about anything. We commit ourselves to believing that tomorrow will be better than today.

7.  Last but not least, we seek to read spiritual texts that form us in every facet of gratitude. One such passage is from St. Paul's first letter to the Corinthians: "So, whether you eat or drink, or whatever you do, do everything for the glory of God. Give no offense to Jews or to Greeks or to the church of God, just as I try to please everyone in everything I do, not seeking my own advantage, but that of many, so that they may be saved. Be imitators of me, as I am of Christ" (1 Cor 10:31–11:1).

Each day we are free to choose between feeling miserable and downplaying every chance of improvement or feeling empowered by grace to engage in positive thinking. We choose between wallowing in dour predictions and seeking more positive perspectives.

Say a question concerning what we should have done but failed to do in a particular circumstance gnaws at us like a nest of termites in a musty cellar. Or what if a person who promised to do us a favor forgets about it? In the first instance we may sink under the weight of false guilt, unable to forgive ourselves for being such failures. In the second instance we may give in to the irritable urges that threaten to destroy our relationships. Before too many accusatory comments rise to our lips, though, we can try to imagine what might have happened. Who knows when or how that person's schedule went up in smoke? The favor we needed can wait a few days. It's better to take life in stride rather than becoming aggravated over nothing. In this way, positivity escalates from an occasional change of tune to a lasting character trait.

Influences like those of parents on children, teachers on students, and pastors on people in the pew can have positive or negative effects on our lives. Some people encourage us to be who we are; others question our integrity and kill our joy. The movement toward positivity may be sidetracked, but it can always be regained through the power of appreciation. Certain interactions may be more harmful than helpful for our unfolding, but growth in good company is a gift that keeps on giving, especially when we momentarily lose our way.

It is as if we stand before two open doors. Going through one brings danger; passing beyond the other leads to opportunity. The first perspective promotes the option of negativity; the second leads to a more positive outlook. Rather than being able to make a clear-cut choice between these two ways, what we experience most often is ambiguity. Uncomfortable as the tension feels, good days may far outnumber the bad. We may have to face the uncertainty of not knowing what to do, but we have to try to go forward anyway, listening as closely as we can to what enhances gratitude. Disappointment in ourselves and others that used to breed negativity may then serve to reinforce a more positive attitude, leading to the conviction that if God is for us, who can be against us?

The bridge from negativity to positivity must be crossed lest the cancer of extreme willfulness ("I want what I want when I want it!") and the equally extreme reaction of apathy ("Nothing I do matters anyway.") overtake us. Our goal must be to find the happy center of authentic willing of the goodness, truth, and beauty embedded in the fabric of everyday life.

To reinforce a positive outlook, we must be open to the expected and unexpected turns life takes. This entails the choice to be aware moment by moment of ways to lighten the heaviness of the atmosphere around us. Demeaning others in the course of trying to discipline them is not an option. Neither is phony praise. It is preferable to take a second look, ensuring that confirmation prevails over condemnation.

Such inner liberation from the bondage of ungrateful living never represents an escape from reality. Far from running away from daily challenges, we choose to live in the midst of them. The liberty of spirit bred in us by the grace of gratefulness lets us face the obstacles strewn on our path without flinching. These obstacles teach us to respect our limits and to look upon them as reminders of our reliance on God. Once we were trapped in the stubborn enclosures we had created; now we are free to let them go and to concentrate instead on the value of every moment of life. From this perspective, the passage of time is no longer reduced to a struggle for power, a goal to be possessed, or an isolated experience of pleasure. Everyone and everything finds its place in the era allotted to it by the Eternal. We take the peaks of life in stride as much as the valleys. We recognize the reality that we belong at once to a community of sinners in need of compassion and a community of saints who, by the grace of God, have learned to handle the dilemmas of the day without losing hope.

One of the most obvious results of living in gratitude is the feeling of belonging, of being welcome, of hearing the Lord say, "Come to me" (Mt 11:28). When we feel weary, it's fine to stop working, as Mary did, and sit at the feet of Jesus. In chiding Martha, Jesus seems to be telling us that work without worship never bears lasting fruit. What if we are so busy, ostensibly doing the Father's business, that we miss what the Master himself wants to tell us? We do not have to make an appointment to see him. He is with us all the time, befriending us when we feel lonely and showing us how to be faithful when we are tempted to go astray. It is foolish to think that we must first attempt on our own to solve every problem and only then ask for his help. In so doing, we put the cart of self-perfection before the horse of Christ's unfolding plan of salvation. In the Lord's presence, there is no need for us to hide our vulnerability under the cover of phony airs of self-sufficiency. The Father wants to be our partner, provided we agree not to be the purveyor of an already set agenda. With the Lord we can be like children confessing our faults to an understanding parent. We may feel ashamed about some of our actions, but we know that the compunction we express will be met with more compassion than we could have imagined.

Jesus gives us bread and wine for the journey when our energy wanes as well as when it abounds. All that matters is the trust he establishes between us as an everlasting covenant (see Isaiah 55:3). From this facet of grateful living comes readiness, alertness, facility, and flexibility. We are more willing to wait upon the Lord rather than merely wait for outcomes we predict. We take a close look in the mirror and see the tight set of a stubborn jaw that demands to know everything. It is so beneficial to switch gears and live like an explorer familiar with the terrain to be crossed yet open to the vistas God still has in store. We listen to our bodies when they tell us to slow down as well as to our brains when they say we must get a move on. We stand at attention, good servants ready to receive our commissions. We try not to be distracted by the barking of countless buyers and sellers promising us spiritual and material prosperity for the price of following their advice. We prefer to listen in awe-filled attention to our Master's voice, not to our own counsels or the stubborn dictates of human reason divorced from the simplicity of childlike faith. Surrendered to the Lord are the vices of rigidity and willfulness that held us in bondage. Offered to us are the virtues of spontaneity and good counsel that lead to liberation. Suddenly we see in apparently impossible situations all that is possible with God's help, and so we pray:

*Lord,* you spoke words weighted with truth that do not pass away. Your words stand fast in the face of evil's defiance of your law. May our responses to forces beyond our control transform a sense of fatalistic surrender into a faithful yielding to the music of eternity. Give us the courage to banish from our vocabulary words used to hurt, not heal; to curse, not console; to batter, not bless. Draw us into those wellsprings of silence out of which words of truth pour forth. Protect us from people who use words as weapons of abuse, as propaganda to subdue free spirits, as tricks of mental and spiritual entrapment. Soften the remnants of hardness in our hearts that we may hear and heed your Word until that day when all words fall silent and we enter into the radiance of your risen presence. Amen.

# QUESTIONS FOR REFLECTION

1. Can we identify points of improvement in our styles of relating to people who used to annoy us? What helped us to change our minds about them?
2. Given the gains we've already made on our journeys to grateful living, what resolutions most help us to maintain them?
3. What are the benefits of positivity we can point to in the recent past, and have we been able to carry them over into the present?

# *COMPANIONS IN GRATEFUL LIVING*

## ST. JOHN OF THE CROSS

For the poor in spirit are happier and more constant
in the midst of want because they have placed their
all in nothingness, and in all things they thus find
freedom of heart.
—*St. John of the Cross (1542–1591)*


Acknowledged as one of the most renowned spiritual masters in
the Western Church, St. John of the Cross knew the meaning of
suffering from childhood on. His father died when he and his
two brothers were young boys; then one of his brothers, Luis,
died too. The other, Francisco, was sent to live with relatives,
leaving John and his mother to find sustenance on their own. To
help make ends meet in their hometown of Medina del Campo,
Spain, John worked in an orphanage-hospital taking care of the
poorest of the poor and, in the process, learning the meaning of
compassion for humanity wounded by sickness and sin.

   After his ordination in 1567, he met the woman who would
change his life as much as he would change hers, St. Teresa of
Avila. She shared with the newly ordained friar her dream of
reforming the Carmelite Order by returning to the original
rule of St. Albert. She would make the distinguishing feature
of her reform the wearing of sandals, not shoes, to symbolize
the poverty she wished her sisters to embrace. They would be
known forthwith as the Discalced Carmelites.

John joined Teresa by reforming the Carmelite friars, and the reformers felt the hostility of the traditionalists from the start, even though the latter group had allowed many mitigations to slip into the rule and its original charism. The wheels were set in motion, politically and ecclesiastically, to squelch the reform. In December 1577, the saint entered what would truly be the dark night of his life. He was kidnapped and imprisoned in the convent at Toledo, where he endured a starvation diet, solitary confinement, and cruel beatings at the hands of his own brothers in the order. Yet it was in this prison that he found his poetic voice, composing there the first of his great lyrics, *The Spiritual Canticle*.

His poetry and prose works—perhaps the greatest ever written in the fields of ascetical and mystical theology—were completed during the last fourteen years of his life when his intellectual and spiritual gifts had come to full flower. He died as he had lived on December 14, 1591, happy to have drunk from the cup of Christ's own suffering and thereby, in his words, to have penetrated "deep into the thicket of the delectable wisdom of God."[4]

For St. John of the Cross, *nada* (nothing but God) always led to *todo* (everything in God). Because we will forever want that which is more than we have attained, we must be wise enough to face the truth that nothing satisfies a heart on fire with love other than Love Divine. Retreating into old protective foxholes of false happiness is no longer an option. Only a leap of faith allows us to accept the paradox that renunciation is the key to liberation.

The benefits of positivity we seek cannot be found unless we cut the thin threads and heavy chains that bind us to anything less than God. Only in God can every want of ours come to fruition. St. John of the Cross challenges us to see not merely the blessings we receive *in God* but to reach the point where we see *God in* every gift and limit. Only then can we remain steadfast and courageous in the midst of failed plans and crosses too numerous to count.

## LET US PRAY

*Lord,* teach us to treasure the virtue of poverty of spirit. Let all illusions of self-sufficiency fade into nothingness. Give us the courage to overcome every obstacle we experience on our journey to you. You are all we need because without you, nothing we do bears lasting fruit. May we taste and savor the freedom that accompanies full surrender. May we respond to your challenge to be grateful always and to accept life's surprises with faith, to carry our crosses with hope, and to rise with you in love. Let us experience the freedom in abandonment and the strength in weakness. Amen.

## JEAN-PIERRE DE CAUSSADE

The divine will is the wholeness, the good and the
true in all things.
Like God, the universal being, it is manifest in
everything.
—*Jean-Pierre de Caussade (1675–1751)*

An outstanding confessor and spiritual counselor, Caussade gave conferences over many years to the nuns of the Order of the Visitation at Nancy in France, and he undertook to direct several of their members. The sisters preserved his conference notes and extensive correspondence, but they remained unpublished for many years. In 1861, his writings found their way into print under the title *Abandonment to Divine Providence*, a book now regarded as a spiritual classic.

Caussade spoke of each passing moment as being not only "the veil of God" but also, when scrutinized and interpreted by faith, "the unveiling of God." He gave the term "sacrament of the present moment" to this understanding of time pierced by the Eternal. As he understood it, duties, temptations, and trials are shadows that hide the action of the divine will in the crevices of the ordinary. For him, the Christian life is a rhythm of active receptivity and receptive action. The kind of prayer he recommended for everyone was a simple waiting upon God, to discern his presence and then to do his will.

Caussade did publish one book in his lifetime. Titled *On Prayer*, it was comprised of a set of dialogues on the art and discipline of contemplative living. According to this experienced director of souls, the aim of prayer is to lead one to the practice of simple recollection and attention to God. Caussade showed little interest in exceptional states of prayer or in complex analyses of the route to perfection. The key to spiritual maturity, he insisted, resides not in self-seeking but in self-giving. Consequently, complete surrender to the will of God is the essence of spirituality and the supreme duty of souls, for "the great and firm foundation of the spiritual life is the offering of ourselves to God and being subject to his will in all things."[5]

Once we rest on this foundation, we come to understand that, in the hands of God, misfortune, illness, and spiritual weakness all bear fruit and can be turned by God into good purposes we had not foreseen. Such happenings are the disguises God assumes so we may reach pure faith, which enables us to recognize him under any appearance. How consoling it is to know, in the words of Caussade, that "in the hands of God everything flourishes and turns to good. . . . He brings life out of the shadow of death, and when, with human weakness, we are afraid, faith, which sees good in all things and knows that all is for the best, remains full of confident courage."[6]

From the beginning to the end of our sojourn on earth, nothing escapes the embrace of God. Every breath we take has been accounted for. Neither the grossest evil nor the collapse of all we hold dear falls outside the sustaining power of God's love, which encompasses all that is, was, and will be.

Evil casts apart; good binds together. Evil is arrogant; good evokes awe. Evil thrives on its own pretended grandiosity; good reaches out in mercy to help the weak. The divine will is not indifferent to our plight but engaged with us in the darkest of nights. We can deny its universality and risk living a lonely, ultimately meaningless existence, or we can live in the divine light manifesting itself in the suffering and joy of each passing moment.

The demands made upon us as disciples of Christ presuppose a positive reply. He asks us not to neglect to visit a sick member of our family, to spend a few extra moments listening to a needy child, to help a frail person who falls in the street. The sheer fact that we are in the world with others means that at some moment they will need us as much as we need them. At first glance, going out of ourselves in service of God and others may seem an impossible request, but that is what we must do. Instead of turning inward in selfish ways that no longer satisfy us or anyone else, we must go forward in self-forgetfulness. This posture of humble surrender is the rule of life Caussade says we must follow in imitation of our Divine Master.

## LET US PRAY

*Lord,* there was no time when you thought of yourself more than others. You forfeited your life out of love for us. You emptied yourself for our sakes. You showed us the way to be released from prisons of our own making. Be with us as we cross the bridge from self-centered passions to that place of grace where we bend our whole beings in the direction of meeting others' needs. Only when we do so can we experience what it means to be and become another Christ. Implant in our consciousness a compass directing us away from focusing only on what we want. Make us more compassionate toward others. Help us remember that in the end, selfishness only causes our hearts to grow cold. Forgive us for being indifferent, for lacking in charity. Let us experience the joy of forgetting ourselves so that we can mirror the light of that self-forgetful, wholly appreciative love enkindled in our souls by you. Amen.

# THREE
# DANGERS OF NEGATIVITY

Pay close attention to yourself and to your teaching;
continue in these things, for in doing this you will
save both yourself and your hearers.

—*1 Timothy 4:16*

I count myself fortunate for having seen firsthand what negativity did to a cousin of mine. She succumbed to this danger in three ways that made me vow never to do the same. The first was *negative identity*. She honed in on what those around her did *not* say. "Yes . . . but" was her favorite phrase. "Yes, you can believe the weather reports all you want, but I know it's about to rain." I'll never forget that righteous look in her eyes when the cloudburst came. When I told her I had decided to major in English literature, she wagged her finger in my face and announced in a tone of unquestionable certitude, "Yes, but you'll never be able to make a decent living on poetry."

The second habit she became known for was *negative exaggeration*. She had a knack for turning molehills into mountains. Without telling us where or how she came by these facts, she concluded that black pepper was the cause of her kidney stones. She went on a rampage of throwing every shaker she could find—even from restaurant tables—into the rubbish. By contrast, when solid research warned her about the dangers associated with consuming excessive amounts of sugar, she furiously proclaimed that the FDA was not going to tell her what she should or shouldn't eat. Under no circumstances would she give up her sweet rolls, candy, and soda.

What followed was her *negative rejection of advice.* Sadly, no one could tell her anything, because she already knew everything. Doctors, nurses, neighbors, and relatives wanted to help her as she aged but to no avail. She nodded as if she were listening to them and then went her own way, sadly dying alone in an apartment filled with boxes of stuff she would never throw away.

Negativity is a fast-growing cancer of the soul. It's a danger zone that kills off joy and thrives on suspicion. If on the sunniest summer day there is a rain cloud in the sky, a negative person will find it. If there is a chicken bone in a pot of soup, it will end up in that person's bowl. If there is a nail in the parking lot, whose tire do you think it will pierce? Because he or she has been attuned for so long to everything that can go wrong, it often does.

We need to listen to our language to see if we overuse negative words and cease doing so. Negativity lessens when we use positive language:

"The sun has to shine one of these days soon!"

"You can always tell a soup is homemade when you find a few bones in it."

"I needed a new front tire anyway, and I'm glad I came to this mall because the dealership here has a sale going on."

Language is as much a house of deformation as it can be one of transformation. If we choose wisely the words we use, more positive results will be forthcoming. Good self-talk may sound like, "I no longer want to suffer needlessly because of negativity," or "So long to that black cloud that followed me wherever I went." The danger of living in an "if only" world is that we tend to mandate what will make us happy. When it does not, the joy we anticipated disappears in a sinkhole of negative predictability. We put on hold any possibility of happiness in the present and switch instead to our usual litany of downers:

"If only I had prayed more, what I wanted would have come to pass."

"If only I had gotten the one job for which I applied, I'd have plenty of money in my pocket by now."

"If only I had joined a gym and gone on a diet, I would have lost that extra weight."

"If only my parents had been more loving, I would not feel like such a loser." The list of negatives our fantasy lives can devise is endless.

This "if only" refrain is the seedbed of some of the impossible-to-fulfill conditions we place before our mind's eye. In their shadow, the possibility of enjoying a fulfilling, purposeful life recedes. What we fail to see is that these refrains themselves

cause the anxiety we feel. Behind them resides the illusory conviction that we cannot be content until they come true. We may
be dead before that happens, but this thought does not cross
our minds. Think of the time and energy we spend spinning in
a whirlpool of negative emotions linked to outcomes we may
never reach. With every disappointment comes a new wave of
anger, bitterness, self-pity, and blame. For every idle hope that
fails to materialize, we forfeit another reason to go on living in
gratitude by training ourselves to appreciate the realistic goals
at hand and to follow their lead.

During winter months in the Northeast, the sun never
seems to shine through clouds as thick as pea soup. I had come
to accept a self-diagnosis of seasonal affective disorder. I felt
sad. I pulled the pillow over my head and wanted nothing more
than to go back to sleep. I lay there thinking I could kick myself
for being too cheap to purchase a sunlamp. I forced myself to
get up, complaining to the four walls that I'd never recover
from this energy drain.

This utterly ungrateful analysis of the day would deplete
the best of us. Discouragement and depression are sinkholes
that swallow any semblance of a good mood. No wonder the
smallest inkling of an intention to be more thankful makes
a world of difference. To help change my attitude, I stopped
by a local lighting store, purchased a sunlamp, and used it for
the prescribed amount of time each day until spring. Another
change I made was watching the clouds out of my bedroom
window and imagining how blue the sky would be this coming
summer. These two improvements generated a better feeling

and let me start the day with a confident, energizing smile. In light of this experience, I saw a whole slew of bad habits that could affect my character formation had I not taken these preventive measures.

With each passing year, I try my best to become more alert to the physical, mental, emotional, and spiritual dangers triggered by negativity. I do not whitewash the painful reality of suffering, but I do accept the age-old truth that through it comes growth in wisdom. By contrast, a negative outlook only serves to increase my misery and worsen the course my life might have taken had I chosen to be more positive.

The problem is that every time we take two steps forward in positivity, a relapse to negativity is always possible. We may praise the Lord with one breath and complain with the next. Anyone who thinks that grateful living happens without a struggle has probably never tried it! Frankly, it is easier to gripe than to express gratitude. Distrust and discouragement are heavy rocks to move out of the way. Becoming a happier person is hard work, especially if we lapse once too often into a sad, somber mood that twists our lips into a scowl rather than a smile.

When it feels as if we have little or no strength left to resist the dangers of negativity, we can turn to the words of scripture and the masters to regain the assurance that when we are weak, then we are strong. The apostle Paul verified this paradox by reaffirming his commitment to interpret the situations in which he found himself—whether hostile or hospitable—as guided by God. He concludes in 2 Corinthians 6:3–10:

> We are putting no obstacle in anyone's way, so that
> no fault may be found with our ministry, but as
> servants of God we have commended ourselves in
> every way: through great endurance, in afflictions,
> hardships, calamities, beatings, imprisonments,
> riots, labors, sleepless nights, hunger; by purity,
> knowledge, patience, kindness, holiness of spirit,
> genuine love, truthful speech, and the power of
> God; with the weapons of righteousness for the
> right hand and for the left; in honor and dishon-
> or, in ill repute and good repute. We are treated as
> impostors, and yet are true; as unknown, and yet
> are well known; as dying, and see—we are alive;
> as punished, and yet not killed; as sorrowful, yet
> always rejoicing; as poor, yet making many rich;
> as having nothing; and yet possessing everything.

Despite such a revelation, we know from experience that ingratitude is resistant to reform. One reason is the know-it-all attitude it breeds. Negativity posing as wisdom is a grave temptation. Its cohorts are the sly gossip that ruins another's reputation and the sweet-sounding put-downs couched in phrases such as "But if you only knew what I know about him . . ." Pride posing as humility can convince us that we are holier than others and that our devaluation of others is justified. In the worst cases, a judgmental attitude escalates to such a degree that it blocks any semblance of empathy and compassion for our own and others' vulnerability. It demands nothing less than total perfection, and that's impossible. Consider the scandal of the Rwandan genocide. Once the Hutus labeled the Tutsis "cockroaches," they concluded that it was necessary to exterminate these vermin. Worthless labels fuel the fires of genocidal madness. The Nazi doctors perpetrated the same lie: their Aryan nation could only be "healed" if they killed the "Jewish vermin" despoiling it.

In the best of times and the worst of times, a grateful heart allows us to steer a steady course away from the rocky shoals of negativity. We remind ourselves that the ship of life is not ours to command; it sails under the direction of a mightier hand. Our place is to muster as much trust as we can without the caveat that everything has to go our way. We step out of the control center and surrender to the Holy Spirit, whose guidance system is fail-safe.

When vices such as rage and envy outweigh virtues such as patience and respect, we may once again be in danger of backsliding into negativity. We may notice in ourselves a repeated tendency to answer challenging questions with curt responses rather than pondering why our very tone of voice can hurt another person. Perhaps we need to install in our hearts a kind of inner radar system that enables us to spot, like bleeps on a screen, the first flare-ups of disparaging looks, to say nothing of verbal lashings, gossip, and grumbling. The sooner we train ourselves to detect signs of negativity, the quicker we can sense them hanging in the air like lingering traces of gas. Now is the time to watch out for cynical smirks, racial profiling, or making fun of a person for his or her body shape or size. We must stop such cruel interactions in their tracks, or before long we may fail to see anything appreciable in other people.

Being aware of negative assessments is the first step toward reforming them. Unless we do so, we may be unable to shake the heavy load of discouragement we feel at day's end. For a conversion of heart to occur, we have to devote whatever time and energy it takes to disentangle ourselves from the tentacles of negativity, no matter how great a challenge this change poses. What counts are not dramatic advances but just noticeable improvements. Once we stand on the threshold of grateful living, there is no reason not to go through the door. Positive steps will follow when we become less attached to outward proofs of success and more inclined to show everyone the love and respect they deserve. We are grateful for the perks that come our way, but we do not allow them to determine our worth. Whenever excessive activity tends to rob us of our need for contemplative presence, we slow down and say a prayer. We do not let worldly gain tempt us to forfeit our integrity or devalue the relationships that make every day worth living. Though our relationships are our greatest blessings, they can also be our heaviest burdens.

Tidal waves of ungrateful living well up when others seem neither to understand us nor to appreciate how hard we work. Rather than trying to express how we feel, we walk away disgruntled, seething with resentment. Once again, our righteous egos rear their negative heads. To defend our turf, we may persist in treating others with disdain rather than continuing our own conversion process through honest self-evaluation.

Getting back on course means becoming less defensive and more willing to confront our own demons. Can we agree to disagree agreeably? Can we treat the upset we feel as an invitation to replace individualistic self-defensiveness with social cooperation?

The more willing we are to examine the motives for acting the ways we do, the more likely it is that we will become more caring than closed, more open than opinionated. We pray for the grace to give up the custom of pouncing on the often-innocent mistakes others make.

Here is a brief but telling incident that I trust illustrates the dangers of negativity:

I was the fourth car attempting to pass through a tollbooth when it became apparent that the person in the first car was short a quarter. The cars behind him were packed too tightly together to change lanes. As the backup built in volume, horns began to squawk. It looked as if the person in the second car was about to blow a gasket. He jumped out and accused the poor driver of being an idiot, demanding to know why he would enter the cash lane without having in advance the correct amount of change. I thought, *He's so angry he's going to jump back into his car and ram the hold-up vehicle from behind*. Before a tollbooth operator could get to their two cars and prevent a road-rage event, the driver in the third car did exactly what I intended to do. He rushed to the first vehicle and handed the driver a fistful of quarters. Flushed but grateful, the first driver paid the toll and the line moved on. The actions of the accuser had embarrassed us all.

Driver Number Three saw in the person who needed change a neighbor in need. Driver Number Two's only aim was to get the line moving. He had no compassion for how mortified Driver Number One felt. The one who gave him the money to pay his way displayed the virtue of neighborliness. The other forfeited courtesy in favor of angrily making his point by calling the other a derogatory name.

*One of these days*, I thought to myself, *it might be my turn to run out of change at a tollbooth. Who do I hope will be in the car behind me?* I'd like to see in the rearview mirror a patient face, lips that smile at the foibles of humanity, and hands stretched out to help. In a climate of negativity, we are unlikely to see in every obstacle a formation opportunity; we do not even think of thanking God for another chance to show compassion to a stranger. First in line is the inclination to put our selfish interests before the needs of others.

Try as we may to stay vigilant to the upsurge of negativity, when we least expect it, a rogue weed may reveal itself. We have to deal with it promptly, relying on the undeserved graces of gratefulness we have received and cooperating with them. Then previously unreflective outbursts may be transformed into less negative outcomes, ranging from courteous responses to a renewed spirit of service to God and neighbor. Rather than letting disappointed expectations harden our hearts, we pray with sincerity that this pushy, impatient mentality will not blind us to what is precious in each person: "God help me not to bypass her creativity. Let me take the time to express at least a simple thank you for the favors she has done for me." In this way we remind ourselves not to attach a sense of urgency to everything we say and do, as if life itself is a deadline we must meet, no matter what.

What goes counter to progress in grateful living is the secret assumption that people are just plain stupid: "How dare they not agree with me when I'm so much smarter than they are!" This disposition produces such statements as "What do you expect of someone with no college degree?" or "One look at that messy mop of hair, and you know that she cannot be trusted to fulfill that task." To assume such a derogatory stance is to pigeonhole anyone who does not live up to the standards we have preset and to label that person inferior. There is not one iota of appreciation in such a statement as "It's a waste of time even to try to teach that person what to do. Once a loser, always a loser."

Ingratitude ignites harsh assumptions like these. It inclines us to feel as if we have to do everything by ourselves. We become micromanagers loathe to delegate a duty to anyone. The savior complex makes us say silently or aloud, "If you want anything done, you'd better do it yourself." That motto strips bare our ability to appreciate the gifts and talents of others. We discourage them from so much as trying to give us a helping hand. We assume in advance that no matter what they do, it will never be good enough.

However deeply these obstacles to grateful living may seem to be rooted in our personalities, they can always be uprooted and reformed. A simple exercise like catching the first sign of tense muscles can tell us that we are in need of relaxing and withholding judgment until we calm down. Taking a few deep breaths is another way of alleviating these pressure points. The second we feel superior to someone, we can remind ourselves that God is behind the steering wheel of life, not us. We relinquish any claim to bragging rights and pray to receive the grace of humility, which means that we walk in the truth that all of us are children of God. Detachment frees us from the illusion of instant gratification. To have what we need is different from acquiring whatever we want—to such a degree that we lose our freedom and end up being possessed by our possessions. Charity is the best way to forget about self-centeredness and instead to reach out and serve others with a grateful heart. The irony is that the less we focus on our defects as obstacles, the more we see them as openings to draw others as wounded as we are into the loving presence of the Divine Healer, Jesus Christ.

An excellent practice is to catch the first flickers of negativity when they flare up. We recognize the danger of fanning those flames or of letting negativity pose as wisdom. Negativity is like a wildfire or a fast-growing weed. It can burn up or choke off our best attempts to be appreciative.

Loss of gratitude blinds us to the truth that all of us are wounded by sin and in need of redemption. In a place as dehumanizing as a prison camp, any manifestation of justice, peace, and mercy was a miracle. When Corrie ten Boom felt downhearted and bereft of joy, she became harsher with herself and less tolerant of others. Only when she practiced the abandonment of a child could she throw herself upon the mercy of God, neither exaggerating her faults nor trying to resolve every problem. Her story, especially what we saw in chapter 1, teaches us that we do not need to have the last word in every argument. For example, instead of feeling hurt by something as innocuous as another's caustic tone of voice, we can try to turn quickly from condemnation to compassion. This movement toward kindness prevents us from falling into the habit of boxing people into cement blocks of our own making. Christ teaches us to love all members of his body in their uniqueness and their diversity since, "If one member suffers, all suffer together with it; if one member is honored, all rejoice together with it" (1 Cor 12:26).

Now is the time to ask ourselves if our actions are Christ-centered or not: Have we trained ourselves to pay attention to the upsurge of ingratitude? Attuned our interiority to signs of depleted enthusiasm or to discouragement or discontent that might override an optimistic outlook? Exercised our potency to say spontaneously, "These sour grapes will dry up if only I do not dwell on them"? Looked beyond obstacles to openings for renewal of our inner and outer demeanors? Widened the spot of light we see rather than focusing on shades and shadows? Shunned the devilish temptation to let despair drown our delights? Said a prayer for others when they mock us for what they dub as naïve faith? Expected some misunderstanding to accompany an overtly thankful life and tried to see such opposition as par for the course? Responded to criticism thankfully by changing it into a chance to forgive others as God has forgiven us?

Another bad habit we might try to break is that of ruminating on past faults and failings that have been confessed and absolved. There are enough crosses we have to carry due to the circumstances of daily life without making self-flagellation one of them. If we do not want bitterness, scrupulosity, and vindictiveness to enter our spiritual bloodstream, we need to commit to memory this by-now-familiar scriptural passage: "See that none of you repays evil for evil, but always seek to do good to one another and to all. Rejoice always, pray without ceasing, give thanks in all circumstances; for this is the will of God in Christ Jesus for you. Do not quench the Spirit. . . . Hold fast to what is good" (1 Thes 5:15–21). And so we pray:

*Lord*, grant us the grace of listening to your gentle yet firm commands to follow you. Remind us that even when we turned away in fear, you turned to us and forgave our failings. Help us to cross over hurdles of self-condemnation that belie the abundance of your mercy. Break through the barriers erected by negativity, and free us once and for all to pursue the peace and joy that accompany grateful living. Amen.

## QUESTIONS FOR REFLECTION

1.  What pressures in the workaday world prevent us from being more positive? What can we do to defuse them before they become habitual causes of negativity?

2. Should we detect in our hearts a penchant to be more negative than positive, can we ascertain where it comes from and begin to change course?

3. What in our experience most helps us to avoid the danger of backsliding into negativity?

## COMPANIONS IN GRATEFUL LIVING

### ST. THÉRÈSE OF LISIEUX

Not wishing to give into the natural antipathy I was experiencing, I told myself that charity must not consist in feelings but in works; then I set myself to doing for this Sister what I would do for the person I loved the most.

—*St. Thérèse of Lisieux (1873–1897)*

The youngest child of Louis and Zélie Martin, Marie-Françoise Thérèse moved from Alençon, France, her birthplace, to Lisieux with her family in 1877. After the death of her mother, her older sister, Pauline, became Thérèse's second mother. The family settled at Les Buissonnets in comfortable surroundings that contrasted with the inner turmoil this young woman was to experience for the next eight years.

Thérèse describes the winter of 1883 as a time of great trial. Pauline had entered the Carmel at Lisieux. Thérèse began to experience continual headaches and insomnia. She got so sick that she went into convulsions, accompanied by nervous trembling, hallucinations, and comas. Then suddenly on May 13, the Feast of Pentecost, while she was praying before a statue of Our Lady of Victory, she said that the smile of the Blessed Virgin Mary cured her.

Spiritual trials followed these physical ones, though Thérèse was deeply consoled when she received her First Communion in May 1884, followed in June by the sacrament of Confirmation. A year later Thérèse experienced liberation from the scruples that had plagued her for so long. Then on December 25, 1886, following Midnight Mass, she received the grace of her complete conversion. Charity entered her soul, and she ceased thinking of herself. She saw the care of others as her mission. Shortly thereafter, as she prayed before a picture of the Crucified Christ, she experienced a burning thirst for souls and the need to pour out upon them Christ's redeeming blood.

At the age of fifteen, Thérèse received special permission to enter Carmel after the bold request she made to Pope Leo XIII. Her first convert was the prisoner Henry Pranzini, a convicted murderer, who embraced the cross prior to his execution. This event seemed to confirm what Thérèse would spend the rest of her life perfecting—an apostolic mysticism that she later named her little way of spiritual childhood. The name she chose to symbolize her new identity in Carmel beautifully expresses the charism of her life: Thérèse of the Child Jesus and the Holy Face. Though she had only nine more years to live before tuberculosis would claim her, Thérèse taught all her sisters, the novices under her charge, and later the tens of thousands of people who embraced her as their strongest advocate in heaven how to live a life of joyful abandonment to Divine Providence, how to turn even the smallest daily event into an occasion of grace, and how to change the darkest trial of suffering into a time of intense mystical transformation.

A prolific letter writer and an exquisite poet, Thérèse agreed, under obedience to her superiors, to write her autobiography, never knowing that it would become one of the most inspiring and best-loved books of all ages with its classic Christian doctrine of the little way. In her autobiography, *Story of a Soul*, she vowed to spend her heaven as she had spent her time on earth: rescuing souls for Jesus.

Though Thérèse never left the enclosure, she became the patroness of the missions of the whole world. She who saw herself as a grain of sand in the immensity of the ocean was, in the words of Pope Pius X, "the greatest saint of modern times." On World Mission Sunday, October 19, 1998, Pope John Paul II named Thérèse a Doctor of the Church.

Although her illness plunged Thérèse into the midnight moment of naked faith, she had absolute confidence that the sun still shone. Dense as this inner darkness was, it deepened her conviction that Christ would never abandon her. The more faults she found in herself, the surer she was of the mercy of God. She did not waste time in an exhausting search for human perfection: she simply accepted her mistakes and continued to operate from her center of humility.

In desolation, when Thérèse probably felt like a lost child, helpless and alone, she clung to the truth of her friendship with the Companion who promised never to desert her. She bypassed the ups and downs of her emotions and relied instead on Christ's promise not to leave her orphaned (see John 14:18). Had Thérèse not exercised the virtue of unshakable confidence in the mercy of God, she might not have been able to carry the crosses he gave her. On bad days, when she sat in the garden amid the beauty of roses in bloom and contemplated the bounty of God's first revelation in creation, she found consolation in knowing that God gives to humble souls an eternity of glory.

This same childlike spirit allowed Thérèse to look lovingly on the virtues her sisters displayed, rather than judging their faults. Fading into the background was for her the best assurance that communal merits would be noted more than her small sacrifices. She had a horror of quarrels and felt that it was better to let the sisters keep their own opinions than to engage in gossip or fighting. It hurt her to think that they might docilely conform to her point of view rather than trying to perceive God's will for themselves. She did her best to restore tranquility whenever trouble arose in the community. Her aim, as God's instrument, was to keep a cheerful countenance; she did this even when the pain of breathing was almost more than she could bear. If misunderstandings by others made her suffer, she remained as silent as Jesus did before his accusers. When certain events did upset her, she learned how to redirect her attention to Christ crucified and to practice, as we all can do, the ministry of the smile.

## LET US PRAY

*Lord,* the desires for deeper union that you awaken in us cannot be crushed by even the most severe disappointments. No matter what happens, we must not settle for less. Every time we drift aimlessly on the surface of life, you beckon us to dive into the ocean depths of your love. On this razor's edge between the finite and the infinite, we have a purpose to fulfill, a destiny to reach. Teach us not to walk with heads lowered to accommodate what is less but to set our eyes on what is always more: the Alpha and the Omega, the beginning and the end. Amen.

## HENRI J. M. NOUWEN

Without care for each other, we forget who we truly are—children of God and each other's brothers and sisters—and so cannot become parents of generations to come.

—*Henri J. M. Nouwen (1932–1996)*

Priest, spiritual guide, author, and counselor, Nouwen insisted that the call of Jesus is a call to conversion of heart and deep healing, addressed not merely to saints but to the most ordinary people. He saw in the brokenness of humanity the wounded and glorified body of Jesus. No matter how lost one felt, he counseled, the way to one's true home could be found through God's unlimited and unconditional love.

Originally from the Netherlands, Nouwen spent most of his life in the United States, teaching at places like the Divinity Schools of Harvard and Yale and taking time off to live in a Trappist abbey as well as to travel and live among the poor in Latin America. He found his lasting home in the L'Arche community called Daybreak in Toronto in a house devoted to the care of handicapped people. His conviction of its importance is clear:

> So we see how loneliness is the minister's wound not only because he shares in the human condition, but also because of the unique predicament of his profession. It is this wound which he is called to bind with more care and attention than others usually do. For a deep understanding of his own pain makes it possible for him to convert his weakness into strength and to offer his own experience as a source of healing to those who are often lost in the darkness of their own misunderstood sufferings. . . . But once the pain is accepted and understood, a denial is no longer necessary, and ministry can become a healing service.[7]

At L'Arche, Nouwen felt the full impact of what it meant to be a "wounded healer" for whom life itself becomes a preparation for death. He died of a heart attack in his native Holland shortly before his sixty-fourth birthday.

When we care for one another as the children of God, we sense the intensity of our interconnectedness. We enjoy a relationship of spiritual generativity that enables us, whatever our state of life, to become "one who is able to transcend the fences of his own predicament and reach out far beyond the concerns of self."[8]

To care means to carry the cross of suffering in compassion for our own and others' vulnerability. To care means not to show mercy sporadically but to place ourselves where love needs us to be and to give to others the gifts we have received. To care means to accept our limits and to guard against pushing beyond them.

Christ, the chief caregiver, shows us how to put our gifts to the best possible use. When caring drained his energy, he paused to replace it in prayer (see Mark 6:31). We risk depletion of our sense of service if we allow our savior complex to get the best of us. Abnormal stress decreases the flow of care that identifies us, to quote St. Teresa of Calcutta, as "tiny pens in a mighty hand."

Care, in Nouwen's view, is a lasting disposition of the heart. Outreach efforts to feed the hungry and shelter the homeless, especially after a natural disaster, edify everyone, but care is not only an emergency measure; it is an outflow of love from one person or group to another, meeting all levels of need and never indifferent to the plight of the poor.

Suffering in any form evokes the giving as well as the receiving of other-centered love through repeated acts of compassion as well as during joyful moments of joint celebration. When we are at home with ourselves and others, we become more aware of the communal bonds that bind us together. Any infringement on our mutual integrity, any bitter plunge to negativity, is out of the question. When we pursue courses of action faithful to Christ's call, we become most truly who we are.

## LET US PRAY

*Lord,* when teachings to the contrary fill the air, let us remember the truth that we are bound together in a brotherhood and sisterhood of compassion and care. Love beyond all telling flows from your wounded hands to heal the sins of the world. Grant us the grace never to clench our fists in indifference to the plight of people abandoned in body and soul. Let no moment pass when we do not hear the cry of those in need of care in nearby neighborhoods and far-distant worlds. Amen.

FOUR

# REDEMPTIVE POWER OF PRAYER

The prayer of the righteous is powerful and effective.

—*James 5:16*

It began as an ordinary day. I gave a lecture in the morning on the literature of spirituality, and, in accordance with the weekly schedule I followed, I proceeded to attend and record Fr. Adrian's class on the foundations of formative spirituality. Though the day was rather cool, I noticed that he began to perspire and seemed to have trouble catching his breath. The entire class knew something was wrong. I jumped into action and phoned the campus switchboard for help. Within moments, first responders were at the classroom door, putting him on a stretcher, and transporting him to the emergency room of the hospital adjacent to the dorms. His primary-care physician met the ambulance and was at his side when he had a heart attack that would have been the death of him had it occurred anywhere else.

Everyone gathered in the waiting room, and we all began to pray for his recovery. It seemed forever until the doctor came through the door and announced, "First of all, thank you for your prayers. Fr. Adrian had an acute myocardial infarction, and for a while, quite frankly, it was 'touch and go.' Thanks be to God," he said, "it was not his time to go, and with good care and lots of rest he'll be with us for many years to come." That happened in 1982, and Fr. Adrian did not go to God until 2007. How could any of us have doubted the redemptive power of prayer?

A few weeks later, Fr. Adrian asked me to bring him a notebook and a pen. I hesitated to do so because the doctor had ordered him to rest, but I could not resist such a simple request. On my next visit, he opened that journal to the first page—on which he had written the words, "The Blessing of a Coronary." In that one phrase, Fr. Adrian demonstrated to me what it means when the attitude of gratitude begins to permeate the spirit, heart, mind, and will.

After he returned to the university, he began to notice aspects of life he had once been inclined to overlook. Behind the frown on a fellow professor's face, he saw a soul so serious he had forgotten how to smile. One colleague confessed that he harbored the morose conviction that the mystery of iniquity overshadowing the human condition was beyond redemption. Fr. Adrian presented him with an example of how to see the beauty behind the ugliest appearances. He reminded him of the classic story *The Hunchback of Notre Dame*. Jumping to conclusions about someone based only on appearances is a big mistake. As a counselor he had trained himself never to label anyone as being beyond redemption. We may not succeed in changing a person, but we can and must continue to ask God to have mercy on him or her.

On the level of logic alone, it seems implausible to say that we have nothing yet possess everything, that the cross is the way to salvation, that the exalted will be humbled and the humbled, exalted (see Luke 14:11). This heart knowledge goes beyond mere reasoning processes that torture us with unanswerable questions. Trust comes to our rescue when we bow in awe before the mystery at the center of everything. From rising in the morning to resting at night, we acknowledge the sovereignty of God with a whispered thank-you prayer on our lips: "Thank you for this food and the roof under which I've prepared it. Thank you for letting me pay my bills on time and for locating the best bank manager to help me. Thank you for the certitude that you direct my every choice of the good and reveal slowly but surely the grand design you have for my life in all its myriad details."

The promise behind these thank-you prayers points to a three-word imperative: *never give up.* A related directive might be "Never become disillusioned with life. Today may be full of shadows, but keep courage because tomorrow a brighter light will dispel them."

The thank-you prayer can be evoked in response to what is both pleasant and unpleasant. Once this prayer is on our lips, we have to complete it: "Thank you for this temporary power outage since it lets me experience what it is like to live by candlelight." The thank-you prayer does not exclude expressing our preferences and imploring God to spare us from what is painful. The difference is that behind this prayer is a blank check backed by the guarantee that only as God wills, let it be done. A thanks of this sort is wholehearted, not half-baked.

As a frequent flyer, I surrender myself totally to the mechanics of flight and the pilot's expertise. Turbulence may petrify me, but I have no choice but to endure it and pray that the feat of engineering in which I sit will carry me to a safe landing. Such trust inflames every thank-you prayer. Through its lens, we see the past in a more hopeful light: "Even in the worst of times, God was there for me." It gives us a more serene view of the present moment: "I'm going to double my portion of trust and see what happens!" It encourages us to face the future with faith: "With each passing day I grow closer to eternity, so why not enjoy what's here and now to the fullest?"

There's a story told about the great evangelist Billy Graham that proves what happens for the good when a person practices thank-you prayers for a lifetime. This event occurred when Graham, at the age of ninety-four, was suffering from Parkinson's disease. At a luncheon in his honor, he told a story the assembly never forgot. It was about Albert Einstein, who had recently been honored as the *Time* magazine person of the year. Einstein was on a train to Princeton University, but when the conductor passed by to punch his ticket, he could not find it in his briefcase nor on the seat beside him. The conductor told him not to worry about it because everyone knew him and no one doubted that he had bought a ticket. On his next pass, the conductor found Einstein on his knees searching for his ticket on the floor, and he again begged him not to worry because he was certain he had bought a ticket. Einstein is purported to have said to him, "Sir, I, too, know who I am. What I don't know is where I'm going."

Graham then told the audience that he had bought a new suit for this occasion, and it would be the one in which he would be buried. Everyone grew still, and then Graham assured them all that he not only knew who he was, but he also knew where he was going.

When we delight in Divine Providence, we *believe* that what we ask of God, if it is in accordance with what God's wisdom wishes to grant, will be done. We *hope* that what we seek, from the meaning of our existence to assistance with the task at hand, will on this or a future day be found. We *love* God so much that we behold in some mysterious way that the door upon which we knocked has already been opened, thanks to the prevenient grace of God.

In this prayerful series of imperatives (*ask*, *seek*, *knock*), we find the best formula for the intercessions and petitions we address to the living God. We know that if we ask our heavenly Father to give us our daily bread (see Matthew 6:11), it will be given to us since Jesus himself is the "bread of life" (Jn 6:35). Even when what we ask for is not immediately forthcoming, we trust that it will be granted to us in God's good time, thanks to the outflow of amazing grace.

When we forget to be grateful, when we refuse to give thanks, we ought not to treat such errors as endpoints.

Temporary relapses to ingratitude ought to prompt us to pray for the grace to start again on a more positive note. When revengeful put-downs pose as sensible solutions, we challenge ourselves to follow Jesus, who even kept company with sinners. We may disagree with an adversary, but we do so without malice. We hold out an olive branch of reconciliation in the hope that he or she will take it.

A sign of peace may be the last gesture we want to extend to an ungrateful, close-minded person, but it may be the only way for God to release through us the virtue of compassion. We could choose to lock ourselves in a tight box of defensiveness, or we can delight in the providential care God wants us to extend to everyone.

Grateful living detaches us from the downward pull of judgmental attitudes and encourages us to give each person respect. We count our blessings, motivated not by ownership but by stewardship. In and behind whatever occurs, we see evidence of the redemptive power of prayer.

A grateful response to life's ups and downs teaches us to accept our own and others' vulnerability. Focusing on the saving grace of God enables us to empathize with the anguish we see everywhere around us and to do what we can to alleviate it. We pray to find the happy medium between caring so sparsely that we become indifferent and caring so much that we become frustrated when there is a scarcity of results. We live more and more in the middle between gentleness and firmness. We see ourselves neither as heroic saviors nor as perfect servants. We are simply pilgrims on the way to Christian perfection. If efforts like these do not emanate from a thankful heart, they may come across as pretenses of charity that humiliate the poor.

Our compassion has to be uplifting, never condescending; empowering, never debilitating. Only then can we help others restore the sense of worth they have lost and take whatever time is necessary to consider their voiced and unvoiced concerns. Gratefulness makes us more tolerant and less judgmental. We do not let our caregiving efforts deteriorate into crippling codependency. Neither do we lose sight of our own vulnerability. Only then can our love remain strong and honest, never a refuge from the reality of suffering, always an invitation to transformation.

It takes only a second or two to picture Jesus beside us when we are inclined to treat every criticism as an insult rather than learning from our mistakes. The Lord gives us the courage to become spiritually mature. This means accepting both compliments and criticisms with grace and equanimity. However troubling a situation may be, we can pray to replace agitation with serenity lest seething cauldrons of rage spill over. That is why we beseech God to clothe us with "heartfelt compassion, kindness, humility, gentleness, and patience" (Col 3:12).

Rather than clinging to willful control, we try to cultivate the virtue of docility. Docility does not mean seeking peace at any price but remaining receptive to what God asks us to do at the present moment. What matters is God's will, not our own agenda. The peaceful inspirations God sends our way do not guarantee the cessation of conflict or the absence of misunderstanding. The difference is that we are now capable of appreciating what we perceived beforehand as only depreciable. We accept the challenge to look upon adversity as an invitation to seek a meaning we hadn't seen when we based our happiness on a fleeting pleasure like worldly acclaim. Now we put on the back burner whatever prevents us from making Christ's example of self-giving love the center of our lives.

We no longer emphasize being busy to such a degree that it excludes simply being. We know when to stop working lest we lose our sense of wonder. We ask God for the grace of abiding in awe-filled attention to the Spirit in the routines of the day. No matter how difficult it may be to discern their meaning, we try to listen and re-listen to these inspirations. We never dismiss them as unimportant or as interruptions in an already overloaded schedule. We release our grip on life and give ourselves over to the surprises of God. Rather than trying to analyze every sign of progress or regression, we choose to go forward, confident that the power of prayer will release us from the spiritual paralysis that results from fear of the unknown. Amid the destructive forces that threaten to derail the practice of appreciation, we choose to pursue the constructive ways that open before us. We interpret the past with faith, approach the present with hope, and usher in the future with love. Time and again, we take comfort in the fact that nothing falls outside the loving embrace of God in whose company we pledge

1.  to see what is appreciable in every person, event, and thing we encounter;

2. to cultivate individually and communally the gifts and fruits of the Holy Spirit;

3. to listen in obedience, to respect in love, and to revere in poverty of spirit all facets of life—inner and outer;

4. to reform as quickly as possible the unthankful conclusions that threaten to overtake us;

5. to lead a calmer, more serene style of life attuned to the transcendent;

6. to integrate contemplation and action wherever we are and in whatever we do; and

7. to pursue the benefits of grateful living and acknowledge how precious souls are in the sight of God.

In all of these ways, we rise above the paralysis caused by a doom-and-gloom mentality. We cannot predict where life will lead us, but we stop worrying about it. Faith in Christ's victory over death rekindles our hope. We trust that the Spirit will reveal what is best for us as individuals and as members of a pilgrim church. The efficacy of this belief reinforces the confidence we feel. It is as if Christ confirms again, "Do not let your hearts be troubled" (Jn 14:1), "I will not leave you orphaned; I am coming to you" (Jn 14:18), and "I am with you always, to the end of the age" (Mt 28:20).

We need to bolster our trust in these consoling promises of Christ day after day. Without thinking about it, as if it were in the blink of an eye, this trust has to become our preferred way of being. When the veil of ingratitude tends to overshadow our joy or erode our peace, we choose at once to block its treacherous tactics by saying silently or aloud, "Thanks be to God for his indescribable [gifts]." (2 Cor 9:15). We may add to this thank-you prayer others, such as "Thank you, Lord, for warning me once again that I need to free myself from these lingering remnants of negativity. Strengthen my belief that I have not been abandoned by you, but that I can and must abandon myself to you."

Another way to strengthen trust is to keep a gratitude journal. In it we record the reasons we had to be thankful today. Every obstacle that caused us to become momentarily negative becomes an opportunity to initiate a more positive approach. We train ourselves to welcome whatever or whomever God sends our way. Before long, we begin to see what may be wrong against the backdrop of all that is right. We lift up for due praise our own and others' achievements and thank God again for the mistakes we've made since we learned so much from them. At day's end, we review all these hindrances and helps to grateful living and feel good about how much we have grown.

In the past, our first response to almost any difficulty may have been to blame ourselves and complain about others. Now we are more likely to accept with equanimity the blessings and burdens that accompany saying with Jesus, "Yes, Father. Your will not mine be done" (see Luke 22:42). We clear the clutter caused by frustration and opt instead to say prayers of thanksgiving.

The process of working through conflicting calls increases our understanding of what it means to be faithful to the daily practice of appreciation. The tension we experience between gratitude and ingratitude brings us to the threshold of a radical choice: to opt for the illusion of self-sufficiency or to trust in the truth that without God we can do nothing. The first response dupes us into denying our powerlessness; the second convinces us to rely on the Cross of Christ, however fragile we may feel.

Instead of caving in to demands on our time, we take more time to pray. Reflective dwelling is not a waste of time or an exercise in withdrawal but a rediscovery of our inescapable connection to the Lord. Instead of turning on the television, leafing through a magazine, or telephoning friends, we listen to the sounds of silence and ponder for a while who it is that God calls us to be. In this way we recast the pain of loneliness into the joy of solitude. To be alone is to recognize that we are unique and at the same time that we have a great deal in common with others. In some ways we are *all-one* while at the same time being *a-lone* with God.

Solitude refreshes our souls and renders us more receptive to what God wants us to be and do in this world. Being alone with God enables us to move from a superficial approach to spirituality, through a time of self-discovery, to a reclaiming of the untapped gifts that let us see into the heart of a problem and address it in a new way.

We could compare this stepping aside in silence and solitude to looking at a painting we appreciate. From afar, we enjoy its beauty and laud the depth of the artist's sensitivity. This distance widens our field of vision to the work as a whole. Were we to stand too close to the canvas, we might see only the chips and cracks on its surface. The harmony of the painting would remain hidden from our view. The same happens when we distance ourselves momentarily from the fast pace of the day and pause for prayer.

We dwell less on life's inevitable imperfections and appreciate again the whole of life in light of the Holy. The gift of stillness lets us drain our minds of restless calculations. Buoyed on waves of peace and the welcome consolation of this inward retreat, we are better able to deal with what awaits us at home and in the marketplace. Openness to the transcendent tells us that life is more than a tabulation of ambitions achieved and problems solved. Silence lets this sense of wholeness and harmony pervade our self-awareness, enabling us to weather the winters of our lives. Solitude teaches us the beauty of being at home with ourselves, others, and God. Solidarity prompts us to go beyond stale, no-longer-viable ways of relating and to seek friendships in the Lord. This springtime of togetherness frees us from the shallowness of the crowd mentality and heightens our attention to where the Spirit invites us to go.

A compassionate nurse cools a fevered brow and whispers words of encouragement. A mechanic touches with pride the car he has just repaired, and the owner cannot thank him enough. Other examples of the fruits of thankful living may be preparing a surprise meal for friends and family or initiating pleasant conversations with local merchants. In and through all of these comings and goings, welcomes and departures, we sense the countless ways in which God's majesty reveals itself, be it in the posture of an old peasant bent in prayer or in a stately cathedral with rows of worshipers. We can connect such expressions of appreciation as listening attentively, loving respectfully, and living simply with the evangelical counsels of obedience, chastity, and poverty that protect us from the misuse of power, pleasure, and possession.

By virtue of our Baptism, we share in the obedience of Jesus to the Father, in his yes to life as a salvation event. We hear or obey the signals sent to us from the Most High in everyday happenings such as making beds and baking bread as well as reaching out to others when a natural disaster destroys what they once held dear. Every time we listen respectfully to events—from awakening in the morning to retiring at night— we deepen our capacity for gratitude. Obedience means listening to more than the practical details of daily life; it invites us to be present to events as providential pointers to God's loving and allowing will.

To become a giver as well as a receiver of gratitude, we pray to grow in chaste, respectful love and be purified of those self-gratifying passions that put our needs above those of others. When God is the center of our attention, care and concern for the persons Holy Providence places on our path become primary. One minute it's an elderly parishioner who needs a lift to the grocery store, the next it's a student who asks for time with us after class. Different as these encounters are, they allow us to express gratitude to God for placing us in situations where we can best exercise Christlike compassion and companionship. Gone is the deceptive illusion that others are there to advance our ambitions—a mentality that signifies the height of ingratitude for who we are in the Lord.

Friendships centered in the Lord are among the greatest of life's gifts; they are the basis for mutually supportive relationships that last a lifetime. What we can count on through thick and thin is an acceptance so unconditional that there is no need to mask our vulnerability. When the Christ in me beholds the Christ in you, it is as if we live in a state of continual thanksgiving. Because our trustworthiness has been tested over time, we do not have to fear betrayal of fidelity or the pain of disappointed expectations. In the safe space of intimacy, we know we are in communion with a beloved other who puts our best interests first. Being together in a relaxing atmosphere of care and concern enables us to converse in confidence about what we think and feel. We do not need to hide our faults and failings or cover up our gifts and goals. These loving exchanges encourage us to go beyond self-centered agendas. I care for you and you care for me because first and foremost, we are cared for by God.

What sets such friendships apart from casual acquaintance-ships is the steady practice of mutual gratitude. We encourage one another to behold the splendor of the ordinary that we ought never to take for granted. We celebrate the hidden lights revealed in the mundane flow of daily life—from bees pollinating flowers to florists creating a birthday bouquet.

To be poor in spirit as Jesus was is to behold all that life offers with a grateful eye. This virtue prevents us from becoming captives of consumerism without any humble admission of our ultimate dependency on God. A generous heart, dedicated to the service of others, avoids being possessed by possessions.

Inner poverty is the seedbed of gratitude. We share what we have not because we are motivated by do-gooder desires but because we know that nothing really belongs to us. All that we have is on loan from the Lord. Whereas a rapacious attitude of possessiveness harms everyone, a reverent disposition of poverty of spirit harms no one. It invites us to behold the beauty that outward appearances often conceal. Ugly as an oyster shell is, open it and there's a pearl!

Living in poverty of spirit also frees us from overanalyzing people, events, and things. We are content to let them be without having to figure them out. What interests us is to enter wholly into what God asks us to do at the moment. Inner stilling prevents us from jumping to wrong conclusions. We stay where we are, awaiting the moment when the Father's will gains clarity and encourages us to go forward no matter how many setbacks may disrupt our plans or leave us feeling discouraged. With joyful abandonment we let go of useless worry and let God take the lead.

Because the word of God is alive and active (see Hebrews 4:12–13), every time we encounter it in prayer, it restores our flagging spirits. We cease trying to predict the outcomes God has in mind for us and flow with the daily lights we receive. From the refreshment that contemplative pauses provide, we are better able to reenter the world of production. We operate not by willpower but in accordance with God's will. Freed from the depleting effects of discouragement, we are free to read the script God writes.

This thankful feeling enhances our capacity to unwrap the meaning of life layer by layer. We begin to explore life's infinite richness not only during an occasional retreat from the din of daily demands but at every moment. Life becomes more like a rhythmic dance than a rubber band stretching us toward momentary contemplation and as quickly snapping us back into action, with no rest in between. A gracious aura permeates our everyday existence, causing us to move in the ebb and flow of presence and participation, of silence and speech, of solitude and new depths of union and communion with God and others. Though there are situations that, humanly speaking, defy comprehension, we remain convinced that God knows the why behind every what. One day we might glimpse the answer, but for now we are content to live in the question while renewing our faith in the promise that God's perfect timing is itself a response to our perfect thanks, and so we pray:

*Lord,* we who are the work of your hands thank you for giving us hands with which to work. When we fold them in prayer, we remember our partnership with you, the source and center of our lives. The smallest act of love sends waves of gratitude through every member of your Mystical Body. May the labor we do on earth mirror in some way what you do without ceasing for our benefit. With the gifts we have been given, let your will be done on earth as it is in heaven. Amen.

# QUESTIONS FOR REFLECTION

1. When is it hardest for you to feel uplifted by the redemptive power of prayer? When is it easiest?
2. As you try with the help of grace to reform the habit of ingratitude ingrained in your heart, what mode of prayer (vocal, mental, contemplative) do you prefer?
3. Despite the dangers inherent in any crisis, can you testify from experience to the blessings in disguise emerging from it?

# COMPANIONS IN GRATEFUL LIVING

## ST. CATHERINE OF SIENA

Oh! How delightful to the soul and pleasing to me
is holy prayer made in the house of self-knowledge
and knowledge of me!
—*St. Catherine of Siena (1347–1380)*

The twenty-fourth of twenty-five children in a prosperous Sienese family, Catherine of Siena was destined to become the patron saint of Italy and one of four women (along with Teresa of Avila, Thérèse of Lisieux, and Hildegard of Bingen) named as a Doctor of the Church. At the age of six, Catherine had a vision of Christ the King that changed the direction of her life forever. Despite her parents' wishes, she refused to marry, cutting off her golden hair as a sign that she would remain a virgin, to be wed only to her heavenly spouse.

In her teenage years, she lived as a contemplative in her own home and was the recipient of many graces associated with mystical espousal and marriage, a favor granted to her in 1367. Unschooled and illiterate, Catherine learned to read through the intervention of the Holy Spirit. Though she remained a laywoman, serving Christ in the world, she sought communal affiliation with the Sisters of Penitence under the sponsorship of the Dominican Order. Like another member of the order, St. Thomas Aquinas, Catherine wanted above all to know and teach the truth, to practice charity, and to adore the presence of Christ in the Eucharist.

As she passed into her adult years, Catherine heard and obeyed the Lord's command to leave her solitude and reach out to the needy of Siena: to its prisoners, to the sick, and to the poor. By 1370, her world had expanded to include people from all walks of life: popes and counselors as well as common folk. When anarchy reigned in Siena, she was enlisted as a peace-maker, as a healer and spiritual director, and even as a brilliant negotiator when she was asked to approach Pope Gregory XI and ask him to return from Avignon to Rome. His successor, Urban VI, also recognized in Catherine a powerful advocate. He appointed her papal emissary to the city-states in revolt. At the beginning of the Great Schism in 1378, she became active in support of Pope Urban, urging both cardinals and monarchs to return to Rome in obedience to him. Her efforts, though, were in vain.

So weary was she by these attempts to restore unity that she died in Rome in her thirty-third year, leaving a legacy of transcribed letters (more than four hundred written to leaders of both the Church and state), a series of poems celebrating her love for the Blessed Trinity and her union with the risen Lord, and most importantly, her masterpiece on the spiritual life, *The Dialogue*. Its central theme is God's truth, of which the soul seeks a deeper understanding not through intellectual mastery but through that humility of mind that is born of pure faith.

In *The Dialogue*, Catherine records her experiences of God as the "gentle and supreme Truth," who has created us in love. In the opening sentences of her masterpiece, she describes herself as being "accustomed to dwelling in the cell of self-knowledge in order to know better God's goodness toward her, since upon knowledge follows love."[9]

St. Catherine sees her essence in God as preceding her existence in time. She situates both of these dimensions in the goodness and generosity of God by revealing that as the soul comes to know itself, it necessarily comes to know and love God. God speaks through her, saying in *The Dialogue*:

> This infinite good cannot be fully contained by anything less than itself any more than the vessel dipped into the sea can contain the whole sea but only as much as it can hold. Only the sea itself can fully contain itself. In the same way I, the sea of peace, am the only one who can fully contain and value myself. And this makes me rejoice in myself and the joy and good that I have in myself I share

with you, with each of you according to your own
capacity. I fill you and do not leave you empty.[10]

She concludes that insofar as God has loved us and sent his Son
to save us, so should Father, Son, and Holy Spirit be loved by us.

Once we receive the grace of this awareness, it follows that
we must seek ongoing conversion by recognizing and relin-
quishing what she calls our "selfish sensuality." When this happens, we live in deeper receptivity to the Lord's goodness. By
means of his grace, we are drawn from darkness into the light
of truth. Hence Catherine prays, "You, eternal Trinity, are the
craftsman; and I your handiwork have come to know that you
are in love with the beauty of what you have made, since you
made of me a new creation in the blood of your Son."[11]

With a grateful heart, Catherine teaches us that the more
we come to know ourselves, the more we realize that our selfish
sensuality has disfigured the reflection of the Divine Beauty
in our souls. This discovery, painful as it may be, motivates us
to grow over a lifetime in union with God and in care for one
another.

## LET US PRAY

*Lord,* in your mercy, awaken in our overly complacent
hearts the virtue of adoration. Wipe away the stains
of arrogance that obscure the radiance of awe. In the presence of
your mystery, place us on our knees and keep us there until we
realize in whose presence we are. Let us search our hearts to find

whether or not they belong to you alone. Transform us, as you did the Samaritan woman, into worshipers in spirit and in truth who believe what we have heard and who bow in gratitude before the Adored One, the Savior of the world. Amen.

## ST. IGNATIUS OF LOYOLA

In the things of God . . . those who are over prudent will hardly achieve anything really great. Those who are constantly brooding and vacillating because they fear the possible outcomes they foresee will never turn their hearts toward real Beauty.
—*St. Ignatius of Loyola (1401–1556)*

Founder of the Society of Jesus, Ignatius was the youngest son of a Basque nobleman. As a young man he dreamt of becoming a soldier. During a long convalescence following a siege in which he was wounded, he read voraciously about the life of Christ and the saints. After a time he felt an irresistible call to give himself to God's service, to be a soldier for Christ. His zeal was unmatched as he exchanged the clothing of a dignitary for the rough garb of a beggar and pledged himself first of all to the service of the Blessed Virgin Mary.

After a year of solitude at Manresa, he made a pilgrimage to Jerusalem. He was certain after this trip that God wanted him to be a priest. That meant continuing his education, which he did from 1524 to 1534, in Barcelona and at the University of Paris. In Paris he inspired seven students, among them St. Francis Xavier, to vow to be missionary disciples in Palestine. Soon this original group increased in numbers and offered their services to the pope. After Ignatius was ordained to the priesthood in 1448, he fulfilled the tasks assigned to him and received inspiration to found the Society of Jesus. Its members would take the usual vows but would add to them one more: to be at the disposal of the papacy and to serve the Church in whatever way they could. In 1540, Ignatius was elected the first Superior General of the Jesuits. His signature work, *The Spiritual Exercises*, guided initiates and professed members of the Society to engage in discursive meditation as an avenue to contemplative prayer.

Understanding as he did the battlefield that goes on in the heart, the future saint strove to discern which of these "bad spirits," that is to say, spirits of devilish origin, was the most cunning. His answer was *brooding*. It is on the prowl whenever we worry so much about ourselves, our mistakes of the past, or our projects for the future that we forget to conform our lives to Christ. This evil spirit attracts one similar to it: *vacillating*. Like puppets on a string, we swing first in one direction, then in another. Back and forth we go, imprudently and without making any progress.

Brooding causes us to regret the past, distrust the present, and predict disastrous scenarios for the future. In every case we are oblivious to the benevolence of God. Vacillating arouses such fear of making a mistake that we bounce from one unrealistic idea to the next since full certitude about anything seems impossible to acquire.

What we miss when such thoughts obsess us is the ability to behold the beauty of God's plan for our lives. What we gain when they are put to rest is a more harmonious outlook. The what-ifs that weakened our trust go by the wayside. We accept with serenity the truth that God's surprises are always better than our plans. St. Ignatius believed that we ought never, under any circumstances, act like cowards or chronic complainers; instead he inspires us to behave always like courageous disciples, willing to comply to the full with the lessons Christ teaches.

## LET US PRAY

*Lord,* brooding, like the blame game, weakens our ability to listen to your Word and the truth it teaches: that useless worry solves nothing. Never let us vacillate because we fear where our faith journeys may lead. Rather, let us run the race to the finish in joyful abandonment to God's loving and allowing will. Amid losses and gains, help us behold the things of God and the real beauty inherent in them. Amen.

# FIVE

# SIGNS OF PROGRESS IN GRATEFUL LIVING

*Do not worry about anything, but in everything by
prayer and supplication with thanksgiving let your
requests be made known to God.*
*—Philippians 4:6*

Sometimes we have to put the people we most love to the test.
Though my mother was as buoyant and upbeat as her mother
most of the time, I detected in her spirit every so often a wave
of sadness. In later years—when we were beyond the usual
mother-daughter relationship and had become good friends—I
heard more about the deepest regret of her life.

Intelligent as she was, she was not permitted by her father to
pursue a higher education. That privilege would go to his eldest
son. She had to go to work immediately after high school, and
that was that. She channeled her talents into being a hatcheck
girl at a private club, wiring electric lamps in a low-budget
hardware store, selling ready-to-wear clothing in the women's section of a department store, and eventually becoming

a manager of a Fashion Hosiery Shops outlet in downtown Pittsburgh, Pennsylvania.

Once she married, she dedicated herself to helping my father with his contracting business and being a full-time mother to my brothers and me. I am sure she encouraged my pursuit of higher education because it represented in some way the realization of her dreams. In addition to her intelligence, my mother had a natural flare for dressing well, beautifying the plainest of rooms, and presenting a delicious meal on a well-decorated table. She created on her sewing machine everything from award-winning Halloween costumes to lovely day and evening dresses.

Off and on throughout the years, she expressed a desire to be an artist, but she never felt as if she could pursue such a dream. On her fifty-sixth birthday, I decided it was time to act. I went to the finest art store in the city and asked the proprietor to put in a large gift box everything a first-time artist would need: a few canvases, an easel, a good set of brushes, tubes of oil paint in primary and secondary colors, a palette, cleaning fluid, and whatever else was suitable for a beginner.

I will never forget the look on my mother's face when she unwrapped that big box. It was as if she already knew—without so much as one lesson—what to do. That night she retired to a corner of our basement, rigged a light to shine on her first canvas, and, by sunrise the following morning, she had painted from her imagination a rendering of my father fishing in his favorite stream, surrounded by trees and wildflowers and with a campfire burning to cook his catch.

I still have the first of what would be her more than four hundred works of art—all lauded by the league she joined and displayed in their local shows. With each creation, and the expertise she gathered from manuals and amateur classes, she made incredible progress. She said she could never thank me enough for believing in her and helping her to pursue her dream. When she sensed the downslide to dementia that made the details of painting impossible (she would die of Alzheimer's disease at the age of eighty-five), she handed me her brushes and we wept together.

From that birthday breakthrough until she was eighty years old, not a day went by when Mother did not do something to advance her artistic gifts. Her progress astonished everyone in the family. Her legacy lives on in the paintings that adorn our homes. A nephew of mine stood before one of her exquisite desert scenes, now hanging on the wall of the entrance to his house, shook his head in wonder, and asked me, "How did she do it?"

"God alone knows," I replied softly, "but how grateful all of us are for the amazing collection she left us. In every completed canvas, her spirit lives on."

The more we live in gratitude, the less inclined we are to reduce the day to a collection of annoying interruptions; we watch with amazement the way the Holy Spirit weaves diverse threads into one grand design. Others benefit from the changes they see in us when we act thankfully, remain in God's presence, and listen to the Good News: "Rejoice in the Lord always; again I will say, Rejoice. Let your gentleness be known to everyone. The Lord is near. Do not worry about anything, but in everything by prayer and supplication with thanksgiving let your requests be made known to God. And the peace of God, which surpasses all understanding, will guard your hearts and your minds in Christ Jesus" (Phil 4:4–7).

In this passage, St. Paul thanks God not only for gifts like good health or special talents but for every treasure life holds—from spring buds on a once-frozen bush to a baby's first steps. In an otherwise ordinary day, we receive uplifting inspirations that point to six signs of progress in grateful living:

1.  Trust your story, and let others know of its positive outcomes.
2.  Train yourself to find a silver lining in every limit.
3.  Never push against the pace of grace lest you lose your peace.
4.  Abandon yourself to the mystery, and never feel abandoned by it.
5.  Let the spiritual hunger you feel be a reminder that, in the words of St. Teresa of Avila, "God alone suffices."
6.  Strive every day, with the help of grace, to overcome the temptation to be ungrateful and instead to practice what St. Thérèse of Lisieux called "the ministry of the smile."

The peace that accompanies a grateful outlook is fragile. What small gains we have made can come under attack by a barrage of negativity and the distress it evokes. The healthy response—"This day was not so bad"—may evoke the dissatisfied refrain, "Don't be an idiot. Practically nothing went right."

Blanket conclusions such as this overlook those times when we need to say no for the sake of a greater yes. Perhaps God is calling us to let go of excessive socializing and empty gossip and to seek instead a little more solitude. The question is, are we willing to detach ourselves from the bad habits we have acquired in favor of the good habits the Gospel asks of us? Maybe we need to modify the functionalistic tendency to judge our worth only by the benchmarks of competition and consumption. Maybe we need to determine to what degree we have begun to live mainly outer-directed, performance-oriented lives inattentive to the cry of the poor. Maybe now is the time to examine our spending habits to assess how much money we waste on frivolous items instead of donating to charitable works.

Despite the progress in grateful living we might be making, new challenges present themselves, with the first being how to maintain the gains granted to us by God. As any new diet reveals, it can end as quickly as it began. In relatively short order, we may find ourselves deviating from the ideals we have pursued. Even the best resolution can go wrong unless we try to incarnate the dispositions that flow from a grateful heart and let them show up in our matching character.

An example may be the way everyday life puts our patience to the test of resisting the irritable impatience that causes us to miss seeing the seeds of goodness in every event. Growth in patience and growth in gratitude expand together. These virtues prevent us from rushing to judgment and labeling this or that happening as hopeless—and from castigating human fallibility and condemning others and ourselves for occasional failures. We can always find reasons to gripe, but would we not rather lift into the light what good there was in the past, is in the present, and will be in the future?

Soon we may find ourselves feeling less agitated and more patient, less distracted and more centered, less fatigued and more rested. We know how to maintain the right rhythm of nearness and distance in our relationships. Too much nearness may lead to the illusion of instant intimacy and its immoral reduction of the other to the object of our pleasure. Too much distance creates a standoffish aura others may perceive as cold, curt, discourteous, and indifferent. To appreciate our shared dignity means neither to invade another's privacy nor to evade our need for community. Rather, we show genuine concern when friends seek our advice and we empathize with them. We avoid any tendency to retreat into our shells or wish only that others would leave us alone.

Thankful living also points to the need for balance between solitude and solidarity. Liking to be alone once in a while is normal, but becoming a recluse who shuns any semblance of spontaneous togetherness is not. Depreciating any solitary moment as inherently self-centered is one extreme. The other is the seductive solidarity that precludes always being on our own. In both cases ingratitude escalates. The opposite happens when the space of solitude we enter makes us sense in a mysterious way that we are in solidarity with others. Being grateful for the silence within makes it easier for us to hear the voices beseeching us from without.

We may then experience life as an ebb and flow between giving of ourselves (our support, talents, prayers) and receiving from others (friendship, hospitality, care). The ebb of giving (effusion) and the inflow of receiving (infusion) move back and forth. Both movements help us to maintain our peace amid the disruptions each day brings. Giving care in noticed and unnoticed ways is our response to the Lord's command that what we do for the least of our brothers and sisters, we do for him (see Matthew 25:45). When this ebb and flow becomes second nature to us, we see life in a new light, proclaiming with the psalmist, "O LORD, I love the house in which you dwell, and the place where your glory abides" (Ps 26:8).

Becoming artisans of appreciative living may grind to a halt if we are prone to be excessively suspicious, refusing, for example, to get involved with others because they may expect too much of us. All such actions belie the commission Christ gave us to be known by our love and the mutual thankfulness we ought to show for one another (see 1 John 3:11). These four counsels may help us to reach this goal:

*Be friendly.* A frown consumes more energy than a smile. While not pushing ourselves on people who obviously want to be left alone, friendliness prompts us to exude an air of hospitality that makes others feel at home. Rather than maintaining a one-track mind-set that shows no interest in those who are different, we avoid as a rule distrustful or discourteous acts of unfriendliness and remain flexible enough to seek and find new friendships.

*Be generous.* If we allow ourselves to become too bound to clock time, we may fail to give others quality time. That is the soil where mutual gratitude takes root. Going that extra mile is a sure sign of a generous heart.

*Don't be judgmental.* The best way to impede appreciation is to profile a person in the light of our own implicit or explicit prejudices. It harms us more than others when we lock them in a box or label them as objects we need to control. Such judgments are always dangerous, for, as scripture says, "Do not judge, and you will not be judged; do not condemn, and you will not be condemned. Forgive, and you will be forgiven; give, and it will be given to you" (Lk 6:37–38).

*Don't withhold blessings.* Withholding well-deserved praise devalues our own and others' worth. All of us welcome spoken or unspoken blessings and the encouragement they convey. *Benediction* means to speak well of or to another. Watch the way others blossom when we discard from our vocabulary condescending words and pejorative phrases and instead try to remind one another of our status as children of God.

Remember how Jesus saved the wedding party at Cana from embarrassment by attending to his mother's observation that they had no more wine (see John 2:1–11)? How about when he allowed a woman of ill repute to break social rank and anoint his feet with expensive perfume (see John 12:1–8)? Imagine how thankful Simon Peter's mother-in-law must have felt when Jesus healed her fever (see Mark 1:30) or how the widow must have felt when he raised her son from the dead (see Luke 7:11–15). To refuse to give of ourselves when we have been given so much by God is a tragedy. To follow Jesus, we must chip off the barnacles of childish narcissism and pursue the path to spiritual maturity. The secret of this transformation is simple: to give of ourselves to God and others to such a degree that the seeds of grateful living blossom to the full, and so we pray:

*Lord,* thank you for staying with me no matter how many times I stray from the path of loving union you've decreed for me. Let this invitation to intimacy be a constant reminder of your forgiveness and acceptance of me. Sensing your grace flowing through me is the surest sign of your care for every wayward child of yours. Teach me day by day to surrender to you in childlike faith, enduring hope, and undiluted love. May these virtues abound in me and fill to overflowing the empty spaces of my life. Amen.

## QUESTIONS FOR REFLECTION

1. If someone known for being thankless wants to become more thankful, what advice would you give to that person?
2. Just as preventive measures help to keep disease at bay in the body, how do grateful dispositions provide good medicine for the soul?
3. As you progress in grateful living, what most facilitates your capacity to treat your imperfections as blessings in disguise?

# *COMPANIONS IN GRATEFUL LIVING*

## ST. BERNARD OF CLAIRVAUX

Lord, you are good to the soul which seeks you.
What are you then to the soul which finds? But this
is the most wonderful thing, that no one can seek
you who has not already found you . . . seek to be
found so that you may be sought . . . sought so that
you may be found.
—*St. Bernard of Clairvaux (1090–1153)*

Over the ages, the abbot of the Benedictine monastery at Clairvaux has garnered many superlative titles, including author of the Cistercian reform, the last of the Fathers, counselor of popes and kings, ecclesiastical statesman and diplomat, mediator between warring factions, and Doctor of the Church. For good reason: St. Bernard was perhaps the most influential person in Europe during the first half of the twelfth century. He was born and educated in Dijon, France. Like his mentor, St. Benedict, he could have pursued a destiny fitting his noble upbringing. Instead, in 1113 he felt drawn to enter the newly reformed monastery of Citeaux. His gifts of persuasion were obvious even then, for he had no trouble convincing thirty of his relatives and friends to enter with him. Under the guidance of the Holy Spirit, they transformed a community on the verge of extinction into a vibrant movement in the Church that would eventually spawn more than three hundred houses across the whole of Europe.

One of the daughter houses of Citeaux was in the town of Clairvaux. There, Bernard became abbot. Though Bernard would have been content to live a hidden life of prayer and work, his reputation for wisdom and holiness soon spread beyond the boundaries of his monastery, drawing him into the thick of ecclesial and political affairs, including the preaching of the Second Crusade.

It should come as no surprise that at the end of the *Divine Comedy*, Dante chose as his spiritual guide to the Love that moves the sun, the moon, and all the stars none other than St. Bernard, who once said, "My purpose is not so much to explain words [as] to move hearts." Perhaps that is why he concluded in one of his sermons on the Song of Songs that "at the slightest sign of amendment of life, I have experienced the goodness of his mercy . . . the remaking and renewing of the spirit of my mind . . . the excellence of his glorious beauty . . . and when I contemplate all these things, I am filled with awe of his manifold greatness."[12] Bernard believed that "truth without grace is bitter; and without the restraint of truth devotion can be capricious, immoderate, and over confident." Such ungrateful presumption is the enemy of our souls, the annihilation of our merits, and the scattering of our virtues. He goes on to say that when we live in the truth of our utter dependence upon God, we "look beyond [our] own needs to the needs of [our] neighbors, and [we] know how to suffer with them in their troubles."[13]

These strong words about love of God and others dispel the myth that we are in charge of our own destinies. A faithless generation might attribute life's ups and downs to mere luck, but not believers like St. Bernard, who are appreciative of God's unfailing love and of the need to purify their hearts of arrogance and ignorance of their grace-filled destinies.

## LET US PRAY

*Lord,* yours is a shepherd's heart that will never reject its own. Give us the grace to stop the foolishness of wandering away from your flock. Remind us when we feel most alone that we are most at one with you. Your appreciation of us overrides any roadblock of ingratitude that gets in the way of discipleship. Our loyal following of you comes to fruition because of your having found us before we lost our way. Amen.

## DOROTHY DAY

We have all known the long loneliness, and we have learned that the only solution is love and that love comes with community.
—*Dorothy Day (1897–1980)*

A native of New York, Dorothy Day returned to the city after living in California and studying in Chicago to work as a reporter for a socialist newspaper. It was in her daily confrontation with the relentless poverty of tenement dwellers that she came to see her call to serve the poor.

Feeling drawn to God after the birth of her daughter, Day was baptized a Catholic. From then on, she maintained a life-long devotion to the Eucharist. Following her conversion, she separated from her common-law husband and stayed on with her daughter in New York, seeking further direction for her life. It was in New York that she met Peter Maurin (1877–1949), with whom she founded the Catholic Worker Movement in the immigrant neighborhoods of New York's Lower East Side. The two opened a house of hospitality that gave credence and concreteness to the corporal works of mercy, which include feeding the hungry, clothing the naked, and sheltering the homeless. The aims of the movement, in addition to person-alist action, were voluntary poverty, a commitment to human rights, and pacifism or a Gospel-oriented commitment to nonviolence.

A gifted writer, Day's autobiography, *The Long Loneliness*, is considered a twentieth-century classic, reflecting the depth of her own yearning toward God. What we know of loneliness as a devastating reality may be seen in hospital wards where patients receive few, if any, visitors; in half-empty funeral par-lors where the departed seems not to have had many friends; in loveless encounters devoid of meaning; in a mobile society where neighbors never make one another's acquaintance and where familial relationships suffer because everyone scatters like dust on a deserted country road.

Dorothy Day learned that the real cure for this disease could not be found by filling the void of loneliness with superficial relationships or by engaging in busy work without a center such as that provided by her Catholic Worker Movement. She insisted that we must pursue the opposite path: to bind ourselves heart and soul to other people, to seek their help and to be sought by them. The hardships of life may at times make us feel as if we are alone, but the truth is we are not. Christ is always with us. If we open ourselves to the people around us, we will come to know his and their love.

In the course of prayer and participation in charitable works, we may experience a movement from a-loneness to all-oneness with our sisters and brothers in the Lord. We realize that we are *one* by virtue of the fact that we stand *alone* before God. Compassion for our failings and forgiveness of our sins creates a bond no trauma can shatter, no disappointment can obscure. The Lord, who calls us forth from the lonely chambers of our losses, reminds us that his love is the creative force behind both solitude and community. Such togetherness in Christ means, in the words of Jean Vanier, to "ask forgiveness of the many I have wounded and of the many I have passed by without seeing their wounds."[14] It is this kind of compassion that draws forth love out of loneliness, that pulls us beyond our self-imposed blindness to relieve with love the plight of the poor.

## LET US PRAY

*Lord,* break through the walls of loneliness behind which we are prone to hide to cover our hurt. Don't let us be afraid to be vulnerable, to admit how much we need one another. Lead us to experiences of community that are healing and freeing, never damaging or coerced. It is our place not to initiate this grace but to respond to your revelation that we must "love one another, because love is from God; everyone who loves is born of God and knows God . . . for God is love" (1 Jn 4:7–8).

# SIX

# LASTING FRUITS OF THANKFULNESS

They are like trees planted by streams of water,
which yield their fruit in its season, and their leaves
do not wither. In all that they do, they prosper.
—*Psalm 1:3*

In 1987, eight years after Fr. Adrian van Kaam and I—with the help of a remarkable group of lay friends, colleagues, and religious—had cofounded the Epiphany Association and attained its nonprofit status under the ruling of the United States Conference of Catholic Bishops, we received our first major contract with the Chaplain Corps of the United States Navy. It would be our duty and privilege to offer their four-day Professional Development Training Program to the 1,200 chaplains serving the navy personnel of our country at that time, representing eighty-six different faith groupings. We would design, develop, and deliver on naval bases in the United States and around the world a course titled "Spiritual Formation and Pastoral Care." We brought to it the expertise we had acquired in our then–masters' and doctoral degree programs in the field of formative spirituality taught at Duquesne University and offered on an outreach basis to the people in the pew under the auspices of the Epiphany Association.

The next two-and-a-half years brought us from Newport, Rhode Island, where the chaplain school was located, to Okinawa, Japan; from Pensacola, Florida, to Rota, Spain, and many other ports of call. At the end of this assignment, we were both made honorary chaplains of the United States Navy and profuse thanks were extended to our entire teaching team for our presentations of these extensive courses.

For years thereafter we received thank-you letters from the chaplains, all of whom seemed to derive lasting spiritual and professional benefits from what we had done. Story after story stayed in our minds regarding how the chaplains applied what they learned from us about the foundations of faith formation while upholding the religious freedom clause of the Constitution. Thanks to our teaching, they had found a way to minister to the spiritual needs of enlisted men and women of whatever rank, no matter their religious tradition.

One of the chaplains told this story: He was sent directly from chaplain school to Vietnam. A devout Southern Baptist, he wore his uniform with pride and trusted the Lord to keep him safe in a war zone such as he had never imagined. No sooner had he gotten off the plane and sought his quarters than he was accosted by a young Marine who was waving a letter and announcing that he was happy to see a "father" because he had to get the rosary beads his mother sent him blessed before he went into battle.

Though he, like all the chaplains, was recognizable by the insignia he wore, Harry told us he apologized profusely to the young lad that he was not a Catholic father and was not accustomed to blessing beads. The lad insisted that at that moment he didn't care what kind of father he was; he just had to get his beads blessed.

Chaplain Harry took him to a quiet corner and asked him to cup the beads in his fist. Then he took the young man's hands in his and said the Lord's Prayer. He hoped that was a good enough blessing. The lad smiled from ear to ear, saluted him, said it was a great blessing, and left to join his unit.

Six weeks later, Chaplain Harry told us he was in the infirmary doing what he could to comfort the wounded and asking if there was anything he could do for them. He noticed a man lying not on his back but on his stomach, looking terribly uncomfortable and obviously in pain. He tapped him on the shoulder to offer his encouragement and to pray with him if he wished. Much to his surprise, it was the same Marine whose rosary beads he had blessed. He quickly apologized to him and said, "Son, forgive me. I told you I wasn't that kind of father, and I guess I didn't do a good job of it." The lad smiled at him and said, "Father, I mean, Chaplain, you did a great job. Can't you see what happened to me? The enemy shot me in my ass, and I'm going home!"

Remembering that episode caused Chaplain Harry to really get what we had been teaching. "After all," he said, "grace does what it has to do despite our inadequacy. When that lad thanked me, all I did for days afterwards, and still do now, was thank God."

Fr. Adrian and I were left speechless. The chaplain had understood from experience all that we had taught about the mystery of grace. We shook hands and assured him, "Harry, please accept our deepest thanks for your service and for the lasting fruit it bore. That soldier needed a father, and God found the best one he could in you."

Once I was about to board a bus from work to home when I felt a tug on my sleeve. A stranger in town asked me for directions to a restaurant where he had promised to meet some friends. I knew where it was, but by the time I finished explaining how to get there, my bus had come and gone. The stranger could not thank me enough for my help and apologized for what had happened. I smiled and told him not to worry. The next bus was due to arrive in about fifteen minutes. I wondered on my way home how many hundreds of unnoticed acts of courtesy happen every day. Embracing the Golden Rule of doing for others what we would like them to do for us is one of the lasting fruits of thankfulness.

It is a rule, not an exception, to compliment others for their achievements, be they spectacular or nondescript. Thankfulness bridges the gap between a functional response and a spiritual blessing. It counters arrogance and teaches us to treat others as kindred spirits. It mellows excessive attachments to me, my, and mine and reminds us to practice self-donating love, even if we have to bear with dishonor, ridicule, and misunderstanding.

God's plan always demands putting aside our avaricious natures and accepting with joy the inescapable limits of finitude. A breakthrough to thankfulness may only happen when something in us or around us breaks down. An addicted person may never go to an Alcoholics Anonymous meeting unless he or she hits rock bottom and uses that devastating experience to reexamine the direction of his or her life as a whole.

Conflicts none of us can resolve without the help of a Higher Power present us with a dilemma: Will we acknowledge our dependency on God or try to solve our problems on our own? Gratitude to God for being with us both on mountaintops of consolation and in valleys of desolation resolves this dilemma. Even if we do not feel the effects of this resolution immediately, we know that in due time God will grant us brief glimpses, passing but unforgettable experiences "coming down from the Father of lights, with whom there is no variation or shadow due to change" (Jas 1:17).

St. John of the Cross, the sixteenth-century Spanish mystic who, along with St. Teresa of Avila, reformed the Carmelite Order, compares this turning point to the twilight hour of initial spiritual awakening. It marks the departure from a former way of life, sunk in selfishness, to the conviction that mere worldly gain is only an empty goal and not worth pursuing.

In these dark nights of sense and spirit that move the soul from the midnight moment of pure faith to the dawning of new hope in the Lord, the deceptive habits that imprison our spirits undergo purgation. The sense of our own unworthiness deepens to the degree that God's love takes the initiative. The irony is that despite this suffering we feel freer. Whereas ingratitude leaves a hole in each of our hearts, gratitude signifies that nothing we possess can fill the empty space in us reserved for God alone.

Spiritual hunger is one of the means God chooses to cut through our clinging to any lesser god for the fulfillment we seek. According to St. John of the Cross, the purpose of this purifying night of faith is to cleanse from our interiors the shadows of confusion, doubt, resistance, and despair. At this turning point from purgation to illumination, what we sense is not a satisfying inrush of consolations but a trickling stream of growth in trust and confidence. In the face of such faith which, according to St. John, is the only proximate means to union with God, vices such as envy, avarice, lust, gluttony, arrogance, and anger are no match for virtues such as respect, generosity, chastity, temperance, patience, and awe.

The admission that we own nothing—that everything is on loan—is the measure of our humility. The willingness to share our goods and services with others is the test of our detachment and charity. It does us no good to wallow in regrets for past mistakes or to focus on the future in fear. In either case we forget to be thankful for the present. Waking or sleeping, working or worshiping, engaged in ministry or pausing for prayer, we need to thank God for the grace to be faithful to our call, to minister to others not as a dreary duty but as an undeserved privilege. Of what use is it to profess our beliefs in private and to stray from them in public?

When the courage to be countercultural wanes, when we succumb to sheer worldliness, that is the exact moment we most need to restore our spirit of gratitude to the Lord, who renews our strength when we weaken and who sends his Spirit to pray in us. To accept failure graciously is another sign that we are ready to deny ourselves and follow Jesus, rejoicing that the grace we need to finish the task set before us has already been granted. Unexpected trials may test us to the limit but not beyond our strength to endure. When they pass, we may surprise ourselves by saying that we would not trade what we went through for all the goods the world has to offer. What we wrongly concluded were energy-depleting detours were revealed to us, thanks be to God, as energy-renewing exercises in discipleship.

With eyes of faith, we submit the past to God's forgiveness, the future to God's mercy, and the present to God's peace. We use our gifts and talents not to bolster our own egos but to respond humbly to the duties of the day, without neglecting Sabbath rest. We are thankful that the signs we see on the drive to work remind us to slow down and live. When we take this advice to heart, when we pause to count our blessings, our lives follow a fourfold pattern of gratitude. It includes *readiness*, which prepares us to acknowledge even the smallest gift; *alertness*, which heightens our sense of indebtedness to God; *facility*, which aids our ongoing transition from ingratitude to gratitude; and *flexibility*, which enables us to give thanks however pressured we may feel to get a task done.

These four dispositions make us more attentive to a beloved face, a glorious sunrise, a freshly blooming rose. We move beyond their temporal meaning to the eternal mystery from whence they spring. We let go of the complexity promulgated by our former rushed and willful ways of acting. Now we gravitate to a godlier, Gospel-guided style of life. We readjust our frantic paces to allow room for needed rest and restoration; we drop our egocentric defenses and remind ourselves that it is time to operate from the center of our humility.

When we look at life through these windows of gratitude, superficial observations no longer fascinate us. Our inner visions of what we ought to do become more acute. Behind the grim faces we encounter, we try to detect a glimmer of goodness. We train our eyes to catch the luminosity of the sacred that surrounds both sinners and saints.

Despite trying to remain upbeat and grateful, there are times in life when the practice of appreciation seems all but impossible. Illness, loss of a loved one, a national disaster, failure of a business—such afflictions can cause a snowball of sadness to turn into an avalanche of depression. We may slide rapidly downhill into self-pity, anger, and depression, but there is an uphill path that we can take. On it we transcend the barrage of bad news that threatens to overtake our hearts and turn to the good news revealed in God's Word about the virtue of hope, which "does not disappoint us, because God's love has been poured into our hearts through the Holy Spirit that has been given to us" (Rom 5:5).

Hope and the sense of gratitude it evokes are lifelines cast in the storm-tossed seas of hopelessness and ingratitude. Even in the bleakest hour, they invite us to have faith. Although the battle between giving thanks and giving up is far from over, we know we can go on, provided we refrain from saying, "This situation is hopeless!"

The message of hope that God etches on our hearts fortifies us whether we are in deserts of aridity or valleys of renewal. We give thanks in all circumstances—for being guided to the street address we needed to find, to the hospital room of a sick friend, to a funeral parlor to pay our last respects to a relative not seen for years. Whether we arrive at these destinations directly or after many detours, we do not feel lost. Hope awakens in us because God guards these comings and goings.

We go on vacation, exhausted and needing rest. We attend a lecture that sheds light on exactly what we hoped to learn. We locate a book that has gone out of print, only to find in it the information we need to prepare a class. We stand in line at a ticket office and behind us arrives a colleague whose address we had lost. A sure sign of thankfulness is not to call these comings and goings coincidental but to see in them the hand of Holy Providence.

When Jesus sits down dead-tired at a well and asks a woman alien to the Jewish people to give him a drink, he erases every shade of hopelessness left in her (see John 4:1–42). Feeling known by him heals her forever and lets her bring a harvest of souls to him. Joy, hope, and gratitude radiate from her to such a degree that she can proclaim to anyone with ears to hear that "this is truly the Savior of the world" (Jn 4:42), and so we pray:

*Lord,* when shadows of doubt cloud our ability to discern the subtle movements that signify your will, clear our vision so that we may follow your lead without fear or hesitation. Let the serene waters of Baptism revive our souls, calming useless worry and the distractions that destroy worship. Remove the blinders from our eyes so that we may behold your face and be healed of whatever has paralyzed our capacity to live in pure faith, especially when the "why" of our lives remains a mystery for which you ask us to be thankful. Amen.

## QUESTIONS FOR REFLECTION

1. What obstructs and what facilitates the decision to let your life be a litany of thanksgiving?
2. What prompted this conversion of heart, and how best can you ensure its continuity?
3. What thread in the ever-unfinished tapestry of thankful living did you weave today?

# COMPANIONS IN GRATEFUL LIVING

## EVAGRIUS PONTICUS

Allow the Spirit of God to dwell within you; then in his love he will come and make a habitation with you; he will reside in you and live in you. If your heart is pure you will see him and he will sow in you the good seed of reflection upon his actions and wonder at his majesty.
—*Evagrius Ponticus (ca. 345–400)*

A contemporary of the three Cappadocian Fathers and saints Basil the Great, Gregory of Nazianzus, and Gregory of Nyssa, Evagrius was an eloquent speaker, a brilliant teacher, and an austere hermit. His own influence and reputation came to rival that of his mentors. His counsels on spiritual living, *The Praktikos* and *Chapters on Prayer*, are storehouses of wisdom, relevant for every age.

Evagrius saw his monastic life, which he lived in Egypt from AD 383 onward, as a blessed though bloodless martyrdom. He had the privilege of coming into contact not only with Hellenic intellectualism in the writings of Origen but also with the practical counsels of the first generation of the Desert Fathers, notably St. Macarius the Great. From this rich treasury of wisdom and discipline, he learned the lesson that mysticism has to be grounded in asceticism just as contemplation has to bear fruit in charity.

The mystical way, as Evagrius understands it, proceeds by degrees from natural contemplation (*theoria*), using the senses and reason, to progressive contemplation (*theologia*), in which the intellect rises beyond forms and figures to behold in pure faith and heavenly luminosity the living God. The main barriers to this ascent are the capital sins. Evagrius is the first to identify *acedia* as the fiercest demon of them all as it is the noonday devil of dejection that preys on the monk's peace of mind. To defeat him is to gain victory over the other vices.

Evagrius reveals that Jesus wants to make his dwelling place in our hearts. The Lord operates by modes of appeal, not by modes of coercion. We are free to accept or reject his friendship. Three conditions enable the state of nearness Evagrius identifies as habitation. For God to reside in us, as in an interior castle, our love for him must be purified of selfish aims. We must never be double-minded, only single-hearted. Then, too, we must turn to the Holy Spirit to pray in us when we feel too depreciative to be devout. Finally, our stance in life must be more meditative than meandering. Wordless awe lifts us beyond doubt and disbelief to adoration of God's mystery.

Once we offer God our full assent, we can look upon our limits without regret. Our task is to do the best we can to contribute to God's reign on earth. Then his indwelling grace will unleash our grateful expressions of love and service.

The fullest expression of our being called, committed, and consecrated to Christ is our being commissioned by him to go and make disciples of all nations (see Matthew 28:19). This final order comes last because first we need to undergo purifying formation to increase our faith, illuminating reformation to boost our hope, and unifying transformation to deepen our love. Preceding being commissioned, with all the dedication it entails, is our acceptance of the call to follow Jesus, our commitment to deny ourselves and take up the crosses he asks us to carry, and our becoming consecrated to him as "a chosen race, a royal priesthood, a holy nation . . . that [we] may proclaim the mighty acts of him who called [us] out of darkness into his marvelous light" (1 Pt 2:9).

## LET US PRAY

*Lord,* give us the courage to follow your plan as faithful friends and loving servants. When impatience cancels peace, teach us to wait upon your Word. Grant that we may unclutter the rooms of our hearts and create space for you to dwell in us now and forever. Let the seeds of self-insight you planted within us yield an abundant harvest of gratitude for our being called, committed, and consecrated to you. Bestow upon us the grace we need to do the tasks entrusted to us now and for ages to come. Amen.

## WALTER J. CISZEK, S.J.

Whatever the trials of the moment, whatever the
hardships or sufferings, more important than all of
these was the knowledge that they had been sent by
God and served his divine providence.
                    —*Walter J. Ciszek, S.J. (1904–1984)*

A Jesuit priest, confessor, and spiritual director whose faith
journey produced two contemporary classics, *With God in
Russia* and *He Leadeth Me*, Fr. Ciszek grew up in Shenando-
ah, a rural mining town in eastern Pennsylvania. Home to
many immigrants, it now counts Ciszek as its most precious
supernatural resource. He left home against his father's wishes
to join the Society of Jesus in 1928. Religious fervor and deep
faith were not foreign to his family; two of his sisters entered
the Bernardine Order. His initial formation in family life left
him with the strong impression that great good can come from
suffering and tragedy as long as one lives in abandonment to
Divine Providence and never ceases trusting in God's will.

During his time of preparation for the priesthood, Ciszek
volunteered to study Russian in the hope of being sent as a missionary to the Soviet Union and became bi-ritual in the Russian
Byzantine Rite in 1937. While on assignment in eastern Poland
in 1938, he watched as Red Army troops invaded the country.
Ciszek, with the naked faith that has become his hallmark of
honor, saw the hand of God in this event. He joined the Polish
refugees disguised as a worker.

Transported to the labor camps of Russia, he intended to carry on his ministry underground, but two years later he was arrested by the Soviet secret police, sentenced to fifteen years of hard labor, and incarcerated in solitary confinement for five years in the notorious Lubyanka Prison in Moscow, where his captors were determined to wrest from him a confession of being a spy. His days in prison consisted of one long, unbroken chain of harassment by his captors, who eventually broke his will and forced him to sign a false confession. As brutal as it was, this breakdown of the last remnant of his all-too-precious pride was the breakthrough he needed to experience true humility.

After serving his entire sentence, he was released in 1963 as part of a prisoner exchange. Ciszek returned to his community in New York City, where he lived as a member of the John XXIII Center for Eastern Christian Studies at Fordham University for the remaining twenty years of his life. There he served as a spiritual guide and a saintly witness to the merits gained through a trial by faith. He shared with all who sought his counsel a word of hope and the secret of his peace and joy: awareness of how little our own efforts mean and how dependent we are upon God's grace for prayer and faith itself. Ciszek died at the age of eighty on the Feast of the Immaculate Conception, a man of heroic virtue whose cause for canonization is now before the Church.

In the face of such horrors as the death of the innocent in war and famine, the inhumanity of concentration camps, the relentless oppression of the poor, and the greed of the powerful, we face a stark choice: either to pursue what is meaningful in these events or to risk falling into a meaningless chasm of grief and despair. Ciszek's story reveals the truth that no one is immune from a sudden illness, a failed mission, or a natural disaster. However successful we may be, suffering and infirmity are our common fate. Loss happens, but it is up to us to derive meaning from it.

Between the Lord and us must be the conviction that there are no coincidences, only providences. However hard this truth is to grasp, nothing about our lives is a pure accident; all events have been sent to us by God as invitations, challenges, and appeals unfolding his plan of salvation. Our role is to seek their significance and to believe, without the shadow of a doubt, that we have a place in this grand design of redemption and an important role to play.

This hope rests not on human power but on the power of God. It lives on when there are no miracles, no consolations. It refuses to take refuge in scornful pessimism. In contrast to hopelessness, resignation, or pessimistic acceptance of a pre-determined fate, hope connotes the expectation of joy. It does not rely on accurate predictions or problem-solving techniques. It is an act of supreme confidence in the word of God, for, as the apostle Paul says, "Hope does not disappoint us, because God's love has been poured into our hearts through the Holy Spirit that has been given to us" (Rom 5:5).

## LET US PRAY

*Lord,* when we lose our footing on the firm ground of faith, show us once again that what happens to us serves a higher purpose. Every moment of life sheds light on our blessed beginning and our destined end. All that obscures your providence is our own inability to believe that you hold us in being, whether we know it or not. To live in your embrace is to feel as safe and sound as we once felt in our parents' arms. The debt of thankfulness we owe them for their finite care is a pointer to your infinite solicitude for us. Amen.

SEVEN

# THANKFUL ACCEPTANCE OF THE MISSION GOD ENTRUSTS TO US

Not that we are competent ourselves to claim anything as coming from us: our competence is from
God, who has made us competent to be ministers
of a new covenant, not of letter but of spirit; for the
letter kills but the Spirit gives life.

—*2 Corinthians 3:5–6*

When Fr. Adrian van Kaam recounted in many conversations just why his experience of the Dutch Hunger Winter of 1944–1945 changed his life, he always began with the fact that he was, so to speak, "catapulted out of the Ivory Tower of the seminary into one of the most devastating and dehumanizing experiences of man's inhumanity to man anyone could have witnessed." In my afterword to his autobiographical memoirs, I noted: "This time of physical and spiritual deprivation, of executions and deportations, was as horrible for him to behold as it was impossible to forget. In this crucible his heart was cleansed of the illusion of independent self-actualization. Reaffirmed was his belief in an ultimately benevolent mystery beckoning us to live in fidelity to our calling in Christ to love and serve all people as children of God."[15]

Being part of the Dutch underground, trying to find food and feed starving people of every walk of life and every religion, taught him that his mission in life after he was ordained would be to find a way to integrate what we believe and how we live these creeds in the peace and pain of daily existence. He had assumed that God's will for him would be to continue to teach philosophical anthropology at the seminary or, if not that, to go with other members of his missionary congregation to Africa or the Amazon. Neither direction was God's will for him.

Instead Fr. Adrian would help to pioneer the Dutch Life Schools of Formation for Young Adults after the war and eventually bring his educational expertise in pedagogy and andragogy to the university level in the United States. He came here in 1954, fully expecting to be assigned to Duquesne University's School of Education. Instead he accepted the top position in the Department of Psychology, where he began a new track of study in psychology as a human science. It appeared to be the final mission entrusted to him, but it was not.

God needed him to open up the new fields of formation science, anthropology, and theology in his own research institute and to bring them to fulfillment under the auspices of the Epiphany Association. He could have died during the Hunger Winter or been transported by the Nazis to a work camp. He survived. He could have been sent to the Belgian Congo or up the Amazon, but health reasons made such assignments impossible. God had another plan. Fr. Adrian had a chance to teach seminary courses for a lifetime, but God brought him to local mills and factories to help lost souls find some meaning in their lives after the war had taken everything they loved from them. He was happy there, but God had another plan for him.

And so it goes.

As Thomas à Kempis reminds us in *The Imitation of Christ*, man proposes, God disposes. My own life changed when I met Fr. Adrian in 1966. Prior to that I had only known him as a professor. At that time, I had a lucrative career in journalism, but God had another course of action in mind for me to follow as well. I was happy doing administrative and editorial work for Fr. Adrian, but he said he needed me to teach courses in the literature of spirituality. I said I would do anything he asked of me except teach. Once inside the classroom door, I never said no again. God had a plan. Years later I won the university-wide award for excellence in teaching.

The lesson we both learned was to accept with thankfulness the mission God entrusts to us. What looked like madness in our minds turned out to be exactly what God destined us to do. We learned from experience that the foundation of effective ministry is the relinquishment of a "What's in it for me?" mentality. Early in his life Fr. Adrian had to put aside the work of studying, teaching, and writing that he loved and do what he could to help the Dutch people and his own family members heal their battle scars. Later he would return to the use of his intellectual and pastoral gifts, but in both cases he cooperated with the grace of gratefulness and completed the mission entrusted to him at the time.

The same outlook awakened my memory of a religion teacher who could not do enough for her students, of a doctor who spent quality time at the bedside of her patients, of a pastor who so loved God's Word that those who listened to his sermons never forgot them. These exemplary servants live on in my memory because others, not themselves, were the center of their attention. Serving not only out of a sense of duty but due to a desire to mirror the goodness of the Lord requires more than talent and thoughtful planning; it challenges us to maintain the motivation to offer our services with or without visible signs of success or guaranteed rewards.

When a neighbor offers to cut our grass on a hot summer day, we show up on the porch with a glass of fresh lemonade. Although we feel tired and want to go to bed, we stay up long enough to write a promised letter to a friend. As soon as we receive an invitation to supper, we ask what we can bring to the table.

The motivation for acting gratefully has to come from a generous heart that is disposed to place others' needs before our own. Contrast this outgoing disposition to what it is like to be with a person who grunts impatiently when we enter the room rather than returning our hello, who never asks how we are feeling, who accepts our gifts but seldom returns the favor, who does what's required but does not find much joy in it.

Giving of ourselves to others is at times draining, but it can also be surprisingly energizing. A profound peace comes over us when we go out of our way to help others, only to find, with tears in our eyes, that they are the ones who helped us. Conflicts associated with our callings can become obstacles that prevent our human spirits from responding to the Holy Spirit or conditions that empower our flights. It all depends on whether we treat these warring tugs in our hearts as dangers or opportunities.

Life is not a ready-made machine with outcomes determined in advance. Such mechanistic images mock the mystery of divine mercy. We cannot confine God to a set of conclusions that we program in advance as if we were robots lacking any semblance of freedom. When a door closes, we can be sure a window will open—one that may prove over time to be a better opportunity for us than any of our previous ventures.

Although we may receive many hints and guesses about where God wants us to go, we cannot master this direction by our own efforts alone. If we are to decrease that Christ may increase, our only choice is to cooperate with grace. No more excuses. No more rationales. No more a divided heart but one united around the sole intention of letting God's providential will take the lead.

Deforming networks of ungrateful living must be unraveled before they entrap us. A never-ending litany of complaints tends to harden like cement. We must adopt the habit of turning off negative talk, whether it is in our own heads or blasted over the airways. To be cultivated for this purpose are dispositions such as patience under pressure and perseverance in unpleasant situations that tempt us to shrug our shoulders and walk the other way. The bad habits of ungrateful living must be reformed at once if we want to reinforce over a lifetime our capacity to give thanks always.

The more we walk in the company of Jesus, the more likely it is that we will see the threadbare tapestry of self-centeredness for what it is. Our decisions and actions, how we feel and what we think, plans executed and projects still to be done all need to be sustained by thanksgiving.

In the past, real or imagined threats to our safety and security may have triggered our survival instincts. To ward off anxiety, perhaps we chose to devise an arsenal of protective devices, and even then we felt uneasy. There is no use pretending anymore. To live fully we have to let trust, not craven fear, be the bridge to formation freedom. Never again do we dare become so enmeshed in the business of the day that we fail to hear the Master when he calls.

That's what happened in the story of the rich young man in Matthew's gospel (19:16–22), who seemed bent on seeking a surefire formula for salvation. Surely Jesus would tell him what he had to do to win eternal life. The Master answered his question with another, more thought-provoking one. After the young man repeated the Great Commandment and pointed to his experience of obeying it, he expected the Teacher to praise him as a paragon of virtue. How sad he was when Jesus asked him, in addition to taking the ancient commandment to its furthest limits, to go, sell all he had, give it to the poor, and then come and follow him. That kind of relinquishment seemed impossible for him, and so, instead of following Jesus to freedom, he turned away sad, returning to his safe but sorry world.

Is it not interesting that, despite the energy and effort we pour out, it seems as if we never have enough time to accomplish what is on our to-do lists? The expression, "The harder I work, the more behind I get," is a good description of how we may feel. To an already overloaded schedule, we add more appointments and meetings. No matter how many technological gadgets we program to save time, we cannot catch up. Deadlines bombard us. Fulfilling them causes sensory overload and abnormal, at times debilitating, stress. We may be too busy to weigh the difference between aspirations to serve the Lord and ambitions to advance our own agendas. Once we set ourselves up as *the* driving force, we dare not fail. Thomas Merton observes in his book *New Seeds of Contemplation* that people who fail to make progress in the spiritual life are "blinded by their desire for ceaseless motion, for a constant sense of achievement, famished with a crude hunger for results, for visible and tangible success, so they work themselves into a state in which they cannot believe that they are pleasing God unless they are busy with a dozen jobs at the same time."[16]

Labor without leisure fails to bear much fruit. Any work we do that proceeds without deference to divine grace is in danger of collapsing like a house of cards. The hurry disease associated with hyperfunctionalism compels us to focus on the fault lines in our characters in an ungrateful way. We demand of ourselves nothing less than perfection, a goal that may well be out of our reach. Such impatient pushing has to be replaced by patient, appreciative perseverance. Otherwise our highest accomplishments may only be empty tributes to human ingenuity lacking humble praise of the Lord.

No matter how many detours ingratitude may cause us to take, we need not be discouraged. Amid the bouts of disbelief that at times assail our souls, we feel confidence in God stirring our hearts once more. As scripture assures us, our heavenly Father knows and will give us exactly what we need.

What appears to be the end of the road through the lens of ingratitude becomes, from the perspective of gratitude, a new beginning. Circumstances beyond our control may shatter our calculations, but behind setbacks and new starts, we try to detect a divine purpose. The force of negative thoughts fades before the overpowering truth of the Paschal Mystery. The risen Lord quiets our doubts and unveils blessings in the most unexpected places: a prison cell, a hospital room, a poor neighborhood.

When Iris Murdoch, one of England's most brilliant writers and teachers of the twentieth century, knew that her memory loss was due to Alzheimer's disease, she made it known to her caregivers that her way of coping with the long goodbye would be to learn what this sad turn of events had to teach her. She would make it her business to overcome despair. She who had relied so much on words would have to learn how to communicate her gratitude in silence. She who welcomed the challenge of a vigorous debate would have to stand by as her memory faded and her astute reasoning process ground to a halt. Mental constructs would have to relocate themselves in the deep caverns of her grateful heart. Murdoch describes in a rare moment of lucidity her sense of the spiritual life as "a long strange business."

At first, the term *business* does not seem to be a good match for describing the life of the spirit. We run our own businesses. We mind the business of others. We like to be busy as bees. Yet another meaning may emerge when we consider that all during his life on earth, the Lord went about doing his Father's business. Here we see the difference between mere activism and endeavors dedicated to doing what God asks of us within the limits of our situations, without losing the courage to conform to Christ and the courtesy to say thanks.

Worldly accomplishments often rest on clever business deals, lots of shoptalk, and endless meetings. The constant companions of corporate types are lengthy memos, electronic communications, and a never-ending stream of words. In the strange business that Murdoch describes, the greatest commodity is silence. Looking busy and important, even if one is not, fuels the fires of functionality, whereas docility replaces doing for ourselves by doing for the "least of these" (Mt 25:45).

Bossy business people schedule power lunches; spiritual seekers enjoy a meal together. Praying on one's knees precedes facing any contingency plan. Meekness is accepted as a prerequisite for discipleship. Without this virtue we remain unwilling to be taught. We act as if we are in charge of the way the world turns, but nothing could be further from the truth. As Murdoch and her husband, John Bayley, discovered, the spiritual life is a strange business punctuated by the faint glimmers of light God sends us in the darkest hours, provided we are wise enough to see them and humble enough to let them lead us.

From Bethlehem to Calvary to the empty tomb, Christ spoke words that came from such a depth of love and wisdom that the disciples dropped everything and followed him. Aligning our character with his is what gives us the faith to conquer every falsehood, the hope to soar beyond every doubt, the charity to love others more than ourselves and to let him lift the heaviest loads from our souls. After all, was it not he who said, "Come to me, all you that are weary and are carrying heavy burdens, and I will give you rest. Take my yoke upon you, and learn from me; for I am gentle and humble in heart, and you will find rest for your souls. For my yoke is easy, and my burden is light" (Mt 11:28–30)?

St. Francis of Assisi added another diamond to the treasury of discipleship in the medieval era. He started brick by brick to rebuild a ruined chapel and ended up restructuring the life of the Church. So did an uneducated laywoman affiliated with the Dominican Order, St. Catherine of Siena. She condemned the corruption she found in prelates who plunged the Church into a schism that stretched from Rome to Avignon. And yet it was she whom Christ chose to find a solution to this calamity. Both saints cleansed the windows of their perception through the power of appreciation. They experienced every deficiency they beheld as an invitation to deepen their dependency on

God, grow in intimacy with the Trinity, and do what they could to advance God's reign on earth.

This Christ-conscious mode of presence enhances our effectiveness. It lets us be at once attached and detached, enjoying what we accomplish while knowing that the outcome of our best efforts is in God's hands. Whether we succeed or not, we have the courage to say, "I am your disciple, and in my servant heart I have only one desire: to do your will. Let me decrease that you may increase. Let me lose myself so I can find myself in you. I am yours, and you are mine."

We may seldom, if ever, foresee what the future holds, but that is unnecessary. What matters when we become wholly thankful is the fidelity that inspires us to act in love and obedience to God's will. What we resist is entrapment in a fast-paced life, lacking reflection. Our intention is not to play a bit part in an action-packed movie with no plot or character development. We may be thrilled momentarily by this spectacle on the screen, but we leave the theater with nothing to remember but its special effects. As believers, the contrast is clear: the whole point of our faith is not to focus on ourselves but to taste and see the goodness of the Lord.

Witness Christ on the Cross. All that was left to him was the agony of abandonment to the Father with not one iota of human honor. Yet from this mysterious place of powerlessness came the power to undo death. Every lash Christ accepted with love released us from fear and showed us how precious we are in the eyes of God. Just as the first blush of dawn dispels the gloom of the night, so this mysterious embrace of the

Divine removes the shadows that obscure the new horizons of joy and hope Jesus wants us to behold with gratitude, and so we pray:

*Lord,* I hear you whisper in my soul, "Remain in me; then I will remain in you." Your loyalty to me, my Lord, can never be questioned. You are fidelity itself. You loved me before I knew how to love you. Your acceptance of me does not depend on impossible conditions. How often you showed all who believed in you the depth of your daily love and care. Please Lord, let the grace of gratefulness abound in me; let it fill the empty spaces in my life and flow forth at every turn. Amen.

## QUESTIONS FOR REFLECTION

1. How can we prevent ourselves from being too busy to notice when others need our care and companionship?
2. When we take the time to be with and for those around us, what spiritual benefits emanate from these encounters?
3. Why is pausing to say thanks to God a condition for the possibility of accepting fully the mission God intends to entrust to us?

# COMPANIONS IN GRATEFUL LIVING

## ST. AUGUSTINE OF HIPPO

To become converted, you must fight your way past
the deceitful voice within.
—*St. Augustine of Hippo (354–430)*

St. Augustine is one of the most influential and prolific of the
Fathers and Doctors of Western Christendom, due in great
measure to his classic works *The Confessions, The City of God*,
and *On the Trinity*. Though brought up by his mother as a
Catholic, Augustine was as famous a sinner before his conversion and Baptism as he was a saint, bishop, and defender of the
faith afterward. He writes of this *metanoia* in his *Confessions*,
of that day in the garden in AD 387 when his admission of sin
gave way to his longing for forgiveness and he read, as if for the
first time, Romans 13:13–14. Then he said, "No further wished
I to read, nor was there need to do so. Instantly in truth, at the
end of this sentence as if before a peaceful light streaming into
my heart, all the dark shadows of doubt fled away."[17]

Augustine was the first to admit that without the prayers of
his mother, St. Monica (ca. AD 331–387), he might never have
been able to escape the "hissing caldron of lust" and the pride
of the intellect that for so long had held him in bondage. Happily for him, the Holy Spirit used the sermons of St. Ambrose,
bishop of Milan, to break the chain that bound his heart and
to turn him toward orthodoxy.

Once caught by grace, Augustine never let go. His "passion for the wisdom of eternal truth" was at long last satisfied. Ordained a priest in 391, he became by 395 bishop of Hippo in northern Africa, an office he held for thirty-five years. He also established a religious community and composed the Augustinian rule as the source of its governance and inspiration. He lived a modest life as companion to his brothers and friend of the poor while using his writing skills to shore up a Church shaken by the very heresies he once espoused, Gnosticism and Manichaeism. He did his utmost to preserve Christian doctrine in the face of barbarian invasions, the collapse of the Roman Empire, and the Dark Ages that were to descend upon the Church.

Augustine died at the age of seventy-six, as the Vandals invaded his episcopal city. What this Doctor of Grace once knew by intuition, he now knew by experience. In what may be the most quoted phrase from his *Confessions*, he proclaimed with full confidence, "You are great, O Lord, and greatly to be praised: great is your power and to your wisdom there is no limit . . . for you have made us for yourself, and our heart is restless until it rests in you."[18]

Though some highly blessed and chosen souls may experience a sudden, dramatic about-face on the road to life's transformation, St. Augustine's tale convinces us that instant *metanoia* is usually not the way God chooses for us. St. Augustine reminds us on every page of his *Confessions* that it takes a long time to become converted. One obstacle after another has to be peeled away.

We must fight our way past the almost impenetrable fortifications erected by our own egos. The illusion by which we live is that, weak as we are, we are really all-powerful. One lie piles up on top of the other until the deceitful castle we have built begins to crack at its foundation. Lights we thought we could trust become dark shadows of sin that stain our souls. Augustine's sins were legion; vainglory, fornication, and disobedience had become such habitual faults that he had no choice but to don the armor of a new knight of faith whose weapons would be humility, chastity, and obedience.

Like good servants we, too, must clean our inner houses before it is too late. Provided we succeed in sorting out the true from the false voices that impinge upon our souls, we may find the peace and joy Augustine experienced. His conversion brought him to the point of attending so faithfully to God's voice within his heart that other alien voices fell silent and Christ became the center of his life.

## LET US PRAY

*Lord,* close our ears to the seductive voices cajoling us to choose self over you. Open our ears to those whispers of your truth resonating in the inmost chambers of our hearts. Let us, like St. Augustine, put on the Lord, Jesus Christ. Only then is our victory over every lying voice we hear from within or without assured. Grant us the gifts of continual conversion and ceaseless prayer that we may fortify our hearts for the journey of faith that will only end when we see you face-to-face. Amen.

## ST. TERESA OF AVILA

The Lord had told me to get started [with the reform
of the Carmelite Order] as best I could, that afterward I would see what His Majesty would do. And
how well I have seen it! Thus, though I knew the
income was small, I believed the Lord would help
us and arrange things through other means.
—*St. Teresa of Avila (1515–1582)*

In her early teens, Teresa lost her mother and fell under the
influence of a frivolous cousin who cultivated vain and worldly ways that would haunt the future saint for years to come
instead of the devotion to which she had previously aspired.
Though attending a convent school directed by Augustinian
nuns helped to reawaken her religious fervor, including the
possibility of a vocation to the religious life, she put off her
decision. The time did come when, against her father's wishes,
she entered the Carmelite Monastery of the Incarnation in her
hometown of Avila.

By 1537, she had professed her vows but didn't experience
the joy she expected to feel. Instead she became severely ill.
The faith healer to whom she was sent nearly killed her. She fell
into a deathlike coma and was almost buried alive. Paralysis
overtook her. Though she returned to the convent, it was not
to fulfill her daily duty but to go to the infirmary.

In 1542, as she tells us in the *Book of Her Life*, St. Joseph
cured her, and she was able to walk again. However, over the

next twelve years, much to her shame, she resumed her old ways and became, in accordance with the customs of her convent, a "parlor favorite," caught in particular friendships and conversations more worldly than godly. All that was soon to change. Already, reading Augustine's *Confessions* had left her dissolved in tears. Then, during the Lenten season of 1554, while meditating before a statue depicting Jesus' scourging at the pillar, Teresa received the grace of radical conversion. Two years later, her spiritual betrothal to Christ took place followed by other mystical graces, including that of the wound of love whereby God alone became the great passion of her life.

Although some of her friends and confessors concurred that she might be the victim of demonic delusion, Teresa knew this was not so. In 1560 she began to compose her autobiography and to open herself without reservation to God's leading. She wrote, "I understood that if the Lord didn't show me, I was able to learn little from books, because there was nothing I understood until his Majesty gave me understanding through experience."[19]

With a daring that would have been impossible without divine intervention, she chose to return to the original rule of Mount Carmel and to live the life of a reformed or cloistered Discalced Carmelite—*discalced* meaning "without shoes," signifying the members' feelings of lowliness in relation to the Master they served—in the utter poverty of the Convent of St. Joseph in Avila. Several daughters followed their "Mother," and the instructions she gave them regarding humility, detachment, and fraternal charity can be found in her book *The Way of Perfection.*

Starting in 1567, she was authorized to found other monasteries, which meant traveling the rough roads of Spain, negotiating with landholders for property, raising considerable funds, and overcoming incredible opposition and misunderstanding. Teresa's courage and cheerful heart prevailed over all obstacles, and new convents arose, including one at Medina del Campo, where she met at last the friar who would understand her call and her spiritual life and who would join her in the reform, St. John of the Cross.

From 1574 to 1576, she established new convents in Segovia, Beas, and Seville, escaped denunciation by the Inquisition, and coped with many persecutions directed at her order. These events strained her already fragile health and caused her much anxiety. And yet at the epicenter of this turmoil, in 1579, she wrote her masterpiece of the ascetical-mystical life, *The Interior Castle.*

Her strength waned severely in 1580, when her heart began to fail. She received the last sacraments on October 3, and the next evening she met "his Majesty," Christ Jesus, whom she so loved and adored. Teresa was canonized in 1622. On September 27, 1970, Pope Paul VI proclaimed her a Doctor of the Church, the first woman to be so honored.

Though St. Teresa was graced with momentary ecstasy, her ordinary lot was agony. She suffered from severe headaches and stomach ailments. She had to defend her life's work before the inquisitors. Her path to God was dangerously disrupted by poor confessors. Yet she persevered. Consolations were occasional, the endurance of crosses continual. What kept her going was meditation on the sacred humanity of Jesus, his Passion, Death, and Resurrection. She called him Savior, Spouse, Majesty. She experienced him in the center of her soul, in the interior castle reached only by way of humility, detachment, and charity. Her life may be seen as a song of faith, a cry of hope, an act of love. Her life assures us that intense prayer (the "Mary" in us) and dedicated ministry (the "Martha" in us) go hand in hand. She was an ideal blend of receptivity and action, of surrender to the will of God and service to his eternal reign. She represents the wholesome, balanced Christian life all of us are called to lead.

Anyone, in any walk of life, seeking liberation from egoism and union with the Lord in this world can benefit from St. Teresa's advice. Her words offer sensible, clear directives that are as applicable today as when she wrote them. Humility assures us that we can find and be faithful to our unique selves in Christ. Detachment enables us to live in each situation in such a way that we can be simultaneously near to others in genuine care while maintaining a certain respectful distance. Charity flows over into compassion for our own weaknesses and for the vulnerability of those who people our world. If we love Christ as the center of our lives, we can serve the Church tirelessly while maintaining inner tranquility.

## LET US PRAY

*Lord,* may my zeal not grow tame or be tempted by idleness, nor may my fervor be dissipated in erratic choices severed from your will. Never let fanaticism sway me from the truths you have revealed. With the zeal of the Lord of hosts, who will accomplish his work in me, I believe I can meet the challenges set before me while attributing to you the power to "put false ways far from me" (Ps 119:29) and to grant me the grace to "meditate on your wondrous works" (Ps 119:27). Amen.

# CONCLUSION

To conclude these reflections, I would like to offer the following tried-and-true ways to foster receptivity to and cooperation with the grace of gratefulness, both personally and culturally.

1. Keep a gratitude journal or write a gratitude letter to someone who has done you a favor. Record in it the reasons you had to be thankful today.
2. Train yourself to see in every obstacle an opportunity to shift from a negative to a positive outlook.
3. Relish moments of achievement as well as the mistakes you've made, since from them you learned so much.
4. Practice appreciative living on the best and the worst of days, and be thankful for the least sign of progress you've made.
5. Appraise the grain of truth in every criticism.
6. Clear the clutter caused by fear and frustration, and opt instead for freedom sustained by the guidance of God.
7. Rather than asking why something happened that crushed your expectations and halted your push to attain self-imposed outcomes, beseech God to show you the meaning of what just occurred.

8.  Trust that the ray of goodness hidden behind every cloud of discouragement will sooner or later reveal itself.

9.  As the shadows of depreciation start to be dispelled, welcome the chances God gives you to turn from being a sourpuss to becoming an epiphanic presence.

10. When the warning signals of depreciative thinking flash with neon intensity, pay attention to them—never deny the dissonance you feel, but search for its source in pursuit of the deeper consonance with Christ you desire.

11. Change your perception of time from *chronos* (clockbound) to *kairos* (the inbreaking of the Eternal), and grow in trusting surrender to God, whose words of truth have the power to touch and transform your life.

12. Take time, despite the functionalistic pressures that may impinge upon you, to unearth the goodness, truth, and beauty embedded in the fabric of daily life.

# COUNSELS ON THE GRACE OF GRATEFULNESS: TWENTY-ONE DAYS WITH THE ANCIENT, MEDIEVAL, AND MODERN SPIRITUAL MASTERS

To live a grace-filled life to such a degree that it becomes second nature to us is the aim of this book. Gratitude ought to be a habit lodged so lastingly in our hearts that it reveals itself in our character. In other words, the spirit of gratefulness, which is God's gift to us, is meant to become a habitual attribute of our human spirit.

One time-tested way to acquire this habit is to turn for help to the wisdom of faith and formation offered by ancient, medieval, and modern masters of the spiritual life. Their classical teachings are as timeless as they are timely.

In this appendix, I begin with a brief biography of these giants of grateful living, followed by a key counsel from each on how to practice this virtue. After each quotation, I pose a guiding question, inspired by its contents and designed to evoke further meditation on the master's counsel on how to acquire the holy habit of living a grace-filled life.

Over the course of these twenty-one days, in accordance with whatever schedule the participant wishes to follow, it is my hope that we will be able to respond with greater ease to God's grace, moving us from the obstacle of ingratitude to the transformative opportunity of giving "thanks in all circumstances" (1 Thes 5:18).

# MEET THE ANCIENT MASTERS

## ORIGEN (CA. 185–254)

Origen's life spanned the turbulent years following the fall of the Roman Empire. In his extensive body of work, he strove to establish a dialogue between the best features of the Roman world, such as beauty and order, and his Christian beliefs. He wanted especially to appeal to thoughtful and educated nonbelievers of his day by works that were as intellectually sound as they were mystically inspiring. In his *Commentary on the Song of Songs*, he became the first Christian to set forth the soul's purgative, illuminative, and unitive ascent to God.

### THE BOUNDLESS EXCELLENCE
### OF THE GRACE OF GOD

Who would not admit that it is impossible for a human being to trace out what is in the heavens?

Nevertheless, this impossibility has become a possibility by the boundless excellence of the grace of God (cf. 2 Cor 9:14). For it is likely that he who was caught up into the third heaven traced out what was in those three heavens, because he heard things that cannot be told, which man may not utter (2 Cor 12:2–4). And who could say that it is possible for a human being to know the mind of the Lord? Nevertheless, even this is given by God through Christ. For He says, "No longer do I call you servants, for the servant does not know what his master is doing; but I have called you friends, for all that I have heard from my Father I have made known to you" (Jn 15:14–15).

—Origen, *Prayer*, 81–82

*What hinders and what helps you to cooperate more fully with "the boundless excellence of the grace of God," especially in the light of your quest to be and become a more grateful person?*

## ST. ANTHONY THE GREAT (CA. 251–356)

An exemplary Desert Father, St. Anthony left his wealthy life in Egypt to seek perfection by uniting himself, body and soul, to Jesus, his Master, Lord, and Redeemer. He sought the secrets of discipleship by pursuing the call to silence and solitude in desert regions around the Nile Valley. There he stayed, praying unceasingly and fending off severe demonic attacks, for more than twenty years. Then, from 306 onward, he accepted disciples seeking a word by which they might live their lives. Called "the Father of Monks," he founded a monastery in the hermetical style and tirelessly served the needs of believers and sincere seekers in the undivided Church until his death at the age of 105.

### THE GRACE OF GOING OUT FOR A WALK

Abba Anthony once went to visit Abba Amoun in Mount Nitria and when they met, Abba Amoun said, "By your prayers, the number of the brethren increases, and some of them want to build more cells where they may live in peace. How far away from here do you think we should build the cells?" Abba Anthony said, "Let us eat at the ninth hour and then let us go out for a walk in the desert and explore the country." So they went out into the desert and they walked until sunset and then Abba Anthony said, "Let us pray and plant the cross here, so that those who wish to do so may build here. Then when those who remain there want to visit those who have come here, they can take a little food at the ninth hour and then come. If they do this, they will be able to keep in touch with each other without distraction of mind." The distance is twelve miles.

—Benedicta Ward, trans., *Sayings of the
Desert Fathers*, 7

*Instead of seeking answers to every question, are you able to "go out for a walk," pray, and quell the distractions that interfere with your commitment to cooperate with grace and grow in gratitude? If you aren't, what might you do to incorporate this practice into your daily life?*

## EPHREM THE SYRIAN (CA. 306–373)

Ephrem was a Christian poet and author of, among others, majestic hymns on the virginity of Mary and the nativity of Jesus. Living in an outpost of the Roman Empire under the reign of Constantine, he promulgated the doctrines of the Nicene Council, proclaiming the oneness of divinity and humanity in Jesus. In opposition to the many Gnostic sects lingering in his time, Ephrem became an outstanding defender of the true faith. Syrian Christianity benefitted greatly from his devotion and literary brilliance. He crafted a form of poetry rich in symbolism and theologically sound. Ephrem, a deacon of the Church at Edessa, established both a school of biblical and theological studies and a women's choir to sing his hymns.

### GIVE THANKS FOR HIS GRACE

Let us thank Him Who was beaten and Who saved
us by His wound.
Let us thank Him Who took away the curse by His
thorns.
Let us thank Him Who killed death by His dying.

Let us thank Him Who was silent and vindicated
  us.
Let us thank Him Who cried out in death that had
  devoured us.

Glory to God the Healer of human nature.
Glory to the One Who plunged in and sank
our evil into the depth and drowned our drowner.
Let us glorify with all our mouths the Lord of all
  means [of salvation].

Blessed is the One Whom our mouth is not sufficient to thank,
Whose gift is too great for those gifted with speech.
Nor are the senses sufficient to give thanks for His
  grace,
for however much we thank Him, it is too little,
and because it is of no use for us to be silent and
  unnerved,
let our weaknesses return [to God] a song of
  thanksgiving.

Sea of glory without needs,
receive in Your graciousness a drop of thanksgiving,
for by Your gift You have moistened my tongue to
  praise You.

> —Kathleen E. McVey, trans., *Ephrem the*
> *Syrian: Hymns*, 87–88

*Have you ever felt that however much you thanked God for the blessings bestowed upon you, it was too little? What drew you to feel so grateful to God for the favors granted to you?*

## ST. GREGORY OF NYSSA (CA. 332–395)

Acknowledged to be one of the leading theologians of the Christian East along with his brother, St. Basil the Great, and their mutual friend, St. Gregory of Nazianzus, St. Gregory of Nyssa has been designated the founder of mystical theology in the Church. His masterpiece of spiritual exegesis, *The Life of Moses*, maintains that the soul in love with God strains ahead to climb the mountain of desire, forgetting what went before and seeking the beauty that lies beyond in what later authors would describe as "the cloud of unknowing" or the apophatic way. Committed as he was to upholding the Trinitarian doctrine of the Church, Gregory revealed in his writing and as bishop of Nyssa that communion with God, difficult as it may at times seem to be, is a constant ascent from glory unto glory. The true enjoyment of the soul consists in never ceasing to ascend toward the "kindred Deity," who draws that which is his own to himself.

## THE GRACE TO GROW
## IN INTIMACY WITH GOD

For the perfection of human nature consists perhaps in the very growth in goodness. . . . The one who is going to associate intimately with God must go beyond all that is visible and (lifting up his own mind, as to a mountaintop, to the invisible and incomprehensible) believe that the divine is *there* where the understanding does not reach. . . . These were the teachings concerning virtue, the chief of which is reverence and having the proper notions about the divine nature, inasmuch as it transcends all cognitive thought and representation and cannot be likened to anything which is known.

—Gregory of Nyssa, *Life of Moses*, 31, 43

*Do you access on a regular basis the Church's teachings on the life of virtue? What connection can you see between the virtue of reverence and the need to cultivate an attitude of gratitude?*

## JOHN CASSIAN (CA. 365–435)

A disciple of Evagrius Ponticus in the East and a contemporary of St. Augustine of Hippo in the West, Cassian's early teachers were the Desert Fathers and Mothers. He continued his study of monasticism in Egypt and became a major force in the formation of Western monastic spirituality, influencing especially St. Benedict of Nursia, who acknowledged the indebtedness of his Rule to the Institutes and Conferences of Cassian. Eventually Cassian founded his own monastery near Marseilles for men and one nearby for women. He challenged his disciples to divest their souls of vices associated with transient, egocentric, and materialistic interests through the exercise of virtue initiated by God's grace, notably solitude, compunction, and uninterrupted communion with God. He insisted, as did St. Benedict, that the essence of perfection is charity, reached by way of asceticism—not as a goal in itself but as a means toward greater love and increasing contemplative prayer. Cassian's ascetic ideals remain grounded in a genial, realistic sense of the everyday, of the need for humility, discretion, common sense, and moderation—all of which may explain why, when he died, he had already attained the reputation of being a saint.

## GOD'S GRACE AVAILABLE TO US
## FROM THE CRADLE

Contemplation of God can be understood in . . . the magnificence of His creation, in the spectacle of His justice, and in the help He extends each day to the running of the world. He can be sensed too when with well-purified minds we consider what He has achieved in each generation by means of His saints. He can be sensed when we gaze with trembling hearts at that power of His which controls, guides, and rules everything, when we contemplate His immense knowledge and His knowing look which the secrets of the heart cannot evade. His presence is known when we meditate on the fact that the sands of the sea are numbered by Him, that He keeps a count of the waves. Astounded, we reflect that every drop of rain, every day and every hour of all the centuries, everything past and everything to come are all facts of which He is aware. Overwhelmed with wonder we think of that unspeakable mercy of His which allows Him to endure with unfailing patience the numberless crimes committed at every moment while He watches. We think of how in His pity for us He has called us to Him, though we had done nothing previously to deserve it. . . . He ordained that our birth was to be such that His grace and the knowledge of His Law would be available to us from the cradle. And having overcome the adversary within us He offers us, in return merely for our goodwill, an eternity of happiness and of rewards.

—John Cassian, *Conferences*, 50–51

*Have you ever been "overwhelmed with wonder" when you thought of the "unspeakable mercy" of God? What does it feel like when you know you have failed to respond to God's grace?*

## JOHN CLIMACUS (CA. 579–649)

Climacus was a master of the contemplative-active life and was influenced by John Cassian. He was a hermit monk of the Monastery of St. Catherine on Mount Sinai. Named the most important ascetical theologian of the East, he was chosen abbot of his community and ruled there until shortly before his death. His book, *The Ladder of Divine Ascent* or *The Stairway to Paradise*, is recognized as a classic in both the Eastern and Western Church. In it, he teaches Christians how to practice a life of virtue by analyzing in thirty chapters or steps—each of which represents one year of the hidden life of Jesus of Nazareth—the vices that deform the soul and the virtues that lead to conformity to Christ. He insists that our natural impulses are not corrupt in themselves but that they must be redirected toward God in total openness to his commandments with no selfish wants blocking the way. If we are striving upward to reach God, then we can be sure that God is reaching downward to draw us to himself. As Climacus said, "The man who leaves the world for love of God has taken fire from the start, and like fire set to fuel, it soon creates a conflagration."[20]

## THE GRACE OF LIVING WITHOUT GUILE

A man called Lawrence who had been about forty-eight years in the monastery . . . genuflected before the abbot and received his blessing. When he stood up the abbot said nothing at all to him but left him standing beside the table and not eating. It was just the start of the midday meal so that he was left standing there a full hour, probably two. I was embarrassed to look this hard-working man in the face, for he was completely white-haired and all of eighty years. He stayed there until we had finished eating, and when we got up . . . I did not let slip the

chance to tease the old man, so I asked him what he
had been thinking about as he stood by the table.
"I thought of the shepherd as the image of Christ,"
he said. "I thought of the command as coming not
from him but from God. And so, Father John, I
stood praying as if I were in front of the altar of God
rather than the table of men; and because I trust and
love my shepherd, I had no malevolent thoughts
concerning him. It is said that love does not reck-
on up injury. But be sure of this much. Father, that
anyone who freely chooses to be simple and guile-
less provides the devil with neither the time nor the
place for an attack."

—John Climacus, *Ladder of Divine
Ascent*, 98–99

*Are there people in your life who exude great patience and grati-
tude for whatever befalls them, people in whom you see the Good
Shepherd and who, by their lives of simplicity and guilelessness,
give "the devil . . . neither the time nor the place for an attack"?
What impact do such encounters have on your life, and what
changes might you make to foster the same impact on others?*

## MAXIMUS CONFESSOR (CA. 580–662)

Called the last great theologian of Greek patristics, Maximus
is one of the most profound mystics of the Eastern Church. It
is thought that Maximus grew up in a distinguished family in

Constantinople and became a secretary of the emperor until he entered a monastery near Carthage in 613. Other traditions say he was born in Palestine and lived there as a monk before coming to Constantinople. In any case, Maximus came under the influence of the patriarch of Jerusalem. There and in Alexandria his brilliance as a defender of the faith became apparent, making him the target of persistent animosity. Though he was mainly concerned with mystical, exegetical, and liturgical matters, he spent most of his energy in the defense of orthodox doctrine against heretical claims that there was a separation of the divine and human nature of God in the second person of the Blessed Trinity.

In addition to his dogmatic and polemic writings, Maximus expounded a doctrine of charity centering on the love of Christ, our Incarnate Redeemer. One of his best-known works is the *Four Hundred Chapters on Love.* In it he shows that it is charity that deifies the soul and enables us to experience our "adoptive filiation" in the family of the Trinity, a relationship ultimately realized in that graced bond of union with God that is mystical marriage or, in a description preferred by the Greek Fathers, "deification."

Maximus paid a high price for his faith. In 662, he was imprisoned in Constantinople where the same heretics he castigated condemned him to be scourged, have his tongue cut off, and have his right hand amputated as a symbol of his commitment as a "confessor," or witness to the true faith. He died that same year, having proclaimed Christ's praises and suffered persecution for his sake. He is revered in the East and the West as a saint and a Doctor of the Church.

## GRACE IS FREE OF OLD AGE

Those who purely pursue the divine way of life find the greatest benefit in knowledge about it. They no longer change their will along with things, but with a sound firmness undertake readily everything which accords with the principle of virtue. . . . The grace of the New Testament is mysteriously hidden in the letter of the Old. This is why the Apostle says that the Law is spiritual. Thus the Law is rendered old and obsolete by the letter and becomes useless, but it is made young and thoroughly active by the Spirit. For grace is completely free of old age.

—Maximus Confessor,
*Selected Writings*, 145

*Do you strive with God's help to pursue virtues such as gratitude and to resist vices such as ingratitude? How do you go about doing so in the humble conviction, whatever your chronological age may be, that "grace is completely free of old age"?*

# MEET THE MEDIEVAL MASTERS

## ST. HILDEGARD OF BINGEN (1098–1179)

The fourth woman named a Doctor of the Church after St. Catherine of Siena, St. Teresa of Avila, and St. Thérèse of Lisieux, St. Hildegard was a Benedictine abbess with incomparable poetic, artistic, musical, and mystical gifts, as well as other gifts that ranged from natural healing methods to preaching and political consultation.

Born into a noble German family of ten children, young Hildegard was placed in the care of a holy anchoress, Jutta, who raised her until she was eighteen and old enough to decide for herself to enter a nearby Benedictine abbey. After Jutta's death in 1136, Hildegard herself became the prioress of a new foundation inspired by the holy woman under whose guidance she had grown in wisdom, age, and grace.

Since her earliest youth, Hildegard had received visions concerning the Word of God in scripture and the imprint of this divine Word in nature. She saw these revelations with the eyes of her spirit; she heard God's voice with the ears of her heart. Although Hildegard had confided in Jutta about the nature of these visions, eventually she sought and received ecclesial approbation from the archbishop of Mainz. The text she wrote inspired by her visions was judged to be orthodox, and so she continued to write her *Scivias*. These texts concerned the relationship between God, humanity, and the cosmos, including powerful insights into the rupturing of creation by sin and its restoration by the Redeemer.

When Hildegard moved her community to a new site near Bingen, the opposition she encountered from the monks who lived nearby sickened her almost to the point of death, but she prevailed. Subsequently, she made preaching tours throughout the Rhineland; shared her spiritual thoughts with many correspondents, including kings and popes; composed original religious music; and divulged her unusual knowledge of medicine and physiology. Hildegard's sensitivity for the ecology of the earth and her commitment to the goodness of creation strike a contemporary note, as does the holistic vision she had of a life lived in gratitude and harmony with God.

## GOD'S REWARDING GRACE

Don't let yourself forget that God's grace rewards not only those who never slip, but also those who bend and fall. So sing! The song of rejoicing softens hard hearts. It makes tears of godly sorrow flow from them. Singing summons the Holy Spirit. Happy praises offered in simplicity and love lead the faithful to complete harmony, without discord. Don't stop singing.

—Carmen Acevedo Butcher,
*St. Hildegard of Bingen*, v

*When you fall under the weight of sin, is your first thought to confess your faults and to thank God for the never-failing grace of forgiveness? What changes need to occur in your life to promote more harmony between you and God?*

## ST. AELRED OF RIEVAULX (1109–1167)

A man of noble ancestry, St. Aelred spent his early years mingling with members of the Scottish court, but worldly success and popularity could not satisfy his restless heart. He became a Cistercian monk, entering Rievaulx Abbey in England in 1134.

Aelred lived in the "Golden Age" of the Cistercian reform, during which there were at least five hundred foundations of the order in Europe alone, thanks to the incredible inspiration and leadership of St. Bernard of Clairvaux. Aelred was an excellent orator and a wise and holy man; his gentle yet firm leadership style attracted more than six hundred monks to his abbey.

From his earliest days in the monastery, Aelred embraced the Rule of St. Benedict, finding in it the key to monastic life: contemplation or resting in God. He regarded contemplation as the ground of Christian charity, the wellspring of spiritual friendship, and the source of social action. Unlike some of his day, Aelred viewed the inclusive style of spiritual friendship as the fruit of charity since friendship in the Lord is based on candor not condescension, on generosity not greed, on gratitude not personal gain.

## THE GRACE OF CONTACT WITH CHRIST

How delightful friends find it to converse with one another, mutually to reveal their interests, to examine all things together, and to agree on all of them! Added to this there is prayer for one another, which, coming from a friend, is the more efficacious in proportion as it is more lovingly sent to God, with tears which either fear excites or affection awakens or sorrow evokes. And thus a friend praying to Christ on behalf of his friend, and for his friend's sake desiring to be heard by Christ, directs his attention with love and longing to Christ; then it sometimes happens that quickly and imperceptibly the one love passes over into the other, and coming, as it were, into close contact with the sweetness of Christ himself, the friend begins to taste his sweetness and to experience his charm. Thus ascending from that holy love with which he embraces a friend to that with which he embraces Christ, he will joyfully partake in abundance of the spiritual fruit of friendship . . . [and] shall rejoice in the eternal possession of Supreme Goodness; and this friendship, to which here we admit but few, will be outpoured upon all and by all outpoured upon God, and God shall be all in all.

—Aelred of Rievaulx, *On Spiritual Friendship*, 131–132

*Do you enjoy the blessing of friends in the Lord? How do these friends help you grow in gratitude for all who long for closer contact with "the sweetness of Christ himself"? Do you thank God for the grace of spiritual friendships that enable you to love all those entrusted to your care as Christ would have you do?*

## JACOPONE DA TODI (CA. 1230–1306)

An aristocrat by birth, Jacopone practiced as a lawyer and accountant. Neither of these functions could suppress his poetic gifts, though. Following the death of his wife in 1268, he converted to Christianity and in 1278 entered the Franciscan Order of Friars Minor. He became embroiled in the controversy between the Conventuals and the Spirituals, which raged following the death of St. Francis of Assisi. A "Spiritual" by virtue of his devotional character, he endured imprisonment for his position until 1303. Beginning during that time and until his death, he wrote exquisite and deeply devotional poems in Latin and in the Umbria dialect, most notably the *Stabat Mater.* His poetic abilities ranged from writing that soared with mystical rapture to pieces that plunged into vulgar directness. His *Lauds* made him the most powerful religious poet in Italy before Dante. In his body of work, he praised the primacy of the love of God, the beauty of Lady Poverty, and the call of grace that all receive to resist worldliness and its impact on the Church itself as the Bride of Christ.

## THE GRACE OF A GRATEFUL HEART

Come, people, come,
And marvel at what you see:
Yesterday the soul was hell,
Today it is paradise!
—Jacopone da Todi, *Lauds*, 91

*In the shortest amount of time you can imagine—in the blink of an eye—do you believe that grace can transport you from a hellish life of ingratitude to a holy life of total thankfulness that reminds you and all you meet of paradise?*

## MEISTER ECKHART (CA. 1260–1327)

A native of the province of Thuringia in Germany, Eckhart was a Dominican friar. His bent toward learning prompted his superiors to send him to the University of Paris to study theology. Recognized as a man of exceptional brilliance, he held the prestigious chair once occupied by St. Thomas Aquinas, and earned in 1302 the title "Meister."

When Eckhart returned to Germany, he became prior of the monastery at Erfurt. Some of his talks were transcribed and circulated as instructions to the faithful, who saw in him an eloquent, honest, and compassionate spiritual master. Around 1320, Eckhart wrote for the bereaved Queen Agnes of Hungary the *Book of Divine Consolation*, which contained his famous treatise "On Detachment." In it he defined his principal ideas on the relationship between the human and the divine and between the Neoplatonic concept of oneness and his Christian belief in the Trinity.

In regard to true detachment, Eckhart simply believed that the detached man or woman is loving and humble, possessing serenity and wisdom, and with a will wholly taken up by God. Eckhart's popularity as a speaker and writer opened him to scrutiny by the archbishop of Cologne, who accused him of heresy. Eckhart defended himself to the Holy See, assuring the pope that he might err in thought but never in will and that he was not a heretic. The defense was not accepted. Twenty-eight propositions in his writings were condemned as part of his ecclesiastical trial in 1326, a ban that has since been lifted by the Church. It has been shown that Eckhart used paradoxical and quite original formulations to try to grasp the unity of the divine and the human and that he never obfuscated the immeasurable difference between the "allness" of the Creator and the "nothingness" of us creatures. He preached that good works can only proceed from a good spirit. This other-centered goodness calls for self-emptying and detachment, indeed for the pursuit of God beyond "gods," or those illusory attachments that impede progress to union and the graced birth of the Word in the soul.

## THANK GOD NOW

If it were the case that someone who had possessed honor and comfort for many years were now to lose these by divine decree, then this person should reflect wisely and thank God. When they become aware of their present injury and hardship, they will realize for the first time how great was their earlier advantage and security and they should thank God now for the security which they previously enjoyed without really being aware of how well off they were, and should refrain from complaining. They should consider that by their natural being men and women possess nothing other than wickedness and weakness. All that is good and goodness has been given on loan to them by God and not for their own possession. For whoever knows the truth, knows that God, the heavenly Father, gives all that is good to the Son and the Holy Spirit, while he does not give but rather only lends goodness to creatures. The sun gives warmth to the air, but it only lends air light. Therefore when the sun sets, the air loses light but warmth remains in it, since it has been given to the air as its own possession.

—Meister Eckhart, *Selected Writings*, 74

*When an unexpected crisis wrenches you out of your comfort zone, is your first response to thank God, or are you more inclined to complain, forgetting that "goodness has been given on loan to [you] by God"?*

## HADEWIJCH (D. 1282)

A Flemish Beguine of the thirteenth century, this visionary mystic and literary genius drew upon the power of poetry commingled with heartfelt prayer to communicate her spiritual message. Graced with the dual gifts of mystical union and poetic communion with God and others, she became a member of the most notable women's movement of her day, dedicating herself to a life of Christian spirituality in the cloister of the world. Hadewijch understood that God had called her to communicate to other seekers the profound knowledge of the mystical theology he granted to her. She directed her words of wisdom and her works of charity to the younger members of her community, for whom she felt a special affection. In her time she knew little fame, preferring to follow the hidden life of Jesus of Nazareth. As a result, her ecstatic writings went largely unknown until the nineteenth century. In her writings, Hadewijch employed a poetic paradoxical style that enabled her to portray at once the humanity and divinity of Christ and the Trinity and unity of God. She believed that the empowerment of human love by divine love enables us to offer ourselves in self-giving love to others. "Therefore," she writes, "works with faith must precede love; then love will set them on fire."[21]

## CONTEMPLATE GOD'S GRACE AND GOODNESS

If you wish to experience this perfection, you must first of all learn to know yourselves: in all your conduct, in your attraction or aversion, in your behavior, in love, in hate, in fidelity, in mistrust, and in all things that befall you. You must examine yourselves as to how you can endure everything disagreeable that happens to you, and how you can bear the loss of what gives you pleasure; for to be robbed of what it gladly receives is indeed the greatest sorrow a young heart can bear. And in everything pleasant that happens to you, examine yourselves as to how you make use of it, and how wise and how moderate you are with regard to it. In all that befalls you, preserve your equanimity in repose or in pain. Continually contemplate with wisdom our Lord's works; from them you will learn perfection.

It is truly fitting that everyone contemplate God's grace and goodness with wisdom and prudence: for God has given us our beautiful faculty of reason, which instructs man in all his ways and enlightens him in all works. If man would follow reason, he would never be deceived.

—Hadewijch, *Complete Works*, 77

*In accordance with the counsel of Hadewijch, do you engage daily in an examination of your conscience? Do you consider how well—and with how much gratitude—you have accepted what was disagreeable to you? Do you assess whether you have tried your best to "preserve your equanimity in repose or in pain"?*

## JOHANNES TAULER (CA. 1300–1361)

Born and buried in Strasbourg, Tauler entered the Dominican Order in 1315, received an excellent education, and spent his entire life in towns and villages along the Rhine. He lived during a time of great turmoil in the Church. The pope was in exile in Avignon, famine and plague ravished the continent, and new lay movements such as the Beguines, the Brethren of the Free Spirit, and the Friends of God were on the rise.

Tauler favored the mystical life as taught by Meister Eckhart with its stress on the indwelling Trinity and imageless contemplation, but he also preached about the beauty of the active life with devotion to Christ's poverty as an antidote to vanity and worldliness. Complementing Eckhart's teaching on the interior life was Tauler's balanced appreciation of prayer in practice, of the right blend of activity and abandonment, thereby revealing the affective and practical side of mystical theology. In this way he avoided the excesses of quietism. He never doubted the importance of asceticism as the virtuous foundation of mysticism and the need to practice the charity that flows from contemplation.

For this reason Tauler, who underwent an interior conversion in his middle years, felt at home with a Flemish contemporary of his, Bl. John Ruysbroeck, whom he met in the Netherlands. He also had an influence on mystics of later ages, notably St. John of the Cross and St. Teresa of Avila. By avoiding rhetorical effect and intellectual subtlety in his sermons, he was able to make his points in a down-to-earth way, which explains why his sermons have survived the test of time. The mystery of the Blessed Trinity with its superabundant unity drew forth some of Tauler's most profound reflections. Its "imageless Image," he says, dwells in the inmost ground of the soul. Here we find by grace what God possesses by nature. That is why over a lifetime of fidelity to God's Word, we should "allow the Holy Trinity to be born in the center of [our] soul, not by the use of human reason, but in essence and in truth; not in words, but in reality."[22]

## PRAISE GOD IN EVERYTHING WITH HEARTFELT GRATITUDE

Those . . . who are God's true witnesses are firmly anchored in Him, in love or in suffering, no matter what God may choose to give or take away. They do not set much store by their own methods; if they prove helpful to their spiritual life, well and good. But God, in His loving foresight, often shatters their foundations and thus they frequently find themselves thwarted. If they want to keep vigil, they are obliged to sleep; if they like to fast, they are made to eat; if they would like to keep silence and be at rest, they have to do otherwise. In this way, everything they cleave to crumbles and they are brought face-to-face with their bare nothingness. Thus they are shown how total is their dependence on God, and they learn to confess Him with a pure and simple faith, with no other support to sustain them. For just as worldly and frivolous people are seduced by the pleasures of their possessions, so these [religious] people take pleasure in their complacency, both in their actions and in their emotions.

And thus they are prevented from an absolute surrender to God and from a true poverty of spirit according to God's will. . . . If we could only learn to praise God in everything—in our thoughts and works and in all events, whether they turn out to our advantage or not. Then we should have discovered the right way. And furthermore, if we could refer everything back to God, with heartfelt gratitude, then we should be true and steadfast witnesses indeed. Beloved, return all things to the ground of Being from which they originated, never come to a standstill at created things, but unite yourselves to the uncreated Source. Within its depth is born true praise of God, and there it grows and blooms and bears fruit.

—Johannes Tauler, *Sermons*, 96

*Do you meditate daily on the awesome truth of your total dependence on God? What, if anything, prevents you from living in "true poverty of spirit according to God's will"?*

## THOMAS À KEMPIS (1379–1471)

Thomas à Kempis was a major figure in a grassroots religious revival movement in the Netherlands known as *Devotio Moderna*, which focused on a return to moral and spiritual values, to the practice of genuine piety, to less stress on abstract information about the faith and more on lived formation in the faith. Thomas entered Mount Saint Agnes in Holland, a monastic community, where he was steeped in the teaching of modern devotion. After his ordination to the priesthood in 1413, he became subprior of the monastery and later novice master.

Widely accepted as the author of *The Imitation of Christ,* it was Thomas who brought this devotion to the universal attention of the Church. In fact, this classic has been dubbed, after the Bible, as the most read text in Christendom. Its perennial popularity is due in great measure to its lucid presentation of a trustworthy pattern of discipleship. Its chapters counsel seekers who want to follow the royal road of the cross by calling to mind at all times Christ's sacrificial love for us.

Throughout the *Imitation,* Thomas derides what he calls "loveless scholarship," learning that only puffs a person up with his own importance but does not feed the interior life or assist in service to one's neighbor. He says, "Search for truth in holy writings, not eloquence."[23] It profits us more to pay attention to what is said than to whether it is said in a lofty manner. Thomas reminds us many times over that "people pass away, but the truth of the Lord endures forever."[24]

## THEN YOUR GRACE WILL BE MINE

If I humble myself, think of myself as nothing, sweep away all self-importance, and account myself as dust, as indeed I am, then your grace will be mine. Then your light will be close to my heart, and all self-importance, no matter how little, will remain submerged in the valley of my nothingness and will perish forever. There, in my nothingness, you show me to myself—what I am, what I have been, and what I have become. I am nothing, and I did not even know it. . . .

But if you turn your face upon me, I am at once made strong and am filled with new happiness. It is wonderful that I am so quickly uplifted and so kindly embraced by you, I who by my own weight am always sinking to the bottom. Your love does this. It freely goes before me and helps me in my many needs. It guards me from grave dangers, too. To tell the truth, your love protects me from so many evils that I cannot count them all! . . . May you be blessed, my God, for though I am unworthy of all the good things you give me, yet your excellence and infinite goodness never cease giving them. Even the thankless and those who have turned their backs on you receive your blessing. Turn us back to you, so that we may be thankful, humble, and devout, for you are our salvation, our courage, and our strength.

—Thomas à Kempis,
*Imitation of Christ*, 95

*How do you feel knowing that God wants you to live in the valley of your nothingness, knowing that you are not alone because Love Divine covers you like a mantle? Unworthy as you may feel, do you believe you are precious in God's sight?*

## MEET THE MODERN MASTERS

### ST. FRANCIS DE SALES (1567–1622)

St. Francis de Sales's priestly life began after his ordination in 1593, when he was sent to minster to Catholics in the region of Lake Geneva. Due to de Sales's compassionate nature and his knowledge of both civil and canon law, in 1599 Pope Clement VII appointed him coadjutor to the bishop of Geneva, a position requiring great grace and diplomatic skills since the area around the lake was predominantly Calvinist. His bent toward reconciliation versus revenge was rewarded, for three years later he became the bishop of that region.

It was in Geneva that de Sales not only foiled several assassination attempts but also began to be recognized as a brilliant preacher and a man endowed with exceptional spiritual gifts. His gentle heart and sense of self-sacrifice endeared him to Protestants and Catholics alike. Many reformers were reconciled to the Church thanks to him. In moments of controversy, he was a model of good manners, sensitive to others, moderate in judgment, clear in expression, dignified, and modest. The depth at which de Sales heard the call to holiness is evidenced in his two most famous books, both spiritual classics, *Treatise on the Love of God* (1607) and *Introduction to the Devout Life* (1608).

In 1604, de Sales agreed to be the mentor and spiritual guide of Jane Frances de Chantel, the saintly widow and spiritual friend with whom he would exchange many letters of direction and found a new religious order for women, the nuns of the Order of the Visitation. His methods of direction were gentle yet firm, stressing moderation instead of excessive forms of piety. He believed in the basic goodness of the human soul and its innate hunger for God. He not only introduced his readers to the devout life as a way to find God wherever one was but he also taught workable methods of meditation based on the instinct of love and fidelity to everyday occasions of grace.

## FIRMLY EMBRACE GOD'S GRACIOUS LOVE

Life on earth flows away like waters that float and undulate in a perpetual diversity of movement. Sometimes they buoy [man] up in hope and sometimes they cast him down in fear. Sometimes they carry him to the right hand by consolation, sometimes to the left by affliction. Not one of his days, not even one of his hours, is completely like another.

For us there is a great lesson in all this. We must try to keep our heart steadily, unshakably equable during such great inequality of events. Even though everything turns and changes around us, we must always remain unchanging and ever looking, striving, and aspiring toward God. No matter what course the ship may take, no matter whether it sails to the east, west, north, or south, no matter what wind drives it on, the mariner's needle never points in any direction except toward the fair polar star. Everything may be in confusion not only around us, I say, but within us as well. Our soul may be overwhelmed with sorrow or joy, with sweetness or bitterness, with peace or trouble, with light or darkness, with temptation or repose, with pleasure or disgust, with aridity or tenderness, it may be scorched by the sun or refreshed by the dew— for all that, ever and always our heart's point, our spirit, our higher will, which is our compass, must unceasingly look and tend toward the love of God, its Creator, its Savior, its sole and sovereign good. . . .

This absolute resolution never to forsake God and never to abandon his merciful love serves our soul as a counterweight to keep it in a holy equilibrium amid all the inequality of the various changes brought to it by the conditions of this life. When caught out in the fields by a storm little bees pick up small stones so that they can keep their balance in the air and not be easily carried away by the wind. So also when our soul has made its resolution and firmly embraced God's [gracious] love, it keeps steady amid the inconstancy and danger that come

from consolations and afflictions, whether spiritual
or temporal and whether exterior or interior.
—Francis de Sales, *Introduction to the*
*Devout Life*, 256–257

*When your life veers from tranquility to tribulation, from clar-*
*ity to confusion, have you so habitually set your inner compass*
*of gratitude on God's guiding will that you are able to remain*
*"unshakably equable during such great inequality of events"?*
*Have you begun to train yourself to try to see in every obstacle*
*a formation opportunity?*

## ST. VINCENT DE PAUL (1580–1660)

Born in France in a peasant family, St. Vincent followed first
his own ambitions and second, if at all, divine aspirations. At
the age of nineteen, his desire to move up in the world led him
to pursue a university education, but he soon realized that God
had other, less worldly plans for him. He came under the influence of one of the masters of the French School of Spirituality,
Pierre de Bérulle. Under de Bérulle, the direction of his life
changed completely, and his intense longing for God resulted in
his ordination to the priesthood. From then on, Vincent would
find his fame not in courtly contacts but in care for the poor.

In 1625, Vincent established a new congregation in the
Church, the Vincentians. They were men of God under religious orders, who were devoted to advancing the formation
of parish priests and to working in rural areas where good

confessors were badly needed. So inspiring was Monsieur Vincent, as he was called, that wealth poured in to support his projects. People of means loved him and the poor he served.

Before long, his influence had spread from France to the entire continent of Europe. He organized a variety of charitable services, to which he attracted the help of St. Louise de Marillac, with whom he founded the Daughters of Charity. Their network of service to the poor, notably through the establishment of hospitals, orphanages, and shelters for the physically and mentally infirm and for the homeless, would eventually span the world, living proof of the efficacy of God's grace poured into hearts that are humble and always ready to serve God and others.

## GRACES RECEIVED FROM GOD
## SINCE CHILDHOOD

My daughters, for the coming week, let the subject of your mental prayer be considerations on the graces you have received from God since the days of your childhood, and the dangers from which you have heard your parents say you have been delivered by the providence of God. . . .

My daughters, say: "From all eternity God has thought of doing good to me even when I had not begun to feel any sentiments of gratitude and thanks." And think over in your hearts the resolution you should select, and resolve to observe for the whole course of your life your rule to serve the sick. . . . When Solomon determined to build God's temple, he used precious stones as a foundation to show the excellence of the work he had decided on. May God's goodness grant you the grace that you who are the foundation of this little company may be eminent in virtue. For, if you were not very virtuous, you would do wrong to those who will come after you, if God be pleased to bless this beginning. As trees bear fruit only according to their nature, it is likely that those who will come after you will not aim at greater virtues than those you have practiced.

—Vincent de Paul and Louise de
Marillac, *Rules, Conferences,*
*and Writings*, 208–209

*Are you ready to engage in a life review to ascertain "the graces you have received from God since the day of your childhood"? How might such a review help you to strengthen your habit of living a grace-filled life for the edification of others seeking the same lasting fruit of faith?*

## ST. ELIZABETH ANN SETON (1774–1821)

A native of New York City, Elizabeth was the daughter of Richard Bayley, an esteemed medical doctor and professor, and Catherine Charlton, daughter of an Episcopal rector. Elizabeth grew up in an atmosphere of wealth and privilege, though, as was the custom in those days, she lived apart from her family while attending school. When she was twenty years old, she married William Seton, a shipping merchant, and eventually became the mother of five children.

Despite the good times Elizabeth enjoyed with family and friends and her work with the poor, trials and tribulations multiplied, including family deaths, sicknesses, and a decline in her husband's business to the point of bankruptcy. Through all these difficulties, Elizabeth practiced faithfully the Episcopalian religion of her youth. To help restore William's failing health, the Setons went on a trip to Italy from which William would never return. He died in 1803, leaving Elizabeth a widow at the age of twenty-nine, having been married just eight years.

It was in Italy under the influence of friends that Elizabeth was introduced to and felt an attraction for the Catholic faith. She returned home, continued to pray about her life call, and finally, in March 1805, converted to Catholicism, even though this meant considerable alienation from friends and family members.

Elizabeth found it hard to earn a living because of the animosity she encountered. When she was offered the chance in 1806 to conduct a school for girls in Baltimore, she did so with joy. She moved to Emmitsburg, Maryland, a few years later. There, together with several companions, she adopted a modified rule of the Daughters of Charity of St. Vincent de Paul and thus became the foundress of the first American religious order, the Sisters of Charity.

In addition to caring for and educating her own children, Elizabeth laid the cornerstone of the parochial school system in the United States. She trained teachers and prepared textbooks. She translated books from French to English, wrote spiritual reflections, visited the poor and the sick, established several orphanages, and developed a deep love for the Eucharist. In 1975, Elizabeth became the first American woman to be canonized a saint.

## MARY FULL OF GRACE

Mary our Mother—What child does not love its mother—the mother of our Eternity—Mother of our redemption—the complacency of the adorable Trinity from Eternity beholding so pure a Vessel to repair the desolation of the fall—announced by all the prophets with our Jesus—her innocence—conceived in perfect purity—we honor her continually with our Jesus, his nine months within her—what passed between them, she alone knowing him, he her only tabernacle!—Mary and Joseph at Bethlehem—the hidden life, the flight, the trial of her humility to bid him and direct him—

*MARY FULL OF GRACE—MOTHER of JESUS*
O! we love and honor our Jesus when we love and honor her. A true proof of our blessed church being the one Jesus only loves—Mary returning our love to JESUS for us, our prayer passing through her heart with reflected love and excellence. Jesus delighting to receive our love embellished and purified through the heart of Mary, as from the heart of

a friend everything delights us. How can we honor
the mysteries of our Jesus, without honoring Mary
in them all—how unhappy they who deprive themselves of such happiness.

—Elizabeth Seton, *Selected Writings*, 328

*When you ponder the life of the Blessed Mother—her courage,
her humility, her suffering, her joy—do you feel in your heart
a surge of gratitude and a renewed desire to emulate in your
own way the fullness of grace poured into her whole being by
God? Name a few ways in which you might try to embody these
Marian virtues in your everyday life.*

## ST. ELIZABETH OF THE TRINITY (1880–1906)

Marie Elizabeth Catez was born to a distinguished family in
Bourges, France, known for its dedication to both civic and
religious concerns. Her father, an officer in the French army,
died when Elizabeth was seven years old, leaving her mother to raise Elizabeth and her sister, Marguerite. The three of
them moved to Dijon, where Elizabeth blossomed under the
firm guidance of her mother into a vivacious and unusually
self-possessed child.

Like St. Thérèse of Lisieux, whose autobiography she read,
Elizabeth would not rest until she entered the cloister. However, her mother made her delay her entrance to the convent
until she was twenty-one and had finished her education. As
a postulant, she began to experience not only a lifelong love

for silence but also interior trials, similar to the dark nights of sense and spirit described by her spiritual father, St. John of the Cross, and her mother in Carmel, St. Teresa of Avila.

Elizabeth also loved the scriptures, especially the epistles of St. Paul. There she found the assurance that she had been chosen by Christ before the foundation of the world. By the time of her religious profession in 1903, she experienced a deep peace of soul, for she had found Christ everywhere and every activity immersed her more in God. A year later, she composed her famous prayer to the Blessed Trinity, which is a synthesis of her experience and her spiritual doctrine. It ends with the unforgettable words: "O my Three, my All, my Beatitude, infinite Solitude, Immensity in which I lose myself, I surrender myself to You as Your prey. Bury Yourself in me that I may bury myself in You until I depart to contemplate in Your light the abyss of Your greatness."[25]

Depart Elizabeth soon would, for by 1905, she had begun to experience the symptoms of the illness that would end her life. For the next several months, she could do nothing but abandon herself totally to the Divine will. After a brief remission of her pain, she suffered yet another relapse, but on May 24, 1906, a few months before her death in November of that year, she reported having received the grace of feeling the presence of God. "I think," she wrote shortly before her death, "that in Heaven my mission will be to draw souls by helping them to go out of themselves, in order to cling to God by a wholly simple and loving movement, and to keep them in this great silence within which will allow God to communicate Himself to them

and to transform them into Himself."[26] Pope Francis canonized
Elizabeth on October 16, 2016.

## ONE WHO IS ALWAYS GIVING THANKS

A praise of glory is a soul of silence that remains like
a lyre under the mysterious touch of the Holy Spirit
so that He may draw from it divine harmonies; it
knows that suffering is a string that produces still
more beautiful sounds; so it loves to see this string
on its instrument that it may more delightfully
move the Heart of its God.

A praise of glory is a soul that gazes on God in
faith and simplicity; it is a reflector of all that He is;
it is like a bottomless abyss into which He can flow
and expand; it is also like a crystal through which
He can radiate and contemplate all His perfections
and His own splendor. A soul which thus permits
the divine Being to satisfy in itself His need to communicate "all that He is and all that He has," is in
reality the praise of glory of all His gifts.

Finally, a praise of glory is one who is always
giving thanks. Each of her acts, her movements, her
thoughts, her aspirations, at the same time that they
are rooting her more deeply in love, are like an echo
of the eternal Sanctus.

—Elizabeth of the Trinity, *I Have Found
God: The Complete Works*, vol. 1, 112

*Do you try to follow the Gospel directive to give thanks always— for movements as customary as making the Sign of the Cross to momentous decisions such as determining how to raise more revenue for your company—all prompting you to live in praise of God's glory as the main motif of your life?*

## ST. TERESA BENEDICTA OF THE CROSS (1891-1942)

Jewish by birth and Catholic by faith, St. Teresa, widely known as the philosopher Edith Stein, was born in Breslau, Germany, on Yom Kippur, the Day of Atonement. She was a woman gifted with a philosophical mind and a writer's heart, and became an assistant to Professor Edmund Husserl at the University of Freiburg, the founder of the phenomenological movement.

In 1922 while studying for her doctorate, she met Jesus Christ, who changed her life forever. To her mother's great sadness, Edith decided to enter the Church. For the next ten years she continued to teach and write, achieving such a high degree of excellence that she was offered a professorship at the University of Muenster. The following year, the Nazis came to power. Many of Edith's scholarly endeavors had to be curtailed, but this no longer disturbed her because she had set her heart on entering the cloistered Carmelite convent in Cologne.

When Edith entered the convent, it seemed to her family that she was betraying them and her people in their hour of greatest need. Yet Edith recognized that to be a Carmelite was not to escape from life but to offer one's life to God as the Lamb did in order to bring spiritual comfort and hope to his people. For her the mystery of the cross was the one guarantee that the suffering of this life, no matter how horrific, can be united with the suffering of the Crucified Christ.

Edith knew that nothing could protect her from the Nazis' hatred of the Jews, certainly not a convent grille. She tells us in her journals and letters that she prayed that God would accept her life and her death in expiation for people's disbelief, for the salvation of Germany, and for world peace. A mere eight years after her profession in 1935, her life would achieve its goal of self-surrender and the cross.

When the Gestapo started persecuting religious orders in Cologne, Edith transferred to the Carmel in Echt, Holland. It was to no avail. In retaliation for a letter read by the Dutch bishops protesting the deportation of Dutch Jews, the Nazis rounded up Catholics of Jewish origin, including Edith, and sent them to concentration camps in July 1942. The death of this prophetic witness to the sacredness of life occurred in Auschwitz on August 9, 1942. On October 11, 1998, she was canonized by Pope John Paul II.

## GOD'S PROOFS OF GRACE

To work in God's grace means for the soul to behold God. Enlightened through grace, the eyes of her spirit deserve to see what previously was concealed by her blindness: "the sublime virtues, abundant sweetness, immense goodness, love and mercy, and the numberless benefits she has received from God. . . ." All of this she was formerly unable to behold or adore. "For great is the rudeness and the blindness of the soul without God's grace!" This soul does not consider the duty she has to recognize God's proofs of grace and to adore him; this does not even enter her mind. "Such is the misery of those who live in sin, or better said, are dead in sin."

Once God has blotted out this sin and ugliness, he no longer reproaches her for it or fails to impart greater favors. But the soul should not forget her former transgressions. Then she will not become presumptuous, will always remain grateful, and her confidence will grow to expect even greater things. The remembrance of her former disgraceful condition increases her happiness at the side of the divine Bridegroom. If of herself she has been *dark* because of sin, now she is arrayed in beauty because God looked at her graciously and thereby made her worthy of new graces. For he gives "grace for grace" (Jn 1:16).

—Edith Stein, *Science of the Cross*, 266

*Do you try to avoid the temptation to presume upon God's mercy and instead to be grateful for the many gifts you have received? In doing so, do you find that, while remembering your "former disgraceful condition," you remain increasingly confident that God will look upon you graciously?*

## ST. MARIA FAUSTINA KOWALSKA (1905–1938)

This modern-day mystic and proponent of the devotion to Divine Mercy grew up in a poor family in Poland during the devastation caused by the First World War. She had only three years of formal education, yet Jesus chose her, as she reveals in her diary, to be his "secretary"—the one through whom his message of mercy would be revealed to the world.

Faustina entered the Congregation of the Sisters of Our Lady of Mercy in Cracow, Poland, and was assigned to do the humblest chores, working in the convent kitchen and the vegetable garden. On February 22, 1931, Christ appeared to this simple sister and revealed a glorious image of himself. The now-famous painting was recorded on that date in Faustina's diary as follows:

> In the evening, when I was in my cell, I saw the Lord Jesus clothed in a white garment. One hand [was] raised in the gesture of blessing, the other was touching the garment at the breast. From beneath the garment, slightly drawn aside at the breast, there were emanating two large rays, one red, and the other pale. In silence I kept my gaze fixed on the Lord; my soul was struck with awe, but also with great joy. After a while Jesus said to me: "Paint an image according to the pattern you see, with the signature: Jesus, I trust in You. I desire that this image be venerated, first in your chapel, and [then] throughout the world."[27]

Later the Lord explained to Faustina what the image meant. "The pale ray," he said, "stands for the Water which makes souls righteous. The red ray stands for the Blood which is the life of souls. . . . These two rays issued forth from the depths of My most tender mercy when My agonized Heart was opened by a lance on the Cross. . . . Happy is the one who will dwell in their shelter, for the just hand of God shall not lay hold of him."[28] Jesus also asked his "little secretary" to issue a call to the whole Church to celebrate the Feast of Divine Mercy on the first Sunday after Easter, for on that day he would open the depths of his mercy to all.

## SHEDDING TEARS OF GRATITUDE

The Lord gave me knowledge of the graces which He has been constantly lavishing on me. This light pierced me through and through, and I came to understand the inconceivable favors that God has been bestowing on me. I stayed in my cell for a long act of thanksgiving, lying face down on the ground and shedding tears of gratitude. I could not rise from the ground because, whenever I tried to do so, God's light gave me new knowledge of His grace. It was only at the third attempt that I was able to get up. As His child, I felt that everything the heavenly Father possessed was equally mine. He himself lifted me from the ground up to His Heart. I felt that everything that existed was exclusively mine, but I had no desire for it all, because God alone is enough for me.

—Maria Faustina Kowalska,
*Divine Mercy in My Soul*, 461

*Do you try to spend some time each day in the solitude of your heart, making acts of thanksgiving, and perhaps, when you least expect it, "shedding tears of gratitude" for the graces bestowed upon you by God? If not, why not? What can you do to increase your attentiveness to the beckoning light of God's grace in your soul?*

## THOMAS MERTON (1915–1968)

A native of France, Merton traveled in his homeland and throughout America during the first years of his life. His mother died of cancer when he was six, and when Merton was ten, his father brought him to Europe to live. In 1934, Merton returned to live permanently in the United States, and four years later, in 1938, Merton converted to Catholicism. Soon thereafter, he applied for admission to the Franciscan Order, but due to his recent conversion, he was asked to detain his novitiate and put his call to the test of time. Though crushed, he accepted the decision with courage, vowing that if he could not live in a monastery, he would become a monk in the world. He taught English at Saint Bonaventure University and worked for a while with Catherine de Hueck Doherty in a settlement house in Harlem, New York.

In 1941, he gave up teaching and followed his true call to be a Trappist monk at the Abbey of Gethsemane, Kentucky. From then on his life was a rhythm of prayer, work, and publication, including the autobiography that brought him fame and brought many readers to the Church, *The Seven Storey Mountain.*

Merton made solemn vows in 1947 and became an American citizen in 1951. He was appointed to the position of master of novices in 1955, a post he held until 1965, when he obtained permission from his abbot to live as a hermit in a wooded area about a mile from the main buildings. There he sought to let go of other preoccupations and to plunge into the divine abyss wherein God's love encircles and takes possession of one's intellect, imagination, and will. He died in 1968 during a trip to the Far East, leaving behind him a lasting legacy as a man of faith, a monk, and a teacher of almost limitless expansiveness, whose writings witness to the truth that "gratitude is therefore the heart of the solitary life, as it is the heart of the Christian life."[29]

## EVERY MOMENT OF EXISTENCE IS A GRACE

There is no neutrality between gratitude and ingratitude. Those who are not grateful soon begin to complain of everything. Those who do not love, hate. . . .

True gratitude and hypocrisy cannot exist together. They are totally incompatible. Gratitude of itself makes us sincere—or if it does not, then it is not true gratitude.

Gratitude, though, is more than a mental exercise, more than a formula of words. We cannot be satisfied to make a mental note of things which God has done for us and then perfunctorily thank Him for favors received.

To be grateful is to recognize the Love of God in everything He has given us—and He has given us everything. Every breath we draw is a gift of His love, every moment of existence is a grace, for it brings with it immense graces from Him. Gratitude therefore takes nothing for granted, is never unresponsive, is constantly awakening to new wonder and to praise of the goodness of God. For the grateful man knows that God is good, not by hearsay but by experience. And that is what makes all the difference.

—Thomas Merton,
*Thoughts in Solitude,* 42–43

*Have you begun to see that "every moment of existence is a grace"? What impact has this insight made on your everyday life in the world?*

# REFERENCES AND RECOMMENDED READINGS

Aelred of Rievaulx. *On Spiritual Friendship*. Translated by Mary Eugenia Laker. Washington, DC: Cistercian Publications, 1974.

Athanasius. *The Life of Antony and the Letter to Marcellinus*. Translated by Robert C. Gregg. New York: Paulist Press, 1980.

Augustine of Hippo. *The Confessions*. Translated by John K. Ryan. New York: Doubleday, 1960.

———. *Augustine of Hippo: Selected Writings*. Translated by Mary T. Clark. New York: Paulist Press, 1984.

Bayley, John. *Iris: A Memoir of Iris Murdoch*. London: Gerald Duckworth, 2002.

Bernard of Clairvaux. *Selected Works*. Translated by G. R. Evans. New York: Paulist Press, 1987.

Bonhoeffer, Dietrich. *The Cost of Discipleship*. Translated by R. H. Fuller. New York: Touchstone, 1995.

Butcher, Carmen Acevedo. *St. Hildegard of Bingen, Doctor of the Church: A Spiritual Reader*. Brewster, MA: Paraclete Press, 2013.

Carretto, Carlo. *Letters from the Desert.* Translated by Rose Mary Hancock. Maryknoll, NY: Orbis Books, 1972.

Cassian, John. *Conferences.* Translated by Colm Luibheid. New York: Paulist Press, 1985.

Catherine of Siena. *The Dialogue.* Translated by Suzanne Noffke. New York: Paulist Press, 1980.

Caussade, Jean-Pierre de. *Abandonment to Divine Providence.* Translated by John Beevers. Garden City, NY: Image Books, 1975.

Ciszek, Walter J. *He Leadeth Me.* Garden City, NY: Image Books, Doubleday, 1975.

———. *With God in Russia.* San Francisco: Ignatius Press, 1997.

Climacus, John. *The Ladder of Divine Ascent.* Translated by Colm Luibheid and Norman Russell. New York: Paulist Press, 1982.

da Todi, Jacopone. *The Lauds.* Translated by Serge and Elizabeth Hughes. New York: Paulist Press, 1982.

Day, Dorothy. *The Long Loneliness.* San Francisco: HarperSanFrancisco, 1997.

de Paul, Vincent, and Louise de Marillac. *Rules, Conferences, and Writings.* Edited by Frances Ryan and John Rybolt. New York: Paulist Press, 1995.

de Sales, Francis. *Introduction to the Devout Life.* Translated by John K. Ryan. New York: Image Books, Doubleday, 1972.

de Sales, Francis, and Jane de Chantal. *Francis de Sales and Jane de Chantal: Letters of Spiritual Direction.* Translated by Péronne Marie Thibert. New York: Paulist Press, 1988.

Dickens, Charles. *A Tale of Two Cities.* New York: Penguin Classics, 2003.

Elizabeth of the Trinity. *I Have Found God: The Complete Works.* Vol. 1. Translated by Aletheia Kane. Washington, DC: ICS Publications, 1984.

———. *I Have Found God: The Complete Works.* Vol. 2. Translated by Anne Englund Nash. Washington, DC: ICS Publications, 1995.

Elizabeth Seton. *Selected Writings.* Edited by Ellin Kelly and Annabelle Melville. New York: Paulist Press, 1987.

Ephrem the Syrian. *Hymns.* Translated by Kathleen E. McVey. New York: Paulist Press, 1989.

Evagrius of Ponticus. *The Praktikos and Chapters on Prayer.* Translated by John Eudes Bamberger. Spencer, MA: Cistercian Publications, 1970.

Francis of Assisi and Clare of Assisi. *Francis and Clare: The Complete Works.* Translated by Regis J. Armstrong and Ignatius C. Brady. New York: Paulist Press, 1982.

Graham, Billy. *Just As I Am: The Autobiography of Billy Graham.* New York: HarperCollins, 1997.

Gregory of Nyssa. *The Life of Moses.* Translated by Abraham J. Malherbe and Everett Ferguson. New York: Paulist Press, 1978.

Guardini, Romano. *The Living God.* Translated by Stanley Godman. New York: Pantheon Books, 1957.

Hadewijch. *The Complete Works*. Translated by Columba Hart. New York: Paulist Press, 1980.

Hammarskjöld, Dag. *Markings*. Translated by Leif Sjoberg and W. H. Auden. New York: Ballantine Books, 1964.

Ignatius of Loyola. *The Spiritual Exercises of Saint Ignatius*. Translated by George E. Ganss. Chicago: Loyola University Press, 1992.

John of the Cross. *The Collected Works of St. John of the Cross*. Translated by Kieran Kavanaugh and Otilio Rodriquez. Washington, DC: ICS Publications, 1991.

John Paul II. *Crossing the Threshold of Hope*. New York: Alfred A. Knopf, 1994.

Julian of Norwich. *Showings*. Translated by Edmund College and James Walsh. New York: Paulist Press, 1978.

Kowalska, Maria Faustina. *Divine Mercy in My Soul: The Diary of the Servant of God, Sister M. Faustina Kowalska*. Stockbridge, MA: Marian Press, 1987.

Lavelle, Louis. *The Meaning of Holiness*. New York: Pantheon Books, 1954.

Lawrence of the Resurrection. *The Practice of the Presence of God*. Translated by Salvatore Sciuba. Washington, DC: ICS Publications, 1994.

Letterman, Rebecca, and Susan Muto. *Understanding Our Story: The Life's Work and Legacy of Adrian van Kaam in the Field of Formative Spirituality*. Eugene, OR: Wipf and Stock, 2017.

Lewis, C. S. *Surprised by Joy: The Shape of My Early Life*. New York: Harcourt, 1956.

Libermann, Francis. *Spiritual Letters to Clergy and Religious.* Translated by Walter van de Putte. Pittsburgh, PA: Duquesne University, 1966.

Lifton, Robert J. *The Nazi Doctors: Medical Killing and the Psychology of Genocide.* New York: Basic Books, 1986.

Maximus Confessor. *Selected Writings.* Translated by George C. Berthold. New York: Paulist Press, 1985.

Meister Eckhart. *Selected Writings.* Translated by Oliver Davies. New York: Penguin Books, 1994.

Merton, Thomas. *New Seeds of Contemplation.* New York: New Directions, 1972.

———. *Thoughts in Solitude.* New York: Image Books, 1956.

Murdoch, Iris. *The Sea, the Sea.* New York: Penguin Books, 1978.

Muto, Susan. *John of the Cross for Today: The Ascent.* Pittsburgh, PA: Epiphany Books, 1998.

———. *John of the Cross for Today: The Dark Night.* Pittsburgh, PA: Epiphany Books, 2000.

———. *Keepsakes for the Journey: Four Weeks on Faith Deepening.* Hyde Park, NY: New City Press, 2010.

———. *One in the Lord: Living Our Call to Christian Community.* Hyde Park, NY: New City Press, 2013.

———. *Twelve Little Ways to Transform Your Heart: Lessons in Holiness and Evangelization from St. Thérèse of Lisieux.* Notre Dame, IN: Ave Maria Press, 2016.

———. *Virtues: Your Christian Legacy.* Steubenville, OH: Emmaus Road, 2014.

Nouwen, Henri J. M. *The Wounded Healer: Ministry in Contemporary Society.* Garden City, NY: Image Books, 1972.

Origen. *An Exhortation to Martyrdom, Prayer, and Selected Works.* Translated by Rowan A. Greer. New York: Paulist Press, 1979.

Peale, Norman Vincent. *Power of the Plus Factor.* New York: Fawcett Crest, 1987.

Petit, Jean. *Descending Fire: The Journal of a Soul Aflame.* Manchester, NH: Sophia Institute Press, 1953.

Pieper, Josef. *Faith, Hope, Love.* San Francisco: Ignatius Press, 2012.

*Sayings of the Desert Fathers.* Translated by Benedicta Ward. London: A. R. Mowbrey, 1975.

Schmidt, Joseph F. *Everything Is Grace: The Life and Way of Thérèse of Lisieux.* Frederick, MD: The Word Among Us Press, 2007.

Sommerfeldt, John R. *Aelred of Rievaulx: On Love and Order in the World and the Church.* New York: The Newman Press, 2006.

Stein, Edith. *The Science of the Cross.* Translated by Josephine Koeppel. Washington, DC: ICS Publications, 2002.

Steindl-Rast, David. *Gratefulness, The Heart of Prayer: An Approach to Life in Fullness.* New York: Paulist Press, 1984.

Tauler, Johannes. *Sermons.* Translated by Maria Shrady. New York: Paulist Press, 1985.

Ten Boom, Corrie. *The Hiding Place.* Edited by John and Elizabeth Sherrill. Grand Rapids, MI: Chosen Books, 1998.

Teresa of Avila. *The Book of Her Life.* In *The Collected Works.* Vol. 1. Translated by Kieran Kavanaugh and Otilio Rodriquez. 2nd rev. ed. Washington, DC: ICS Publications, 1987.

———. *The Way of Perfection.* In *The Collected Works.* Vol. 2. Translated by Kieran Kavanaugh and Otilio Rodriguez. 2nd rev. ed. Washington, DC: ICS Publications. 1987.

Teresa of Calcutta. *Come Be My Light.* New York: Doubleday, 2007.

———. *Essential Writings.* Maryknoll, NY: Orbis Books, 2005.

Thérèse of Lisieux. *Story of a Soul.* Translated by John Clarke. Washington, DC: ICS Publications, 2005.

Thomas à Kempis. *The Imitation of Christ.* Edited by William C. Creasy. Notre Dame, IN: Ave Maria Press, 1989.

Underhill, Evelyn. *Practical Mysticism.* Canal Winchester, OH: Ariel Press, ND.

van Kaam, Adrian. *Formation of the Human Heart.* Formative Spirituality Series. Vol. 2. Pittsburgh, PA: Epiphany Books, 2002.

———. *The Life Journey of a Joyful Man of God: The Autobiographical Memoirs of Adrian van Kaam.* Edited by Susan Muto. Eugene, OR: Wipf and Stock, 2010.

———. *A Light to the Gentiles: The Life Story of the Venerable Francis Liberman.* Eugene, OR: Wipf and Stock, 2009.

———. *The Roots of Christian Joy.* Denville, NJ: Dimension Books, 1985.

———. *Spirituality and the Gentle Life.* Pittsburgh, PA: Epiphany Books, 2005.

van Kaam, Adrian, and Susan Muto. *Formation of the Christian Heart.* Formation Theology. Vol. 3. Pittsburgh, PA: Epiphany Books, 2006.

———. *The Power of Appreciation: A New Approach to Personal and Relational Healing.* Pittsburgh, PA: Epiphany Books, 1999.

Vanier, Jean. *Tears of Silence.* Toronto: Griffin House, 1970.

# NOTES

1. International Commission on English in the Liturgy, *Liturgy of the Hours* (Totowa, NJ: Catholic Book Publishing Corp., 1975).

2. Julian of Norwich, *Showings*, trans. Edmund Colledge and James Walsh (Mahwah, NJ: Paulist Press, 1978), 262–263.

3. Lawrence of the Resurrection, *The Practice of the Presence of God*, trans. Salvatore Sciurba (Washington, DC: ICS Publications, 1997), 53.

4. John of the Cross, *The Spiritual Canticle*, in *The Collected Works of St. John of the Cross*, trans. Kieran Kavenaugh and Otilio Rodriguez (Washington, DC: ICS Publications, 1991), 613–614.

5. Jean-Pierre de Caussade, *Abandonment to Divine Providence*, trans. John Beevers (Garden City, NY: Image Books, 1993), 72.

6. Ibid., 95.

7. Henri J. M. Nouwen, *The Wounded Healer: Ministry in Contemporary Society* (Garden City, NY: Image Books, 1972), 87.

8. Ibid., 17.

9. Catherine of Siena, *The Dialogue*, trans. Suzanne Noffke (New York: Paulist Press, 1980), 25.

10. Ibid., 360.

11. Ibid., 365.

12. Bernard of Clairvaux, *Selected Works*, trans. G. R. Evans (New York: Paulist Press, 1987), 256.

13. Ibid., 115.

14. Jean Vanier, *Tears of Silence* (Toronto: Griffin House, 1970), i.

15. *The Life Journey of a Joyful Man of God: The Autobiographical Memoirs of Adrian van Kaam*, ed. Susan Muto (Eugene, OR: Wipf and Stock, 2001), 312.

16. Thomas Merton, *New Seeds of Contemplation* (New York: New Directions, 2007), 206.

17. Augustine of Hippo, *The Confessions*, trans. John K. Ryan (New York: Doubleday, 1960), 202.

18. Ibid., 43.

19. Teresa of Avila, *The Book of Her Life*, in *The Collected Works of St. Teresa of Avila*, vol. 1, trans. Kieran Kavanaugh and Otilio Rodriguez (Washington, DC: ICS Publications, 1987), 192.

20. John Climacus, *The Ladder of Divine Ascent*, trans. Colm Luibheid and Norman Russell (New York: Paulist Press, 1982), 76.

21. Hadewijch, *The Complete Works*, trans. Columba Hart (New York: Paulist Press, 1981), 81.

22. Johannes Tauler, *Sermons*, trans. Maria Shrady (New York: Paulist Press, 1985), 104.

23. Thomas à Kempis, *The Imitation of Christ*, ed. William C. Creasy (Notre Dame, IN: Ave Maria Press, 1989), 35.

24. Ibid.

25. Elizabeth of the Trinity, *I Have Found God: The Complete Works*, vol. 1, trans. Aletheia Kane (Washington, DC: ICS Publications, 1984), 184.

26. Ibid., 28–29.

27. Maria Faustina Kowalska, *Divine Mercy in My Soul: Diary of Saint Maria Faustina Kowalska* (Stockbridge, MA: Marian Press, 1987), 24.

28. Ibid., 139.

29. Thomas Merton, *Thoughts in Solitude* (New York: Image Books, 1956), 101.

**Susan Muto**, executive director of the Epiphany Association, is a renowned speaker, author, teacher, and dean of the Epiphany Academy of Formative Spirituality.

Muto earned a master's degree and a doctorate in English literature from the University of Pittsburgh, where she specialized in the work of post-Reformation spiritual writers. Beginning in 1966, she served in administrative positions at the Institute of Formative Spirituality at Duquesne University and taught as a full professor in its programs, edited its journals, and served as its director from 1981 to 1988. An expert in literature and spirituality, she continues to teach courses on an adjunct basis at a number of schools, seminaries, and centers of higher learning.

Muto is a frequent contributor to scholarly and popular journals such as *Mount Carmel* and *Spiritual Life Magazine,* and served as editor of Epiphany's online journals and courses, including *Growing in, with, and through Christ.* She is the author of more than thirty books, among them *Twelve Little Ways to Transform Your Heart, Table of Plenty, Then God Said,* and *Virtues: Your Christian Legacy.* She is the coauthor—with Rev. Adrian van Kaam, C.S.Sp. (1920–2007)—of more than forty books, including *Commitment: Key to Christian Maturity,* and *The Power of Appreciation.*

Muto lectures and leads conferences, seminars, workshops, and institutes nationally and internationally. She has received many distinctions for her work, including a doctor of humanities degree from King's College, Wilkes-Barre, Pennsylvania. She was one of four Catholic writers to be honored in 2009 with a lifetime achievement award by the Catholic Historical Society of Western Pennsylvania. Muto also is the recipient of the 2014 Aggiornamento Award presented of the Catholic Library Association. She lives in Pittsburgh, Pennsylvania.

1976

# Understanding Homosexuality:
# Its Biological and Psychological Bases

# Understanding Homosexuality: Its Biological and Psychological Bases

Edited by
**Dr J A Loraine**
Department of Social Medicine
University of Edinburgh

AMERICAN ELSEVIER PUBLISHING CO., INC.
NEW YORK

Published in the United States by
AMERICAN ELSEVIER PUBLISHING CO. INC.
NEW YORK

Published in the United Kingdom by
MTP
MEDICAL AND TECHNICAL PUBLISHING CO. LTD.
LANCASTER

Library of Congress Catalog Card No: 74-18960

ISBN 0-444-19519-X

First published 1974

# Contents

# List of Contributors

**The Revd. Kenneth M. Boyd,** M.A., B.D., Ph.D.
*The Chaplaincy of the University of Edinburgh, Edinburgh*

**Alan J. Cooper,** M.D., M.R.C.Psych., D.P.M.
*Medical Director, E. Merck Ltd., Wokingham, Berks;
Hon. Senior Lecturer in Psychiatry, St. Mary's Hospital Medical School,
London Hon. Consultant Psychiatrist, St. Mary's Hospital, London*

**Nicholas H. Fairburn**
*Fordell Castle, Dunfermline, Fife*

**Professor Kurt W. Freund**
*Clark Institute of Psychiatry, Toronto, Canada*

**Anthony Grey**
*Managing Trustee, The Albany Trust, London*

**F. Edwin Kenyon,** M.A., M.D., F.R.C.P.(Ed.),
F.R.C. Psych., D.P.M.
*The Warneford Hospital, Oxford*

**Ambrose John King,** T.D., M.B.B.S.(London), F.R.C.S.
*London*

**Dr. John A. Loraine**
*Medical Research Council External Scientific Staff,
Department of Social Medicine, Usher Institute, Edinburgh*

**Ronald W. Ramsay,** B.A., M.A., Ph.D.,
*Psychological Laboratory, University of Amsterdam, Holland*

# Aetiology of Homosexuality

## A.J. Cooper

## INTRODUCTION

The purpose of the present chapter is to discuss some of the more recent and credible work on factors which may be important in causing homosexuality. Although much of what follows probably applies equally to the female, the majority of specific references concern the male. Indulging a personal criticism, a brief historical introduction is presented which moralises how man's judgement has in the past, and continues in the present, to be clouded by prejudice and bigotry. No attempt is made to review the voluminous earlier literature much of which was misguided and irrelevant. Instead a holistic psychosomatic approach is offered which argues that homosexuality is acquired by various learning processes in individuals possibly sensitised by hormonal and early life experiences.

It should be conceded immediately that despite over 50 years of intermittently intense research hard data on aetiological factors are sparse and much of what follows would be unacceptable as evidence by most branches of science. Implicit in this presentation is an indictment of the past, recent and even current research on the subject, much of which is unsystematic, uncontrolled and therefore of limited value; indeed, the bulk of it may eventually prove to be irrelevant. It seems axiomatic that real advance will require a multidisciplinary approach involving the respective skills of psychologists, physiologists, endocrinologists and possibly other specialists. If, and when, we do find satisfactory answers, as the sexual attitudes of society evolve, it may ultimately be decided that these are not worth having (at least in a medical sense) being of academic or curiosity value only.

## HISTORICAL THEORIES OF HOMOSEXUALITY

Some of the views of early writers, medical and non medical alike, are of interest since they tell us something about 'official' and public opinion at the time. In addition they allow a measure of judgement as to how sexual attitudes have developed over the past two thousand years. It is perhaps not too surprising although it is personally depressing that the general views of yesteryear remain somewhat similar to those of today; although many of the half truths and myths have been dispelled, society at large has changed little in its generally condemnatory attitude to homosexuality. Homosexuality was widely prevalent in the ancient classical world. Indeed it is almost certain that such eminent Grecian scholars as Plato and Socrates were, at least latent and probably practising homosexuals; despite this however the behaviour was never openly condoned. Tacit acceptance was by no means general and some authorities were quite vociferous in their criticism, especially in respect of the passive partner who was generally considered to be grossly abnormal. He was often believed to be suffering from a 'hereditary disorder' of the anus which had become the primary erotic zone replacing the genitals (Aristotle). Mettler[1] quoted Aretaeus who stated that: 'impotence . . . . . . . and effeminisation resulted from excessive sexual indulgence'. It is clear from the context that Aretaeus was referring to homosexuality. During the middle ages Christian societies were remarkably silent on the subject. This was possibly due to the legal definition of homosexuality, which mirroring the churches position, saw it as 'a sin so horrible that it should not be put into words by Christians'.

In the early nineteenth century basic attitudes towards homosexuality had changed little, but medical explanations for its cause had become rather more fanciful. Thus, it became bracketed with masturbation and as such was considered as a 'kind of insanity'. Benjamin Rush[2], who was professor of medicine at Philadelphia University, provides a good example of the way in which prejudice and bigotry can fashion medical philosophy. In 1830 he said 'if one indulged in undue or a promiscuous intercourse with the female sex or in onanism. it produces seminal weakness, . . . . . . . fatuity feminisation . . . . . . . and death'. It is clear that Rush, a pillar of the establishment, was merely giving vent to his rather narrow religious beliefs without any supporting evidence. However ludicrous it might seem today his utterances and those of some infamous European predecessors including Tissot[3] placed medical thinking in a strait jacket for almost

100 years. Obsessions over moral turpitude and the conviction that masturbation was a cause for virtually everything, extended into the twentieth century. Indeed even the noted liberal sexologist Havelock Ellis[4] said 'in the constitutionally disposed, masturbation may lead not only to neurasthenia but to premature ejaculation, impotence and aversion to coitus—the latter helping to furnish a soil on which the inverted impulse may develop'. Krafft-Ebing[5], and Moreau and Block[5] were also numbered amongst those who believed disapprovingly that masturbation might lead to homosexuality. Other commentators at the time, seemingly convinced of the essentially heinous nature of homosexuality, included a Dr Morrison, a London consultant. He righteously referred to homosexuality as 'being of so detestable a character it is a consolation to know that it is sometimes the consequence of insanity'. This consolation seemed to be based on the observation that people of high breeding and standing were not immune from the 'detestable' disease[6].

Havelock Ellis later[4] rejected the idea that homosexuality was acquired and promulgated a mainly genetic aetiology. At the time this had certain advantages to the physician and the homosexual alike. Thus being 'inborn' it was *ipso facto* largely untreatable, this being professionally face saving to the doctor; similarly, the homosexual could not (or should not) be blamed or castigated for his behaviour, since this had already been (genetically) determined at birth. Unfortunately Havelock Ellis was never able to explain why some homosexuals became heterosexual spontaneously or as a result of treatment. He argued (unanswerably) that they could not have been proper homosexuals in the first place.

## THE CONCEPT OF SEX DRIVE

Sex drive maybe considered under two separate headings:
(i) Strength
(ii) Direction
Although these words seem straightforward enough, agreement as to their meaning is far from unanimous.

(i) In respect of strength Kirkendall's[7] suggestions have much to commend them. He sub-divides strength into three components; 'sexual performance'—what one actually does, 'capacity'—what one can do, and 'drive'—how strongly one desires or strives to do.

According to Kirkendall sexual capacity is determined by the ability of the nervous and musclar systems to respond to sexual stimuli by orgasm and to recuperate from that experience to the point where orgasm can again be experienced. This ability varies greatly from person to person, and Kirkendall believes that it probably represents the actual physical sex difference between individuals. Performance, although limited at its upper extreme by capacity, generally varies according to physical and psychological factors operating at the time. Performance is not an accurate measure of capacity because few, if any, persons perform to full capacity. Kirkendall's concept of performance roughly acquaints with Kinsey's' statistic of 'strength of sex drive'. Kinsey simply charted the actual frequencies of sexual outlets to orgasm and ejaculation, from all sources for various age groups. He found that 'sex drive' was normally distributed (like intelligence) and varied inversely with age, reaching a peak in the late teens and declining thereafter. It was remarkably constant throughout life—high responders retaining their potency longer than low responders. Because of these facts Kinsey concluded that there was a very strong genetic component. In some respects Kinsey's concept is much more useful since it relates to what a particular individual actually does rather than some hypothetical capacity which may or may not be achieved.

Drive according to Kirkendall is the strength or the intensity with which the individual wishes to perform. This seems to be largely a psychologically conditioned component, varying markedly from individual to individual as a personality trait. However, it is entirely possible that sex hormones operating both during intrauterine life, as well as later, play a significant role.

Drive and performance are usually closely correlated although at certain times of life, i.e. particularly in the senescence, they may be discordant. Clinically the elderly male who still gets feelings of 'desire' whilst being physically incapable of developing erections, is a common enough phenomenon. The difference in the rate of decline of drive and performance suggests a different genesis. Cooper *et al.*[9] have suggested that sexual physiology, i.e. erections and ejaculations, is probably dependent to a greater degree on hormones than desire, which is largely cortical in origin. Sex drive is an interesting subject which is worthy of further study.

(ii) The direction of sex drive is much easier to define since it relates to the nature of the preferred sexual object. Thus in our culture it is most often heterosexual although it may be homosexual, bisexual or multisexual. The remainder of this chapter is concerned with factors which may be causally relevant in homosexuality.

**Genetic Factors**
Genetic theories for homosexuality have been prevalent since early times and continue to attract proponents today. The initial appeal of an 'inborn cause' was probably moralistic to counter the blast of the masturbation—insanity—homosexual school, i.e. hereditary sin being less heinous and preferable to acquired sin. However, the persisting absence of a credible

alternative aetiology also played its part and heredity was invoked by default.

Later supporters of the importance of genes were often homosexuals themselves and/or unable to make any sense out of the extremely complex psycho-analytical explanations which abounded at the time. Although data from many sophisticated genetic studies have been recently available the conclusions are far from definitive.

Earlier genetic theories are of historical interest only and will not be discussed further.

The largest and probably the best known genetic study is that of Kallman[10]; he reported a 100% concordance rate in thirty-seven monozygotic twin pairs and a 12% rate in twenty-six dizygotic pairs. Kallman drew attention to the major difficulties of investigating homosexuals. In retrospect he would probably accept that he chose rather an atypical group and his criteria were such as to make distortion more likely. Thus the data were collected via psychiatric, correctional and charitable agencies and also from contacts with the underground homosexual world. These sources are often known to be unreliable. Moreover he attempted to limit his sample to exclusive homosexual cases (i.e. Kinsey Grade 5 or 6) who were also over the age of thirty. For these reasons (or perhaps because of others failing to replicate his findings) Kallman later conceded that his very high concordance rate for the monozygous twins was a 'statistical artifact'. Consistent with this admission he later reported a pair of monozygous twins one of whom was schizophrenic and homosexual and the other normal[11].

Lange[12] described two sets of monozygous twins who were part of a much larger criminal twin population. In one pair, both were homosexual, in the other pair one twin only, who had brain damage. Brain damage especially involving the limbic system has been seen to be associated with various types of sexual inversion and personality disorder[13]. In this latter case it seems that no firm genetic conclusions can be made.

Koch[14] performed a 25-year follow-up examination of 495 pairs of non-psychiatric non-deliquent twins. In this series there was one female monozygotic and one male dizygous twin who was homosexual, the co-twins being quite normal.

In a recent study Heston and Shields[5] reported a family with a sibship of fourteen who were thoroughly investigated both clinically and in respect of genetic polymorphisms (blood groups and plasma proteins). Among the siblings were three pairs of male monozygotic twins in two of whom both twins were homosexual and in the third both were heterosexual (i.e. a concordance rate of 100%). In discussing his findings Heston calls upon data derived from homosexuals on the Maudsley psychiatric clinic twin register. In summary, out of five monozygous pairs only two co-twins were also homosexual; whilst in seven dizygous pairs only one co-twin was also homosexual.

A study reported within the last several months mainly concerned with endocrine function in homosexuals is particularly interesting from a hereditary standpoint. Margolese and Janiger[16] presented biographical data obtained during a psychiatric interview on 63 male subjects, including two sets of identical twins. These authors demonstrated a very significant difference in the incidence of consanguineous homosexual relatives. Of 24 heterosexuals (Kinsey 0 - 2) two reported homosexual relatives. Of 28 homosexuals (Kinsey 4 - 6) seventeen reported homosexual relatives, five of whom had two each. Both sets of identical twins were concordant for homosexuality.

Looking through this array of information it can be stated that although Kallman's original study greatly overestimated the resemblance generally found in monozygous pairs it seems beyond dispute that they are significantly more often alike in respect of male homosexuality than are dizygous pairs. Since there is no evidence that monozygocity itself predisposes to homosexuality, genetic factors seem proven. Salter[17], looking for specific factors, found that male homosexuals tended to be the last born of older mothers and suggested an autosomal abnormality. However, this is not supported by a more statistically detailed study of 291 male homosexuals which demonstrated a significantly higher paternal age with a correspondingly higher maternal age, secondary to the shift in paternal age[18]. These investigators concluded that their observations provided no support for a hypothesis that a cause of male homosexuality may be found in a biological factor related to the mother's age, e.g. by causing a chromosomal abnormality. Additionally it has been shown in a large number of homosexuals that there is *no* sex chromosomal abnormality. Loss of an X chromosome has no significant association with homosexuality or mental illness generally. Although at present the precise mode of genetic transmission is undetermined it is almost certain that it will prove to be heterogeneous and non-specific, i.e. perhaps via an influence on personality rather than direction of libido. In individual cases the relative importance of genetic and environmental factors remains uncertain[20].

## HORMONAL THEORIES
Due to the advent of sophisticated technology which for the first time allows accurate measurements of small concentrations of sex hormones in body fluids, these are currently much in vogue. The importance of sex

hormones in the foetal circulation during development and functional organisation of the brain has recently been demonstrated in animal experiments. In sub-primates the position has been summarized by Donovan and Bosch[21]. They conclude 'in general terms it appears that sub-primate females suitably treated with androgens during sexual differentiation develop external genitalia closely resembling those of the normal male. As such pseudohermaphroditic females mature they show an exaggerated tendency to pursue and mount females in oestrus, and, like normal males, they manifest a marked resistance to the display of receptive behaviour when treated with female hormones during adult life'. Along similar lines pregnant female rats treated with the anti-androgen cyproterone acetate* produce offspring chromosomally male, but with external female genitalia; although of course these did not have uteri and were sterile[22]. In humans, Money and Ehrhardt[23] noted that girls exposed to androgens *in utero* and born hermaphrodite, developed a tendency towards tomboyish behaviour, being more 'rough, spirited, combative and aggressive' than girls with Turners syndrome. They point out, however, that tomboyishness was not associated with lesbianism or trans-sexualism. Neither was lesbianism encountered among a large number of older adrenogenital female hermaphrodites who had not been treated.

These recent investigations, whilst undoubtedly interesting and important, are not remotely commensurate with recent reports in various sections of the lay press (e.g. *Times (London)* 13.3.69) which stated that 'the cause of homosexuality had been discovered and that it will soon be possible to prevent "congenital homosexuality" by means of injections during foetal development'.

The great stumbling block with all animal work is its relevance to the human situation. Hormonal manipulation resulting in male rats mounting male rats and female rats, female rats, cannot by any stretch of the imagination be equated with homosexuality in which the psychological components especially motivation is as crucial, or more so, than the physical act. Furthermore in human subjects, functional evolution of the organism has made 'sex' a cortical rather than a gonadal experience with a duality of function, i.e. biological-procreative and psychosocial-pleasure. Despite these cautionary remarks however in the past five years or more investigations into the endocrine function of homosexuals have flourished and some of it is worthy of presentation. Prior work concerned with the measurement of various urinary oxosteroids is considered largely irrelevant and with one exception is not discussed.

*Cyproterone acetate (i)blocks the action of testosterone on hypothalamic receptors (ii) suppresses the production of pituitary gonadotrophins and therefore testosterone synthesis and (iii) antagonises the effects of androgens on peripheral receptor sites.

Loraine[24], and Kolodny's[25] work is fairly typical of the type of investigation currently being conducted in many centres. Loraine studied three male homosexuals aged 19, 29 and 33 years. The homosexual role adopted was variable, being active and passive at different times. Total urinary output was collected for a period of time ranging from 19 to 26 days. Two of the subjects were exclusively homosexual while the third was engaged in both homosexual and heterosexual activities. A control group of 14 heterosexual males was included in the experiment. In the exclusively homosexual subjects urinary output of testosterone was significantly lower than in the case of the heterosexuals. The bisexual male did not differ from the control group. Loraine also studied four female homosexuals and a control group of 14 heterosexuals. Oestrone was significantly lower in all the homosexuals and testosterone excretion was significantly higher than in the controls. Although only a small number of cases was studied the results are suggestive.

More recently Margolese and Janiger[16] have comprehensively examined a group of 63 males clinically and endocrinologically. They devised an androsterone/etiocholanolone equation which discriminates between heterosexual and exclusively homosexual individuals. Androsterone and etiocholanolone are metabolites of testosterone being stereo isomers which are conjugated mainly as glucuronides and excreted in the urine. These two compounds plus DHA are the principal urinary 17-oxosteroids. Of the total 17-oxosteroids about two-thirds come from the adrenal cortex mainly as DHA. When assayed biologically, almost all of the androgenic activity is due to androsterone. Margolese and Janiger classified their subjects as: 24 controls (Kinsey Grade 0, 1); 23 homosexuals (Kinsey 5, 6);—nine intermediate (Kinsey 2 - 4); one trans-sexual. Five heterosexual subjects were classified as non-healthy, three because of depression, one because of hypothyroidism and one because of hypercorticoadrenalism. One homosexual was classified as non-healthy because of a raised SGOT level.

The mean androsterone/etiocholanolone ratio of the Kinsey Grade 5 and 6 homosexuals differed significantly from the controls, this being due to a relatively low androsterone level. There was no difference between the mean weekly sexual outlets of the healthy controls (4.1) and the homosexuals (3.7). This is an important point because other workers have suggested that androgen levels rise and fall with sexual activity[9,27,28]. It should be mentioned, however, that for some inexplicable reason in this particular analysis Margolese and Janiger grouped all the homosexuals together; whether or not exclusive homosexuals (Kinsey 5 and 6) had significantly lower outlets is not stated. The authors tentatively concluded that a relatively low androsterone level is associated with a sexual preference for males by either sex, whereas a relatively high androsterone reading is associated with a preference for females by either sex. There is only one case, in the literature—a medical curio—which suggests that homosexuality may be due exclusively to a neuro-endocrinogical factor[28]; it is mentioned merely to endorse the view that such rarities will probably be found from time to time, but in perspective they have no general aetiological significance. Lief's[28] patient displayed cyclical alterations of male and female behaviour of 3 - 4 days duration. Urinary 17-oxosteroids were unaltered during the two phases, although an increased growth of facial hair together with other obviously masculine features were noted during the predominantly male periods. The cessation of these cyclical sexual phases at the age of 23 coincided with a striking increase of 17-oxosteroids.

The currently available evidence suggests that with the exception of the critical periods of intra-uterine and (possibly) neonatal life, sex hormones produce little, if any effect on the direction of sexual drive. Homosexuality does not complicate castration either in men or women, although libido and general energy level may be reduced. It is possible that during foetal development the brain is sensitised to abnormally high/low/or altered ratios of various sex hormones and later at puberty the increased production activates patterns of sexual behaviour laid down during foetal and neonatal life.

Unfortunately however there is more speculation than hard data at present, and it will be necessary to redress the balance if genuine advances in this area are to be made. Another way of looking at the functional importance of testosterone and other sex hormones and the direction of sex drive is simply to observe the effects of these compounds administered to various groups of patients and normal subjects. In normal individuals and impotent males, although there might be some slight increase in the strength of drive and improvement in potency, this is unpredictable. However the direction of the drive remains unchanged. Giving testosterone to homosexual men is quite without effect on sexual preference although again there might be some slight increase in libido and feelings of well-being. The latter is probably due to the anabolic effect of the hormone. Oestrogens administered to male homosexuals usually reduce libido and potency but do not make them more homosexual.

The effect of testosterone on heterosexual females, is sometimes to increase the strength of the libido without influencing its direction. This is equally true in lesbians. In summary, sex hormones whilst occasionally increasing the strength of the drive have no influence on its direction in either sex. Although this point seems clear, it should be borne in mind that the neurophysiology of sexual drive probably involves transmitters other than the sex hormones. For example recent work in animals points to the possible importance of various catechol and indole amines[29,30]. Since *a priori* it seems that the subject will be shown to be much more complex in humans than in animals, much work obviously lies ahead.

## ANDROGENS AND AGGRESSIVENESS?

It is becoming increasingly obvious that androgens play some role in 'aggressiveness' and 'explosive physical activity'. For instance, it has been shown in rhesus monkeys that aggressiveness and social order correlate with testosterone levels; the more aggressive and dominant males having significantly higher levels of this hormone than the passive, placid ones[31]. Recently in the human male explosive athletic activities involving maximal physical and psychological effort have been found to be associated with elevated androgen levels. No response was seen with submaximal exercise[32]. The authors commented that physiologically the rise might be associated with an increase in muscle carbohydrate metabolism, and psychologically with the 'aggressiveness and drive necessary to perform physical exercise and may also contribute to the feeling of well being experienced by athletes approaching peak fitness'.

In other studies an XYY genotype (extra Y chromosome) has been associated both with an elevated testosterone level and marked aggressiveness[33]. It has been postulated that the Y chromosome mediates the production of testosterone and that the presence of excess androgen in the circulation 'primes' the CNS to aggressive tendencies[34]. A double Y pattern might thus be expected to potentiate this.

Entirely consistent with this hypothesis is the observation that some tranquillising drugs also reduce testosterone levels; probably via the hypothalamico testicular axis[35]. The new anti-androgen, cyproterone acetate which has been used primarily in deviant hypersexuality has also been found to be effective in patients exhibiting aggressive and assaultative behaviour. In particular chronic schizophrenics subject to explosive violent outbursts have been controlled with this medication. All of this evidence whilst not conclusive points to an important functional role for androgens in aggressive behaviour.

### Organic Factors

Although clincial case reports on the co-existence of temporal lobe epilepsy and various sexual deviations have appeared from time to time Kolarsky *et al.*[3] point out that this could be pure coincidence; therefore a definite aetiological relationship should not be assumed. Kolarsky *et al.*[13] suggest that in order to be significant any brain lesion would have to have been present since early childhood and throughout the period of psychosexual development. Using neurological and psychosexual parameters these workers made a comprehensive study of a sample of 86 male epileptic patients in an attempt to relate sexual deviations to a specific cerebral localisation (i.e. temporal versus extra temporal) and the age of onset of the brain lesion. They found a significant relationship between sexual deviation (including homosexuality) and temporal lobe damage before the end of the first year of life. Another finding was that subjects with non-deviant sexual disturbances such as hypoactivity or frank impotence also had temporal rather than extra-temporal lesions. Support for the functional importance of the temporal lobes in sexual functioning is provided by Gastaut and Collomb[36], Johnson[37] and Hierons and Saunders[38], all of whom reported hyposexuality and impotence in patients with various lesions in this area. However, damage to the temporal lobes is by no means always accompanied by sexual impoverishment since, following partial or total (surgical) extirpation, some individuals have shown an increase in libido and the frequency of sexual activities[39]. More recently it has been shown that the ventromedial and dorsomedial hypothalamic nuclei are important both in animals and humans in mediating sexual behaviour. For instance, three uncontrollable and compulsive male homosexuals subjected to ablation of the ventromedial hypothalamic nucleus showed a marked reduction in sexual drive and, possibly of greater importance, complete abolition of homosexual tendencies[40]. This is an important difference from drug treatments (e.g. oestrogens, and antiandrogens) which tend to influence the strength, but *not* the direction of the sexual drive. General conclusions from the above data are far from easy to draw, but it seems as with many of the aforementioned factors, that 'natural or 'acquired' organic lesions of the brain and particularly the limbic system may in some way sensitise an individual to his environment and thereby predispose him to homosexuality, or indeed to other forms of sexual dysfunction.

The role of drugs in 'releasing' overt homosexual behaviour has not been adequately studied. However, it seems reasonable to conclude that in some cases alcohol may be used, at least initially to suppress inhibitory guilt, ambivalence, etc. However, once the behaviour is firmly established and the individual has accepted it as 'normal', then alcohol becomes redundant. However, there are probably a minority of homosexuals who are never able to accept fully their homosexuality and in these, alcohol may continue to be used sporadically as a means of support or escape. There is no evidence that alcohol itself causes or predisposes to homosexuality.

**Homosexuality and Other Deviations**

It has been widely asserted that transvestism and trans-sexualism usually represent a homosexual orientation. This view has been challenged by Kinsey[8] and Randell[41]. The latter in a detailed study showed that the majority of his transvestites were at the heterosexual end of the hetero-sexual-homosexual scale[9]. In fact, many were married and had children and apart from their desire to cross-dress, their sexual function was normal. Clinically, some had a tendency towards obsessive personalities and some had frank obsessional compulsive neuroses. A few were psychopathic personalities, but proportionately these would probably be similar to any other sample selected according to sexual orientation. Physically transvestites and trans-sexuals, unless taking sex hormones, are generally entirely normal, although in a minority of cases there are non-specific changes in their EEG's.

It would appear that although homosexuals and transvestism/trans-sexualism may co-exist and are probably both acquired by aberrant conditioning they should be viewed as aetiologically independent.

The incidence of psychiatric disease in homosexuals has usually been overstated because of a sampling bias. Taken as a whole there is no reason to believe that psychiatric morbidity in homosexuals is any higher than in heterosexuals.

**Strength of Sex Drive and Homosexuality**

Unlike some of the other deviations, the strength of libido in homosexuals seems to be on a par with heterosexuals[42,43] Therefore, the hypothesis that deviations represent an overcompensation for a feeble sex drive[44] does not fit the admittedly meagre facts pertaining to homosexuality. On the contrary, one may speculate that if it were possible to examine whole populations, then the sex drive in homosexuals would be normally distributed and similar to that of heterosexuals (Kinsey *et al*[8]). Saghir *et al*[43] suggest a fascinating difference. In the case of heterosexuals it is generally accepted that there is a decline with age from the late teens until senescence. This appears to be a relentless and inevitable progression which according to Kinsey[8] is due in the main to biological factors. In contrast, Saghir and colleagues, reporting on 89 homosexuals drawn from a homophile organisation, showed that the number of sexual outlets was greatest between the ages of 40 and 49. Even after the age of 50 the mean sexual outlets (four times weekly) were the same as in the 20-year olds[43]. It is difficult to account for this phenomenon, other than in terms of the greater availablity of partners in the older age group. Although in part, it may reflect the variability of activity possible for homosexuals (i.e. both passive and active) in many respects it would appear that Saghir's group was not typical of homosexuals generally (is there indeed an average homosexual?), and his data suggest that they were much more sexually active than the average. It may well be that in high outlet homosexuals libido and performance actually increase with age up to a ceiling of 50 approximately. Whatever the explanation Saghir's observations endorse the importance of regular sexual outlets in maintaining potency.

### Body Build

The view has been put forward that 'typical homosexuals' are either of feminine body build—that is, with broad hips, rounded contours and relatively narrow shoulders—or thin and weakly, of the physique corresponding to Sheldon's[45] ectomorph. However, the available evidence does not support this stereotype. Thus in Hemphill's series of convicted cases who were somatyped, almost two-thirds were of good physique (Mesomorph) and only ten of thin linear physique (Ectomorphs); none of these cases showed a typical feminine distribution of fat. Hemphill concluded that in terms of physique the group was normal. This was also so in the development of secondary sexual characteristics, which followed the usual pattern in age and appearance[42]. Coppen[46], studying homosexuals who were also psychiatric patients, showed that they had the same androgyny scores as other neurotic psychiatric patients. The androgyny score, which is probably largely dependent upon androgen/oestrogen ratios was devised by Tanner (1951)[47] (1955)[48] and defines android (masculine) features in women and gynaecoid (female) features in men. The score is arrived at by measuring the bi-acromial and bi-iliac diameters and substituting them in the formula: 3 x bi-acromial – 1 x bi-iliac diameter (centimetres). Using this more sophisticated technique Coppen was unable to demonstrate any differences in physique between his homosexuals and neurotic subjects.

It is perhaps of some interst that Johnson[49] found a significant difference in androgyny in a group of early onset (i.e. never competent) impotent subjects who showed a tendency towards gynandromorphy. This may be explicable in terms of the correlation between early onset impotence and reduced testosterone levels[9] which may have beenaetiologically important both for the impotence and the gynandromorphy. Although not definitely proven, it seems likely that body build is closely related to the levels of male/female hormones present at puberty and throughout adolescence and is independent of the direction of sex drive.

## SOCIAL FACTORS, INTELLIGENCE AND PERSONALITY

There are comparatively few adequately designed studies on the relationship of these factors to homosexuality, and in those that are reliable the diversity of the groups makes generalisations impossible. This point is illustrated by a brief comparison of three good studies conducted by 'middle of the road' psychiatrists of a somewhat similar orientation (Table 1. 1).

It can be seen from Table 1. 1 that apart from promiscuity and an early age of homosexual awareness the results of the two male studies[42,43]differ sharply. On the other hand Kenyon's[50] data for lesbians are remarkably similar to those for Saghir's male homosexuals[43]. Both groups were drawn from organisations dedicated to the advancement of homosexuality.

The main point emerging from investigations into socio-economic factors and homosexuality is that as in heterosexuality all classes of people, personality, etc. may be represented; although arising out of common interests some groups may be identifiable as more alike than others. Therefore at present there is no evidence that there are any socio-ecomic factors specific for homosexuality.


## PSYCHOLOGICAL FACTORS

Despite literature of encyclopaedic proportions the importance of various psychological factors in the aetiology of homosexuality remains undetermined.

No attempt is made to review the voluminous contributions which have accumulated over the years, but instead there is a discussion of more recent trends which seem to offer promising leads for the future.

The general framework adopted by Bancroft[6] seems an eminently sensible way of looking at the subject. He refers to 'push' factors whichhave a negative effect on the development of heterosexual behaviour and'pull' factors which are positive for homosexuality. Such a model is not of course specific for sexual orientation; it can be equally applied to any behaviour pattern which may be represented along a continuum, the poles of which reflect opposites; for instance dominance-submissiveness, passive-aggressive, etc. Before discussing some of the more popular recent theories about the causes of homosexuality it has to be stressed again that in most cases there is no supporting scientific evidence, at least in the accepted sense of the word. Clinical feelings and impressions abound, and although the relevance of some of these would be accepted by most psychiatrists they remain subjective and as such suspect. There is an undoubted need for more 'scientific studies'. However, whether or not the very nature of the matter under examination will ever really lend itself to such methods remains to be seen.

Despite uncertainties over specific causal factors the consensus of

TABLE 1. *Comparison of three studies on social factors, intelligence, personality and homosexuality*

| Variable | Saghir et al.[43] | Hemphill et al.[42] | Kenyon[50]. |
|---|---|---|---|
| Sample | 89 American males 75% recruited from a homophile organisation | 64 males recruited from an open prison | 123 females drawn mainly from homophile organisations |
| Mean age | 35 years | 40.5 years | 36.4 years |
| Marital status | 18% married, or had been at time of investigation | 40% married, or had been at time of investigation | 18% married, or had been, at time of investigation |
| Social class | 56% upper classes - e.g. professional, managerial | 21% upper classes | 56% upper classes |
| Intelligence | above average | below average | above average |
| Personality | 50% outgoing, confident stable | 56% neurotic or schizoid | Not stated |
| Prior psychiatric illness | Nil | 15.8% | 19.5% |
| First awareness of homosexuality | <14 to > 19 years | Mean age 12.3 years range 5 - 15 years | Mean age 16.1 + 5.31 years range 15 - 34 years |
| Initial homosexual experience | most often with adult males | most often with boys of same age | most often with partner of same age or older |
| Subsequent homosexual pattern | 100% promiscuous 94% had more than 15 partners | 83% promiscuous | Promiscuous; mean number of partners 3.73 + 3.04 |

opinion leaves no doubt that the basic homosexual drive (like the heterosexual drive) is fashioned in childhood or at the latest in adolescence. The *de novo* appearance of homosexuality after the age of thirty is singularly rare.

**The Push Factors**

1. *Anxiety and fears*
In individual cases fear of contracting venereal disease, fear of causing pregnancy and fear of being injured by the female sex organs, etc may be present[51]. There are undoubtedly a large number of homosexuals who feel threatened by women as sexual objects. Interviews with some individuals suggest that 'fear of impotence', 'fear of ridicule', 'fear that the penis is too small', etc may be important. It is an interesting speculation that an increasingly vociferous woman's lib movement which disparages males could increase the prevalence of homosexuality.

2. *Hostility and Resentment*
Many homosexuals express deep hostility or rivalry towards women, but the problem is one of knowing whether these feelings preceded and were causal or contributory to the homosexuality or whether they followed as a consequence. It is a strong clinical impression that in many exclusive (Kinsey Grade 5 and 6) homosexuals, hostility or at least dislike towards females had been present from the earliest (pre-sexual) days. With the passage of time and an increasing commitment to homosexuality this feeling had hardened and become more intense. Some even rationalise the antipathy towards woman as being responsible for their homosexuality. In reality the opposite is probably true. Gutheil[52], who considers that male-female hostility accounts for a good deal of sexual morbidity, has coined the apt phrase the 'war between the sexes'.

At the other end of the spectrum, however, the strongly bisexual homosexual may harbour no such feelings towards woman. Some married subjects express affection towards their spouses, and continue to have satisfactory coitus, as well as homosexual relationships. Clinical interviewing of such men often reveals them to be driven by strong libidinous needs which are only satisfied by varied homo- and heterosexual outlets. Bisexuality may be associated with a personality disorder characterised by egocentricity, narcissism and excessive self gratification needs. Some bisexuals are frankly psychopathic.

3. *Disgust*
It has been suggested that feelings of disgust about the female sex organs may turn some men away from females and in the predisposed make

homosexuality more likely[53]. El Senoussi *et al.*[54] have pointed out that many men who feel that sexual intercourse is shameful dirty and may masturbate to various fantasies. This has obvious relevance in the light of McGuire's hypothesis concerning the central importance of masturbation in the development of deviant behaviour[55].

## 4. *Inhibition*

Heterosexual inhibition may begin in childhood and be consolidated by events throughout adolescence and into adulthood. This may take the form of an over protective mother who may express regret for not having had a girl; she may treat the little boy as if he were a girl, forbidding masculine pursuits and fostering dependency. Heterosexual contacts may be represented as being sinful or dirty and any attempts to develop such may meet with strong disapproval and resistance. Alternatively sex may not be mentioned at all, and the absence of factual knowlege may predispose to various distortions, fears and disgust which may hamper heterosexual development. In such circumstances it is easy to see how 'fearing the unkown' (female), a male may direct or have drawn what libido he has towards a member of his own sex.

Although its central aetiological significance cannot as yet be proven, the commonest general finding which recurs time and again is an abnormality of parent/child relationships. The stereotype is a father who is weak and inept and who may be physically absent from the home for varying periods of time; the mother on the other hand is often stated to be forceful, overprotective and fostering dependancy. She will tend to discourage 'normal boyish activities', such as football, athletics, etc on the grounds that they are dangerous, thus denying the little boy an important opportunity of developing masculine patterns of behaviour. Subconsciously or even consciously seeing other females as rivals for her son's affection such a mother would steer him away from developing heterosexual relationships[56]. This type of protective upbringing, which disparages normal heterosexual relationships, could play an important role in the development of negative feelings towards young women and a compensatory turning towards males for physical and psychological sexual satisfaction. However, abnormal parental relationships may figure in other types of sexual abnormality[57,58] as well as in other types of psychiatric morbidity. It seems likely therefore that such factors are not specific for homosexuality acting merely in some general way as a precursor. It is hard to believe that the dominant mother-weak father scenario is equally important in *all* types of homosexuality, and it is possible that its emphasis reflects a current reseach preoccupation. Clinical experience suggests that all permutations of parental abnormality may be encountered; alternatively, as far as it is possible to tell, there may be no abnormality of any sort. The only generalisation which presently fits the admittedly sparse facts is that a percentage of homosexuals may have been brought up in a weak father-dominant mother home environment.

**The Pull Factors**
These have been adequately described by Bancroft[8] and include the following:

1. *Strength of sexual drive*
The desire for sexual contact with another person seems to be basic for the vast majority of humans, although precisely why this should be so is not known; neither is it understood why self masturbation is generally not an adequate substitute. Sex drive is probably undifferentiated at birth, but given that such a drive exists, this results in a psychobiological need for its release. A homosexual object choice is one alternative.

2. *Need for warmth*
If, as is often the case, the father-child relationship has been unsatisfactory there may be a need for an emotionally and physically warm relationship with an older male. This may be doubly important if a heterosexual alternative is unfulfilling or not possible.

3. *Fulfilment of basic human needs*
Where great feelings of heterosexual inadequacy are present one means of bolstering self esteem lies in developing and maintaining a successful homosexual relationship. The homosexual male may actively praise his partner or be praised just like heterosexuals. Fulfilment of these basic human needs, i.e. of 'possessing and of being possessed', whether in a heterosexual or homosexual relationship makes consolidation of the initial sexual object choice more likely. In some cases homosexuality may just happen 'passively' following a proposition from an affluent dominant male who quite often is willing to pay for the services of somebody who attracts him. This may even amount to formally setting up house together in which the roles of the 'provider' and the 'provided' are clearly delineated. This type of arrangement which might have strong emotional components may last for years.

## EVOLUTION OF A HOMOSEXUALITY IDENTITY

If a concept of 'variable homosexual predisposition' is accepted, according to the relative prominence of push and pull factors, overt behaviour must still be acquired by learning. Whether or not this happens and becomes a permanent response depends upon the positive-negative-reinforcement equation. In its simplest form this states that the more homosexual behaviour is rewarding, physically and emotionally, the greater the likelihood of it being repeated and ultimately established. Similarly if negative consequences outweigh the rewards then it is less likely that the behaviour will persist; these include feelings of guilt, fear of detection, depression, etc. Whether homosexuality becomes exclusive presumably depends upon the level of reward and the absence of gratifying heterosexual experiences. Bisexuals derive pleasure from both types of outlet, which are thereby reinforced. Some degree of heterosexual arousal and physical contact may be found in up to 50% of homosexuals during preadolescence, this figure falling parallel with an increase of homosexual interests in adulthood[43]. A minority of homosexuals may have actual intercourse with females; but by the age of thirty up to 75% are likely to stop this activity, never to resume[43]. The reasons for heterosexual intercourse are most often curiosity, experimental marriage or temporary disenchantment with homosexuality. In a proportion hetero-sexual arousal may be experienced.

Although a surprisingly large number of homosexuals may have some degree of physical sexual experience with females, overwhelmingly their sexual fantasies are homosexual and have been for as long as they can remember. The pattern of sexual fantasies rather than overt behaviour seems a much more reliable indicator of basic sexual preference. Mutual masturbation is the commonest outlet during the teens and early adult-hood. Hemphill *et al.*[43]—100% prevalence by 16.6 years, Saghir *et al.*[42] 88% by the age of 15. However with reinforcement and as a homosexual identity becomes established practices become more elaborate and include fellatio and anal intercourse, both in passive and active roles. *Pari passu* any residual heterosexual leanings fade in most cases.

It has been suggested that homosexuality may be acquired following a single accidental or contrived sexual experience[59]. Different authorities assert the importance of adult seduction[43] and mutual experimentation by boys of like ages respectively[43,42]. Whether one of the other prevails clearly depends upon personality and circumstances. The obvious prerequisite is for a willing and sexually attractive male partner to be available and for an emotionally and physically satisfying response to result.

More recently Maguire *et al.*[55] have presented a somewhat different view as to how homosexuality might be acquired. They believe that the learning takes place *after* the initial seduction or experience, which plays its part only in supplying a fantasy for later self masturbation. Although masturbation has been seen by various workers to have a part to play in the perpetuation of homosexuality, it has not previously been assigned a role in the formation and shaping of sexual stimuli. Maguire and colleagues answer the question:- Why do prospective homosexuals choose to masturbate to homosexual fantasies rather than to thoughts of heterosexual intercourse in terms of the precipatating (homosexual) incident which was the first *real* sexual experience as opposed to stories from others or from books or other means? Maguire believes that this must give the incident stronger initial stimulus value as a masturbatory fantasy. Illustrating his theory with case histories Maguire points out the important finding that most of his patients believed that a 'normal sex life was not possible for them'. This apparently arose from a variety of events such as early aversive heterosexual experiences, feelings of physcial or social inadequacy, etc. Whatever the precise role of masturbation in the genesis of homosexuality, the practice has been found to be widely prevalent, at an early age. It seems likely that the habit[42 43] becomes associated with pleasurable homosexual fantasies which later extend into real life[42 43]. Maguire's hypothesis is an interesting variation on the usual explanations and it satisfies many clinical and therapeutic observations without invoking separate theories[56].

## CONCLUSIONS

Traditionally, homosexuality has been studied by the medical sciences, particularly endocrinology and psychiatry, with methods which assumed the pleasant of medical and/or psychological pathology. The generally inconclusive findings in such studies must cast doubt on this view. It is clearly of crucial importance to decide whether or not homosexuality is a 'disease' in its own right since this must determine the nature of, indeed the relevance of, future research. Although homosexuality is still comparatively rare (about 2 - 5% of the male population but increasing) this is not sufficient to brand it as a 'disease'. At present the best way of viewing homosexuality is as a sexual variant practised by the minority which despite the Wolfenden Report is disapproved of and misunderstood by the majority. But, is an idiosyncrasy necessarily sickness?

Most of the homosexuals who present to psychiatrists or other doctors do so, not because of the nature of their sexual preference *per se*, but because of complicating factors. These, most often guilt feelings, depression, etc which may require treatment in their own right are usually the result of a harsh public and the homosexual's inability to live with himself. Few actually wish to become heterosexual. Another complicating factor, which although obvious needs to be restated is the assumption that homosexuality is a unitary and homogeneous condition. It is surely expecting too much to find many, indeed any, common aetiological features in, on the one hand the psychopathic polyperverse homosexual and on the other the passive exclusive homosexual. Clearly these are poles apart, and this is so even if they both belong to a homophile organisation or share the same prision cell; to study them as if they belong to a common group is unlikely to produce any worthwhile findings.

If homosexuality is to be studied aetiologically then it is necessary to be much more discriminating in population selection; only then are we likely to begin to obtain meaningful data.

Despite the very real methodological problems which bedevilled the past and which will undoubtedly affect future work there are some aetiological clues worthy of mention and replication. It seems beyond reasonable doubt that genetics and possibly hormonal influences may sensitise an individual to the environment. In particular, it has been found that a dominant, over protective and often seductive mother and a weak or absent father, figure prominently in many cases. Generally however, it must be conceded that in spite of a great deal of work and many ingenious theories the causes of homosexuality remain undetermined. It may well be that the complexity of society will defeat all investigative efforts and keep it this way.

# REFERENCES

1. Mettler, F. In Mettler, C.C. (1947); ed. *History of Medicine* (Philadelphia: Blakiston)
2. Rush, B. (1830). *Medical Inquiries and Observations upon the Diseases of the Mind* (Philadelphia: Grigg)
3. Tissot, S.A. (1764). *L'Onanisme: Dissertation sur les maladies produites par la masturbation* 3rd edit: (Lausanne: Marcus Chapius et cie)
4. Ellis, H. (1901). *Studies in the Psychology of Sex,* Vol. 1, (New York: Random House)
5. Quoted by Hare, E. (1962). *Brit. J. Psychiat.,* **108,** 2
6. Bancroft, J. (1968). *Brit. J. Hosp. Med.,* (Feb) 168
7. Kirkendall, L.A. (1967). In *Encyclopaedia of Sexual Behaviour* (A. Ellis and A. Abarbanel editors) (New York: Hawthorn)
8. Kinsey, A.C., Pomeroy, W.B. and Martin, C.E. (1948). *Sexual Behaviour in the Human Male* (Philadelphia: Saunders)
9. Cooper, A.J., Ismail, A.A.A., Smith, C.G. and Loraine, J.A. (1970). *Brit. Med. J.,* **3,** 17
10. Kallman, F.J. (1952). *J. Nerv. Ment. Dis.,* **115,** 283
11. Kallman, F.J. (1953). *Heredity in Health and Mental Disorder,* (New York: Norton & Co.)

12. Lange, J. (1931). *Crime as Destiny* (trans. Haldane, C.) (London: Allen & Unwin)
13. Kolarsky, A., Freund, K., Machek, J. and Polak, O. (1967). *Arch. Gen. Psychiat.*, **17**, 735
14. Koch, G. (1965). *Die Bedeutung genetischer Faktoren fur das menschliche Verhalten. Arzliche Praxis*, **17**, 823 and 839
15. Heston, L.L. and Shields, J. (1968). *Arch. Gen. Psychiat.*, **18**, 149
16. Margolese, M.S. and Janiger, O. (1973). *Brit. Med. J.* **3**, 207
17. Slater, E. (1962). *Lancet*, **i**, 69
18. Abe, K. and Moran, P.A.P. (1969). *Brit. J. Psychiat.*, **115**, 313
19. *Lancet* (1968) Leading article, **ii**, 1066
20. Pare, C.M.B. (1965). in *Sexual Inversion* (J. Marmor, editor) (New York: Basic Books)
21. Donovan, B.T. and Bosch, J.J. van der Werff Ten (1965). *Physiology of Puberty* (London: Arnold)
22. Briggs, M.H. (1970). *Sexual Behaviour and Antiandrogens. Pharmacology of Cyproterone and related compounds, Symposium* Royal Society of Medicine, London
23. Money, J.E. and Ehrhardt, A.A. (1968). in *EndocrinologyandHuman Behaviour* (R.P. Michael, editor) (London: Oxford University Press)
24. Loraine, J.A. (1972). *New Scientist*, 3rd Feb. 270
25. Kolodny, R.C. (1971). *New Engl. J. Med.* **285**, 1170
26. Ismail, A.A.A. and Harkness, R.A. (1967). *Acta Endocrinol. (Kbh)*, **56**, 469
27. Dewhurst, K. (1969). *Brit. J. Psychiat*, **115**, 1413
28. Lief, H.I., Dingman, J.D.F. and Bishop, M.P. (1962). *Psychosomat. Med.*, **24**, 357
29. Tagliamonte, A., Tagliamonte, P., Gessa, A. and Brodie, B.B. (1969). *Science N.Y.*, **166**, 1433
30. Gessa, G.L. (1970). *Nature*, 616
31. Rose, R.M., Holaday, J.W. and Bernstein, J.S. (1971). *Nature*, **231**, 366
32. Sutton, J.R., Coleman, M.J., Casey, J. and Lazarus, L. (1973). *Brit. Med. J.*, **1** 520
33. Abdullah, S., Jarvik, L.F., Kato, T., Johnston, W.C. and Lanzkron, M.D. (1969). *Arch. Gen. Psychiat.*, **21**, 497
34. Maccoby, E.E., editor (1966). *The Development of Sex Difference* (Stanford: Stanford University Press)
35. Beaumont, P.J.V., Corker, C., Friesen, H.G., Kolakosska, T., Mandelbrote, B.M. and Marshall, J. (1974). *Brit. J. Psychiat.* (in press)

36. Gastaut, H. and Collomb, J. (1954). *Ann. Medicopsychol (Paris)* **112,** 657
37. Johnson, J. (1965). *Brit. J. Psychiat,* **111,** 300
38. Hierons, R. and Saunders, M. (1966). *Lancet,* **ii,** 761
39. Falconer, M.A., Hill, D., Meyer, A., Mitchell, W. and Pond, D. (1955). *Lancet,* **i,** 827
40. *Brit. Med. J.* (1969). Leading article, **2,** 250
41. Randell, J. (1959). *Brit. Med. J.,* **2,** 1448
42. Hemphill, R.E., Leitch, A. and Stuart, J.R. (1958). *Brit. Med. J.,* **1,** 1317
43. Saghir, M.T., Robins, E. and Walbran, B. (1969). *Arch. Gen. Psychiat.,* **21,** 219
44. Allen, C.A. (1962). *A Text Book of Psychosexual Disorders* (London: Oxford University Press)
45. Sheldon, W.H. (1940). *The Varieties of Human Physique* (New York and London: Harper)
46. Coppen, A.J. (1959). *Brit. Med. J.,* **2,** 1443
47. Tanner, J.M. (1951). *Lancet,* **i,** 574
48. Tanner, J.M. (1955). *Growth at Adolescence* (Oxford: Blackwell)
49. Johnson, J. (1965). *Brit. Med. J.,* **2,** 572
50. Kenyon, F.E. (1968). *Brit. J. Psychiat.,* **114,** 1337
51. Cory, D.W. (1967). In *The Encyclopaedia of Sexual Behaviour* (A. Ellis and A. Abarbanel, editors) (New York: Hawthorn)
52. Gutheil, E.H. (1959). In *American Handbook of Psychiatry* (New York: Basic Books)
53. Jones, E. (1919). *Papers on Psycho-Analysis,* (New York: Wood)
54. El-Senoussi, A., Coleman, D.R. and Tauber, A.S. (1959). *J. Psychol.,* **48,** 3
55. McGuire, R.J., Carlisle, J.M. and Young, B.G. (1965). *Behav. Res. Ther.,* **2,** 185
56. O'Connor, P.J. (1964). *Brit. J. Psychiat.,* **110,** 381
57. Roth, M. and Ball, J.R.B. (1964). In *Intersexuality in Verebrates, including Man* (C.N. Armstrong and A.J. Marshall, editors) (London: Academic Press)
58. Stroller, R.J. (1969). *Sex and Gender,* (London: The Hogarth Press)
59. Jaspers, K. (1963). *General Psychopathology* 323, (Manchester: Manchester University Press)

# 2

# Male Homosexuality:
# An Analysis of the Pattern*

## K. Freund

## INTRODUCTION

### Definition of some basic terms

Homosexuality is the sustained erotic preference for same sexed persons when there is a free choice of partner as to sex and other attributes which may co-determine erotic attractiveness. In this definition the term 'sex' denotes male type or female type of externally visible gross somatic features ('body shape'), particularly the type of external genitalia, whereas male *v.* female types of behaviour patterns fall among 'other attributes'.

The terms homo- and hetero-sexuality, according to this definition, denote only an erotic preference for body shape and not a preference for the type of sexual behaviour of a potential partner, or for the type of one's own preferred sexual behaviour. A particular male may erotically prefer female body shape, i.e. he is heterosexual, and have at the same time a preference for male type behavioural or attitudinal components in his partner, and for female type components in his own sexual behaviour, which is so in some masochistic males and in heterosexual trans-sexual males. The definition of bisexuality is based on the same set of observations which was used for the definition of hetero- and homo-sexuality, i.e. an erotic preference for sex type of body shape. The smaller the relative

* Thanks are due to Dr R. Langevin for invaluable criticism and help in preparing the manuscript and to the Laidlaw Foundation, Toronto, Canada, which made writing this chapter possible.

erotic preference for the body of one sex over that for the other, the higher the degree of bisexuality. The highest degree, i.e. about equivalent bisexuality, is reached when there is virtually no difference between erotic responses to the body shapes of females and males. However, as will be shown later, a subject's capacity to become sexually aroused by true or imagined interaction with persons of both sexes need not necessarily be based on any considerable degree of bisexuality proper.

### Assessment of erotic preferences

In the foregoing the concepts of heterosexuality, homosexuality and bisexuality were defined in terms of erotic preference, the assessment of which, from self reports on erotic attitudes and feelings, poses great difficulties, and the same is true for behavioural analysis in its present state. Systematic behavioural observation is quite advanced in work with animals and is just starting to develop in work with children under 5 years of age[1,2]; however it is almost nonexistent as yet in work with humans above that age. Therefore a specific method for assessment and measurement of the degree of erotic preference has been introduced which adds a further reference system in a field still almost devoid of reliable dimensions.

This method, the so-called phallometric test[3-5] makes it possible to define the degree of erotic preference for various stimulus configurations, in terms of their sexual arousal value, indicated by the degree of penile volume change. The validity of the phallometric method, when used with cooperating subjects, appears to be satisfactory.

Basically it is, of course, possible to suppress penile responses, or to provoke, by erotic fantasies, spurious responses at presentation of non-arousing objects. This has also been confirmed experimentally[4,6]. However, in such experiments a high proportion of selected intelligent subjects, who were asked to and told how to suppress or fake responses, had not been successful either. In another investigation it was possible to detect, in normal heterosexual males, penile tumescence response to the pictures of 6- to 8-year-old girls[7]; and in a further study it was possible by means of the phallometric test, to diagnose paedophilia even in some of those recidivist pedophilic sex offenders who claimed to prefer physically mature females[8]. The above-indicated limitations of the phallometric method (in its present stage) are to be taken into account when considering the conclusiveness of results, but its degree of validity, as tested in the above-mentioned studies, warrants acceptance until better methods are available. In the context of the following, various studies carried out by means of this method will be reported[1]

## An outline of the chapter

The aim of this chapter is to bring up to date the analysis of the pattern of male homosexuality by taking into account recent pertinent information. This implies a general discussion of erotic preferences for body shape of potential partners and of preferences for particular types of erotic interaction. An attempt will be made to present the material in the appropriate social and biological framework.

Section 1 will illustrate the fact that sexual interaction quite frequently occurs with the non-preferred sex. In heterosexual subjects, such inter-action appears to be mostly due to insufficient availability of the opposite sex, whereas in homosexual subjects, interaction with the non-preferred sex is, in the majority of such cases, an attempt to adjust to a heterosexual society. It will be argued that any successes reported by therapists who try to change homo- to hetero-erotic preference are most likely due to a facilitation of interaction with the non-preferred sex, and not to any considerable change in erotic preference.

Studies will be reviewed which show that, not only in humans but in vertebrates generally, sexual interaction with the non-preferred sex occurs when interaction with the preferred sex is not possible. This raises the question whether, under usual conditions, there is a sexual response to body shape (in sub-human mammals to phemerones as well) of either sex or whether mainly other factors are responsible for this phenomenon. This topic will be discussed in Sections 2 - 4.

Section 2 investigates whether, in human males, the virtually universal arousability by members of either sex can be explained by bisexuality proper, i.e. in terms of sexual responses to sex type of body shape. In this context the results will be reported of assessments of such responses in homosexual and heterosexual males, and in those clinical cases where there was conspicuously high arousability by either sex. It will be argued that, in males who prefer physically mature partners, arousability by members of the non-preferred sex finds little explanation by bisexuality proper, i.e. in terms of sexual responses to body shape, and must therefore be attributed to the erotic impact of behavioural patterns and, in particular, to body contact. The latter part of this hypothetical explan-ation will be supported by a report on assessment of sexual responses of homosexual males to imagined heterosexual interaction.

Section 3 considers an alternative explanation of erotic arousability by members of either sex, based on a Freudian point of view. The Freudian concepts of latent homo- or hetero-sexuality are explored and an experi-ment will be reported which was an unsuccessful attempt to elicit considerable bisexual responses in cases where they should be expected, if the Freudian point of view were valid.

The above-mentioned investigations concerned males who prefer physically mature partners. Section 4 addresses itself to the problem of bisexuality as it occurs in males who prefer pubescents or children. It will be pointed out that, at least in some of these cases, bisexuality proper (i.e. in terms of responses to body shape) appears to play a much greater part than in males who prefer physically mature partners, and erotic age preference in homosexual males will be briefly discussed.

The earlier-mentioned finding, that imagined heterosexual body contact has a positive sexual impact on homosexual males, poses the question whether there is not in fact a sexual aversion to female body shape, which might strongly preclude any such intimate body contact. This question is of particular importance because many therapists still assume that male homosexuality is caused by an aversion against the female as a sexual partner. Section 5 reports an experiment which shows that in homosexual, as well as in heterosexual, males there is *no* gross general sexual aversion against the non-preferred sex.

There is only one phenomenon in erotic attitudes towards the non-preferred sex on which homosexual males appear to differ from heterosexual males, i.e. a shift from heterosexuality to homosexuality, as claimed in retrospective self reports of some homosexual males, which is not parallelled by analogous statements of heterosexual males.

The discussion in Sections 1-5 centres mainly on erotic preference for body shape, whereas questions concerning erotic preferences for one's own or a partner's sex type of behavioural and attitudinal patterns will be considered in more detail in Sections 6-8. The only such variable known to date, on which homosexual and heterosexual males appear to differ, is feminine gender identity; but there is obviously substantial overlap. Section 6 discusses gender identity in general and explores the occurrence of feminine gender identity in males.

It will be concluded that there is support for the notion that there is more feminine gender identity in homosexual than in sexually normal males and that, in homosexual males who erotically prefer physically mature partners, there is more feminine gender identity than in those who prefer physically immature partners.

In a search for the socially more invariant components in feminine gender identity, Sections 7 and 8 explore the biological roots of sex type behavioural patterns. In Section 7 studies will be reviewed which show that, in sub-human vertebrates, male *v.* female mating behaviour is influenced by concurrent agonistic* constellations and that both, type of mating behaviour and agonistic behaviour, are developmentally de-

---

*Agonistic behaviour is fight and flight behaviour and includes threatening or signalling dominance or submission.

termined (or co-determined) by the amount of androgens available at particular critical periods. In Section 8 the study of human intersexes will be discussed in the given context, the result of which seems to indicate that in humans there are culturally invariant androgen-dependent components in gender identity and preferred partner sex.

# 1. INTERACTION WITH THE NON-PREFERRED SEX

Homosexual interaction, even if occurring regularly, is not by itself a very reliable indicator of homosexuality, and this applies conversely to heterosexual interaction as well. In the following, material will be reviewed from which it is evident that not only in humans, but throughout vertebrates generally, sexual interaction with the non-preferred sex occurs quite frequently. It will be argued that, in heterosexual subjects, such interaction is mostly due to insufficient availability of the opposite sex. It will be further argued that any success of therapeutic attempts to make a homosexual male heterosexual is most likely due to a facilitation of interaction with the non-preferred sex.

## Homosexual behaviour in heterosexual males

The high incidence of homosexual behaviour in predominantly heterosexual males, within contemporary Western society, has been demonstrated by the well-known and often-quoted Kinsey report[9] which showed that about 37% of the white male population of the United States had at least some homosexual experience to the point of orgasm, between adolescence and old age. Approximately 7% among the white male population of the United States had more than incidental homosexual experience or reactions over at least a 3-year period between the ages of 16 and 55, but were still predominantly heterosexual.

Homosexual behaviour, as exhibited by adult heterosexual persons, probably occurs at its highest frequency in prisons and reform institutions. According to Kinsey *et al.*, between 35% and 85% of the male inmates at various prisons admitted some sort of homosexual activity. Ward and Kassebaum[10] have described the ways in which newcomers, who were previously heterosexual, have been introduced by homosexual inmates of a women's prison to homosexual activities. According to Ward and Kassebaum, it was the homosexual inmates' firm conviction that their formerly heterosexual partners would, upon leaving prison, generally revert back to their heterosexual pattern of behaviour, and parole officers indicated that this appears to be what happens.

A second typical instance of homosexual interaction between heterosexual persons is mutual masturbation among young adolescents. This also occurs where suitable partners of the other sex are available, and may be mainly due to insufficient erotic communication between the sexes.

Another condition where heterosexual persons may become involved relatively easily in homosexual interactions is alcoholic intoxication, which tends also to facilitate heterosexual interaction in homosexual persons. Alcoholic intoxication enhances the probability of sexual interaction with objects of a non-preferred category in general, probably by dulling the subject's discrimination, though the actual number of such instances is likely to be exaggerated by the tendency of sex offenders to attribute their deviant behaviour to alcoholic consumption rather than admitting that they, in fact, acted in their erotically preferred, though socially un-accepted, way, e.g. by exposing themselves.

One further instance of heterosexual persons exhibiting homosexual behaviour is homosexual prostitution; such behaviour occurs in a basically non-erotic context. Before homosexual interaction among con-senting adults ceased to be an indictable offence, a considerable number of young male prostitutes, apprehended for such interaction but obviously thoroughly heterosexual, were interviewed by the present writer, and since the phallometric test had become available, such diagnoses arrived at by interview were confirmed by the test result.

**Crosscultural comparisons**
Historical[11] and ethnological data reveal a wide variation in attitudes among various communities towards homosexual interaction[12]. Same-sexed interaction among heterosexual males, under particular conditions, has been accepted in a variety of cultures as respectable and sometimes even as a regular component in a male's sexual life. It appears that, in the majority of such communities or societies where homosexual interaction was general and accepted, females were unavailable as sexual partners for young males for prolonged periods of time. In some tribal societies, certain types of homosexual interaction and/or attachments among heterosexual males have even been institutionalised, in particular, attach-ments between 10- to 14-year-old boys and physically mature persons. In a number of societies male children were formally regarded as females, and the pubertal rites were believed to endow them with maleness. In a few of the communities investigated, a significant part of those rites involved adult males performing anal intercourse upon boys, and in other communities obvious remnants of these rites were present[11,13-16]. According to Williams[16] working with the Keraki on New Guinea, girls were being betrothed or married in early childhood (or even before having been born) and given into the custody of the fiance's family, who made sure that the girl had no intimate contact with males until the marriage was consum-

mated. Layard[15] encountered a similar situation on the island of Malekula in the New Hebrides and added that, in the northern parts, the relative lack of females was particularly severe because rich chieftains had purchased most of them. Deacon[14] found that sexual interaction among males, in this northern region of the island, was particularly frequent. These facts seem to warrant the interpretation that, in tribal societies, acceptance and institutionalisation of homosexual interaction served as surrogates for insufficient heterosexual opportunities, when and where socio-economic traditions severely inhibited heterosexual interaction. It is hoped that cultural anthropologists will be able rigorously to test the validity of this contention for, if it were borne out, a simple explanation would be available for most of the homosexual activity which occurs among heterosexual pesons. Then, however, a more crucial question is to be asked: under what conditions is interaction with same-sexed partners a better surrogate than automasturbation for heterosexual people? This may be so only at high drive level and under deprivation in regard to any kind of erotic communication with the preferred sex.

### Heterosexual activity in homosexual males
Sexual interaction with the non-preferred sex seems to occur in homosexual males at least as frequently as in heterosexual males, but it is not easy to arrive at an estimate of this frequency. According to the data of Kinsey *et al.*, approximately 13% of the white male population of the U.S.A. seemed to respond predominantly, but not exclusively, in a homosexual way for at least a 3-year period between ages 16 and 55. This extremely high number raises the suspicion that it might be an artifact caused by the complexity of Kinsey's definition of the hetero-homosexual continuum.

Kinsey *et al.* used a seven-degree scale for the assessment of the hetero-homosexual balance. The scale estimates self-reported sexual responses to members of the same sex *v.* those to members of the opposite sex, and sexual response is defined as 'erotic arousal or orgasm through physical contact and/or erotic 'psychic' responses'. With the exception of degrees 0 and 6 of the scale, the confounding of arousal effected by body contact and that effected by real or imagined visual (or auditory) stimulus configurations makes it difficult to understand what this scale really measures. The additional provision of giving priority to 'psychic responses' and of differentiating between various qualities or intensities of such responses appears to bias the scale towards measuring erotic preference, but poses new difficulties by increasing the ambiguity of the basic data.

Judging from relevant statements made by homosexual males[5], the motive of sexual interaction with females was very rarely the unavailability of suitable male partners, but rather 'curiosity' or the desire to adjust to a heterosexual life in order to escape the frustrating social situation of a homosexual male in a heterosexual society. Some homosexual persons also indicated that they desired a family life. Many homosexual males are married, have families and are able to hide their true inclination quite well. Some of them have reached this high degree of heterosexual adjustment during or after some therapy, but the present writer is inclined seriously to doubt the validity of reports which claim that homosexual males have been rendered heterosexual by some kind of therapy[17-28]. The present writer's doubts are based on a study of reports on the treatment of homosexuality and on his own therapeutic study which included follow-up over an extended period of time[5].

In this latter project, aversion therapy was used, combined with attempts positively to reinforce heterosexual behaviour. Several homosexual males achieved, during or after treatment, a remarkable degree of heterosexual adjustment. They married, had children and seemed to be very happy for about a year but, in the course of time, the heterosexual adjustment usually deteriorated and they were left with a virtually non-functional marriage and greater problems than those which they had had prior to therapy. Our information about the fate of heterosexual marriages involving homosexual males is limited to those where the homosexual husbands came to the attention of the psychiatrist, i.e. where the homosexual husbands had been 'successfully' treated and had married afterwards or where the homosexual husbands were seen because they spontaneously asked for help or because there were charges against them for homosexual offences[29]. Those homosexual males who do not need the clinician's help might be able to make a better marital sexual adjustment.

The effect, if any, of our therapeutic effort was that of having enabled a male who still remained homosexual (in preference) to interact sexually with females. The favourable 'effects' very much resembled the 'bisexual' outcome reported by earlier psychotherapists.

Contrary to the overwhelming majority of his followers, Freud[30] did not really believe that it is possible to turn a homosexual person heterosexual through psychotherapy. He thought that the most favourable outcome of such treatment was achieved if the patient became 'bisexual', i.e. if the therapy 'restored' the patient's 'full bisexual function'. After that it was the patient's decision to 'choose' to be hetero- or homo-sexual. Freud complained that, as a rule, it is not possible 'to convince' the patient that by choosing heterosexuality he will regain, when interacting with partners of the other sex, all the satisfaction he loses by abandoning the same-sexed object. Stekel[31,32] was more optimistic in regard to the effect of psycho-therapy of homosexuality but he had his doubts whether one should try at all because 'by turning him (the homosexual patient) heterosexual, he will repress his homosexuality. . . . . . .and if one would make him bisexual one would be ostracised by society'. The view that the outcome of effective psychotherapy of homosexuality is 'bisexuality' has been explicitly in-dicated also by several later authors[33,34] and has obviously been implied by many others. However, it is to be noted that, at the time of Freud and his early followers, the terms hetero- and homosexuality were not yet clearly defined as preferences, and therefore any evaluation of the patient's hetero-homosexual balance posed even greater difficulties than at present.

Bieber *et al.*[19] are the authors most frequently quoted by those who believe in the possibility of effecting, by psychotherapy, a real change from homo- to hetero-sexuality. However the information on which they base their favourable appraisal of the therapeutic outcome is in fact scanty and the original diagnosis of the patients involved, not very precise. The behaviour therapy experiment of Feldman and MacCulloch[21] was incom-parably better documented but the patient histories with follow-up notes, contained in these authors' book, does not appear to be in strong support of their therapeutic optimism. Feldman and MacCulloch depended basically on the patients' own progress reports, and the follow-up rarely had continued longer than one year. It is hoped that these authors will continue their follow-up and find means other than the patients' own statements, for evaluting therapeutic effects. Until strong evidence is presented for the possibility of turning homosexual males heterosexual, it is safer to assume that all heterosexual adjustment of homosexual males is due to their basic ability to interact with the non-preferred sex. The limitations of such surrogate activity have to be taken into account when the question of therapy arises.

**Homosexual interaction in animals**
Apart from Schutz's[35] highly interesting series of experiments on in-duction of a preference for same-sexed pair formation in male ducks, by means of imprinting, there are no fully reliable reports on homosexual preference in sub-human vertebrates[36] and the frequently observed homo-sexual interactions represent interaction with the non-preferred sex which occurs, as in humans, most often when there is high sexual arousal and a partner of the opposite sex is not available. Such homosexual behaviour may occur without or with a concurrent sex type reversal of mating pattern, depending on drive level and, as will be seen later (Section 7), on agonistic constellations.

Morris[37] made a pertinent observation on tenspined sticklebacks in all-female tanks. The females were well fed, which enhances maturing of the eggs and increases the readiness for mating. In this situation Morris observed the typical male zigzag dance (see Section 7) appearing in females. Beach[38,39] created an analogous situation for male rats, in which he showed that unavailability of the preferred partner sex leads to interaction with the non-preferred sex, and that high drive level may lead, in such situations, even to reversal of sex type of mating behaviour. Male rats, after having been aroused by sexual interaction with females and after their heterosexual activity had been interrupted in an early phase, vigorously mounted each other, but if the drive level was not extremely high, none of the mounted partners replied with any of the reactions typical of receptive females. This experiment was repeated with the difference that now the males had been pretreated by male hormone to increase their drive level. Under these conditions some among the mounted animals showed female type responses.

The virtually universal potential for sexual interaction with the non-preferred sex poses the question whether it is to be attributed to bisexuality in a Freudian sense, as mentioned in the foregoing, to bisexuality proper (i.e. in terms of arousal to body shape) or to other factors. This topic will be pursued in Sections 2-5.

## 2.   BISEXUALITY PROPER

In the following section it will be shown that the universal potential for sexual interaction with the non-preferred sex, as documented in the foregoing section, appears not to be based on any considerable degree of bisexuality proper. The definition of homo- or hetero-sexuality and bisexuality in the Introduction of this chapter has been based on (relative) sexual arousal value of body shape. A study was carried out on hetero-sexual and on androphilic* males in whom sexual responses to the non-preferred sex were compared with those to sexually neutral stimulus configurations[40]. Figure 1 shows the order of erotic preference of various visually presented sex-age categories for 36 normal heterosexual and 36 androphilic male volunteers. Pictures were presented of nude females and males of various ages. Each sex-age category was represented by six photographic subjects, shown on slides as well as on a film strip.

In both groups of subjects there was a big difference between responses to shape of body of preferred and non-preferred sex. Results showed that, for the heterosexual group, the age categories of females were all distinct; the sexual responses to each of them were greater than those to the various age categories of males, and there were no significant differences

* Erotic preference for physically mature males.

(*P* > 0.05) between responses to the various age categories of males. The androphilic group responded more to physically mature males than to pubescent boys and more to pubescent boys than to male children, and there were no reliable differences between responses to male children and the various age categories of females (Figure 1).

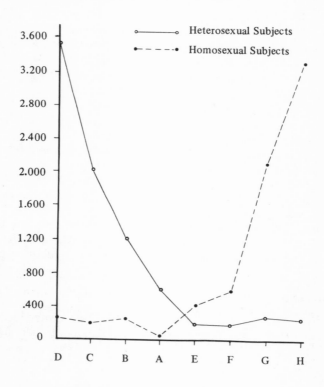

FIGURE 1.   Penile responses of homosexual and heterosexual males to pictures of females and males of various ages. *Key:* D—adult females, C—pubescent girls, B—8- to 11-year-old girls, A—6- to 8-year-old girls, E—6- to 8-year-old boys, F—9- to 11-year-old boys, G—pubescent boys, H—adult males. Reproduced from *Brit. J. Psychiat.* (1973), **122,** 163-9, with permission from the Editor.

For the comparison of sexual responses to the non-preferred sex and those to sexually neutral stimulus configurations, the same slides were shown to 32 heterosexual and 32 homosexual males, with one change: the youngest age category in both sexes was replaced by sexually neutral pictures (landscapes). The result showed that penile responses to the non-preferred sex were not different from those to the sexually neutral pictures. This fact indicates that, among normal heterosexual, as well as among androphilic males, there is *no* substantial degree of bisexuality, in terms of penile volume changes, to visually perceived body shape. This does not fully rule out the existence of some positive erotic value of body shape of the non-preferred sex. It only shows that if there is any such arousal value, its order of magnitude is very low and that substantial positive responses of this kind, if any, occur only very rarely in members of the groups which were tested. The well-documented fact that homosexual interaction occurs with a considerable number of normal heterosexual males (see Section 1), received little explanation from these results. Either there are other factors, e.g. behavioural patterns or body contact, which set the scene for heterosexual males to interact sexually with male partners or there are situations where the pattern of erotic responses to body shape might change substantially.

### Bisexuality in anomalies where there is conspicuously high sexual arousability by the non-preferred sex

Not even in those cases of anomalies in sexual preferences where there was a conspicuously high arousability by either sex, was there any conspicuous bisexuality proper.

Heterosexual masochistic males sometimes show such an unusual arousability by either sex, but in the few cases in whom there was an opportunity to employ the phallometric test, no conspicuous response to male body shape was observed. Such a case of masochism has been published elsewhere[5]. This patient preferred heterosexual interaction but sporadically sought homosexual anal intercourse as well, he being the receptive partner. At the time of the investigation he was married. He said that he had loved a number of women and had never felt any erotic tenderness for males. When refused by a female he was approaching, he used to indulge in the fantasy that he was this female himself, and that in this role he was suffering various tortures as a punishment for having refused. This elicited 'sweet pain'. He did not choose his male partners for handsomeness, etc., 'it did not matter' if they were ugly or crippled, etc. His female partners were usually quite pretty, as was his wife. In childhood he had had the fantasy that he and his classmates were being beaten by their female teacher on their bare rear ends, and later his favourite fantasy was that he was a prisoner of and maltreated by girls of his own age. This topic appeared often in his masturbation fantasies. From the age of 27 he had occasionally aroused himself by imagining he was being beaten by a male. This fantasy, including the shift of the imagined tormentor from female to male, occurs also in some masochistic males who report they never imagine themselves as females.

A further category of subjects with an abnormally high sexual arousability by either sex are heterosexual trans-sexual males. The differentiation between heterosexual trans-sexualism and transvestism is not an easy one. There are many variations of the combination of heterosexuality and high feminine gender identity in males. Transvestite males are 'fetishistic' towards female clothing in that they not only put on such attire for the purpose of orgastic activities (masturbation or sexual intercourse) but in that they are erotically aroused by female garments. When masturbating or when having heterosexual intercourse, they indulge in the fantasy that they themselves are females. The majority of transvestite patients does not feel at all like females when not involved in orgastic activities. In some transvestite patients the fetishistic factor is particularly strong and their need for a partner is minimal. Some transvestite patients may also have erotic fantasies, other than about orgastic activities, in which they appear in female clothing and feel as if they are females. One of our patients[41] erotically preferred (female) woollen garments which had already been worn. During his masturbatory activities, when clad in such garments, he used to rip them apart and fondle his imaginary breasts. One of his favourite erotic fantasies was that he was on a walk with a girlfriend, arm in arm, and both wore the same woollen outfits. In real life he had little erotic interest for males and not much more interest for females. This was borne out by the result of the phallometric test.

The transvestite syndrome may develop into trans-sexualism which is characterised by *sustained* feelings of cross-gender identity, combined with the subject's wish that his body were that of the other sex. Sometimes heterosexual trans-sexualism may develop (similar to homosexual trans-sexualism) without passing through a stage of only temporary feelings of cross-gender identity (i.e. without passing through a transvestite or masochistic stage).

An example of the development of trans-sexualism in heterosexual males similar to that found in homosexual males, i.e. without being combined with transvestism proper or masochism, could be seen in a patient of Nedoma[42] whom we were able to observe for a long period[5]. The patient was 57 years old and had had five children. He had been separated from his wife for many years. According to his statements he had never felt sexually aroused by female clothing. In his youth he had felt sexually attracted to females and never to males. His wife confirmed both statements in a letter. The phallometric test indicated heterosexuality without any conspicuous bisexuality. The patient claimed that from childhood he used occasionally to wear female attire. In the course of time male attire was worn less and less, and at the time we were seeing him, he had lived for many years as a female. A similar case has been described by Gelder and Marks[43].

In particular those heterosexual patients, with whom feminine gender identity is not temporally limited to orgastic activities, often indicate a considerable degree of bisexual potential. However, sometimes such statements appear to be merely the subject's demonstrations of his femininity as, e.g. the above-mentioned 57-year-old male's repeated complaint that he was desperately in need of a male. When hospitalised and observed for a prolonged period of time on a ward where there were several quite handsome males, some of them homosexual, he did not show the slightest interest in them. In contrast, the above-mentioned trans-vestite patient who had an inclination towards woollen garments, repeatedly invited, during his hospital stay, a homosexual patient to remain with him when he masturbated in female attire.

There was obviously a high degree of heterosexual potential in a 36-year-old male patient with high permanent feminine gender identity. He claimed that he always would have very much preferred having a female body; however, he did not request sex reassignment surgery, so that this validation of his trans-sexual inclination was lacking. According to his report, since the age of 8 or 9 he had felt more at ease with girls than with boys his age, but he did not prefer girls' toys or games to boys' toys or games. At age 13 or 14 he occasionally put on female clothing, which often by itself provoked an ejaculation. When in female clothing he felt as though he was a female. First homosexual intercourse was at age 18 or 19, first heterosexual intercourse at about age 20. He became very excited by the female and very little by the male. He married at the age of 25. When seeing his wife in the nude he was strongly aroused. They had intercourse frequently, but after a time he asked his wife to be on top of him during intercourse, and to allow him to wear female attire on such occasions. The wife did not wish to comply. He was still living with her but they had not had intercourse for 5 or 6 years. They had no children. He was charged several times for breaking and entering (this was always to steal female garments). The most recent charge was of a different nature. He was following a woman on the street; it was at night and he could not see her well. She was tall and, he thought, of male-like body build. He 'thought she could easily be a male clad as a woman'. He threatened her with a knife, threw her to the ground and dragged her behind a house where he had her, under threat, masturbate him. When hospitalised, this man experienced difficulties with other patients who had observed his keen interest in a handsome 18-year-old boy who was also in the ward. Not even the phallometric test of this patient indicated a conspicuously high degree of bisexuality.

## Bisexuality in non-masochistic and non-trans-sexual males who prefer physically mature partners

We tried in vain for years to find heterosexual non-trans-sexual male subjects with conspicuously little difference in erotic preference for either male or female body shape. A few such supposed 'bisexuals' were located and given the phallometric test. All proved to be thoroughly heterosexual. It would seem, from the verbal information received from these men, that they took part in homosexual activities only in order to gain social or material advantages. Kraff-Ebing[44], Ellis[45], Hirschfeld[46] and Kronfeld[47] pointed out a different kind of 'bisexual' male, namely homosexual persons who, according to their own admission, attempted to adjust to and stay adjusted to heterosexual relationships but who at time could not resist having homosexual intercourse.

## Sexual arousability by the nonpreferred sex and bisexuality

According to our above-mentioned clinical experience with individual cases, unusually high arousability by either sex may be accompanied at most by a slight degree of bisexuality proper. However it may be expected that a comparison of *groups* of males with such disorders with normal subjects, using penile responses to body shape, would render significant differences in the expected direction.

There is no reason to expect a greater difference in this regard between homo- or hetero-sexual males who had many contacts with the non-preferred sex and those who had none. Our phallometric data do not show any conspicuous bisexuality in the former, but a rigorous comparison of the above-indicated groups has not yet been carried out.

As already mentioned in Section 1, there may be another more or less universal factor responsible for the considerable arousability by the non-preferred sex encountered in heterosexual as well as in homosexual males. Body contact at high sexual arousal level may trigger same-sexed interaction, without the presence of bisexuality proper. In a series of experiments which tested whether there is, in androphilic males, any substantial aversion against females as sexual partners, or whether the female is only sexually neutral to them (see Section 5), the subjects' sexual responses to imagined heterosexual body contact, including intercourse, were assessed. The subjects were pre-aroused by slides of male nudes and, at a certain level of sexual arousal indicated by penile volume increase, statements were presented spoken by a female voice, describing the various phases of heterosexual interaction as if the subject were the male partner in this interaction. The statements described the various phases[48] of such interaction: location of a female partner, pretactile interaction, tactile interaction and intercourse. Statements describing the subject's involvement in sexually neutral situations were also presented. After each presentation the subject rated the situation on a 4-point scale of disgust. As expected, the descriptions of the androphilic subject's involvement in heterosexual intercourse were rated more disgusting than that in other heterosexual body contact, and the latter was rated more disgusting than heterosexual partner location, pretactile interaction, or the sexually neutral statements. There was no significant difference among penile responses to sexually neutral situations, location of a potential partner and heterosexual pretactile interaction. However the penile response to the situation of tactile interaction was significantly different from those to sexually neutral situations, and the penile response to the imagined situation of heterosexual intercourse was significantly different from those to all the remaining stimulus categories. In fact, the penile responses to imagined heterosexual body contact, including intercourse, showed a volume increase above the level at start of presentation of these stimuli. Thus, imagined involvement in heterosexual body contact, including intercouse, either did not prevent a substantial further increase of the tumescence response to the preceding arousing male nude stimuli or, by themselves, might have effected a further increase of penile tumescence. This indicates that, in androphilic males who are in a state of heightened sexual arousal, imagined heterosexual body contact, including intercourse, appears to have some positive sexual impact. This is not so in regard to location of a prospective female partner or pretactile heterosexual interaction. The discrepancy between verbal ratings and responses in penile volume changes appears to correspond to statements of those homosexual males who had experienced heterosexual intercourse, during which they had felt as if masturbating[46] and had not felt 'personally' or 'emotionally' involved[5,49] or had experienced negative feelings even when obviously sexually very aroused. This discrepancy also resembles the reports of heterosexual males who in early adolescence had interacted homosexually. Here also 'no personal involvement', no tender feelings towards the partner, and sometimes concomitant negative feelings are reported.

No comparable experiment could be carried out with normal males, but if venturing a hypothetical generalisation from the incomplete available data, the expectation was confirmed that in a situation of increased sexual arousal, body contact tends to facilitate sexual interaction with the non-preferred sex, and therefore contributes greatly to a subject's sexual arousability by members of the non-preferred sex.

However, from a Freudian point of view, it could be argued that bisexuality may only show under particular conditions because usually the homosexual component in partner appetance is blocked off in heterosexual persons and the heterosexual component is blocked off in homosexual persons. Section 3 attempts to explore the Freudian concept of bisexuality.

## 3.   THE FREUDIAN CONCEPT OF BISEXUALITY

Freud[19] was the first to draw the attention of psychologists and psychopathologists to the phenomenon that humans can be sexually aroused by members of either sex. Freud[30,50] speculated that every human being is bisexual and that the homosexual component is usually being blocked off during the final stages of early sexual development. According to his earlier quoted views on the therapy of homosexuality, Freud obviously assumed that, apart from this block, the structure of the homosexual and heterosexual components are comparable, i.e. they may manifest themselves in a similar way.

Contrary to Freud, the adaptational school of psychoanalysis does not believe in such general bisexuality and claims instead that only homosexual people are latently heterosexual whereas heterosexual people are not latently homosexual[51,52]. Ovesey[53-56] and co-authors, for instance, do not invoke latent homosexuality even in such cases where heterosexual non-psychotic males develop an intense fear of being or becoming homosexual, of being approached sexually by a male, neither do they in cases in whom there is the feeling of a compulsion to approach another male sexually. These authors denote such conditions as pseudohomosexual anxiety states and explain them by the current concepts of Sullivan's[57] line of the adaptational school. (Ovesey assumes that pseudohomosexual anxiety ensues from feelings of social inadequacy which make the patient doubt his masculinity.)

The meaning of the term 'latency' has been explained by Freud[58] simultaneously with the term 'non-conscious' (das Unbewusste) by the example of a post-hypnotic command, i.e. an instruction given during hypnosis which requires an action to be carried out at some time after awakening from the hypnotic trance. During the period between command and such action, certain relevant psychic contents (or images) are present of which there is no awareness. It is further assumed that the system of non-conscious images or attitudes is composed of two parts—the preconscious part, the contents of which can be readily brought to consciousness, and a second part, composed of actively repressed materials, i.e. of such material which is being prevented, by censoring mechanisms, from entering consciousness. From Freud's discussion of his theory of 'paranoia' it is quite clear that by 'latent homosexuality' he is referring to some such repressed tendencies. 'Paranoia' was to be seen as an attempt of the patient to defend himself against extremely strong homosexual desires, which were breaking through a weakened censoring system. Such defense was thought to be achieved by a transformation of the homosexual desires into persecutory delusions. The erotic attitude is transformed to hate, which in turn is projected onto the erotically desired same-sexed partner who, by the same token, becomes the persecutor[59,60].

However Freud obviously did not assume that all the repressed homosexual strivings which break through a weakened censoring system, in 'paranoia', are fully transformed into persecutory delusions. A considerable amount of this originally repressed homosexuality should rather just be set free. This is clear from Freud's arguments based on the autobiographical case history of Schreber. This patient's illness manifested itself by hallucinations, episodes of catatonic excitement[61], persecutory delusions and by a symptom which had been described by Krafft-Ebing[44] as 'metamorphosis sexualis paranoica', i.e. the delusion that the patient's body is changing into a body of the opposite sex. More recently MacAlpine and Hunter[62] pointed out that this syndrome represents a change in gender identity.

Schreber voiced the desire 'to succumb' to a male. that he would like to be a female prostitute, etc. and at the same time he complained about being approached homosexually by a certain person he did not want to name. Freud interpreted this picture as indicating abnormally strong homosexual urges which, prior to the illness, had been successfully repressed.

In contrast to Kraepelin's[63] original viewpoint, which was later shown not to be valid[64], Freud[50] understood Kraepelin's paranoia as belonging among the schizophrenic syndromes, but he did not believe that his theory held also for such cases of schizophrenia where there was no persecutory delusion. On the other hand he also applied his theory, with some small modifications, to jealousy delusions, which appear to occur particularly in alcoholics.

Freud's theory of the homosexual origin of the persecutory syndrome has been found to be valid by many of his followers[65]. Attempts have also been made, by methods other than psychoanalysis proper, to validate the claim that there is a connection between persecutory delusion and decreased repression of homosexual tendencies. However, projective tests were often applied as validational methods[66-70], or poorly formalised interpretations of the patients' statements were made[71-73]. Miller[74], who used a more controlled interpretation, thought that the Freudian theory accounted for only a fraction of his cases. Klein and Horwitz[75], Klaf and David[76,77] and Rossi *et al*.[78] worked with uninterpreted statements of their patients, and their results were mainly negative.

## A test of the Freudian theory of bisexuality

It is difficult to test the validity of Freud's concept of bisexuality because, for this purpose, it has to be translated into operational language and the accuracy of any such translation of psychoanalytic theories can be easily questioned.

We attempted to test the assumption that strong latent homosexual strivings are set free in such patients as specified by Freud, by employing the phallometric method of erotic object preference. If Freud's hypothesis were valid, conspicuous bisexuality, in terms of responses to body shape, should be expected in such subjects. This study was a comparison of patients suffering from persecutory or jealousy delusions with 'neurotics'. It had to be terminated before completion because of the advent of the tranquillisers which naturally were given to all the delusional, but not to the 'neurotic', patients, this made further comparisons impossible. In 14 cases there were persecutory delusions. Two of these 14 patients also had jealousy delusions. In 4 additional subjects there was only delusional jealousy with no persecutory delusion, and in the remaining 8 subjects there were particular delusional ideas which made an investigation as to increased homosexual tendencies worthwhile, e.g. hypochondriacal delusions of sexual content, impotence during heterosexual coitus combined with the idea of being suspected by everyone of masturbation. One schizophrenic patient claimed that he had been a homosexual prostitute and that since that time there had been a marked general interest in his person; another schizophrenic patient attempted suicide because he thought he was homosexual. He was unable to reach orgasm during heterosexual intercourse and complained that he felt the urge to examine the rear end of males. Another among the schizophrenic patients in that study had been hospitalised because he had requested amputation of the penis.

The patient group was very heterogeneous and therefore each phallo-metric record was compared individually with those of 30 'neurotics'. No substantial evidence could be found for increased bisexuality. A detailed description of this study, including the response scores, has been given elsewhere[5].

It could be argued that the patients successfully suppressed responses to males but, in view of the earlier-mentioned difficulty of response suppression in the original set-up of the phallometric test (see Introduction), it is very likely that the majority of our patients would not have been able substantially to suppress such responses.

The above-described investigation can only serve as a first orientation towards the problem in question. The use of 'neurotic' patients as controls (necessitated by the fact that funds were not available to use to recruit a normal control group) is unacceptable, particularly to psychoanalytically orientated readers because, according to Freud[50,79,80] neuroses are the result of various insufficiently integrated infantile sexual desires, and homosexuality belongs, according to Freud, in this category. However, there were also no conspicuous differences in respect to bisexuality between 'neurotics' and normal control groups which were used later.

If Freud's theory of bisexuality were valid and our operational translation of this theory appropriate, a gross increase in bisexuality would have been expected in the kind of patients tested; however the results were negative. On the basis of our data we have to conclude that we were not able to integrate Freud's concepts of bisexuality and latent homosexuality into an operational conceptual framework. It may be worth mentioning that some psychoanalytic authors[81-84] reject the original theory of persecutory delusion and, on the contrary, view homosexuality as being the result of paranoid anxiety.

## 4. BISEXUALITY AND EROTIC PREFERENCE FOR IMMATURE PERSONS

In Section 2 it has been shown that in males who erotically prefer physically mature partners there is virtually no bisexuality, in terms of responses to body shape, and that even in those rare cases where there is conspicuously high arousability, by imagined or true interaction with the non-preferred sex, there is usually no conspicuous degree of true bisexuality either. Contrary to that, such a conspicuously high degree of bisexuality in terms of responses to body, shape did appear in some paedophilic or paedo-ephebophilic*males[8]. This may give us a lead for research on erotic preference for physically mature partners where, with the exception of the work of Mohr et al.[85] and of Gebhard et al.[86], very little has so far been done.

Highly bisexual phallometric responses also occurred in a group of homosexual paedophilic patients who probably had not approached female children, who admitted an erotic preference for boys, and who seemed unaware of any attraction to girls[8,87].

There are also some paedophilic males admitting homosexuality who seem not to be aware of any general erotic attraction towards girls, but who exceptionally approach girls; this applies also to some heterosexual paedophilic males. In such cases there was generally no unusual degree of bisexuality in terms of phallometric responses to body shape.

*Paedophilia is the erotic preference for children, ephebophilia that for male and hebephilia that for female, pubescents.

For paedophilic males who show clearly bisexual phallometric responses to the body shape of children, the erotic value of some sexually neutral features of the child's physique seems to be comparable to that of the sexual characteristics proper[87]. However the question of the connection of paedophilia and bisexuality in terms of responses to body shape is obviously very much in need of further clarification.

There has not yet been an opportunity to compare fairly large samples of the various above-mentioned offender groups on bisexuality in terms of responses to body shape. In the present writer's opinion such a project could possibly provide valuable information on various kinds of preferences for immature partners. Such an inquiry could also indirectly contribute to the problem of male homosexuality, because of the overlap of these two areas.

## Homosexual preference for immature partners

Hirschfeld[46] was probably the first to point out that, in adult homosexual males, a preference either for children, pubescents or physically mature partners remains fairly stable throughout their lives. The vast majority of androphilic males have hardly any sexual contacts with pubescents, and virtually none with children. The main sources of our knowledge of erotically preferred age brackets are the ages of victims of recidivist offenders, the homosexual males' own statements, or the result of the phallometric test. In respect to victims listed in police or court files, there appear to be three crudely discernible types of offenders, those who approached children only, those who approached children as well as pubescents, and those who approached only pubescents[5].

In terms of phallometric responses to body shape, male children did not effect any considerable sexual arousal in androphilic males, but pubescents did (see Section 2). For normal heterosexual males female children were definitely arousing. Ephebophilic males respond sexually not only to male pubescents but also, to a lesser degree, to male children and physically mature males, whereas homosexual paedophilic subjects did not respond to physically mature males[87,88].

However, neither ephebophilic nor homosexual paedophilic males respond substantially more to physically mature females than do androphilic males[87,88]. This is not only of theoretical but also of immediate practical interest with respect to the results to be expected from therapeutic attempts to change the erotic preference of ephebophilic or homosexual paedophilic males into that for physically mature females.

Apart from the still open question in respect to bisexuality, there are only a few further, mainly tentative findings which concern differences between homosexual males who erotically prefer immature partners and those who prefer mature partners. Two of these will be mentioned in the appropriate places*.

## 5. ATTITUDES OF HOMOSEXUAL MALES TOWARDS FEMALES AS SEXUAL PARTNERS

### Heterosexual aversion

In the foregoing exploration of erotic arousability by the non-preferred sex, and of bisexuality proper, no gross differences were found between homosexual and heterosexual males. However there is the phobic theory of homosexuality which, if valid, would contradict this conclusion.

In this theory, aversion against sexual interaction with females has been assumed to be the main factor in the causation of male homosexuality. This phobic theory of homosexuality was originally formulated by Freud[66,79] and Rado[51,52] and to date is adhered to explicitly or implicitly by many psychotherapists[19] or behaviour therapists[89]. If this theory were valid, one would expect to find such an aversion in homosexual males generally.

Some homosexual males in fact indicate they feel aversion against females as sexual partners, and particularly against heterosexual intercourse, whereas others say they just do not feel any heterosexual attraction but there is no aversion. In an earlier investigation of 222 homosexual males[90] who sought help either because they wanted to become heterosexual or because they were in trouble with the law, 67.6% indicated they never had felt any sexual curiosity towards the female body. The remaining subjects claimed they had. 26.1% of the subjects indicated that even when sober they had experienced some erotic attraction towards females, and an additional 5.4% indicated that this had happened only when drunk. 68.5% indicated they had at some time attempted heterosexual intercourse (51.8% successfully, 16.7% unsuccessfully). 42.3% indicated they felt an aversion against heterosexual intercourse, whereas 47.7% said they never had, and about 10% said they could not answer this question. 26.1% of the homosexual males claimed that at some time they had loved a female.

In Section 2 the finding was reported that, as expected, androphilic males did not respond sexually to female body shape. However, in prearoused homosexual males, imagined heterosexual body contact including intercourse elicited .positive sexual responses, accompanied by

---

*At this point it might be of interest to note that on the basis of many years of clinical and forensic experience and from the literature, the present writer has gained the impression that in heterosexual, as well as in homosexual females, true erotic preference for children or pubescents appears either not to exist at all or to be very rare. The exceptional relevant cases can be explained as surrogate activity because there is virtually no recidivism.

reports that aversion was felt against such interaction. This may raise the suspicion that the impact of the body shape may in fact be rather negative, i.e. may effect an erotic aversion which may prevent heterosexual body contact.

In an earlier-described study on the erotic effect of body shape, little provision was taken to make possible the assessment of aversion. Therefore two experiments were carried out to test the hypothesis that homosexual males have an aversion to females[40,91].

The subjects were prearoused to a predetermined fixed level of penile tumescence by slides of nudes of their preferred sex-age category. At this point a potentially aversive stimulus was exposed and the penile response measured.

The first experiment compared the responses of androphilic and normal heterosexual males to body shape of the non-preferred sex. To androphilic males who had been prearoused by male nudes, slides of nude pubescent and physically mature females were presented. To heterosexual males who had been prearoused by female nudes, male adults and pubescents were shown. All subjects were shown landscapes and other sexually neutral slides, and potentially aversive pictures of skin diseases from a dermatological textbook. After each presentation the subjects rated the picture on a 4-point scale of disgust. The experiment showed that, in both homosexual and heterosexual males, detumescence responses to pictures of skin diseases were larger than those to anything else, there was no difference between homosexual and heterosexual males in penile responses to the non-preferred sex and, with both subjects' groups, there was no difference between detumescence responses to the nudes of the non-preferred sex and those to sexually neutral pictures (Figure 2). Both subjects' groups rated the pictures of skin diseases more disgusting than all the other stimuli, and the heterosexual group rated the male nudes more disgusting than the neutral pictures; however, no such difference was found among the ratings of homosexual males.

However, Freud[60,79] and Rado[51,52] assumed that only a particular part of the female body is aversive to a homosexual male, i.e. the vagina (in fact the vulva) which, according to this hypothesis, is perceived by the homosexual male in his alleged unconscious phantasies, as the threat he tries to avoid. Therefore a second experiment was designed as a test of this original version of the phobic theory of male homosexuality. To androphilic males who had been prearoused by male nudes, pictures of various parts of the female body were presented,—the face, the breasts, the fully exposed vulva, as well as sexually neutral pictures of landscapes. There were no significant differences among penile responses to the various parts of the female body and neutral slides, but the vulva was rated more disgusting

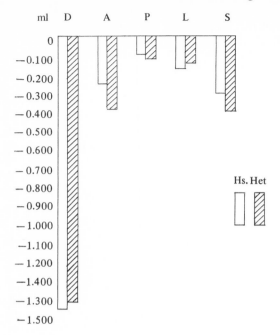

FIGURE 2. Detumescence responses of homosexual males and heterosexual controls. _Key:_ ml—millilitres, D—dermatological pictures, A—pictures of adult persons of the non-preferred sex, P—pictures of pubescent persons of the non-preferred sex, L—pictures of landscapes, S—white drawings on black background, Hs—homosexual males, Het—heterosexual controls. Reproduced from _Brit. J. Psychiat._ (1973), **122**, 163-9, with permission from the Editor.

than the breasts, which in turn were rated more disgusting than anything else.

There appears to be no general strong aversion among androphilic males towards females as sexual partners, certainly not more than there is in heterosexual males against same-sexed partners. Therefore any variation in heterosexual experience or attitudes towards females as sexual partners, which is encountered in homosexual males, is probably comparable to the corresponding variation in heterosexual males in respect to same-sexed partners.

### Reports on shifts from hetero- to homosexuality

However, there is one such phenomenon on which homosexual males appear to differ from heterosexual males. Some homosexual males indicate that within a particular period of time a gradual shift had occurred from hetero- to homo-sexuality, which means that there probably was a phase of about equal arousability by females and males. These claims are not parallelled by comparable statements of hetero-sexual males. The period for which such a shift is reported is usually at attaining puberty or shortly afterwards. Exceptionally the claim was made that this had happened in the late teens or early twenties. In the present writer's clinical experience, those of his homosexual patients, who claimed a shift from heterosexual to homosexual preference had occurred at such a late date, always had a good reason for pretending that they had become homosexual only recently, although there remained exceptions where no such reason could be found. In some of these cases there was very good contact with the patient and only in these few cases was the writer inclined to take this claim seriously. Krafft-Ebing[44] originally thought that this shift shows that homosexuality is solely acquired by adverse experiences but later[92] he revoked this interpretation. Näcke (1899, quoted from Hirschfeld[46]), denotes this phenomenon 'late homosexuality'.

An example of a late shift from hetero- to homo-sexual preference—as indicated by self reports—is the case of a 26-year old labourer who sought our help because he was being blackmailed by a young man to whom he had made advances. His first emission was at age 15. Since then he felt an erotic attraction towards females, and there were only females in his emission dreams. Until his 20th year he felt no attraction towards males. At age 17 he became intimate with a girl of the same age. When they kissed he got very aroused sexually. After one year they had sexual intercourse repeatedly, but the relationship was broken off after two years, when the girl moved to another town. When in military service he had another girlfriend and they had intercourse once in 14 days. His mother and sister did not approve of this girlfriend and he therefore left her. From then on he had several shortlived affairs with various girls. Recently he had fallen in love with a 20-year-old boy. Comparing his present erotic feeling towards the young male with his former erotic attitudes towards females, he thought that he in fact had never loved any girl. When his present girlfriend visited from a neighbouring town where she had been living, he pretended to be ill and tried his best to get her back to the train as soon as possible.

The patient indicated that he had never automasturbated. When asked what he would wish to do with his boyfriend, should he be willing to interact, the patient replied 'What could I do with a male? If he had an operation to change him into a female, yes I would, but that is just nonsense'.

At that time the present writer had the impression that this was just a homosexual episode in a basically heterosexual male but, after psychotherapy, he was followed up for 6 years and did not shift back to heterosexual preference. He used to fall in love with late-teen-age males but only initiated homosexual intercourse 5 years after he had first been seen. This is one of the few reports on hetero-homosexual shifts where the present writer thought it might be valid. The contact with this patient had been maintained for a prolonged period of time, and no charge for an offence was involved. However, as mentioned above, when the patient came to seek our help, he was in a difficult situation because he was being blackmailed.

Reports on hetero- to homo-sexual shifts in the later teens are much more frequent. A patient, a 32-year-old officer, reported that when 10 to 12 years old, he had played 'father and mother' many times with a girl of the same age, whereby they made unsuccessful attempts at intercourse. This came to an end when they were observed by a boy who threatened to tell their parents. However, during the same period of time the patient participated frequently in mutual masturbation with other boys. While still at a pre-pubertal age the patient observed heterosexual intercourse among adults, felt very aroused at the time and wished he were in the place of the male in this interaction. When 13 he had a crush on his 19-year-old teacher of religion. Together with other children he used to accompany her home. He attended church only because of her and used to await her lessons impatiently. The patient did not remember having had any erotic interest in a male, prior to age 14. When 15 years old, he participated several times, with another boy, in overpowering a female classmate and intimately touching her against her will. On these occasions he got very sexually excited and masturbated afterwards regularly with the other male participant in these heterosexual activities. At that time he started automasturbation and indulged in fantasies, of mutual masturbation while hugging and kissing the above mentioned boy or other boys he knew. At 18 he realised that his inclination towards boys was not normal and that girls ceased to attract him at all. Since that time he erotically preferred boys about 16 years old (more extensive digests of these two histories are given in Freund[5]).

Hopefully there will be an opportunity at some time in the future to analyse such hetero-homosexual shifts concurrently with their occurrence, mainly in pre- and post-pubertal males. For the time being we can only hold out such reports as a possible source of future information.

There appears to be a difference between androphilic and non-androphilic homosexual males in regard to claims that such a hetero-homosexual shift had occurred. In an earlier study[88], the subjects were explicitly asked whether, up to a certain age, they had felt attracted exclusively to females. In analysing the data, age 15 was chosen as a cutoff point, since puberty should have set in by this age. Ten amongst 54 androphilic non-patient volunteers and 14 among 45 ephebophilic and paedophilic offenders, who admitted their preference for young boys, indicated that until this age they had felt attracted exclusively to females. This result did not reach significance (Fisher test, $P = 0.1115$) but, when the 8 paedoephebophilic subjects were included in the comparison who had originally been left out because they could not be categorised as either ephebophilic or paedophilic, the difference did reach significance ($P = 0.0356$). However, this finding should be replicated before being accepted as reliable.

In Sections 1-5, sexual interaction with and erotic attitudes towards the non-preferred sex were explored. The present Section has elaborated further on such sexual responses and erotic attitudes of homosexual males towards their less preferred sex, i.e. females. The next two Sections will investigate erotic preferences in regard to the subject's own behaviour.

# 6. FEMININE GENDER IDENTITY AND MALE HOMOSEXUALITY

In Section 2 the problem of erotic preference for a subject's own behavioural and attitudinal sex type, and for that erotically preferred in a partner, was briefly introduced in general and demonstrated on clinical cases. In the present Section such preferences will be explored which appear to be linked to male homosexuality.

There is no reason to assume that there is less variability in homosexual than in heterosexual males, in patterns of verbally conveyed attitudes, feelings, etc. and in behavioural patterns. Among the many variables which could possibly be isolated, there is one, namely masculine *v.* feminine gender identity, on which homosexual males differ conspicuously from heterosexual males, even if there is apparently substantial overlap. This variable is not yet well defined but the phenomena in question clearly deserve considerable attention.

The term gender identity was introduced by Money *et al.*[93] to denote a subject's sex role adaptation and, in the course of time, has been increasingly used by Money himself and others, in the context of erotic motivation. In the following the term will be used in its later narrower sense and also will no longer cover preferred partner sex. The reason for the latter provision is the amply available evidence that a subject's erotically preferred own sex role and preferred sex of partner do not always correspond. In this narrower sense the term gender identity denotes an erotic preference for the sex type (male or female) of one's own behaviour and attitudes in erotic interaction, which mostly implies a preference for the opposite attitudinal and behavioural sex type in the partner. The concept of gender identity is based on the notion of a high degree of invariance of behavioural and attitudinal differences between the sexes, i.e. on the concept of masculinity *v.* femininity. This concept seems to be, at first glance, reasonably clear, but attempts to measure this implied unitary and bipolar trait have posed difficulties which contradict the original assumptions[94-96].

**Cultural variation of masculine *v.* feminine patterns**
The items used in masculinity-femininity tests are obviously culture bound and lead to results which vary with educational level[97]. Anthropologists[13,98] have shown that attitudes and behavioural patterns, seen as typically masculine or feminine, differ in various societies. In many tribal communities there is a trend to stress behavioural sexual differences to a high degree[99]. In some of these societies, males and females differed even in the words they used to denote the same objects[13]. There obviously was elaboration of sexual differences in earlier phases of the more developed cultures also, but in our present society the trend towards male-female educational and occupational differentiation has been reversed and the better psychological indicators of masculinity or femininity in adults, i.e. occupational preferences and verbally expressed emotional and ethical attitudes, which appear to heavily depend on education, may become more and more obsolete.

Attempts to improve measurement of masculinity-femininity should be geared towards developing indicators of a higher degree of cross-cultural invariance than those represented by the items of the present masculinity-femininity scales.

On a cross-cultural level, according to Mead, there seemed to be one invariant differential male *v.* female pattern over all tribal societies: only males were warriors and hunters of big game. They differed from females in that they shared together all the preparatory and accessory activities which are related to these occupations, and in none of the investigated tribal societies was the power or dominance status of the females comparable to that of the males. This finding corresponds with observations on sub-human vertebrates, including primates[100] and points at a fairly universal difference between the sexes in agonistic behaviour. Corresponding differences between the sexes have been observed in children.

**Development of behavioural and attitudinal sexual differences in humans**
There is a substantial body of knowledge on behavioural sexual differences which are present from infancy[101,102]. Gesell[103] was one of the first to

report on such very early differences in motor skills. These can be interpreted as differences in the mobility of distal *v.* peripheral joints. Male infants tend to be more active or better in gross movement patterns, girls in fine motor skills such as handwashing, door-opening, buttoning, unbuttoning etc. Several observers have found early-appearing differences in agonistic behaviour, between the sexes. Terman[104] reports on two relevant early studies, one by Goodenough and one by Hattwick. The study by Goodenough of 19 girls and 26 boys, in the age bracket of 7 to 82 months, revealed that more rough and tumble play, threat and assertion were observed in boys than in girls. The study by Hattwick on 4,579 kindergarten pupils showed that boys, more often than girls, take away toys from other children and more often refuse to share toys, whereas girls tend to avoid conflicts and tend to give in more easily. Later studies by Mischel[105] had comparable results and, in a more recent investigation by Jones[2] on 2- and 4-year-old children, boys were found to wrestle and hit more during rough and tumble play than girls.

The existence of such an early difference between the sexes in agonistic behaviour does not by itself indicate whether it is primarily biological, and therefore of high cross cultural invariance, or learned only on the basis of social traditions because, in humans as well as in other vertebrates, it is not possible to exclude the effects of rearing. However, Harlow's[106] observations on rhesus monkeys showed that, at least in this primate species, the basic sex differences in agonistic behaviour are not due to an unequal treatment of male or female offspring by the parents. This does not rule out that, even in rhesus monkeys, upbringing can effect further elaboration of such biologically anchored patterns.

Harlow observed infant rhesus monkeys who were brought up without a live mother but with surrogate mothers, namely dummies of wiremesh and cloth with a wooden headpiece. The male infants showed much more fighting and threat behaviour than did the female infants. They threatened other males as well as females, whereas females only exceptionally threatened males. The female infants threatened other females much less than did males. Rough and tumble play was usually initiated by males and was much more frequent in males than in females. Females, on the other hand, responded to threats more often than did males, by remaining motionless (passive) with or without visibly increased muscle tone (rigidity) or by retiring with averted face. Harlow is of the opinion that in rhesus monkeys the agonistic patterns are among the precursors of the later reproductive behaviour. We shall return later (see Section 7) to the discussion of the biological roots of masculinity *v.* femininity and their relationship to agonistic behaviour. At present the question of gender identity will be pursued further.

Gender identity is part of general sex role adoption. There is a series of studies on the development of the latter and of the ability to discriminate between the sexes. Probably the first investigation of this kind was Rabban's[107] study which assessed children's preferences for typically male or female toys, whether children assign the right sex to dolls according to sex typed clothing and hairstyle, whether they like the male or female dolls best, and whether they wish to become a mother or father when grown up. Brown's[108] -[110] 'It' scale uses similar indicators and this is true as well for the more recent work on development of masculinity-femininity or of gender identity in children (for an overview see Mischel[105] and Thompson and Bentler[111] ). This work is still in its infancy, and there is not yet any reliable information on the development of the various aspects of gender identity and their relationship to various components of agonistic behaviour in humans.

**Feminine gender identity in males**
Self reports of and observed behaviour in some homosexual males indicate a conspicuous adoption of various parts of the female role in erotic interaction or in developmental precursors of such patterns[112] - [118] To date there is little information available on whether feminine gender identity in homosexual males has some biological roots in common with true femininity as it appears in females. Therefore a first attempt has been made to measure, in homosexual males, feminine gender identity in a more direct way than by masculinity-femininity scales because, as mentioned above, feminine gender identity in homosexual males need not necessarily correspond to femininity as assessed by masculinity-femininity tests validated on the differentiation between males and females.

Those items which have been pointed out by experienced clinicians[44,46] as being indicative of 'femininity' in homosexual males and which, at their face value, appear to be relatively direct indicators of gender identity, are not contained in the current masculinity-femininity tests. Therefore a scale has been assembled of such items derived from clinical experience with homosexual males, and has been validated on groups of sexually normal controls and on trans-sexual and non-trans-sexual androphilic males[119] (the reason for the choice of androphilic males will be given later). This scale measures a male's position as to femine gender identity on a continuum which extends from a lower limit, where there is a clustering of the scores of sexually normal controls, to an upper limit which is occupied by the scores of homosexual trans-sexual males who, by definition, are those among the homosexual males with the most pronounced feminine gender identity. Thus rather than using females as a referent, as is the case in masculinity-femininity scales, the scores of homosexual trans-sexual males have been used instead. According to the results of a comparison of non-trans-sexual and trans-sexual homosexual males[120], it is very likely that homosexual trans-sexual males do not differ much from non-trans-sexual homosexual males in any way other than in degree of feminine gender identity, and the present writer is inclined to assume that the further differences are also related to this main difference. This statement does not imply any beliefs or guesses as to why some homosexual males reach such an extreme degree of feminine gender identity. Hoenig *et al.*[121-124] conceive of trans-sexualism as a disorder comparable to an overvalued idea.

In an attempt to assess gross differences between trans-sexual and non-trans-sexual homosexual males, 52 homosexual applicants for sex reassignment surgery were compared with 185 non-trans-sexual homosexual males[120]. All the applicants had indicated a preference for physically mature partners and, therefore, only androphilic males had been included among the controls as well.

Apart from degree of feminine gender identity, there appeared only one conspicuous difference between trans-sexual and non-trans-sexual androphilic males. All the homosexual applicants for sex reassignment surgery indicated that they preferred heterosexual male partners. The only one who did not answered that he did not care whether his partner was homosexual or heterosexual. In contrast, approximately three-quarters of the non-trans-sexual androphilic controls indicated that they preferred homosexual partners, and only 14% indicated a preference for heterosexual partners. An additional 13% answered that for them it did not make any difference whether the partner was homosexual or heterosexual. The strong preference of trans-sexual homosexual males for heterosexual partners seems to be easily explained as only reflecting their strong feminine gender identity, which may imply equally strong masculinity in the partner.

Various degrees of feminine gender identity can be observed in homosexual males and, as indicated above, there are some such males with apparently no feminine gender identity at all. Only a very small minority of homosexual males are trans-sexual. This is borne out by comparing the order of estimated prevalence of homosexuality and Wålinder's[125] estimate of prevalence of homosexual and heterosexual trans-sexualism.

In homosexual males the diagnosis of trans-sexualism is not as easy as it appears at first sight. Some of them socialise predominantly in female attire, but do not intend to undergo sex reassignment surgery. Some of them indicate that for a long time they had wished to do so but that since then they have changed their minds. In an earlier-mentioned study[120], 6%

among the non-trans-sexual controls indicated that at some time they had also wished they had a female body. It would not be easy to test the validity of such statements, but they should alert us to the possibility that trans-sexual leanings might disappear. Trans-sexualism in homosexual males appears to be just an extreme of a frequently occurring attribute.

In validating the feminine gender identity scale, the trans-sexual and non-trans-sexual homosexual males were compared with the sexually normal controls, only on those 12 items where there was no reason to expect that they could be offending to the normal subjects, and trans-sexual and non-trans-sexual androphilic males were compared on the full scale of 19 items as well. The scores for the various subjects' groups are shown in Figures 3 and 4.

In Figure 3, about one third of the androphilic males had a feminine gender identity score well within the range of that of the sexually normal controls. This is in agreement with results of comparisons of homosexual and heterosexual males on the current masculinity-femininity scales. Terman and Miles[94] had already reported that there were groups of homosexual males who, on their scale, scored conspicuously high on femininity, and other homosexual groups which scored more masculine than did normal controls. It therefore appears warranted to assume that both the usual masculinity-femininity tests and the above-mentioned new test, measure feminine gender identity in homosexual males and that there exist such homosexual males with whom virtually no feminine gender identity can be detected.

Nonetheless, feminine gender identity and male homosexuality are related. This was shown in two studies[126,127] which compared heterosexual and homosexual males on feminine gender identity. In the second study, age preference was taken into consideration as well. The groups compared were heterosexual males who preferred physically mature partners, such who preferred children, homosexual males who preferred physically mature partners and such who preferred children. The homosexual males had the higher scores on feminine gender identity, but there was a considerable interaction of sex preference and age preference, and there was no significant effect of age preference *per se,* because the *heterosexual* paedophilic group scored almost as high on feminine gender identity as did the androphilic group. This indicates that not only trans-sexual, but also paedophilic heterosexual males, tend to differ from normal heterosexual males in that they show a considerable degree of feminine gender identity.

In homosexual males there appears to exist a relationship between preferred partner age and feminine gender identity. Historically, Ferenczi[128] thought that, on clinical grounds, he had clearly established two

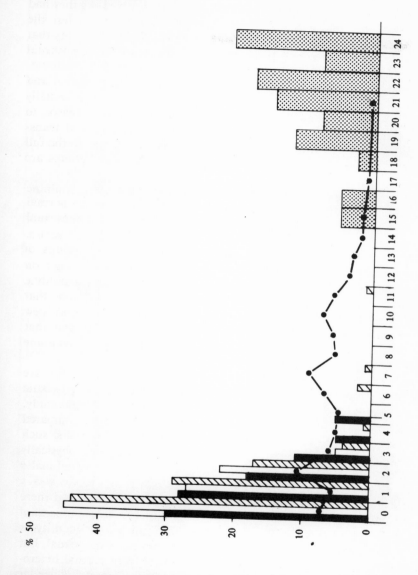

FIGURE 3. F.G.I. Part A scores for all subjects. Black columns: alcoholic patients; White columns: staff of Correctional Services; Striped columns: students; Dotted columns: trans-sexual patients; Line: non-trans-sexual androphilic males

On the x-axis the weighted scores are given on Part A of the F.G.I. scale. Maximum possible score: 24. On the y-axis the percentage of subjects who achieved the corresponding F.G.I. score marked on the x-axis. Reproduced from *Archives of Sexual Behavior,* Vol. III, No. 3, with permission of the Plenum Publishing Corporation, New York.

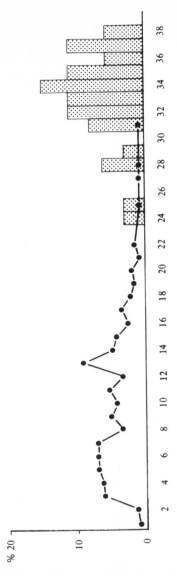

FIGURE 4    Full F.G.I. scale scores (Part A plus Part B combined) of non-trans-sexual and trans-sexual homosexual males. Dotted columns: trans-sexual patients. Line: non-trans-sexual androphilic males. On the *x*-axis the full-scale scores on the F.G.I. scale (Part A plus Part B combined) are given. Maximum possible score: 38. On the *y*-axis the percentage of subjects who achieved the corresponding F.G.I. score marked on the *x*-axis. Reproduced from *Archives of Sexual Behavior,* Vol. III, No. 3, with permission of the Plenum Publishing Corporation, New York.

types of homosexual males. One type combined masculinity and a preference for pubescents, and the other type combined femininity with a preference for physically mature partners. However, Hirschfeld[46] who had examined a very large number of homosexual persons, doubted the existence of a relation between femininity and age preference.

In an earlier-mentioned study[127] which compared androphilic, ephebo-philic and homosexual paedophilic males on the Feminine Gender Identity scale, the androphilic group scored considerably higher than the ephebophilic and paedophilic groups, and there was virtually no dif-ference in this respect between the ephebophilic and paedophilic males.

A comparison of the three groups on one of the better current masculinity-femininity scales, Gough's[129] Fy scale from the California Personality Inventory, had a similar result. However, a high degree of feminine gender identity (or 'femininity') does not preclude an ephebo-philic or paedophilic preference in homosexual males. In a sample of 92 such males there were three subjects with very high scores on feminine gender identity[120]. Conversely, as mentioned earlier, there are androphilic males in whom no feminine gender identity could be detected.

The fact that there are heterosexual males with high feminine gender identity and that in some homosexual males no feminine gender identity could be found indicates that feminine gender identity is not a necessary condition for the development of male homosexuality, and *vice versa*. The relationship between these two anomalies is either a relationship between their causal factors, or the presence of one of the two anomalies enhances the probability of the acquisition of the other. A similar alternative of explanations seems to hold for the relationship between the degree of feminine gender identity and the preferred age of the partner.

## 7. BIOLOGICAL ROOTS OF MASCULINITY-FEMININITY

Section 6 discussed gender identity as the only known behavioural and attitudinal variable on which homosexual males appear to differ from heterosexual males. However, measurement of feminine gender identity in males is very much in need of further development; and the factors measured by masculinity-femininity tests appear not to be well defined either. There is some relationship of feminine gender identity and femininity in males, as shown by some parallellism of results of the application of masculinity-femininity tests and the feminine gender identity scale, but the structure of this relationship is still unclear.

The search for cross-culturally more or less invariant factors in gender identity and masculinity *v.* femininity, which may be of help in developing these concepts, leads to an exploration of masculine and feminine behavioural patterns in sub-human vertebrates.

The masculinity-femininity concept, applied to humans, centres on attitudinal and behavioural patterns other than those particularly involved in mating, whereas in sub-human vertebrates, behavioural sex type is mainly defined by type of mating behaviour proper. However there are other behavioural patterns, i.e. agonistic (see Section 6) and parental behaviour in sub-human vertebrates, which appear to be sex typed. Parental behaviour and its development, i.e. its precursors occurring in childhood, have not yet been thoroughly investigated, either in humans or in animals, and therefore only agonistic behaviour will be discussed.

Two links between mating behaviour and agonistic behaviour have been observed in vertebrates: the link between particular situational agonistic constellations and inhibition *v.* facilitation of male *v.* female mating behaviour and the developmental link, in particular the parallel effects of androgens, at certain developmental phases, on later agonistic and mating patterns. These links suggest the presence of common components in sex type of mating behaviour and predominantly fight or flight type of agonistic behaviour, which may render a suitable basis for measuring masculinity or femininity. In the following, an attempt will be made to support this view by results of pertinent studies.

**Agonistic behaviour and male *v.* female mating patterns in subhuman vertebrates**

Lorenz[130], in his analysis of the behaviour of ravens, jackdaws and geese, remarks that, where sexual dimorphism (as to gross body shape and colour) is limited to a difference in 'degree', the female behaves in a female way only if the male is more 'impressive' (size, strength, intensity of colouring, readiness for threat display and fight) and the same is true, *vice versa,* for the male. In such avian species, the sex roles in pair formation and copulation depend heavily on dominance and submission. The bigger, more impressive, stronger animal will adopt the male role, the smaller, less impressive, weaker animal will adopt the female role, whatever its physiological sex. Craig[131] had already reported that if the cage of a male laughing dove is near that of a bigger male of the same species, the first male ceases to display in a male fashion and begins to respond in a female way. These factors are not as crucial, but are nonetheless important even in mammals, where usually the accessory genitals are clearly visible and are being explored by the potential partner, and where sexual dimorphism is complemented by sex-specific body odours.

External conditions which decrease a male's potential for responding to an 'enemy' with threat display and, if necessary with fight, will also facilitate cross gender mating behaviour, and the same seems to be true, *vice versa,* for females. There are certain situations, i.e. the possession or non-possession of a territory, which tend to function as facilitators or inhibitors of aggressive agonistic behaviour as well as of the male pattern of mating behaviour. In species in which reproductive activities are linked to the possession of a territory, a male on his own territory is usually more ready to threaten or fight than is an intruder, and would probably win the battle. Males without a territory are neither in good fighting condition nor very inclined to execute male type pair-formation activities. The ten-spined stickleback belongs to such territorial species. After having occupied a territory, he digs a nest for the deposition and care of the eggs. Females are lured into the territory by a typical male behavioural pattern, the zig-zag dance. Morris[37] put male sticklebacks in a container which was too small to allow each of them to take possession of a territory and in this situation some of the males, who had lost the ensuing battle, let themselves be led by the victor's zig-zag dance to the nest and behaved exactly in a female way, with the exception, of course, of the deposition of eggs. Similar observations on occurrence of female behaviour in males have been made by Morris[132] in the zebra finch.

According to Tinbergen[33] there is a close relationship between agonistic and courtship display patterns in male fish and birds, and they may have many components in common. Morris[134] conceives of pair-formation behaviour in general as a resultant of three vectors—a tendency to attack, a tendency to flee and a tendency towards copulation. There is con-siderable variation among the genus and species as to the particular balance of the vectors which result in female type or male type sexual behaviour, but for most species it appears to be true that a tendency towards flight decreases, or entirely blocks off, male pair-forming and preserving or copulatory behaviour, and facilitates the appearance of female patterns, whereas in females, dominance relative to the male partner tends to decrease, or entirely block off, female (pair-forming and preserving or copulatory) behaviour and to faciliate the appearance of male behaviour.

## The signalling and testing of agonistic constellations in terms of male *v.* female mating patterns

Another instance of a situational relationship between agonistic and reproductive behaviour is the use of male and female mating patterns, by males of many primate species, when signalling and testing their relative standing in the social power structure within the group[106,135,136]. The observed same-sexed interaction may partly serve a sexual surrogate function as well, but until now differentiation between same-sexed interaction "proper" and primarily socially motivated sexual activity was not possible. The former may be an environmentally induced artifact, and very rare under natural conditions.

As a general rule, young male monkeys in captivity have little access to sexually mature females, who are being jealously guarded by the overlord to whom they belong. However this may be quite different in free-living animals[137]. According to DeVore[138], under natural conditions, the domineering males among baboons will take possession of a female for themselves solely at the time when the swelling of her sex skin is at a peak. During the phases of low sexual receptivity the younger males will often interact sexually with these females, without being threatened or punished by the overlords. In rhesus monkeys also, homosexual interaction is very frequent and the socio-sexual constellation within the group, at least in captivity, is similar to that in baboons. Among free-living chimpanzees the influence of the social hierarchy on such same-sexed interaction seems to be similar to that reported on other primates[100].

It appears that at least under natural conditions copulatory interaction between sub-human primate males serves mostly the function of signalling non-sexual agonistic relationships. In the following, the developmental hormonal link between agonistic and mating patterns will be discussed.

**The developmental effect of androgens on male *v.* female mating and agonistic behaviour**

In vertebrates the presence or absence of male sex glands at critical stages of foetal development determines whether an otherwise male or female organism will ensue[139–142], including the difference between the female type cyclic and male type 'tonic' release of gonadotrophic hormones from the pituitary[143]. Harris and Jacobson[144] showed that the change in pituitary function which occurs under the influence of the male hormone is a result of a change in a nervous steering system, whereas the pituitary gland itself retains the capacity for cyclic gonadotrophin release. This system was later found to be located in the hypothalamus.

The presence or absence of androgens at a critical period in the early stages of development also determines the later mating and agonistic patterns. There exist many comprehensive reviews on the impact of androgens at such periods and on the development of various components of male *v.* female mating behaviour in vertebrates[145–147]. Most of this work has been carried out on rodents. Generally, at a critical period, androgens or very large amounts of oestrogen or progesterone were administered to females, and males were either given oestrogen or were castrated and later, prior to testing, the remaining animals were also gonadectomised.

Then both sexes were tested (in adulthood) for male as well as female mating behaviour. Male type mating was tested by presenting the animal with a female partner after concurrent pretreatment with testosterone, female type mating by presenting the animal with a male partner after concurrent pretreatment with oestrogen and progesterone.

Under these conditions various kinds of 'feminisation' of the males' mating behaviour and 'masculinisation' of the females' mating behaviour appeared.

The presence or absence of androgens at certain foetal or postnatal periods appear to have a developmental effect on agonistic behaviour as well. This effect varies with species and strain[148-149]. Its presence in primates has been shown by Goy[150] who reported on somatically masculinised female rhesus monkeys. Their mothers had been treated by androgen in pregnancy. The female rhesus infants were not only somatically quite masculinised, but they resembled young males in regard to the frequency of rough and tumble play and threat behaviour.

Very little is known to date about *how* androgens influence the development of mating patterns, and nothing is known about how androgens influence the development of agonistic patterns. Young *et al.*[151] propounded the theory of the organising action of androgens on the central neural tissue, destined to mediate mating behaviour after the attainment of adulthood. Several authors have tried to test this hypothesis against the alternative that the changes in sexual behaviour are due to decreased phallic or enhanced clitoral development. The results were mostly ambiguous[152-154]. However one experiment, using two different androgens, seems to support strongly the hypothesis that the developmental effect of androgens is due to its action on the nervous system[155]. (The relevant details will be given later.) This would also be in keeping with more recent studies where two separate systems were found in the rat hypothalamus—one the integrity of which is necessary for mounting behaviour to appear—the other being necessary for the appearance of (the female type) lordotic behaviour[156&158].

In female rats, early post-natal androgen administration decreases or abolishes the facilitating effect of oestrogen on the lordosis response to the mounting male. This fact was the basis of Beach's[159,160] hypothesis that neonatal androgen renders the rodent's central nervous system less sensitive to a later influx of oestrogen, and increases its sensitivity to androgen. However, Södersten[162] found that androgenised females responded to later oestrogen application with an increase in mounting behaviour. Södersten therefore concludes that the developmental effect of androgen is behaviour specific and is not the result of a change in sensitivity to hormones.

The administered androgen was almost always testosterone, but various androgenic compounds are known to exist in the vertebrate organism. Only more recently, experimentation begins to focus on their differential effects, and results strongly support the expectation that different androgen metabolites are differentially effective in the various target tissues, the induction of the various components of sexual behaviour[155,163,164]. The effect of androgens can also be modified by other sexual hormones[165] as well as by particular binding proteins in the blood[166]. It also appears that these effects vary over species and their strains[167,168]. Among these studies, the previously mentioned experiment by Feder appears to give strong support to the hypothesis of a developmental effect of androgens on some neural structures, which mediate mating behaviour. Male rats, castrated at birth and treated during the first 20 days of life with androstenadione, retained the ability to display lordotic behaviour in adulthood, and normal male accessory reproductive organs, i.e. the female type pattern, appeared in spite of a sufficiently developed male external genital. From experiments on animals there is no evidence to date that partner sex preference also depends directly on foetal or neonatal androgenisation.

This Section was an attempt to document the contention that male type mating behaviour is related to fight threat and dominance in agonistic behaviour, and that female type mating behaviour is related to flight, retreat, submission type of agonistic behaviour. Studies were reviewed which showed that this relationship is situational and developmental, and that the development of male type mating and agonistic pattern is dependent on the effects of androgens at certain critical periods. Therefore it seems likely that, apart from sex type mating patterns, sex type of more general behavioural and attitudinal patterns in humans may be best represented by such components which agonistic and courtship behaviour have in common. A search for such components is likely to provide a wider and firmer base for the masculinity-femininity and gender identity concepts than is at present available.

## 8.  HUMAN INTERSEXES

One of the areas which appear to hold considerable promise in a more direct search for factors which determine gender identity, and possibly preferred sex of partner as well, is the study of human intersexuality. In these conditions unusual relations are often present between type of sex chromosome set, sex hormone levels, reproductive glands, the appearance of the external genitalia and upbringing (as a boy or girl). Money *et al.*[33] supplied a comprehensive overview of these conditions and demonstrated the apparent incongruities among the above-mentioned components in the sexual make-up of their patients. However, the above-mentioned experiments amply demonstrate that our knowlege of hormonal development and its relationship to masculinity and femininity in sub-human vertebrates is still very scanty, not to mention the corresponding relationships in humans. Therefore, to date, the informational value of case studies on intersexual persons is still quite limited.

Among the most striking intersexual conditions are the testicular feminisation syndrome and congenital virilising adrenal hyperplasia. In cases of complete testicular feminisation, sex chromosome pattern, gonads and sex hormone pattern are male type, while external genitals, body build, gender identity and partner-sex preference are female type (somatically: the vagina is short and ends blindly; the testes are located in the abdomen or labia and there are male internal ducts, whereas uterus and oviducts are absent). A comparable condition also exists in rats and mice and there is a strong hereditary factor which, at least in mice, is X-linked [169]. For mice, a deficiency of a particular enzyme has been reported which normally enables the organism to utilise dehydro-testosterone [170]. In human testicular feminisation the enzymatic defect has not yet been located [171,173-175].

The testicular feminisation syndrome shows that the development of male or female type of gender identity and preferred partner sex is only indirectly based on the type of sex chromosome set and that, under the usual external conditions, either sex hormones or upbringing are the direct determiners of such development. The earlier-indicated experiments on sub-human mammals point, of course, to the hormones, but the development of male or female type behaviour in humans may proceed in a different way.

There are reports on cases of incomplete testicular feminisation, i.e. on cases where there is a somewhat better utilisation of testosterone, a fact which is indicated by the presence of pubic and axillary hair. In these cases, sometimes male type gender identity or partner sex preference have been observed. König [176] reported on a pair of siblings with incomplete testicular feminisation, one of which had male type gender identity and partner sex preference, and Ledermayer and Delucca [177] describe another such patient with male type partner preference whereas there was feminine gender identity. Both patients were reared as females. However, not even this psychological difference between complete and incomplete testicular feminisation renders conclusive support to the hormonal hypothesis of gender identity and preferred partner sex, because it could also be argued that in complete cases there is usually a somewhat larger clitoris than in incomplete ones, and the role of the type of external genitals in the development of psychological maleness or femaleness is not yet clear (see Money[178]).

Congenital virilising adrenal hyperplasia affects chromosomal females. An abnormally increased production of adrenal androgens leads to the appearance of male type secondary sex characteristics inclusive of clitoral enlargement, which may reach such proportions that it is mistaken for a penis. These most virilised females are usually brought up as males and have male type gender identity and partner preference and, for the least virilised, the opposite is true. However in some cases there are apparent discrepancies in this regard. Particularly such cases have been recorded by authors who favour the hypothesis that gender identity and preferred sex of partners are mainly the result of whether the subject had been reared as a boy or a girl. There is no point in including into this review the remaining types of human intersexes, which are usually invoked in the context of discussions on the roots of feminine gender identity.

The contention that the example of intersexes shows that male or female type gender identity and partner preference in general are basically determined by type of rearing (as a boy or girl) has been most cogently refuted by Zuger[179] who pointed out the scarcity of information on hormonal make-up and development which can be made available in any individual case. Zuger also assembled a great number of case reports of patients erroneously reared in a way opposite to their biological sex (because of their under- or over-developed phallic structure) who longed for and arrived at sex reassignment.

Of particular interest are cases of intersexuality with known aetiology, where medication was instituted in time and, where warranted, the external genitals adjusted to type of rearing. There are two such thoroughly investigated samples[180,181]. Both consisted of girls, exposed as foetuses to androgens or related compounds. One group was made up of patients suffering from virilising adrenal hyperplasia, the other of girls whose mothers had been given large amounts of progestin during pregnancy. Under these circumstances the foetal hormonal effect on gender identity and preferred partner sex was not contaminated by either the postnatal effect of masculine-looking genitals or by the persistence of incongruous hormonal functioning. Self reports and reports of the girls' mothers were evaluated. Boys' toys were preferred over dolls, motherhood play was missing or low in priority of interests. There was a high incidence of tomboyism. The authors indicate that there was no incidence of incipient male type partner sex preference, but only a low priority rating for interest in boys as compared with the control group. However, in this regard not all the necessary information was available as yet.

A possibly comparable study is that of Yalom *et al.*[182]. These authors report on decreased masculinisation of male children who had been exposed prenatally to exogenously administered oestrogen and progesterone. They were the sons of diabetic mothers who had received these hormones to prevent the complication of pregnancy. Almost all had fully normal external genitals. These boys were compared with matched normal subjects on a wide variety of measures which comprised teachers' ratings, the experimenter's ratings from clinical interviews with these boys and their mothers, a battery of masculinity-femininity and personality tests, ratings of athletic coordination in throwing and catching a ball, swinging a bat and running. A second control group had also been included, made up of the sons of diabetic mothers who had not received the oestrogen progesterone treatment. The prenatally treated group turned out to be less aggressive, less assertive and had less athletic skills and grace. The details of this very richly designed experiment cannot be reported here and the reader is referred to the original.

The vast majority of homosexual persons do not show any gross somatic intersexuality and the occasional findings, published by some authors on hormonal anomalies[183, 188], could not be replaced later[189, 190]. More recently, when valid methods had become available, hormonal investigation has been resumed, but the results are still conflicting. Loraine *et al.*[191] reported reduced urinary testosterone readings in homosexual males and raised levels of luteinising hormone in the urine of homosexual women. Margolese *et al.*[192] found a difference between homosexual and heterosexual males, in the ratio of urinary androsterone *v.* aetiocholanolone, and Kolodny *et al.*[193–194] reported reduced plasma testosterone levels and raised plasma luteinising hormone levels in groups of homosexual males. Birk *et al.*[195] and Brodie *et al.*[196] and Doerr *et al.*[197] also studied plasma testosterone levels but could not repeat the results of Kolodny *et al.*

Human intersexes were considered because of the developmental anomalies in regard to the involvement of androgen. In these cases the development of gender identity can be studied directly. Our knowledge of the hormonal anomalies themselves, in critical developmental periods, is still too scanty to offer reliable information. Particularly the more recent results of animal experimentation show that hormonal development is complex and that the various types of androgens may exert their effect at various loci and at various critical periods. The example of the testicular feminisation syndrome further points at the enzymes which are necessary for androgen utilisation, and there may even be particular enzymes for the various tissues involved. On the other hand it is, of course, not easy to imagine that type of rearing should not have any effect at all, and the problem of biological or experimental causation will probably have to be solved separately for particular components of the complex phenomena of gender identity and partner preference. However, the study of human intersexes appears to point at the dependence of masculine *v.* feminine gender identity and, possibly even of preferred partner sex, on the effect of androgens.

## SUMMARY AND CONCLUSIONS

The terms homosexuality and heterosexuality denote a subject's erotic preference for the male or female body shape. The term bisexuality has been defined analogously. The term erotic preference has been based on relative sexual arousal value of male and female body shape. In humans there is a virtually universal capability of responding with an increase of sexual arousal to actual or imagined interaction with the non-preferred sex. This capability is not based on any considerable degree of bisexuality in terms of sexual responses to body shape, and therefore an enhancement by guidance, or some other kind of treatment, of a homosexual male's capability to interact sexually with females does not necessarily imply that a comparable shift has been accomplished from homosexuality towards bisexuality proper. The main components of the capability of sexually interacting with members of the less preferred sex appear to be body contact (which might concurrently increase a sub-threshold arousal value of body shape of the non-preferred sex) and, in particular cases, gross behavioural and attitudinal deviations from a subject's own sex type (e.g. those present in heterosexual trans-sexualism and in some cases of masochism in males). With the exception of some cases of paedophilia, true bisexuality (i.e. about equivalent sexual response to male and female body shape) does not exist at all or is very rare.

The attitudes of homosexual males towards females, as sexual partners, vary considerably and, in the retrospective self reports of some homosexual males, a shift from heterosexuality is stated, which had occurred at an early post-pubertal age, or exceptionally, later. However the validity of these reports has not yet been established. Some homosexual males indicate they feel an aversion towards females as sexual partners. However, a series of experiments showed that in pre-aroused androphilic males there was *no* corresponding penile detumescence response to gross female body shape or to various parts of the female body, including the fully exposed vulva, and, in contradiction to statements indicating aversion, sexually prearoused homosexual males responded with further arousal increase to imagined heterosexual tactile interaction including intercourse.

The only known behavioural and attitudinal variable on which homosexual males differ from homosexuals is feminine gender identity. However, in many homosexual males no feminine gender identity could be found, and a high degree of feminine gender identity occurs, exceptionally, in heterosexual males as well. Feminine gender identity appears therefore not to be a necessary condition of male homosexuality, and *vice versa.*

This means that in homosexuality and cross-gender identity either there are related causal factors or the presence of one of these two anomalies predisposes an individual towards the acquisition of the other.

In homosexual males there is also a relationship between feminine gender identity and preferred partner age. There is a higher degree of feminine gender identity in homosexual males who prefer physically mature partners than in those who erotically prefer pubescents or children, but again, there were androphilic males with whom no feminine gender identity could be found, and there were ephebophilic or homosexual paedophilic males with a considerable degree of feminine gender identity. This suggests an explanation for the relationship between preferred partner age in homosexual males, and feminine gender identity, analogous to that for the relationship between feminine gender identity and homosexuality.

The degree to which gender identity overlaps with masculine *v.* feminine behavioural sex type is not yet known, as it is not yet clear to what degree feminine gender identity, when occuring in males, is comparable to feminine gender identity in females. Operational analysis of these concepts is still in its initial phase. A search for the biological roots of behavioural and attitudinal sex type may provide information which may prove useful in such an analysis. In sub-human vertebrates, behavioural sex type has been intensively investigated for mating behaviour and, to a lesser degree, for agonistic and parental behaviour. Cases have been reported of opposite sex type mating behaviour caused by atypical agonistic situations and, in humans as well as in animals, the development of agonistic behaviour appears to be different in the sexes.

Both sex type of mating behaviour and agonistic behaviour depend on the effect of androgens at particular critical developmental periods. This is so in sub-human vertebrates, and it may therefore be hypothetically expected that anomalies in the effect of androgens during foetal development may also dispose a human subject towards later cross-gender behavioural patterns. From studies on sub-human vertebrates, there is little evidence that this also applies for the development of partner sex preference. However, under natural conditions no true homosexuality, comparable to that occurring in humans, has as yet been observed in animals. The study of human intersexes will probably render useful and pertinent information at some time in the future, because there the development of gender identity proper can be investigated. To date the necessary data on the hormonal disorders at critical developmental phases are mostly not well enough known in these cases. Nonetheless the relevant material seems to indicate that there are androgen-dependent components in the development of gender identity and, possibly also, in that of preferred partner sex.

The reliability of the results reported in this Chapter are, of course, limited by the degree of validity of the methods used in the various investigations. Throughout the Chapter I have attempted to indicate these limitations. More problems have been shown than hard facts offered, because research on homosexuality is still at an early stage.

## REFERENCES

1.  Hutt, S.J. and Hutt, Corinne (1970). *Direct Observation and Measurement of Behavior.* (Springfield, Illinois: Charles C. Thomas)
2.  Jones, N. (1972). *Ethological Studies of Child Behaviour.* (London: Cambridge University Press)
3.  Freund, K. (1957). Diagnostika Homosexuality u mužů. *Čs. Psychiat. (Prague),* **53,** 382
4.  Freund, K. (1963). A laboratory method for diagnosing predominance of homo- or heteroerotic interest in the male. *Behav. Res. Therapy,* **1,** 85
5.  Freund, K. (1965). Die Homosexualität beim Mann. (Leipzig: S. Hirzel Verlag)
6.  Freund, K. (1961). Laboratory differential diagnosis of homo- and heterosexuality—an experiment with faking. *Rev. Čs. Med.,* **7,** 20
7.  Freund, K., McKnight, C.K., Langevin, R. and Cibiri, S. (1972). The female child as a surrogate object. *Arch. Sex. Behav.,* **2,** 2, 119
8.  Freund, K. (1967). Diagnosing homo- or heterosexuality and erotic age-preference by means of a psychophysiological test. *Behav. Res. Therapy,* **5,** 209
9.  Kinsey, A.C., Pomeroy, W.B. and Martin, C.E. (1948). Sexual Behavior in the Human Male. (Philadelphia—London: W.B. Saunders Co.)
10. Ward, D.A. and Kassebaum, G.G. (1964-5). Homosexuality: A mode of adaptation in a prison for women. *Soc. Prob.,* **12,** 159
11. Bethe, E. (1907). Die dorische Knabenliebe. *Rheinisches Museum für Philologie,* **62,** 438
12. Ford, C.S. and Beach, F.A. (1951). *Patterns of Sexual Behavior.* (New York: Harper and Row)

13. Davenport, W. (1965). Sexual patterns and their regulation in a society of the Southwest Pacific. In : *Sex and Behavior* (Ed. F.A. Beach) (New York: John Wiley Inc)
14. Deacon, A.B. (1934). *Malekula, a Vanishing People in the New Hebrides.* (London: G. Routledge & Son)
15. Layard, J. (1959). Homoeroticism in primitive society as a function of the self. *J. Anal. Psychol.,* **4,** 101
16. Williams, E.G. (1944). Homosexuality: A biological anomaly. *J. Nerv. Ment. Dis.,* **99,** 65
17. Allen, C. (1952). On cure of homosexuality. *Internat. J. Sex,* **5,** 139
18. Allen, C. (1958). *Homosexuality.* (London: Staples Press)
19. Bieber, I., Dain, H.J., Dince, P.R., Drellich, M.G., Grand, H.G., Gundlach, R.H., Kremer, M.W., Rifkin, A.H., Wilbur, C.B. and Bieber, T.B. (1962). *Homosexuality: A Psychoanalytic Study.* (New York: Basic Books)
20. Buki, R. (1964). A treatment program for homosexuals. *Dis. Nerv. Syst.,* **25,** 304
21. Feldman, M.P. and MacCulloch, M.J. (1971). Homosexual Behaviour—Therapy and Assessment. *International Series of Monographs in Experimental Psychology.* (Oxford—New York—Toronto: Pergamon Press)
22. Hadden, S.B. (1957). Attitudes towards and approaches to the problem of homosexuality. *Pennsyl. Med. J.,* **60,** 1195
23. Hadden, S.B. (1958). Treatment of homosexuality by individual and group psychotherapy. *Amer. J. Psychiat.,* **114,** 810
24. Hadfield, J.A. (1958). The cure of homosexuality. *Brit. Med. J.,* **1,** 1323
25. Martin, A.J. (1962). The treatment of twelve male homosexuals with LSD followed by a detailed account of one of them who was a psychopathic personality. *Acta Psychother.,* **10,** 394
26. Poe, J.S. (1952). The successful treatment of a 40 year old passive homosexual, based on an adaptional view of sexual behavior. *Psychoanal. Rev.,* **39,** 23
27. Prince, G.S. (1959). The therapeutic function of the homosexual transference. *J. Anal. Psychol.,* **14,** 117
28. Stevenson, I. and Wolpe, J. (1960). Recovery from sexual deviations through overcoming nonsexual neurotic responses. *Amer. J. Psychiat.,* **166,** 737
29. Freund, K., Pinkava, V. and Březinová, V. (1959). Zur Frage der Eheschlieszung homosexueller Männer. *Beitr. Sex. Forsch.,* **Nr.** 16, 25
30. Freud, S. (1926, orig. 1920). Über die Psychogenese eines Falles

von weiblicher Homosexualität. In: *Studien zur Psychoanalyse der Neurosen* (1913-1925). (Leipzig-Wien-Zurich: I.P.V.)

31. Stekel, W. (1923). Onanie und Homosexualität. (Berlin-Wien)
32. Stekel, W. (1929). Ist die Homosexualität heilbar? *Nervenarzt*, **2,** 337
33. Serog, M. (1931). Analyse eines Homosexuellen. *Zbl. Psychother.,* **4,** 750
34. Ellis, A. (1956). The effectiveness of psychotherapy with individuals who have severe homosexual problems. *J. Consult. Psychol.,* **20,** 191
35. Schutz, F. (1971). Prägung des sexualverhaltens von Enten und Gänsen durch Sozialeindrücke während der Jugendphase (Imprinting of sexual behaviour of ducks and geese through social experience during their juvenile period). *J. Neuro-Visceral Relations,* Suppl. X, 339
36. Inhelder, E. (1962). Skizzen zu einer Verhaltenspathologie reaktiver Störungen bei Tieren. *Schweiz. Arch. Neurol. Neurochir. Psychiat.,* **89,** 276
37. Morris, D. (1952). Homosexuality in the ten-spined stickleback *(Pygosteus pungitius). Behaviour,* **4,** 233
38. Beach, F.A. (1941). Female mating behaviour shown by male rats after administration of testosterone propionate. *Endocrinology,* **29,** 409
39. Beach, F.A. (1944). Experimental studies of sexual behaviour in male mammals. *J. Clin. Endocrinol.,* **4,** 126
40. Freund, K., Langevin, R., Cibiri, S. and Zajac, Y. (1973). Heterosexual aversion in homosexual males. *Brit. J. Psychiat.,* **122,** 163
41. Freund, K. (1969). *Homosexualität.* (Hamburg: Rowohlt)
42. Nedoma, K. (1956). Příspěvek k problematice utváření lidského chování. *Čs. Psychiat.,* **52,** 20
43. Gelder, M. and Marks, I. (1969). Aversion treatment in transvestism and transsexualism. In: *Transsexualism and Sex Reassignment* (Eds. Green and Money). (Baltimore: Johns Hopkins Press)
44. Krafft-Ebing, R. (1890). *Psychopathia Sexualis.* 5th edition. (Stuttgart)
45. Ellis, H. (1950, orig. 1915). *Studies in the Psychology of Sex—Sexual Inversion.* 2 vols. (London)
46. Hirschfeld, M. (1920, orig. 1914). *Die Homosexualität des Mannes und des Weibes.* (Berlin).
47. Kronfeld, A. (1923). *Sexualpathologie.* (Leipzig-Wien)
48. Freund, K. and Kolářský, A. (1965). Grundzüge eines|einfachen Bezugssystems für die Analyse sexueller Deviationen. *Psychiat. Neurol. Med. Psychol.,* **17,** 221

49. Freund, K. and Srneć, J. (1953). K otázce mužské homosexuality, analysa změn sexuální apetence během pokusné léčby podmiňováním. *Sbornik lék.*, **55**, 125
50. Freud, S. (1922, orig. 1917). *Vorlesungen zur Einführung in die Psychoanalyse.* (Leipzig-Wien-Zurich: I.P.V.)
51. Rado, S. (1940). A critical examination of the concept of bisexuality. *Psychosom. Med.*, **2**, 459
52. Rado, S. (1969) *Adaptational Psychodynämics: Motivation and and Control.* (Eds. J. Jameson and H. Klein). (New York Science House).
53. Ovesey, L. (1955). The pseudohomosexual anxiety. *Psychiatry*, **18**, 17
54. Ovesey, L. (1955). Pseudohomosexuality, the paranoid mechanism and paranoia. *Psychiatry*, **18**, 163
55. Ovesey, L. (1956). Masculine aspirations in women. *Psychiatry*, **19**, 341
56. Kardiner, A., Karush, A. and Ovesey, L. (1959). A methodological study of Freudian theory, 111: Narcissism, bisexuality and the dual instinct theory. *J. Nerv. Ment. Dis.*, **129**, 207
57. Sullivan, H.S. (1946). *Conceptions of Modern Psychiatry.* (Washington)
58. Freud, S. (1931, orig. 1913). Einige Bemerkungen über den Begriff des Unbewuszten in der Psychoanalyse. In: *Theoretische Schriften (1911-1925)* (Wien)
59. Freud, S. (1911). Psychoanalytische Bemerkungen über einen auto-biographisch beschriebenen Fall von Paranoia (Dementia paranoides). *Jahrb. Psychoanal. Psychopathol. Forsch.*, **111**, 1, 9
60. Freud, S. (1926, orig. 1922). Über enige neurotische Mechanismen bei Eifersucht, Paranoia und Homosexualität. In: *Studien zur Psychoanalyse der Neurosen (1913-1925)* (Wien-Berlin-Zurich: I.P.V.)
61. Baumeyer, F. (1955). Der Fall Schreber. *Psyche Nr.* **91, 1X**, 513
62. MacAlpine, I. and Hunter, R.A. (1955). Commentary to D.P. Schreber—*Memoirs of my Nervous Illness.* (London: W. Dawson)
63. Kraepelin, E. (1915). *Psychiatrie,* **1V**, 3
64. Kolle, K. (1931). Über paranoische Psychopathen. *Z. ges. Neurol. Psychiat.*, **136**, 97
65. Fenichel, O. (1945, orig. 1930). The psychology of transvestism. *Internat. Z. Psychoanal.*, **16**, 21 In *The Collected Papers of Otto Fenichel* (New York)
66. Aronson, M.L. (1952). A study of the Freudian theory of paranoia by means of the Rorschach test. *J. Proj. Tech.*, **16**, 397

67. Aronson, M.L. (1953). A study of the Freudian theory of paranoia by means of the Blacky Pictures. *J. Proj. Tech.,* **17,** 3

68. Chapman, A.H. and Reese, H.M. (1953). Homosexual signs in Rorschachs of early schizophrenics. *J. Clin. Psychol.***9,** 30

69. Davids, A., Joelson, M. and McArthur, C. (1956). Rorschach and TAT indices of homosexuality in overt homosexuals, neurotics and normal males. *J. Abnorm. Soc. Psychol.* **53,** 161

70. Lindzey, G., Tejessy, C. and Zamansky, H.S. (1958). Thematic apperception test: An empirical examination of some indices of homosexuality. *J. Abnorm. Soc. Psychol.* **57,** 67

71. Gardner, G.E. (1931). Evidences of homosexuality in one hundred and twenty unanalyzed cases with paranoid content. *Psychoanal. Rev.* **18,** 57

72. Norman, J.P. (1948). Evidence and clinical significance of homosexuality in 100 unanalysed cases of dementia praecox. *J. Nerv. Ment. Dis.* **107,** 484

73. Moore, R.A. and Selzer, M.L. (1963). Male homosexuality, paranoia and the schizophrenias. *Amer. J. Psychiat.* **119,** 743

74. Miller, C.W. (1941). The paranoid syndrome. *Arch. Neurol. Psychiat.* **45,** 953

75. Klein, H.R. and Horwitz, W.A. (1949). Psychosexual factors in the paranoid phenomena. *Amer. J. Psychiat.* **105,** 697

76. Klaf, S.F. and Davis, C.A. (1960). Homosexuality and paranoid schizophrenia. *Amer. J. Psychiat.* **116,** 1070

77. Klaf, F.S. (1961). Female homosexuality and paranoid schizophrenia. *Arch. Gen. Psychiat.* **4,** 84

78. Rossi, R., Delmonte, P. and Terracciano, P, (1971). The problem of the relationship between homosexuality and schizophrenia. *Arch. Sex. Behav.* **1,** 4, 357

79. Freud, S. (1925, orig. 1905). *Drei Abhandlungen zur Sexualtheorie.* 6th Edition. (Leipzig-Wien)

80. Freud, S. (1922, orig. 1914). Zur Einführung des Narziszmus. In: *Sammlung kleiner Schriften zur Neurosenlehre (4).* 2nd Edition. (Berlin-Leipzig-Zurich: I.P.V.)

81. Klein, M. (1932). *The Psychoanalysis of Children.* (London: Hogarth Press)

82. Nunberg, H. (1938). Homosexuality, magic and aggression. *Internat. J. Psychoanal.* **19,** 1

83. Knight, R.P. (1940). The relationship of latent homosexuality to the mechanism of paranoid delusions. *Bull. Menninger Clin.* **4,** 149

84. Rosenfeld, H. (1949). Remarks on the relation of male homo-

sexuality to paranoia, paranoid anxiety and narcissism. *Internat. J. Psychoanal.* **30,** 36

85. Mohr, J.W., Turner, R.E. and Jerry, M.B. (1964). *Pedophilia and Exhibitionism.* (Toronto: University of Toronto Press)
86. Gebhard, P.H., Gagnon, J.H., Pomeroy, W.B. and Christenson, C.V. (1965). *Sex Offenders.* (New York: Harper & Row and Paul B. Hoeber Inc.)
87. Freund, K. (1967). Erotic preference in pedophilia. *Behav. Res. Therapy* **5,** 339
88. Freund, K., Langevin, R., Wescom. T. and Zajac, Y. (1974). *Heterosexual interest in homosexual males.* To be published in *Arch. Sex. Behav.*
89. Ramsay, R.W. and Van Velzen, V. (1968). Behaviour therapy for sexual perversions. *Behav. Res. Therapy* **6,** 233
90. Freund, K. (1960). Aus den Krankengeschichten homosexueller Männer. *Psychiat. Neurol. Med. Psychol.* **12,** 213
91. Freund, K., Langevin, R. and Zajac, Y. (1974). Heterosexual aversion in homosexual males: A second experiment. *Brit. J. Psychiat.* In press.
92. Krafft-Ebing, R. (1901). Neue Studien auf dem Gebiete der Homosexualität. *Jahrb. Sex. Zwischenstufen* **3,** 1
93. Money, J., Hampson, G.J. and Hampson, J.L. (1955). An examination of some basic sexual concepts: The evidence of human hermaphroditism. *Bull. Johns Hopkins Hosp.* **97,** 301
94. Terman, L.M. and Miles, C. (1936). *Sex and Personality: Studies in Masculinity and Femininity.* (New York-London)
95. Lunneborg, P.W. (1972). Dimensionality of MF. *J. Clin. Psychol.* **28,** 3, 313
96. Constantinople, A. (1973). Masculinity-femininity: An exception to a famous dictum? *Psychol. Bull,* **80,** 5, 389
97. Grygier, T.G. (1957). Psychometric aspects of homosexuality. *J. Ment. Sci.* **103,** 514
98. Mead, M. (1935). *Sex and Temperament in Three Primitive Societies.* (New York: W. Morrow & Co)
99. Bateson, G. (1936). *Naven.* (Cambridge, England: The University Press)
100. Van Lavick-Goodall, J. (1971). *In the Shadow of Man.* (London: Fontana-Collins)
101. Kagan, J. and Moss, H. (1962). *Birth to Maturity: A Study in Psychological Development.* (New York: John Wiley & Sons, Inc.
102. Walker, R.N. (1962). Body build and behavior in young children:

1. Body build and nursery school teacher's ratings. *Monogr. Soc. Res. in Child Develop.* **27**, 1, (3)

103. Gesell, A. (1940). *The First Five Years of Life.* (New York-London: Harper & Brothers)

104. Terman, L.M. (1946). Psychological sex differences. In: *Manual of Child Psychology* (Ed. L. Carmichael). (London-New York: John Wiley & Sons Inc.)

105. Mischel, W. (1972). Sex-typing and socialization. In: *Carmichael's Manual of Child Psychology,* 3rd ed. 3 (Ed. P.H. Mussen). (New York: John Wiley & Sons, Inc.)

106. Harlow, H.H. (1965). Sexual behaviour in the rhesus monkey. In: *Sex and Behaviour* (Ed. F.A. Beach). (New York: John Wiley & Sons, Inc.)

107. Rabban, M. (1950). Sex role identification in young children in two diverse social groups. *Genet. Psychol. Monogr.* **42**, 1

108. Brown, D.G. (1957). Masculinity-femininity development in children. *J. Cons. Psychol.* **21**, 197

109. Brown, D.G. (1957). The development of sex-role inversion and homosexuality. *J. Pediat.* **50**, 613

110. Brown, D.G. (1958). Sex-role development in a changing culture. *Psychol. Bull.* **55**, 232

111. Thompson, Spencer K. and Bentler, P.M. (1973). A developmental study of gender constancy and parent preference. *Arch. Sex. Behav.* **2**, 4, 379

112. Friend, M.R., Schiddel, L., Klein, B. and Dunaeff, D. (1954). Observations on the development of transvestitism in boys. *Amer. J. Orthopsychiat.* **24**, 563

113. Green, R. and Money, J. (1960). Incongruous gender role: Non-genital manifestations in prepubertal boys. *J. Nerv. Ment. Dis.* **130**, 160

114. Green, R., Fuller, M., Rutley, B.R. and Hendler, J. (1972). Playroom toy preferences of fifteen masculine and fifteen feminine boys. *Behav. Therapy.* **3**, 3, 425

115. Zuger, B. (1966). Effeminate behavior present in boys from early childhood. 1. The clinical syndrome and follow-up studies. *J. Pediat.* **69**, 1098

116. Lebovitz, P.S. (1972). Feminine behavior in boys: Aspects of its outcome. *Amer. J. Psychiat.* **128**, 10, 1283

117. Bates, J.E. and Bentler, P.M. (1973). Play activities of normal and effeminate boys. *Develop. Psychol.* **9**, 1, 20

118. Bates, J.E., Bentler, P.M. and Thompson, S.K. (1973). Measure-

ment of deviant gender development in boys. *Child Development*, **44**, 591

119. Freund, K., Nagler, E., Langevin, R., Zajac, A. and Steiner, B. (1974). Measuring feminine gender identity in homosexual males. *Arch. Sex. Behav.* **3**,|249

120. Freund, K., Langevin, R., Zajac, Y., Steiner, B. and Zajac, A. (1974). The trans-sexual syndrome in homosexual males. *J. Nerv. Ment. Dis.* **158**, 145

121. Hoenig, J., Kenna, J. and Youd, A. (1970). A follow-up study of transsexualists: Social and economic aspects. *Psychiatr. Clin.* **3**, 2, 85

122. Hoenig, J., Kenna, J. and Youd, A. (1970). Social and economic aspects of transsexualism. *Brit. J. Psychiat.* **117**, 537, 163

123. Hoenig, J., Kenna, J.C. and Youd, A. (1971). Surgical treatment for transsexualism. *Acta Psychiatr. Scand.* **47**, 106

124. Hoenig, J. and Kenna, J. (1974). The nosological position of trans-sexualism. *Arch. Sex. Behav.* **3**, 273

125. Wålinder, J. (1971). Incidence and sex ratio of transsexualism in Sweden. *Brit. J. Psychiat.* **119**, 195

126. Ferenczi, P.S. (1911). Über die Rolle der Homosexualität in der Pathogenese der Paranoia. *Jahrb. Psychoanal. Psychol. Forsch.* **3**, 101

127. Freund, K., Langevin, R., Laws, R. and Serber, M. (1974). *Feminine gender identity and preferred partner age in homosexual and heterosexual males.* To be published in *Brit. J. Psychiat.*

128. Gough, H.G. (1970). *California Psychological Inventory.* (California: Consulting Psychologists Press)

129. Freund, K. and Pinkava, V. (1960). K otázce femininity u homosexuálních mužů. *Čs. Psychiat.* **56**, 386

130. Lorenz, K. (1935). Der Kumpan in der Umwelt des Vogels. *J. Ornithol.* **83**, 137, 289

131. Craig, W. (1909). The voices of pigeons regarded as a means of social control. *Amer. J. Sociol.* **14**, 86

132. Morris, D. (1954). The reproductive behaviour of the zebra finch (Poephila guttata) with special reference to pseudomale behaviour and displacement activities. *Behaviour* **6**, 271

133. Tinberger, N. (1965). Some recent studies of the evolution of sexual behaviour. In: *Sex and Behaviour* (Ed. F.A. Beach). (New York: John Wiley & Sons)

134. Morris, D. (1955). The causation of pseudofemale and pseudomale behaviour: a further comment. *Behaviour* **8**, 46

135. Carpenter, C.R. (1942). Sexual behaviour of free ranging rhesus monkeys (Maccaca mulatta). *J. Comp. Psychol.* **33**, 133, 143

136. Ploog, D.W. and MacLean, P.D. (1963). Display of penile erection in squirrel monkey (Saimiri sciureus). *Anim. Behav.* **11,** 32

137. Zuckermann, S. (1932). *The Social Life of Monkeys and Apes.* (London: Kegan, Paul, Trench, Trubner and Co.)

138. De Vore, I. (1965). Male dominance and mating behaviour in baboons. In: *Sex and Behaviour* (Ed. F.A. Beach). (New York: John Wiley & Sons)

139. Jost, A. (1954). Über der Erzeugung fötaler Zwitterbildung bei der Ratte mit Methylandrostendiol. *Geburts. Frauenhk.* **14,** 687

140. Jost, A. (1956). Les bases biologiques de l'interprétation de certaines anomalies sexuelles. *Ann Endocrinol.* **17,** 479

141. Jost, A. (1957). L'étude physiologique de la différenciation embryonnaire du sexe et l'interprétation de diverses anomalies sexuelles. *J. Suisse Méd.* **87,** 275

142. Jost, A. (1957). La fonction endocrine du testicule foetal. In: *La fonction endocrine du testicule* (8-18). Publication du colloque sur la fonction endocrine du testicule (Eds. A. Gilbert-Dreyfus, J.C. Savoie, J. Sebaoun). (Paris)

143. Pfeiffer, C.A. (1936). Sexual differences of the hypophyses and their determination by the gonads. *Amer. J. Anat.* **58,** 195

144. Harris, G.W. and Jacobsohn, D. (1951/2). Functional grafts of the anterior pituitary gland. *Proc. Roy. Soc. Biol.* **139,** 263

145. Money, J. and Ehrhardt, A.A. (1971). Fetal hormones and the brain: Effect on sexual dimorphism of behaviour—a review. *Arch. Sex. Behav.* **1,** 241

146. Neumann, F. and Steinbeck, H. (1972). Influence of sexual hormones on the differentiation of neural centers. *Arch. Sex. Behav.* **2,** 147

147. Reinisch, J.M. (1974). Fetal hormones, the brain and human sex differences: A heuristic, integrative review of the recent literature. *Arch. Sex. Behav.* **3,** 51

148. Payne, A.P. and Swanson, H.H. (1972). Androgens—effect of neonatal administration on aggressive behaviour. *Nature,* **239,** 5370, 282

149. Vale, J.R., Ray, D. and Vale, C.A. (1973). Interaction of genotype and exogenous neonatal estrogen: Aggression in female mice. *Physiol. Behav.* **10,** 2, 181

150. Goy, R.W. (1968). Organizing effects of androgen on the behaviour of rhesus monkeys. In: *Endocrinology and human behaviour* (Ed. R.P. Michael), pp 12-31. (London: Oxford University Press)

151. Young, W.C., Goy, R.W. and Phoenix, C. (1964). Hormones and sexual behaviour. *Science,* **143,**212

152. Nadler, R.D. (1968). Masculinization of female rats by intracranial implantation of androgen in infancy. *J. Comp. Physiol.* **66,** 157

153. Nadler, R.D. (1969). Differentiation of the capacity for male sexual behavior in the rat. *Horm. Behav.* **1,** 1, 53

154. Ward, I.L. (1972). Female sexual behavior in male rats treated prenatally with anti-androgen. *Physiol. Behav.* **8,** 1, 53

155. Feder, H.H. (1971). The comparative actions of testosterone propionate and $5\alpha$-androstan-$17\beta$-ol-3-one propionate on the reproductive behaviour, physiology and morphology of male rats. *J. Endocrinol.* **51,** 241

156. Singer, J.J. (1968). Hypothalamic control of male and female sexual behavior in female rats. *J. Comp. Physiol. Psychol.* **66,** 738

157. Modianos, D.T., Flexman, J.E. and Hitt, J.C. (1973). Rostral medial forebrain bundle lesions produce decrements in masculine, but not feminine, sexual behavior in spayed female rats. *Behavioral Biology,* **8,** 5, 629

158. Hendricks, S.E. and Scheetz, H.A. (1973). Interaction of hypothalamic structures in the mediation of male sexual behavior, *Physiol. & Behav.* **10,** 4, 711

159. Beach, F.A. (1948). *Hormones and Behaviour.* (New York: Paul B. Hoeber Inc.)

160. Beach F.A. (1949). A cross-species survey of mammalian sexual behavior. In: *Psychosexual Development in Health and Disease* (Eds. P.H. Hoch and J. Zubin). (New York: Grune & Stratton)

161. Pfaff, D.W. and Zigmond, R.E. (1971). Neonatal androgen effects on sexual and non-sexual behavior of adult rats tested under various hormone regimes. *Neuroendocrinology,* **7,** 3, 129

162. Södersten, P. (1973). Increased mounting behavior in the female rat following a single neonatal injection of testosterone propionate. *Horm. Behav.* **4,** 1

163. Goldfoot, D.A., Feder, H.H. and Goy, R.W. (1969). Development of bisexuality in the male rat treated neonatally with androstenedione. *J. Comp. Physiol. Psychol.* **67,** 41

164. Hart, B.L. (1972). Manipulation of neonatal androgen: Effects on sexual responses and penile development in male rats. *Physiol. Behav.* **8,** 5, 41

165. Diamond, M., Llacuna, A. and Wong, C.L. (1973). Sex behavior after neonatal progesterone, testosterone, estrogen or anti-androgens. *Horm. Behav.* **4,** 73

166. Burke, C.W. (1972). Oestregen—Amplification by sex-hormone-binding globulin. *Nature*, **240**, 5375, 38

167. Luttge, W.G. and Whalen, R.E. (1970). Dihydrotestosterone, androstenedione, testosterone: Comparative effectiveness in masculinizing and defeminizing reproductive systems in male and female rats. *Horm. Behav.* **1**, 4, 265

168. Luttge, W.G. and Hall, N.R. (1973). Differential effectiveness of testosterone and its metabolites in the induction of male sexual behavior in two strains of albino mice. *Horm. Behav.* **4**, 31

169. Lyon, Mary F. (1970). Genetic activity of sex chromosomes in somatic cells of mammals. *Phil. Trans. Roy. Soc. Lond.* **B259**, 41

170. Gehring, T. (1971). Testosterone action—Effect of androgen-insensitivity mutation on cytoplasmic receptor and nuclear uptake. *Nature, New Biol.* **232**, 106

171. Charreau, E. and Villee, C.A. (1968). Steroid metabolic pathways in feminizing testicular tissue. *J. Clin. Endocrinol.* **28**, 1741

172. Mauvais-Jarvis, P. and Bercovici, J.P. (1968). Donnees nouvelles sur la physiopathologie du syndrome de feminisation testiculaire. *Pathologie et Biologie*, **16**, 965

173. Mauvais-Jarvis, P., Bercovici, J.P. and Gauthier, F. (1969). In vivo studies on testosterone metabolism by skin of normal males and patients with the syndrome of testicular feminization. *J. Clin. Endocrinol.* **29**, 417

174. Mauvais-Jarvis, P., Crepy O. and Bercovici, J.P. (1971). Further studies on the pathophysiology of testicular feminization syndrome. *J. Clin. Endocrinol. Metabol.* **32**, 4, 568

175. Mauvais-Jarvis, P., Charransol, G. and Bobas-Masson, F. (1973). *J. Clin. Endocrinol. Metabol.* **36**, 3, 452

176. König, P.A. (1960). Genetische, endokrinologische und psychosexuelle Probleme bei testikularer Feminisierung. *Geburts. Frauenhk.* **20**, 166

177. Ledermair, O. and Delucca, A. (1969). Inkomplete testiculare feminisierung. *Gynaecologia* **168**, 49

178. Money, J., Hampson, G.J. and Hampson, J.L. (1957). Imprinting and the establishment of gender role. *Arch. Neurol. Psychiat.* **77**, 333

179. Zuger, B. (1970). Gender role determination: A critical review of the evidence from hermaphroditism. *Psychosom. Med.* **32**, 5, 449

180. Ehrhardt, A.A., Epstein, R. and Money, J. (1968). Fetal androgens and female gender identity in the early-treated adrenogenital syndrome. *Johns Hopkins Med. J.* **122**, 160

181. Money, J. (1970). Sexual dimorphism and homosexual gender identity. *Psychol. Bull.* **74,** 6, 425

182. Yalom, I.D., Green, R. and Fisk, N. (1973). Prenatal exposure to female hormones: Effect on psychosexual development in boys. *Arch. Gen. Psychiat.* **28,** 554

183. Lundsberg, E. (1935). *Est-il possible de constater la présence d'une homosexualité constitutionnelle par injections de folliculine?* XV. Internat. Physiol. Congr. Leningrade—Moskva. Biomedigiz

184. Wright, C.A. (1938). Further studies of endocrine aspects of homosexuality. *Med. Record.* **147,** 449

185. Glass, S.J., Deuel, H.J. and Wright, C.A. (1940). Sex hormone studies in male homosexuality. *Endocrinol.* **26,** 590

186. Myerson, A., Neustadt, R. and Rak, J.P. (1941). The male homosexual, hormonal and clinical studies. *Arch. Neurol. Psychiat.* **45,** 572

187. Severinghaus, E.L. and Chornyak, J. (1945). A study of homosexual adult males. *Psychosom. Med.* **7,** 302

188. Williams, E.G. (1944). Homosexuality: A biological anomaly. *J. Nerv. Ment. Dis.* **99,** 65

189. Appel, K.E. and Flatherty, J.A. (1937). Endocrine studies in cases of homosexuality. *Arch. Neurol. Psychiat.* **37,** 1206

190. Myerson, A. and Neustadt, R. (1946). Essential male homosexuality and results of treatment. *Arch. Neurol. Psychiat.* **55,**291

191. Loraine, J.A., Ismail, A.A.A., Adampoulos, D.A. and Dove, G.A. (1970). *Brit. Med. J.* **4,** 406

192. Margolese, M.S. and Janiger, O. (1973). Androsterone/ etiocholanolone ratios in male homosexuals. *Brit. Med. J.* **3,** 207

193. Kolodny, R.C., Masters, W.H., Hendryx, B.S. and Toro, G. (1971). Plasma testosterone and semen analysis in male homosexuals. *New Engl. J. Med.* **285,** 21, 1170

194. Kolodny, R.C., Jacobs, L.S., Masters, W.H., Toro, G. and Daughaday, W.H. (1972). Plasma gonadotrophins and prolactin in male homosexuals. *Lancet,* 18

195. Birk, L., Williams, G.H., Chasin, M. and Rose, L.I. (1973). Serum testosterone levels in homosexual men. *New Engl. J. Med.* **289,** 23, 1236

196. Brodie, H.K., Gartrell, N., Doering, C. and Rhue, T. (1974). Plasma testosterone levels in heterosexual and homosexual men. *Amer. J. Psychiat.* **131,** 1, 82

197. Doerr, P., Kockott, G., Vogt, H.J., Pirke, K.M. and Dittmar, F. (1973). Plasma testosterone, estradiol, and semen analysis in male homosexuals. (1973). *Arch. Gen. Psychiat.* **29,** 829

# 3

# Female Homosexuality—
# A Review

## F.E. Kenyon

The word homosexuality is derived from the Greek prefix 'homos'
meaning 'same', and not the Latin for man; there is no special name for
male homosexuality. Female homosexuality is variously described as
lesbianism, sapphism or tribadism. The first is derived from Lesbos, the
Greek island in the Aegean; one of its more famous inhabitants was the
lyric poetess Sappho (born about 612 BC) who founded a sort of female
literary society. The popular term tribadism is a misnomer as it refers to a
particular sexual practice (from Greek 'to rub') and not to lesbianism in
general. A now obsolete term 'urninde' was proposed by Ulrichs in 1862.
The first person to use the term lesbian in the sexual sense would seem to
be Aristophanes (fourth century) in his play 'The Frogs' (405 BC).

There are many problems of definition, but the essential feature is a
definite preferential erotic attraction to another female. This usually, but
not inevitably, also involves some physical expression of the attraction; so
we can then speak of homosexual behaviour, overt homosexuality or a
practising lesbian. This is in contrast to what has been described (mainly
by psychoanalysts) as latent or repressed homosexuality.

## CLASSIFICATION

An entirely satisfactory classification is not yet possible. However, it is
more practicable to study homosexual behaviour, which may be transient
or life-long, and which may be associated with psychiatric morbidity or
may occur in an otherwise well-adjusted personality. Kinsey's rating scale

— from 0 (entirely heterosexual) to 6 (entirely homosexual) with various grades in between — is now well known and is a reminder that homosexuality is a matter of degree. The popular dichotomy into 'femme' and 'butch' is not helpful, as few actually fit these stereotypes.


## GENERAL SURVEYS

There is, as yet, no satisfactory monograph on lesbianism giving a comprehensive, unsensational and reliable account of the condition in all its complexity. One widely read book on homosexuality contains much more material on females than previous editions, and the whole is a sensible, humane and 'middle-of-the-road' account; but the author tries to cover the whole field and inevitably there is little room for much detailed discussion.

The book by Caprio[2], a medically qualified American psychoanalyst, is very uneven, poorly written and has an undiscriminating and unreliable bibliograph. Cory[3] is the pseudonym of an American male homosexual who has written sympathetically 'from the inside' about homosexuality and who has now produced a book on lesbianism which is endorsed by A. Ellis. It is a popular account with a useful classified list of references. An intelligent layman's perceptive account of the problem[4] grew out of a television documentary on the subject.

'Love Between Women'[5] is an idiosyncratic account by a German psychiatrist with a background of poetry, literature and philosophy. She stresses the overall emotional rather than sexual attraction, but the many facets of the subject are given scant coverage, nor are previous findings appraised or compared with her own. Although the appendix of 28 statistical tables comparing 106 lesbian subjects with a control group gives a scientific gloss to the work, there is an elementary lack of appreciation of scientific methodology, e.g. no information is given on the source of the control group. Feldman and MacCulloch[6] give a selective but useful review of factors predisposing to homosexual behaviour in the light of recent advances in behavioural psychology. There is a brief 'speculative' section on female homosexuality.

The BMA Family Doctor booklet on homosexuality[7] gives good coverage of the special problems of lesbianism. A novelist's account[8] of bisexuality is also concerned with female cases. A well written account from 'real life' is given in the recently published 'Portrait of a Marriage'[9], a frank account of the turbulent sex life of Vita Sackville-West. A survey of all important papers published between 1907 and 1972 has already been made[10].

## PREVALENCE

It must be said at the outset that this is not definitely known as the basic epidemiological study has yet to be carried out. Such figures as are quoted are mostly inspired guesses from impressions or inadequate data, sometimes extrapolating from what is known of male homosexuality.

The best known and most thorough investigation to date was made by Kinsey *et al.*[11]. They had 5940 females in their sample; however 58.2% had never married, and this would give a bias towards a greater incidence of lesbianism than in a more representative sample of the general population. They found that although by the age of 45 homosexual experience to orgasm had occurred in 13%, relatively few remained predominantly homosexual for many years, and nearly all who did were unmarried. About 4% of the single women remained more or less exclusively homosexual from 20 to 35 years of age.

It is impossible to arrive at an accurate figure for the size of the present-day lesbian population of England, but it is likely to be a sizeable minority. The present author's estimate would be somewhere in the region of 1 in 45 of the adult female population who are persistently and exclusively homosexual.

### Comparison with Male Homosexuality

Much unsubstantiated argument has ensued as to whether homosexuality is more common among males or females.

When the more modern studies are taken into consideration it is clear that overt homosexuality is much rarer in the female. This applies not only to animals[12] but also to so-called primitive people[13]. Indeed, this would be expected for sexual behaviour, given some of the more fundamental psychosexual differences between the sexes. This, too, may also account for other differences between lesbians and male homosexuals; lesbians are less promiscuous, have more stable and longer-lasting relationships and have no organised prostitution. So that within broad limits, the lesbian, apart from her sexual orientation, retains most of the basic female characteristics.

### Animal studies

It is now accepted that homosexual behaviour is widespread in the animal kingdom, particularly among mammals and primates. It is a common observation that cows may attempt to mount other cows especially in oestrus. However, the matter is complicated by other factors which must call for caution in extrapolating to human behaviour. For instance, animal homosexual behaviour may well be influenced by such variables as dominance-submission, degree of maturity, territorial behaviour and crowding. Lip service is often paid to anthropomorphism, which is then overlooked when interpreting experiments (it is relatively easy to forget love, tenderness and loyalty, in the 'scientific' study of human sexual behaviour).

But it should also be noted that no exclusively homosexual patterns have been reported for female mammals; homosexual contacts between sub-human females never appear to result in orgasm, and homosexual arousal is much less frequent among female sub-human primates. There is also good evidence that sexual learning and conditioning are much greater in males.

Animal observations have been given a greater impetus since the advent of ethology, with the introduction of such concepts as critical periods and imprinting. Animals have been 'made' homosexual although more recent experiments have suggested that with the onset of sexual maturity imprinted objects are abandoned in favour of more adequate sex partners. Also many experiments have not been reproducable by others; some behavioural patterns seem to be species-specific and other important variables have been neglected.

Again, how relevant this is to the development of human homosexuality has still to be established. Some have seen a possible analogy between the establishment of gender role in early childhood and imprinting. The complex interrelationship between gender and homosexuality is the subject of a chapter in a comprehensive survey on recent ideas on gender differences [44].

## ANTHROPOLOGICAL AND SOCIOLOGICAL ASPECTS

### Cross-cultural studies

There have been several surveys of sexual customs and behaviour among different races, cultural groups and primitive societies. In general, it has been shown that homosexuality is more often found in the more restrictive communities where sexual behaviour is subject to formal rules.

In the Yale survey [37] of 76 societies, in 64% homosexual activities were considered normal and socially acceptable for certain members of the community. Specific information on female homosexuality was obtained in only 17 societies. Even allowing for such obvious sources of error as both investigators and informants usually being male, lesbianism would still seem to be less frequent than male homosexuality. The Mohave Indians seem to be one of the few pre-literate groups for whom there are records of exclusively homosexual patterns of behaviour among females, and the only group in which such activity was openly sanctioned. A study of lesbianism in the New Zealand Maori [16] supports the importance of social and cultural aetiological factors.

Female homosexuality in classical times has been commented upon by various authors[16], but its (apparent) relative rarity may be due in part to the social position of women at the time and the male sex of most commentators. Fisher[17] noted the lowly position of women with no political or economic rights, minimal education and exclusion from cultural activities. The extent among females of the equivalent idealised 'platonic' relationships between males is not known for sure; if it did exist to any extent, it was either ignored or ridiculed. Licht[18] in his famous monograph on 'Sexual Life in Ancient Greece' devoted a whole chapter to lesbianism. Little seems to have been written about it in ancient Rome[19]. In ancient China[20] however, female homosexuality was quite common, viewed with tolerance and even encouraged in the women's quarters of the household.

## Modern Social Contributions

It will be obvious from work already quoted that there is a tremendous variation between different societies and indeed in the same society at different epochs, as to what kinds of sexual behaviour are considered normal, deviant, pathological or sinful and which need to be accepted, ignored, punished or treated.

Social factors play an important part in the development of sexually appropriate behaviour whether one adopts the social-learning hypothesis[21] or the cognitive-developmental one[22]. The former emphasises the fact that acquisition of sexual behaviour can be described by the same learning principles used to analyse any other aspect of behaviour — for example, conditioning, reward, punishment; the latter stresses the cognitive aspect in the active nature of the child's thought as he organises his role perceptions around his basic conceptions of his body and his world. The general characteristics of any minority group will also apply to lesbians as a group, whether organised or not, perhaps reinforced in the case of lesbians by the inequalities of a woman in a man's world. Such factors as loneliness, feelings of rejection, paranoid attitudes, over-sensitivity and hostility may all be seen with the additional problem of childlessness. The stereotype of the 'typical' lesbian may grow out of such social factors. The non-sexual factors in their adjustment are sometimes forgotten; as Simone de Beauvoir[23] has emphasised, women without men has a literal meaning as well — most lesbians must take responsibility for a whole range of activities and skills that ordinarily fall to the male in the family. The non-sexual factors have also been emphasised by other workers[24].

## Popular Movements

A modern phenomenon is the formation of homophile organisations to foster the special sub-culture of the 'gay' world, and to offer help, guidance and companionship to those in need. The first in England to be specifically devoted to the interests of the lesbian was formed in 1963 — at first called the Minorities Research Group, later changed to Trust — but now apparently defunct. They published a magazine called 'Arena Three'. A similar organisation in the U.S.A. is the Daughters of Bilitis, who publish 'The Ladder'.

It is difficult to keep up to date with these organisations as some disappear as rapidly as they are formed. Two of the currently best known ones campaigning for a better deal for all homosexuals are the Campaign for Homosexual Equality (CHE) and the Gay Liberation Front. There is now, in fact, a National Federation of Homophile Organisations with some 18 affiliated organisations representing a combined membership of more than 5000 men and women.

A further measure of society's attitude is the amount and quality of popular literature permitted and disseminated, as well as the treatment of lesbianism by the mass media. In the last few years there has been an ever-increasing popularisation and acceptance, amounting at times to commercial exploitation. It is of interest to note that unlike males there is virtually no erotic literature written by lesbians for other lesbians. The great mass of semi-pornographical literature which is allegedly intended for lesbians is in fact written by men for other men, not necessarily homosexual[25]. The ex-librarian of the Kinsey Institute has written a scholarly account, with 304 references, of the 'sex-variant' woman in poetry, literature and drama[26]. A further bibliography of literary references to lesbianism was compiled by Damon and Stuart[27]. An interesting biography[28] of Radclyffe Hall, the author of the famous lesbian novel 'The Well of Loneliness', gives the background history of both the author herself as well as the fate of the novel. On the 'literary fringe' and well illustrating the lifelong devotion of two women is the fascinating tale of the two 'Ladies of Llangollen[29].

**Institutional lesbianism**
The best paradigm here is prison, an institution much studied by sociologists. That lesbianism should be found with such frequency among prisoners is no surprise in view of the one-sex closed establishment and the often psychiatrically disturbed inmates. This may provide one of the situations for the development of so-called 'situational' or 'facultative' homosexuality which only lasts as long as the situation, in contrast to 'obligatory' homosexuality. One recent American monograph on prison life is mainly devoted to lesbianism and bears the general subtitle 'Sex and Social Structure'[30]. Another monograph[31] on a different American prison,

contained an interesting chapter on 'The Homosexual Alliance as a Marriage Unit' as well as a fascinating glossary of prison argot and a useful bibliography. Yet another American work[32], entirely devoted to the problems of homosexuality in prisons, has a chapter on lesbianism.

## Religious aspects

There is only one (ambiguous) reference to lesbianism in the Bible: Romans 1,26, 'For this cause God gave them up unto vile affections; for even their women did change the natural use into that which is against nature'. In a scholarly review on the relationship between Christianity and homosexuality and after pointing out the reference to St. Paul just quoted, Bailey[33] summarised the position: 'The Penitentials punish tribadism, including the use of the artificial phallus; councils at Paris in 1212 and at Rouen in 1214 prohibit nuns from sleeping together, and there is no doubt that the *concubitus ad non debitum sexum* which Aquinas includes among the species of *vitium contra naturam* relates to female no less than to male homosexual acts. But these, and a few other references of similar import . . . more or less exhaust the allusions to lesbianism in theology and ecclesiastical legislation prior to the Reformation'. Nevertheless, the Catholic codes explicitly condemn male and female homosexuality. But the Church's more recent conciliatory approach is exemplified by Pittenger's[34] account. The Talmud regarded lesbianism as a mere obscenity, and the only penalty incurred was that of disqualification from marriage to a priest. While some authors comment on the absence of Jewish lesbians others present series with predominantly Jewish patients[35]. In one controlled study[36] it was found that more lesbians had no nominal religion, but in the stated denominations lesbians were proportionately overrepresented in the Roman Catholic group and underrepresented in the Church of England. On the other hand, 16% had experienced some guilt feelings over their lesbianism and 19.5% some religious conflicts.

## The Law

English common law has evolved out of ecclesiastical law and hence is still permeated by the Judaeo-Christian tradition. As is well known, there have been few attempts to punish lesbianism while quite savage penalties have been the traditional lot of the male homosexual. The reasons for this are complex as can be seen from the discussion in Kinsey *et al.*[37]. According to these same authors there are specific statutes against female homosexuality only in Austria, Greece, Finland and Switzerland. Although a number of American statutes are so worded as to apply to either sex they have rarely been implemented in the case of lesbians.

It was rumoured that when further legislation was contemplated nobody dare raise the subject of lesbianism with Queen Victoria! But a little known attempt was made in 1921 under a private member's Criminal Law Amendment Bill to include acts of 'gross indecency between females'. This clause was actually passed by the House of Commons but subsequently rejected by the House of Lords[37]. The Sexual Offences Act, 1967 applies only to male homosexuals.

The apparent increase in female criminality has been partly blamed on the accelerated pace of emancipation. Some workers with special forensic experience think that lesbian girls are particularly violent.

## PSYCHOANALYTICAL THEORIES

The psychoanalytical literature on female psychology, sexuality and homosexuality is extremely complicated, diffuse and at times difficult to follow. No attempt can be made here to evaluate it in great detail. A word should be said at the outset about the psychoanalytical use of the term. 'sexual' which is not synonymous with genital but has a much wider connotation implying pleasure derived from various bodily zones.

Freud himself admitted on more than one occasion that female sexuality was a closed book but established an anti-feminist psychology which, with a vengeance, brought woman down from her Victorian pedestal. She was passive, vain, jealous, narcissistic, rigid, with a poor sense of justice, and weak in social interests, had less capacity for sublimation, was lacking in creativity and full of shame for her genital deficiency.

The pillars of the freudian case are biological bisexuality, the libido theory and infantile sexuality, the Oedipus complex, penis envy and the transfer of 'masculine' clitoral sexuality to feminine (passive) vaginal sexuality. Unfortunately little of this theoretical background has stood the test of time.

The oedipal phase of development takes place around age 3-5 years. In the female this was modified (it was Jung, in 1913, who suggested that it be called the Electra complex, but characteristically this was rejected by Freud) as the result of 2 complementary processes, the acceptance of castration and the later (oedipal) wish for a child from the father, being derived from an earlier fantasy of the mother possessing the desired penis, which was also equivalent to a child. It was only later and due to the influence of a series of female analysts that the importance in the girl of the extended pre-oedipal phase of attachment to the mother was conceded. One of the most brilliant reformulations of psychoanalytical theories in the light of modern scientific discoveries was also made by a woman[38].

Freud only published 3 cases of female homosexuality[39-41] but in none was there any physical expression and in only 1 was it consciously acknowledged, the other 2 being unconscious and latent. In his review of female sexuality, Freud[42] outlined three lines of development, one of which could lead to homosexuality. She acknowledges castration, her own inferiority and the superiority of the male but rebels, and from this divided attitude she can either:

1. Develop a general revulsion from sexuality; 2. Cling with defiant self-assertiveness to her threatened masculinity, this masculinity complex resulting in a manifest homosexual choice of object; 3. Take her father as the object and find her way to the normal feminine form of Oedipus complex.

In his final lecture Freud[43] highlighted the constitutional factor and that even after the apparently successful passage through the oedipal phase, disappointment with the father could lead to regression back to the earlier masculinity complex. The phases are well mimicked in the practices of some lesbians who play the parts of mother and baby with each other as often and as clearly as those of husband and wife. There is much to be said, though, for a view put forward by Clara Thompson[44] who summarised her notion of the changing concepts of homosexuality in psycho-analysis:

'In short, homosexuality is not a clinical entity, but a symptom with different meanings in different personality set-ups . . . overt homosexuality may express fear of the opposite sex, fear of adult responsibility, a need to defy authority, or an attempt to cope with hatred of or competitive attitudes to members of one's own sex; it may represent a flight from reality into absorption in body stimulation very similar to the auto-erotic activities of the schizophrenic, or it may be a symptom of destructiveness of oneself or others.'

## ADLER AND JUNG

Adler makes use of his concept of 'masculine protest' in that some women compensate for their sense of inferiority by being very aggressive and masculine. The competitiveness is not necessarily sexual and differs from Freud's penis envy in that they do not want to possess the male organ but envy men for the many advantages they have. This resentment often leads to the development of a preference for their own sex and what is sometimes seen in lesbians, an overt expression of hatred for all men. Other factors may also operate, such as the life style and fear of inadequacy in one's proper sex role[45]. But Adler seems to invoke the same mechanisms to explain all the neuroses, including homosexuality.

Jung postulated a type of psychological bisexuality in his animus-anima concept, the former being the unconscious masculine side of a woman and the latter being the feminine side of a man. Specific references to female homosexuality are found in two of his lectures, one being on the love problem of a student and the other on woman in Europe[46] . The unconscious masculinity (animus) can become overdeveloped and prevent the development of her true femininity. But he also spoke of the exchange of tender feelings and intimate thoughts and 'Generally they are high-spirited, intellectual, and rather masculine women who are seeking to maintain their superiority and to defend themselves against men. Their attitude towards men is therefore one of disconcerting self-assurance, with a trace of defiance. The effect on their character is to reinforce their masculine traits and to destroy their feminine charm. . . Normally the practice of homosexuality is not prejudicial to later heterosexual activity. Indeed the two can even exist side by side. I know a very intelligent woman who spent her whole life as a homosexual and then at 50 entered into a normal relationship with a man.'

## OTHER EARLY ENVIRONMENTAL THEORIES
### Parental Attitudes
Many sorts and combinations of parental relationships[47] have been postulated in the aetiology of homosexuality, some being variants of the oedipal situation and some not. One fairly consistent theme centres around the girl's difficulty with her father, which may involve hatred, rejection or fear.

To test some of these theories Bene[48] gave the Bene-Anthony family relations test to 37 lesbians and 80 married controls. She found the lesbians were more often hostile towards and afraid of their fathers and also felt more often that their fathers were weak and incompetent, compared with controls. Kenyon[36] compared 123 lesbians and controls with the following significant differences; more lesbians had poor relationships with their mothers (21% compared with 0.8%) and also with their fathers (30% compared with 8%); fewer thought their parents happily married (46%compared with 84%); and more had parents who had been separated or divorced (23% compared with 5%). Although fewer lesbians rated their fathers as the more dominant partner, this was not significant. Finally there was a positive psychiatric history in 15% of the mothers of the lesbians (4% controls), but there was no significant difference in the fathers, which was 6% and 7% respectively.

### Early Seduction
It has always been a popular theory that the girl is seduced into homosexuality by an older lesbian but the evidence for this belief is poorly

documented. Kenyon[36] found seduction to be a factor in only 8% of his series. It is also relevant to point out that very few lesbians desire very young sexual partners; in fact of those who expressed a preference 70% preferred a partner of the same age or older. This is yet another difference from the male; there is no female equivalent of the seducer of prepubertal boys or the paedophile.

## Sex preference of parents
Bene[48] adduced some evidence to suggest a relationship between the parents' wish for a son and the homosexuality of their daughter. Also Caprio[2] suggested that a girl who senses her father would have preferred a son may try to fulfil that role in order to win his affection. There was also a significant difference in Kenyon's series[36] in that 28% lesbians and 10% controls thought their parents would have preferred a boy to them, although 81% lesbians and 100% controls thought they were brought up and treated like a girl.

## Early sexual influences
Another popular notion is that an early traumatic experience with the opposite sex might have a lasting effect in provoking fear or hostility towards men. In fact there was a significant difference in that 41% of lesbians and 25% of controls said they had, as small girls, been disgusted or frightened by the sexual behaviour of a man[36]. It would seem that in a number of cases an important factor is fear of or inhibition in developing heterosexual drives, which may or may not be aided and abetted by the parents. Kaye *et al.*[38] found a good deal of evidence for a basic and fundamental heterosexual drive in the lesbians they studied, and felt that this drive had been blocked or interfered with by anxiety, inhibition, or threat. In confirmation of this Kenyon[36] found that 46% of the lesbians had at some time in their lives wanted to get married, 58% admitted sexual intercourse with a man and 20% had been pregnant. On current attitudes towards men, 32% of lesbians compared with 6% of controls said they felt indifferent or embarrassed in male company. Another common finding in the backgrounds of homosexuals is a puritanical upbringing as regards sexual matters, which may link up with inhibition of later sexual drive. In one investigation[36] only 22% of lesbians compared with 40% of controls considered that their family's attitude towards sex was a normal and accepting one.

## Measurement of sex differences and femininity
In recent years there has been an ever increasing volume of literature dealing with femininity in all its aspects; much of the impetus has come

from the Women's Liberation movement. The concept of femininity is largely a sociocultural one but, as outlined in Klein's[49] scholarly review, there are many different approaches. In her summary, she stated:

'The impression one gains from this variety of disciplines is definite on only one point, namely the existence of a concept of femininity as the embodiment of certain distinctive psychological traits. What, however, is considered essential to this concept depends to a large extent on personal bias and valuations and on the social-historical vantage point of the observer.'

She outlined three historical stages: 1. Woman is denied a soul and femininity is considered a kind of natural defectiveness; 2. Woman is thought to be in every respect the reverse of man; 3. The recognition of two factors: personality traits are by-products of immediate interests and incentives and develop in accordance with social role in a given culture, and the view that individual differences prevail over differences between whole groups. These ideas are very relevant to the construction of psychological tests purporting to measure masculinity-femininity.

A recently published symposium[50] was concerned with differences between the sexes in behaviour other than specifically sexual behaviour, with the focus on how sex differences in temperament and ability developed in young children. It also provided an annotated bibliography of some 500 articles of relevant research. Another review[5h] concentrated on homosexuality and divided testing devices into questionnaires distinguishing masculinity-femininity (MF), semantic tests, projective tests and tests measuring personality in developmental terms. The dynamic personality inventory[51] (DPI), is a projective test founded on psycho-analytical theory and consists of 325 items to which the subject gives his first reaction in terms of like or dislike.

One interesting study, using the DPI, was on masculinity-femininity as a possible factor underlying the personality responses of male and female art students. Among other findings was that female art students showed sex-role deviation over a wider range of scales than males, and assumed a greater number of opposite sex characteristics[52]. The DPI was also used to study lesbians[5f] but data were imcomplete, although those investigated scored higher on masculinity; it was also found that masculinity of interests in women was significantly correlated with intelligence and professional status. But the DPI itself has recently come in for a certain amount of criticism. The nature and origin of feeling feminine was investigated by Wright and Tuska[50] by studying 2650 middle class and university women on a self-rating semantic differential test. The 'feminine' women rated themselves more narcissistic, confident and comfortable and had recollections of an emotionally satisfying mother and a successful father. The 'masculine' women rated themselves more forceful, intelligent and responsive, and had recollections of an emotionally satisfying father but a frustrating unsympathetic mother.

One of the most popular tests both in the U.S.A. and here, is the MMPI (Minnesota multiphasic personality inventory) and there is an enormous literature on it. It has an Mf scale which seems to be based on rather dated stereotypes of an (American) ideal man and woman. In spite of its extensive usage, there are no published reports on a series of lesbians.

An ingenious attempt to investigate the psychoanalytical theory of latent homosexuality in women was made by Goldberg and Milstein[54]. They divided 25 college students into high-latent ($n = 10$) and low-latent ($N = 15$) homosexuals on the basis of their MF scores on the MMPI. They were then shown tachistoscopically 6 pictures chosen as being threatening or non-threatening on the basis of psychoanalytical theory. Compared with those not showing signs of latent homosexuality the group with marked latent homosexuality had longer latencies on each of the most highly threatening pictures and shorter ones on each of the non-threatening pictures. Results are accepted as supporting psychoanalytical theory concerning female homosexuality although scores were not statistically significant for group differences on any picture.

There are no known differences on Rorschach responses between men and women and up to 1951 there were no published studies on lesbians. Fromm and Elonen[55] mentioned 2 new Rorschach signs of homosexuality on the basis of an extensive study of one 22-year-old lesbian. Armon[56] used both figure-drawing tests and Rorschach tests with 30 overt lesbians and a matched heterosexual control group. None of the judges was able to make a 'blind' distinction of homosexual records significantly better than by chance. Failure to find many clear-cut differences suggested that homosexuality was not a clinical entity and was not necessarily associated with gross personality disturbance. Hopkins[57] in a carefully controlled study found three 'lesbian signs' in the Rorschach protocol: 1. Average of 3 or less responses per card. 2. Deprecated female response to Card VII. 3. Omission of Card VII from the top 3 'like' cards. An exhaustive and well documented survey[58] of the psychology of women provides a very useful source book of empirical data.

Maslow[59] investigated dominance-feeling or self-esteem by interviewing 139 female subjects, of whom 5 had had overt homosexual experience. The overall conclusion was that a finding of very high dominance-feeling in a woman pointed either to active homosexual episodes in her history or else conscious tendencies, desires or curiosity. He further considered that an interpretation of homosexual behaviour in terms of dominance, which was in close accord with previous work on primates, was a more valid and useful concept than a purely physiological one.

Terman and Miles[60] introduced a multiple choice test of 910 items in 7 parts and included data on 18 lesbians. They found the lesbians gave a unique profile with a contrast between a high degree of femininity in word association and an even higher masculinity in activity and occupational choice. In word response they were excessive in femininity of score, although in information and in their expression of emotional attitudes and in censure their MF scores did not differ from the norms. In activity choices they reached a peak otherwise characteristic of adolescents. Henry[61] used this test on 21 of his female 'sex variants' only 6 of whom were classed as homosexual, the others being called either bisexual or narcissistic. Nevertheless, he concluded that a mean score of $-25 \cdot 62$ (normal mean $= -70$) was in agreement with the proposition that sex-variant women were intermediate between male and female.

Hirschfeld[62] proposed the term 'third sex', a sexual intermediary stage between man and woman. Havelock Ellis[63] tried to collate the views of others but also advocated the congenital theory in spite of quoting case histories which showed the importance of psychological factors. It is of interest to note that his own wife was a lesbian and with true scientific detachment (although factually inaccurate in certain key areas) included her as 'Miss H' in an extended case history in his book, 'Studies in the Psychology of Sex'.

*Genetic and chromosomal studies*

Genetic theories have a long ancestry with the more extreme views now being mainly of historical interest as they are based on outmoded ideas such as a universal bisexuality, the theory of degeneracy and a congenital or hereditary basis for the male component in female homosexuals.

The theory that homosexuals were genotypical of the opposite sex was later proved to be false when nuclear sexing and more sophisticated chromosomal study became possible. Although a large series of lesbians has not been investigated, it has been conclusively shown in male homosexuals that there is no sex chromosomal abnormality. An extra X chromosome confers a double expectation of psychosis, but loss of an X has no association with mental illness, while neither has any consistent association with homosexuality. There is one published case[64] of a lesbian trans-sexual showing XO/XX mosaicism but the association could well be fortuitous.

That there might be an autosomal abnormality was suggested by Slater[65] who found that male homosexuals tended to be the last born of older mothers, rather like mongols. In his results the mean maternal age at birth for a group of 53 female homosexuals is given as 30.3 with a variance of 40.3. Also shown was a shift to the right in the birth order. But another study,[66] using more sophisticated statistical techniques (in 291 male homosexuals), found a significantly higher paternal age and a high maternal age secondary to this shift and concluded that this ruled out a causative biological factor related to maternal age. In his controlled study, Kenyon[36] found no significant differences between lesbians and controls for either mean maternal or paternal ages at the birth of the subjects. Gundlach and Riess[67] obtained data on 217 lesbians and controls and found proportionately more lesbians who were either 'only' or first born of 2 siblings and fewer lesbians who were the third child of 3 sibling families.

Family histories are difficult to compile for sexual deviations, and, in any case, even if hereditary factors were of supreme importance they are likely to be multifactorial. The strongest plank in the argument has been twin studies, and always quoted in this context are the phenomenally high but frequently criticised concordance rates found by Kallman in male homosexuals. The most recent review[68] of female cases presented a pair of 36-year-old identical twins concordant for overt and persistent homosexuality who also had a history of mutual homosexual contact with each other. The authors also gave a survey of the psychiatric literature on female monozygotic twins which concluded: 1. There were no clearly documented case reports of overt homosexuality in both members of a female monozygotic pair; 2. There were no clearly documented case reports of persistent overt homosexuality in even one member of a female monozygotic pair; and 3. There were no clearly documented case reports of mutual homosexual contact between female identical twins in childhood, adolescence or adulthood.

Unfortunately, they missed at least 2 papers. Parker[69] described a female monozygotic pair aged 39 discordant for homosexuality, and Koch[70] another female pair also discordant. There is no evidence that monozygotic twins *per se* are particularly prone to homosexuality[71].

## Hormones and Homosexuality

The fundamental hormonal difference between the sexes is not in the nature of the hormones themselves but in their manner of production, this being established very early in the female on a cyclical basis while there is more constant production in the male. Technological advances have been very important in the study of this field as more refined methods of assay and greater recognition of the many complex variables involved have left many earlier claims unsubstantiated. Clear-cut male and female sex hormones (androgens and oestrogens) were thought to exist and an earlier theory of homosexuality postulated imbalance between them. By 1954 one survey stated.[72] 'There is no convincing evidence that human homosexuality is dependent upon hormonal aberrations. The use of sex hormones in the treatment of homosexuality is mainly disappointing.'

Eleven years later another review[73] of the subject included details ofthe investigation of a 27-year-old lesbian but physical and endocrinological studies, including repeated urinary oestrogen assays, were all normal. The general conclusions were: 'We have never observed any correlation between the choice of sex object and the level of hormonal excretion. Oestrogenic substances administered to homosexual females do not alter the sexual drive or the choice of sex object . . . Androgenic substances, particularly testosterone, do not change the choice of sex object of either male or female homosexuals. They do however when employed in large amounts, tend to increase the sexual activity of females and hypogonadal males. These observations lead us to believe that steroid hormones of the oestrogenic and androgenic types have nothing to do with choice of sex object and therefore with the determination of homosexuality. . . It must be concluded that homosexuality is a purely psychological phenomenon neither dependent on a hormonal pattern for its production nor amenable to change by endocrine substances'. Using urinary measures only, Loraine *et al.*[74],[75] in 4 lesbians found testosterone and L.H. raised, oestrogens (especially oestrone) lowered and FSHand pregnanediol normal. However, numbers were small, 3 out of 4 had menstrual irregularities and normal values for the hormones assayed were extremely variable. But even if endocrine abnormalities are demonstrated they are not necessarily of primary importance.

However, with further technical advances the wheel is tending to come full circle again. The whole field of neuroendocrinology, with differential hypothalamic responses to minute doses of hormone and particularly the greater understanding of intrauterine endocrine sexual differentiation are now throwing some doubts on the former firmly negative conclusions. Much of the recent work was summarised in the monograph by Donovan and Bosch[76]. They pointed out that in behavioural development the individual androgens loomed large, this being especially shown by the sexual responses of female guinea-pigs born to mothers treated with testosterone during most of the gestation. The embryonic and foetal periods are periods of organisation or differentiation in the direction of masculinisation or feminisation. Adulthood when gonadal hormones are being secreted is a period of activation; neural tissues are the target organs and mating behaviour is brought to expression.

There is always a critical phase of development when hormonal influences exert their effects: 'In general terms it appears that sub-primate females suitably treated with androgens during sexual differentiation develop external genitalia closely resembling those of the normal male. As such pseudohermaphroditic females mature they show an exaggerated tendency to pursue and mount females in oestrus, and, like normal males, they manifest a marked resistance to the display of receptive behaviour when treated with female hormones during adult life.'

The human equivalent has also been investigated. Money and Ehrhardt[77] have stated: 'Girls affected by androgens *in utero* and diagnosed with either progestin induced hermaphroditism or hyper-adrenocortical hermaphroditism showed more of a developmental tendency towards tomboyish behaviour than girls with Turner's syndrome. The latter have no gonads and are not, therefore, exposed to foetal gonadal hormones. Tomboyishness appeared to be independent of lesbian inclination.' They also noted that 'one does not find a prevalence of homosexuality among a large number of older and long-untreated androgenital female hermaphrodites'.

All these more recent observations and experiments are very relevant to German claims, widely publicised in the lay press, that the cause of homosexuality had now been discovered and that it will soon be possible to prevent 'congenital homosexuality' by means of prenatal injections (The Times 13.3.69). This refers to Dörner's work[78] on rats. He showed that androgen treatment of newborn female rats during the critical organisa-tion phase of the hypothalamus, followed by androgens in adulthood, resulted in predominantly male sexual behaviour. This could be prevented by anti-androgens given during the critical hypothalamic phase. He concluded that the direction of sex instinct is completely determined — independently of genetic sex — by the androgen level during the critical hypothalamic differentiation period. In the normal development of mammals, testosterone represents the mediator between the sex chromo-somes and the neural differentiation of sexual behaviour.

This may well be so in rats but does not necessarily have direct relevance for the vastly more complicated human situation. A much more cautious and perceptive review[79] of hormonal influences in the female sexual response (although not mentioning Dörner's work) concluded: 'Current information about the role of hormones in human female sexuality indicates that it is a factor of importance for: 1. The early developmental organisation of the neural substructures subserving sexual behaviour; and 2. Activation of these neural substructures to adult functional levels at puberty. . .

There is also evidence that pharmacological agents which affect catecholamine metabolism may influence sexual behaviour. None of the studies reviewed is entirely satisfactory, being lacking on one or more of the important pieces of information necessary (knowledge of intrapsychic conflict about sex, systematic study of manifest behavioural data, manifest sexual data broadly representative of the population, appropriate placebo studies, and knowledge about variation in metabolic handling of hormonal agents, especially with regard to the synthetic agents). Suggestions are made for future research in this area.'

## Body Build

Few studies on the physique of female homosexuals have been carried out on sufficient numbers or with satisfactory techniques and controls. Henry and Galbraith[80] examined 105 lesbians and found they had fine adipose tissues, deficient fat on shoulders and abdomen, excess bodily and facial hair and underdevelopment of the breasts. In a further study[61] of 40 cases (14 homosexual, the remainder classified as either bisexual or narcissistic) it was found that half had an athletic habitus, a mean biacromial diameter of 368 mm and bi-iliac diameter of 229 mm with the conclusion: 'the sex variant tends to have broad shoulders and narrow hips, an immature form of skeletal development.'

Kenyon[81] in 123 lesbian subjects and heterosexual controls found lesbians were significantly heavier, with bigger breasts and waists; however they were less tall than controls and had slightly bigger hips. This may be better correlated with their higher neuroticism scores than their sexuality as was found in a study of male homosexuals[92]. In a further study[88] of a subgroup of 46 exclusively homosexual females (Kinsey 6) compared with 77 predominantly homosexual, the former were less heavy and smaller on all measurements, thus showing a tendency to revert to control (heterosexual) measurements, except in their height, which was even shorter. In another investigation[84] of 42 lesbian volunteers and controls it was found that the lesbians were significantly greater in stature and shoulder width, but the latter difference disappeared when the difference in sheer size was allowed for. A discriminant androgyny score showed a significant though minor difference in the masculine direction for the lesbians, but it was concluded that there was no such thing as a lesbian physique.

## Clinical psychiatric aspects

The precise findings on psychiatric associations depend a great deal on where and what type of population sample is being studied and patients may have little in common apart from homosexual behaviour. Lesbianism is compatible with mental health, happiness and as good a social adjustment as society will allow. On the other hand, it is naïve to suppose that in those who are seriously neurotic or otherwise psychiatrically disturbed it is simply a reaction to a hostile environment. In 123 non-patient lesbians 19.5% had a previous psychiatric history compared with 6% of controls; the commonest type of illness in lesbians was depression followed by an anxiety state. Nearly 5% had required inpatient treatment[36]. Their previous medical and surgical histories were no different from controls, but menstrual histories differed in two respects; 51% of lesbians resented menstruation as compared with 14% controls although fewer lesbians had symptoms of premenstrual tension[87]. In another series[85] of 25 patients referred with homosexual problems there was a high incidence (60%) of depressive symptoms. Presenting symptoms had been present, on average, for just over 4 years. There was a significant medical or surgical history in 48% and a previous psychiatric history in 44%.

### Personality disorder and immaturity

Lesbians would be considered abnormal personalities by Schneider as they certainly are in the statistical sense. In adults psychopathy is more likely to be associated with promiscuous bisexuality and to be only one facet of the more generalised personality disorder. The association with delinquency in general depends on which particular offenders are studied and where.

It is sometimes claimed that lesbians are simply immature personalities, without defining what is really implied. It could be said that the classical psychoanalytical theory and some derivatives of it point to a degree of immaturity in that an earlier developmental phase has either not been adequately passed through or, if it has, regression back to it has occurred.

Some of the difficulties were reviewed by Saul and Pulver[86] who pointed out the confusion between value-determined and developmental concepts of maturity. Some include heterosexual adjustment as part of the definition of maturity and indeed spell out the conditions in great detail.

Homosexual behaviour in the adolescent may be part of a 'crisis of identity', a passing phase, and should not in itself be looked upon as evidence of a fairly fixed sexual orientation. Schoolgirl 'crushes' are very common and may cause very little disturbance if sensibly handled.

A report[87] on rootless adolescent girls also highlighted their chaotic sexuality. 23 (60%) of the girls thought themselves to be lesbians, 8 had illegitimate children or were pregnant, and all except one had been on drugs. 'The most obvious characteristic is clearly that of sexual deviation. However, the worker recorded that their expression of sexuality was often so infantile in character that it hardly warranted the description of homosexuality. What perhaps requires explanation is the way in which these girls come to accept and act out the 'label' of sexual deviant.'

An American survey[88] of 25 lesbian girls aged from 12 to 17 showed nearly all of them to have personality problems (50% aggressive personalities) but a different home background from the commonly described close-binding father and dominant puritanical mother. The fathers were hostile, exploitative, detached and absent, and the mothers were mainly overburdened and inadequate. But before too many generalisations are made it should be noted that this adolescent group came from a deprived lower socio-economic area of New York and all presented significant behavioural problems in addition to their lesbianism.

It is of some interest to note, in retrospect, at what age adult lesbians thought they first became aware of homosexual feelings and had their first physical experience. In Kenyon's series[36,83] the mean ages were 16.1 ± 5.3 years and 21.4 ± 7.6 years, respectively; for the subgroup of exclusively homosexual individuals it was even earlier, being 14.6 ± 4.2 and 20.4 ± 6.3 years.

### Association with other sexual deviations

All sexual deviations, except homosexuality, sadomasochism and prostitution, are very uncommon in females. The most favoured methods of sexual gratification among lesbians are mutual masturbation, oral-genital contacts and tribadism. In spite of popular fantasy the use of a dildo (artificial penis) is rare. But sadomasochistic practices, for example the use of a whip, are not all that uncommon. Although Saghir and Robins[89] went into great detail on the sexual development and practices of their 57 non-patient lesbians they made no mention of other deviant sexual behaviour.

### Transvestism and trans-sexualism

Both these are very difficult to define, particularly the former in women. Few lesbians actually wear 'full drag', in other words, complete male attire. But apart from the actual clothes worn both the motivation and affective state while doing so are frequently ignored. According to Stoller[90] transvestism is found only in men. In Kenyon's series[36] all subjects were asked 'Do you like to dress in male-type clothing?' Only 2.4% of controls answered in the affirmative compared with 42% of lesbians. In another (unpublished) series all lesbians were asked, if it were possible, would they like to be changed into a man and 24% said they would.

Barahal[91] in a review of female transvestism and homosexuality, mentioned a number of cases historically documented, without discussing one of the most interesting transvestites of all; Joan of Arc (Kenyon[92], has recently reviewed Joan's life and health). One long case history is analysed — a lesbian of 22 who was married to a homosexual. He concluded: 'Female transvestism, therefore, is not a manifestation of homosexuality, but of a drive for masculinity. Qualitatively, it does not differ essentially from other similar motivated disturbances in the sphere of feminine psychology. The supposedly happily married woman who is eternally competing with her husband is the more subtle prototype of the same problem. Homosexuality has no meaning except as a multi-determined manifestation of neurosis.'

Schultz[93] asserted that true trans-sexualism occurred only in men but at the same time cited a female case in a footnote. Roth and Ball[94] on the other hand, stated that women seeking a surgical change of sex were invariably active and dominant partners in a homosexual relationship. Vogt[95]described 5 female cases of trans-sexualism who were all helped. after failure of psychiatric treatment, by testosterone, mastectomy, suppression of ovarian function and assistance in change of name. The quoted case histories show some of the difficulties in defining lesbianism: Case 1 'She strongly denied being a homosexual. She explained that when she approached girls, fondled themand kissed them, it was because she really was a male. Homosexuality was something she held in abhorrence. She could not stand homosexual girls; they had to be heterosexual and feel for her as a male. From a psychological point of view she considered herself heterosexual.'

Pauly[96] reviewed the literature on female trans-sexualism, described further cases and concluded the condition was 3—4 times less frequent than male trans-sexualism. She also doubted the existence of female transvestism . . . 'rather there are female trans-sexuals who wear men's clothes, not intermittently for their erotic value, but continuously as a manifestation of belonging to the male sex. They demonstrate less psychopathology, and their requests for help are not so demanding . . . Female trans-sexuals consider only normal, heterosexual women as sexual partners'. In another series[97] of 60 cases there were 14 females all of whom were rated entirely homosexual as opposed to 74% of the males, but this rating was made on the sole criterion of their sexual fantasies.

**Prostitution**
Lesbian prostitutes for other lesbians are virtually unknown but the allegation of frequent lesbian practices among ordinary prostitutes has often been made. Glover[98] in a psychoanalytical study gave unconscious homosexuality and unconscious antagonism to the male as the most important factors in the psychopathology of prostitution. Gibbens[99] agreed with this following an assessment of a group of juvenileprostitutes. A recent review[100] of the literature on delinquency in girls stated: 'A large part of the delinquencies of girls consists in sexually ill-regulated behaviour of a type not to demand social sanctions in the case of an adult'.

In a wide-ranging and scholarly study of prostitution, Henriques[101] surveyed some of the published accounts of the association of lesbianism and prostitution. But as Walker[102] astutely pointed out, with examples, the amount of psychopathology found in prostitutes depended not only on where the sample is selected but also on the sex of the investigator, with females tending to find less pathology than males. Those seen in prison are a very highly selected sample.

## Frigidity

One of the psychodynamic explanations frequently brought forward to explain sexual frigidity is latent homosexuality. Gluckman[103] writes: 'Frigidity in the female is frequently a defense against unconscious lesbian drives. The female homosexual can get by fairly well in marriage by passive acceptance of her status, especially if there are phantasies that are emotionally satisfying in association with coitus or auto-erotic expression.' Indeed one author[104]. gave this as one of the reasons for there being fewer female than male homosexuals.

One of the difficulties here and for other formulations based on it is the concept of latent homosexuality. Salzman[105] ended his review of the subject: 'the looseness of the term "latent homosexuality" and its abuse by professionals as well as laymen demands that the validity of the concept be definitely demonstrated or the term completely abandoned'.

In a study of overt lesbians[36] only 7% had been married, half unhappily and also half had a poor sexual adjustment; but 71 (58% of the sample) had had heterosexual intercourse at some time in their lives. These and controls were asked to rate, on a 5-point scale, their enjoyment of sexual intercourse, when 10% of lesbians compared with 45% of controls had experienced regular orgasm.

## Neurosis and Neuroticism

Clinically one of the most commonly associated disorders is a neurotic depressive reaction; this may be precipitated by conflicts over being a lesbian, a broken love affair, or some other environmental stress. This may reach the point of a suicidal attempt. The present author has encountered 3 cases of the recrudescence of lesbian impulses as part of a puerperal depression. In the American group[35] treated by psychoanalysis the primary reason for the lesbians entering analysis in the first place was because of depression and anxiety, although only 5 out of the 23 (22%) were diagnosed as psychoneurotic. Rarely is overt lesbianism part of a clear-cut phobic or compulsive neurosis.

Naturally psychiatric morbidity is to be expected in patient samples but what of those who were not psychiatric patients at the time of study? In the 57 subjects reported on by Saghir and Robins[99] one criterion for selection was no previous hospitalisation for psychiatric illness; yet nevertheless 30% had received psychotherapy in the past. In the Bilitis Study[166] 64%

had not found it difficult to adjust to their homosexuality, 83% considered themselves well-adjusted at the time of the survey, and less than 30% had had psychotherapy. Gundlach and Riess[107] in 226 lesbian subjects found that only 8% had ever been in a psychiatric hospital but 41% had at some time had psychotherapy. In these American studies due regard must be paid to sociocultural influences on such important variables as indications for and acceptance of psychotherapy and hospitalisation.

Using the Maudsley personality inventory (MPI) and the Cornell medical index (CMI) as tests of neuroticism, Kenyon[108] found that lesbians scored significantly higher on both tests compared with controls. If certain scores are accepted as dividing the neurotic from the non-neurotic then on the CMI between 42—44% lesbians scored above these (controls 16—21%). This admittedly crude measure at least highlights the fact that over half do not come into the neurotic range. It could also be argued that more neurotics would volunteer for a research project of this nature or even join an organisation (from which the subjects were recruited) but to try and offset any such trend, controls were also obtained in a similar way.

Another group[109] of 21 lesbian subjects (not patients) were given three tests: Cattell's 16 personality factor questionnaire (16 PF), the Eysenck personality inventory (EPI) and the dynamic personality inventory (DPI). On the EPI lesbians were slightly higher on Neuroticism and significantly lower on Extraversion. The 16PF profile showed few outstanding differences from the norms whilst scores on Cattell's 'neurotic profile' all fell within the average range apart from a slight increase in apprehensiveness. The DPI profile was more akin to the normal than the neurotic one, but as with 16 PF scores standard deviations tended to be larger, which supported the general conclusion that lesbians do not form a homogeneous group. Eisenger *et al.*[84] in their group of 42 lesbian volunteers, also found higher mean neuroticism and lower mean extraversion scores. Hopkins[110] also used the 16 PF and found similar trends; she concluded that the traditionally applied 'neurotic' label was not necessarily applicable. Siegelman[111] investigated lesbian volunteers and a control group using a Questionnaire compounded of several different scales which purportedly measured 12 dimensions related to mental health. Overall he found the homosexuals to be as well adjusted as the heterosexuals.

**Psychosis**

The psychoanalytical theory of psychosis is based on Freud's analysis of the Schreber case whose diagnosis was paranoia. Actually Freud never personally examined the patient and went entirely off his written memoirs. It is likely, too, that Schreber really suffered from paranoid-schizophrenia and recent evidence shows the important influence of his father's highly abnormal training[112] . At the heart of the Freudian theory is latent homosexuality and three basic mechanisms of denial, reaction formation and projection. The homosexuality is denied, the love is turned into hate and finally to persecution. If this formulation is correct then theoretically the supposed persecutor should be of the same sex as the patient. This and other deductions have been tested in various studies of schizophrenics. Klaf [113] compared 75 female paranoid schizophrenics with 100 non-psychotic controls and concluded that of four deduced consequences of Freud's hypothesis two were verified (delusions and hallucinations prominently sexual, and religious preoccupation), but 83% of those with sexual delusions were heterosexual and the largest proportion (61%) had male 'persecutors'. However it is not clear why non-psychotic instead of non-paranoid schizophrenics were used as controls. In another study[114] of 100 overt homosexual patients paranoid ideation was prominent in 18% of the females. It was concluded that an association between homosexuality and paranoid defences had been shown but 'this association need not be limited to repressed homosexuality'.

In his review of the previous literature Klaf ignored the work of Klein and Horwitz [115] who recorded earlier German views that homosexuality as a basis of paranoid delusions was not found in women with the same regularity as in men. Their own study concerned 40 females, selected at random from a group diagnosed as paranoid psychosis. But there were no controls and the whole account and comparison with the 40 male cases is anecdotal and difficult to follow. Their overall conclusion was that the paranoid mechanism could not be explained solely by homosexual conflict despite the convincing evidence of its pertinence in some cases.

Even when paranoid mechanisms are associated with lesbianism there may be other explanations. For instance, they already belong to a minority group which is regarded by many with a mixture of ridicule and suspicion. One recent psychological study[116] (on male homosexuals) was an attitudinal one to test the state of cognitive dissonance. One way of reducing this is to derogate somebody or something and this might explain a paranoid attitude. Differences were found but the attitudes of the homosexuals were not paranoid.

A special form of schizophrenia that has been associated with homosexuality is acute homosexual panic, sometimes called Kempf's disease. This was described by Glick[117] as 'an acute schizophrenic reaction, usually temporary in duration, displaying the usual schizophrenic symptoms accompanied by sensations of intense terror manifesting in wild excitement or catatonic paralysis. It is based on the patient's fear of loss of control of unconscious wishes to offer himself as a homosexual object which he feels will result in the most dire consequences.'

One of the earlier manifestations of schizophrenia may be difficulties over sexual orientation or overt homosexual behaviour coupled with (if especially enquired for) vague feelings of changing sex or other odd bodily sensations. As schizophrenia commonly starts in adolescence this may initially pose a difficult diagnostic problem. The author has recently seen two adolescent girls of schizoid personality and minor degrees of facial hirsutes, who felt attracted to other girls and wondered whether they were turning into lesbians.

There does seem to be a rather high proportion of psychotics — not all schizophrenics but manic-depressives as well — among the reported series of female homosexual patients. But Landis *et al.*[118] found no difference between patients (57% psychotic, half of these schizophrenic) and controls for homosexuality and concluded: 'One fact of significance to the present study does stand out, namely, there were no more homoerotic individuals among the abnormal group than among the normal. Seemingly homoeroticism acted as a factor or set of factors independent of mental disease.'

## Alcoholism and drug addiction

Yet another facet of the psychoanalytical concept of latent homsexuality is its connection with orality and the tendency to addiction. The position was summarised by Rosenfeld[119] : 'The majority of authors mention some perversion such as homosexuality, masochism or sadomasochism as appearing frequently in drug addicts and alcoholics, some stating specifically however that such perversions are only to be seen as part of the general picture. Thus Juliusburger stresses that homosexuality is only one of the factors in alcoholism. Glover believes that only very mild cases are due to unconscious homosexuality while Rado emphasises the fact that the homosexuality of the addict is only of secondary importance, developing under the influence of severe masochism'. These writers seem unaware of the only prospective study of the subject, the Cambridge-Somerville Survey, U.S.A. where a random sample of 500 boys was followed into adult life; 10% became alcoholic by their 30s. But it was found that those with the most marked feminine tendencies (the latent homosexuals) had the least chance of becoming alcoholic, which is contrary to psychoanalytical theory[120] .

## Organic cerebral pathology

Very occasionally homosexual behaviour is associated with cerebral organic pathology, for example following head injury or dementia. In many such cases it is looked upon as a release phenomenon in the already predisposed.

In discussing the relationship to brain damage Scott[121] suggested an alternative hypothesis to the 'release' one, namely experiences or altered perceptions caused by brain lesions may affect the early learning situation and so modify sexual behaviour. He described a lesbian patient of 20, who from childhood had suffered from temporal lobe epilepsy with vaginal aurae and suggested that sexual excitement followed by the unpleasant experience of a seizure may have effected strong conditioning with consequent disturbance of sexual orientation.

An association with temporal lobe pathology is of great theoretical interest as this part of the brain has been connected with sexual activity since the description of the Kluver-Bucy syndrome in monkeys produced by bilateral temporal lobectomy. Among the many manifestations of this syndrome was a degree of hypersexuality which could also include homosexual behaviour. Later more refined techniques showed the pyriform cortex to be the most important area concerned with sexual behaviour. Although the syndrome, as originally described, and particularly the hypersexuality, has not been seen in man, there is considerable evidence that the neural basis of sexual behaviour is closely connected with the limbic system.

**Prognosis and treatment**
Relatively few lesbians come for psychiatric treatment and fewer still with a direct request for a change in sexual orientation. In the author's investigation[36] of non-patient lesbians 19% had at some time had psychiatric treatment and 23% stated that they would like to be changed into a heterosexual.

The aims of treatment must be clarified; is it to help the patient to become a better adjusted lesbian, to reassure her that she is not in fact a lesbian, to manage an incidental crisis presenting as a depression, to treat other associated symptoms or syndromes, or attempt a change of orientation to heterosexuality? Much time and ink has been wasted on semantic quibbles as to whether or not homosexuals can be 'cured'. It is more a question of who can be helped and in what way. It is hoped that such well-meaning but naïve advice as 'find yourself a man', 'get married' or 'have a baby' is no longer meted out since the consequences can be disastrous to all concerned.

As there are so many different types it is difficult to give a general prognosis which has any real meaning apart from stating rather obvious factors such as the young, intelligent, well-motivated, non – psychopathic and those with some previous heterosexual interest, tend to have a much better prognosis. Priority for treatment should be given to those with a favourable prognosis, those tortured by guilt, depression or anxiety, the bisexuals, the married and those coming of their own volition asking for help.

Treatment methods, which can be used singly or in various combinations, can be divided into the psychotherapies, behaviour therapies and physical methods. Psychotherapy includes counselling, support, environmental manipulation and insight therapies. The National Council for Social Services has published a booklet [122] on counselling homosexuals male and female. After outlining what they consider to be in the medical/psychiatric and personal/social domains they state: 'The others (i.e., the vast majority) need neither doctor nor psychiatrist, but rather a range of services from simple information giving to skilled and lengthy work aimed at releasing them from the hell of alienation from themselves and their fellow men and women. It is these services that are collectively known as 'counselling services'. The booklet is marred, in this writer's opinion by its advocacy of 'befriending' which could end in 'full, unconditional mutual friendship'.

Counselling overlaps with what is more traditionally called supportive psychotherapy. This includes such things as explanation, reassurance and acceptance without moralising. Putting in touch with a suitable homophile organisation may also be indicated. In other cases it may be reassurance that she is not really a lesbian after all. This can occur, for instance, in an adolescent, with a crush on an older more sophisticated girl when there is confusion over admiration of that person's role and what they stand for and the person herself; an example of such a case history has already been published [7]. In some instances the girl's family may also be in need of counselling. Married homosexuals present special problems, particularly if it comes to divorce when the question of a lesbian's suitability to have custody of the children may be raised.

On the other hand, if it is a question of tipping the scales in a heterosexual direction longer term support may be necessary. Here encouragement will be needed in overcoming social and sexual fears of the opposite sex as well as controlling masturbation fantasies. Hypnosis had a vogue at one time but is dangerous in inexperienced hands and is useless if used in any such a blunderbuss fashion as 'suggesting' change of sexual orientation.

For more profound types of insight therapy, including psychoanalysis itself as well as short-term psychoanalytically orientated psychotherapy, psychiatric referral will usually be necessary. The latter can often be combined with physical methods of treatment, e.g. with drugs as in the series of 25 female patients referred to the author with homosexual problems [86]. Of these 19 were taken on for further treatment, 4 with psychotherapy only and the rest combined with other methods. Results showed that 63% were improved, that in 16% there was no change and that in 21% treatment was unsatisfactory.

Various reports have been published on the efficacy of psychoanalytical therapy but the experience of any one analyst is necessarily limited. An effort was made, along the lines of Bieber *et al.*[73] for male homosexuals to collate information from the Society of Medical Psychoanalysts in New York, which had over 150 members. Unfortunately the report[35] is extremely disappointing both in numbers, methodology and presentation. Only 24 cases and controls were included with a follow-up of 19. Only 7 had originally stated at the outset that they wanted their homosexuality to be cured and curiously one of the 19 followed up had been rated as exclusively heterosexual at the outset. Of the 9 patients rated exclusively homosexual at the beginning only 4 were still so at the time of the follow-up. The authors' final evaluation was 'We have indications for therapeutic optimism in the psychoanalytic treatment of homosexual women. We find, roughly, at least a 50% probability of significant improvement in women with this syndrome who present themselves for treatment and remain in it'.

In an elaborately planned and executed follow-up study[124] of 19 homosexuals treated by psychotherapy there was only 5 lesbians and results for these are extremely difficult to disentangle from the published tables. They found no significant differences in overall improvement between females and males; the mean duration of therapy was 1.7 years and at follow-up (mean interval 4.5 years) 47% were found to be 'apparently cured or much improved'. Ellis[104] maintained that lesbians were easier to treat than males because it was easier for them to relate to a male therapist, easier for them to consummate coitus, that prior to therapy more females had had heterosexual experiences, and that their therapeutic motivation was greater. He described, with appropriate statistical evaluation, the results of treating 28 male and 12 female homosexuals. However, 2 of the females were not overt homosexuals although obsessed with the thought that they might become so. His further assertion that lesbians were more emotionally disturbed than males is not self-evident from data quoted, as no length of history or clearly formulated diagnostic assessments are given. Eight of the lesbians had between 20 and 220 sessions of psychotherapy and by the end of therapy 4 (33%) were 'distinctly improved' and 8 (67%) 'considerably improved'.

The treatment currently in vogue is behavioural therapy. This has evolved with a great deal of unnecessarily bigoted rivalry with psycho-analysis, the behavioural therapists frequently perpetuating the same mistakes of which they accuse the analysts, for example reporting isolated cases, often atypical and under controlled conditions, and then making sweeping generalisations from the results. Happily there now seems a spirit of rapprochement exemplified by a recent paper[125] which explored the common ground between the 2 approaches in relation to the treatment of homosexuality. It was suggested that a combination of analytical and behavioural techniques may be more emotionally satisfying for the patient and encourage persistence.

Actually the published record of the use of behavioural therapy in the treatment of lesbianism is practically nonexistent. Feldman[126] reviewed the position of aversion therapy for sexual deviations up to that time in a long critical paper, but none of the studies surveyed was concerned with lesbians. He omitted the anecdotal but amusing account by Gebhard[127] of how a confirmed lesbian, during the course of a drunken party at the home of a predominantly homosexual male, underwent a process of 'conditioning', not unlike a desensitising technique, which led her to accept a full heterosexual life.

Among the 43 homosexual patients treated by aversion therapy by MacCulloch and Feldman[128] there were only 2 females. They were both aged 18, partners in a lesbian affair, had completed treatment and both 'were practising heterosexual intercourse with a variety of partners. Neither patient found this pleasurable, and both felt a considerable degree of contempt for their male partners'. Results at follow-up after 1 year were graded as 'very good improvement' in spite of the fact that one no longer practiced heterosexual intercourse. One further American case has been published[129] of a 22-year-old college student who in any case had a good prognosis and was only followed up for 2 months.

It now seems that any simple type of aversion therapy is bound to fail, unless desired heterosexual behaviour is also encouraged. This approach is probably better when there is less general anxiety but considerable anxiety over homosexuality. Systematic desensitisation is indicated for those with more obvious heterosexual anxiety. Some of the more common doubts over the whole approach have already been summarised[7], as well as theoretical speculations about possible mechanisms involved[130]. There are more technical problems in the female—e.g., how to measure sexual arousal. Accordingly the precise place for this type of therapy in the management of lesbianism has not yet been firmly established, but it is likely to be a limited one and will fail to initiate any heterosexual development in the absence of any such previous tendencies.

As there is no consistent relationship with any specific endocrine disorder, there are no indications for any routine hormonal therapy. Occasionally in males and exceptionally in females, help is required in damping down unacceptably strong sexual impulses. Recently introduced, and of great theoretical interest are the anti-androgens, e.g. cyproterone acetate. This is a synthetic progestogen with anti-gonadotrophic properties, which reduces plasma testosterone. It is closely related to one class of contraceptive pill, and some workers have particularly implicated those with strong progestogenic properties in causing both a diminution of libido and depression. One of the neuroleptic butyrophenone group of drugs, benperidol ('Anquil'), is claimed to have a specific antilibidinal action.

Other drugs may well be needed for the treatment of associated conditions, e.g. anxiety, depression and schizophrenia. Electroconvulsive therapy is only indicated if the patient is seriously depressed. When the lesbian behaviour is merely part and parcel of a more generalised personality disorder, it cannot be treated in isolation and the management becomes that of the personality disorder.

**References**
1. West, D.J. (1968). *Homosexuality*. 3rd edn. (London: Duckworth)
2. Caprio, F.S. (1957). *Female Homosexuality; a Psychodynamic Study of Lesbianism*. (London: Owen)
3. Cory, D.W. (1964). *The Lesbian in America*. (New York: Citadel)
4. Magee, B. (1966). *One in Twenty*. (London: Secker and Warburg)
5. Wolff, C. (1971). *Love Between Women*. (London: Duckworth)
6. Feldman, M.P. and MacCulloch, M.J. (1971). *Homosexual Behaviour: Therapy and Assessment*. (Oxford: Pergamon)
7. Kenyon, F.E. (1973). *Homosexuality*. A Family Doctor Booklet. (London: British Medical Association)
8. MacInnes, C. (1973). *Loving Them Both: A Study of Bisexuality and Bisexuals*. (London: Brian and O'Keefe)
9. Nicolson, N. (1973). *Portrait of a Marriage*. (London: Weidenfeld and Nicolson)
10. Kenyon, F.E. (1974. *Homosexuality in the Female in Contemporary Psychiatry: Reviews from the British Journal of Hospital Medicine, 1966-1972*. (T. Silverstone, and B. Barraclough, editors) (Kent: Headley Bros. Ltd.)
11. Kinsey, A.C., Pomeroy, W.B., Martin, C.E. and Gebhard, P.H. (1953). *Sexual Behaviour in the Human Female*. (Philadelphia: Saunders)
12. Churchill, W. (1967). *Homosexual Behaviour Among Males; a Cross-Cultural and Cross-Species Investigation*. (New York: Hawthorn Books)
13. Ford, C.S. and Beach, F.A. (1952). *Patterns of Sexual Behaviour*. (London: Eyre and Spottiswoode)
14. Bancroft, J. (1972). The relationship between gender identity and

sexual behaviour. Some clinical aspects, Chpt. 4 in *Gender Differences: Their Ontogeny and Significance.* (C. Ounsted and D.C. Taylor, editors) (London: Churchill Livingstone)

15. Gluckman, L.K. (1967). Lesbianism in the Maori. *Aust. N.Z. J. Psychiat.*, **1,** 98

16. Atkins, J. (1973). *Sex in Literature.* Vol. 2, (London: Calder and Boyars)

17. Fisher, S.H. (1965). *Sexual Inversion,* 165 (J. Marmor, editor) (New York: Basic Books)

18. Licht, H. (1932). *Sexual Life in Ancient Greece.* (London: Routledge and Kegan Paul)

19. Kiefer, O. (1934). *Sexual Life in Ancient Rome.* (London: Routledge and Kegan Paul)

20. Gulik, R.H. van (1961). *Sexual Life in Ancient China.* (Leiden: Brill)

21. Mischel, W. (1967). *The Development of Sex Differences* (E.E. Maccoby, editor) (London: Tavistock Publications)

22. Kohlberg, L. (1967). *The Development of Sex Differences* (E.E. Maccoby, editor) (London: Tavistock Publications)

23. Beauvoir, Simone, de (1953). *The Second Sex* (H.M. Parshley, translator and editor) (London: Jonathan Cape)

24. Simon, W. and Gagnon, J.H. (1967). *Sexual Deviance* (J.H. Gagnon and W. Simon, editors) (New York: Harper and Row)

25. Freeman, G. (1967). *The Undergrowth of Literature.* (London: Nelson)

26. Foster, J.H. (1958). *Sex Variant Women in Literature.* (London: Muller)

27. Damon, G. and Stuart, L. (1967). *The Lesbian in Literature: A Bibliography.* (California: The Daughters of Bilitis)

28. Brittain, V. (1968). *Radclyffe Hall: A Case of Obscenity.* (London: Femina Books)

29. Mavor, E. (1971). *The Ladies of Llangollen: A Study in Romantic Friendship.* (London: Michael Joseph)

30. Ward, D.A. and Kassebaum, G.G. (1965). *Women's Prison: Sex and Social Structure.* (London: Weidenfeld and Nicolson)

31. Giallombardo, R. (1966). *Society of Women; a Study of a Women's Prison.* (New York: Wiley)

32. Vedder, C.B. and King, P.G. (1967). *Problems of Homosexuality in Corrections.* (Illinois: Thomas)

33. Bailey, D.S. (1955). *Homosexuality and the Western Christian Tradition.* (London: Longmans)

34. Pittenger, N. (1970). *Time for Consent: A Christian's Approach to Homosexuality.* (London: S.C.M. Press Ltd.)

35. Kaye, H.E., Berl, S., Clare, J., Eleston, M.R., Gershwin, B.S., Gershwin, P., Kogan, L.S., Torda, C. and Wilbur, C.B. (1967). Homosexuality in women. *Arch. gen. Psychiat.*, **17**, 626
36. Kenyon, F.E. (1968). Studies in female homosexuality IV & V. *Brit. J. Psychiat.* **114**, 1337 and 1343
37. Hyde, H.M. (1970). *The Other Love: An Historical and Contemporary Survey of Homosexuality in Britain.* (London: Heinemann)
38. Sherfey, M.J. (1966). The evolution and nature of female sexuality in relation to psychoanalytic theory. *J. Amer. Psychoanal. Assoc.*, **14**, 28
39. Freud, S. (1905). *The Standard Edition of the Complete Psychological Works.* vol. VII, 7 (London: Hogarth Press (1953)
40. Freud, S. (1914-16) *ibid.* vol. XIV (1957) p. 147
41. Freud, S. (1920) *ibid.* vol. XVIII (1955) p. 147
42. Freud, S. (1927-31) *ibid.* vol. XXI (1961) p. 225
43. Freud, S. (1932-36) *ibid.* vol. XXII (1964) p. 7
44. Thompson, C. (1947). Changing concepts of homosexuality in psychoanalysis. *Psychiatry,* **10**, 183
45. Adler, A. (1917). The homosexual problem. *Alienist, Neurol.,* **38**, 268
46. Jung, C.G. (1964). *The Collected Works.* vol. 10, 97, 113, (London: Routledge and Kegan Paul)
47. Robertson, G. (1972). Parent-child relationships and homosexuality. *Brit. J. Psychiat.,* **121**, 525
48. Bene, E. (1965). On the genesis of female homosexuality. *Brit. J. Psychiat.,* **111**, 815
49. Klein, V. (1946). *The Feminine Character; History of an Ideology.* (London: Kegan Paul, Trench and Trubner)
50. Maccoby, E.E. (1967). Editor, *The Development of Sex Differences.* (London: Tavistock Publications)
51. Grygier, T.G. (1957). Psychometric aspects of homosexuality. *J. ment. Sci.* **103**, 514
52. Stringer, P. (1967). Masculinity-femininity as a possible factor underlying the personality responses of male and female art students. *Brit. J. soc. clin. Psychol.,* **6**, 186
53. Wright, B. and Tuska, S. (1966). The nature and origin of feeling feminine. *Brit. J. soc. clin. Psychol.,* **5**, 140
54. Goldberg, P.A. and Milstein, J.T. (1965). Perceptual investigation of psychoanalytic theory concerning latent homosexuality in women. *Percept. Motor Skills,* **21**, 645
55. Fromm, E.O. and Elonen, A.S. (1951). The use of projective

techniques in the study of a case of female homosexuality. *J. Project. Techn.,* **15,** 185

56. Armon, V. (1960). Some personality variables in overt female homosexuality. *J. project. Techn.,* **24,** 292
57. Hopkins, J.H. (1970). Lesbian signs on the Rorschach. *Brit. J. Proj. Psychol.,* **15,** 7
58. Sherman, J.A. (1971). *On the Psychology of Women : A Survey of Empirical Studies.* (Illinois: Charles C. Thomas)
59. Maslow, A.H. (1942). Self-esteem (dominance-feeling) and sexuality in women. *J. soc. Psychol.,* **16,** 259
60. Terman, L.M. and Miles, C.C. (1936). *Sex and Personality: Studies in Masculinity and Feminity.* (New York: McGraw-Hill)
61. Henry, G.W. (1951). *Sex Variants; a Study of Homosexual Patterns.* (London: Cassell)
62. Hirschfeld, M. (1952). *Sexual Anomalies and Perversions.* (N. Haire, editor) (London: Encyclopaedic Press)
63. Ellis, Havelock (1936). *Studies in the Psychology of Sex.* vol. II, part II Sexual Inversion. 3rd edn. (New York: Random House)
64. James, S., Orwin, A. and Davies, D.W. (1972). Sex chromosome abnormality in a patient with transsexualism. *Brit. med. J.,* **3,** 29
65. Slater, E. (1962). Birth order and maternal age of homosexuals. *Lancet,* **i,** 69
66. Abe, K. and Moran, P.A.P. (1969). Parental age of homosexuals. *Brit. J. Psychiat.,* **115,** 313
67. Gundlach, R.H. and Riess, B.F. (1967). Birth order and sex of siblings in a sample of lesbians and non-lesbians. *Psychol.Rep.,* **20,** 61
68. Pardes, H., Steinberg, J. and Simons, R.C. (1967). A rare case of overt and mutual homosexuality in female identical twins. *Psychiat. Quart.,* **41,** 108
69. Parker, N. (1964). Homosexuality in twins: a report on three discordant pairs. *Brit. J. Psychiat.,* **110,** 489
70. Koch, G. (1965). Die Bedeutung geustischer Faktoren für das mensehliche Verhalten. *Arztl. Prax.,* **17,** 839
71. Heston, L.L. and Shields, J. (1968). Homosexuality in twins: a family study and a registry study. *Arch. gen. Psychiat.,* **18,** 149
72. Swyer, G.I.M. (1954). Homosexuality: the endocrine aspects. *Practitioner,* **172,** 374
73. Perloff, W.H. (1965). *Sexual Inversion,* 44 (J. Marmor, editor) (New York: Basic Books)
74. Loraine, J.A., Ismail, A.A.A., Adamopoulos, D.A. and Dove, G.A.

(1970). Endocrine function in male and female homosexuals. *Brit. med. J., 4, 406*

75. Loraine, J.A. Adamopoulos, D.A., Kirkham, K.E., Ismail, A.A.A. and Dove, G.A. (1971). Patterns of hormonal excretion in male and female homosexuals. *Nature, 234, 552*

76. Donovan, B.T., and Bosch, J.J., van der Werff Ten (1965). *Physiology of Puberty.* (London: Arnold)

77. Money, J. and Ehrhardt, A.A. (1968). *Endocrinology and Human Behaviour, 32* (R.P.Michael, editor) (London: Oxford University Press)

78. Dörner, G. (1968). Hormonal induction and prevention of female homosexuality. *J. Endocrinol., 42, 163*

79. Kane, F.J., Lipton, M.A. and Ewing, J.A. (1969). Hormonal influences in female sex response. *Arch. gen. Psychiat., 20, 202*

80. Henry, G.W. and Galbraith, H.M. (1934). Constitutional factors in homosexuality. *Amer. J. Psychiat., 13, 1249*

81. Kenyon, F.E. (1968). Physique and physical health of female homosexuals. *J. Neurol. Neurosurg. Psychiat., 31, 487*

82. Coppen, A.J. (1959). Body-build of male homosexuals. *Brit. med. J., 2, 1443*

83. Kenyon, F.E. (1968). Studies in female homosexuality, VI—the exclusively homosexual group. *Acta psychiat. scand., 44, 224*

84. Eisinger, A.J., Huntsman, R.G., Lord, J., Merry, J., Polani, P., Tanner, J.M., Whitehouse, R.H. and Griffiths, P.D. (1972). Female homosexuality. *Nature, 238, 106*

85. Kenyon, F.E., (1972). Some characteristics of female patients referred with homosexual problems. In *Psychosomatic Medicine in Obstetrics and Gynaecology.* p. 379 (N. Morris, editor) (Basel: Karger)

86. Saul, L.J. and Pulver, S.E. (1965). The concept of emotional maturity. *Comprehens. Psychiat., 6, 6*

87. Timms, N. (1968). *Rootless in the City.* National Council of Social Service, London.

88. Kremer, M.W. and Rifkin, A.A. (1969). The early development of homosexuality: a study of adolescent lesbians. *Amer. J. Psychiat., 126, 91*

89. Saghir, M.T. and Robins, E. (1969). Homosexuality—1. Sexual behaviour of the female homosexual. *Arch. gen. Psychiat., 20, 192*

90. Stoller, R.J. (1969). *Sex and Gender.* (London: Hogarth Press)

91. Barahal, H.S. (1953). Female transvestism and homosexuality. *Psychiat. Quart., 27, 390*

92. Kenyon, F.E. (1971). The life and health of Joan of Arc. *Practitioner,* **207,** 835

93. Schultz, J.H. (1963). *Intersexuality* (C. Overzier, editor) (London: Academic Press)

94. Roth, M. and Ball, J.R.B. (1964). *Intersexuality in Vertebrates including Man.* (C.N. Armstrong and A.J. Marshall, editors) (London: Academic Press)

95. Vogt, J.H. (1968). Five cases of transsexualism in females. *Acta psychiat. scand.,* **44,** 62

96. Pauly, I.B. (1969). Adult Manifestations of Female Trans-sexualism. *In Trans-sexualism and Sex Reassignment.* (R. Green and J. Money, editors) (Baltimore: The John Hopkins Press)

97. Hoenig, J., Kenna, J. and Youd, A. (1970). Social and economic aspects of transsexualism. *Brit. J. Psychiat.,* **117,** 163

98. Glover, E. (1943). *The Psycho-Pathology of Prostitution.* Institute for the Study and Treatment of Delinquency, London.

99. Gibbens, T.C.N. (1957). Juvenile prostitution. *Brit. J. Delinq.,* **8,** 3

100. Cowie, J., Cowie, V. and Slater, E. (1968). *Delinquency in Girls.* (London: Heinemann)

101. Henriques, F. (1962, 1963, 1968). *Prostitution and Society: A Survey.* 3 vols. (London: Macgibbon and Kee)

102. Walker, N. (1965). *Crime and Punishment in Britain,* 295 (Edinburgh: University Press)

103. Gluckman, L.K. (1966). Lesbianism—a clinical approach. *N.Z. med. J.,* **65,** 443

104. Ellis, A. (1956). The effectiveness of psychotherapy with individuals who have severe homosexual problems. *J. cons. Psychol.,* **20,** 191

105. Salzman, L. (1965). *Sexual Inversion,* 234 (J. Marmor, editor) (New York: Basic Books)

106. Bilitis Study (1959). One Institute Quarterly: Homophile Studies, **11,** 113

107. Gundlach, R.H. and Riess, B.F. (1968). *New Directions in Mental Health,* vol. I, (B.F. Riess, editor) (New York: Grune and Stratton)

108. Kenyon, F.E. (1968). Studies in female homosexuality—psychological test results. *J. cons. clin. Psychol.,* **32,** 510

109. Kenyon, F.E. (1971). Personality neuroticism and female homosexuality. *Proc. Vth World Congr. Psychiat.*

110. Hopkins, J.H. (1969). The lesbian personality. *Brit. J. Psychiat.,* **115,** 1433

111. Siegelman, M. (1972). Adjustment of homosexual and heterosexual women. *Brit. J. Psychiat.,* **120,** 477

112. Schatzman, M. (1973). *Soul Murder: Persecution in the Family.* (London: Allen Lane)

113. Klaf, F.S. (1961). Female homosexuality and paranoid schizophrenia: a survey of seventy-five cases and control. *Arch. gen. Psychiat.,* **4,** 84

114. Klaf, F.S. (1961). Evidence of paranoid ideation in overt homosexuals. *J. soc. Ther.,* **7,** 48

115. Klein, H.R. and Horwitz, W.A. (1949). Psychosexual factors in the paranoid phenomena. *Amer. J. Psychiat.,* **105,** 697

116. Kendrick, D.C. and Clarke, R.V.G. (1967). Attitudinal differences between heterosexually and homosexually oriented males. *Brit. J. Psychiat.,* **113,** 95

117. Glick, B.S. (1959). Homosexual panic: clinical and theoretical considerations. *J. nerv. ment. Dis.,* **129,** 20

118. Landis, C., Landis, A.T. Bolles, M.M., Metzger, H.F. Pitts, M.W., D'Asopo, D.A., Moloy, H.D., Kleegman, S.J. and Dickinson, R.L. (1940). *Sex in Development.* (New York: Hoeber)

119. Rosenfeld, H.A. (1965). *Psychotic States: A Psycho-Analytical Approach.* (London: Hogarth Press)

120. McCord, W. and McCord, J. (1960). *Origins of Alcoholism.* (London: Tavistock Publications)

121. Scott, P. (1964). *The Pathology and Treatment of Sexual Deviation,* 87 (I. Rosen, editor) (London: Oxford University Press)

122. Righton, P. (1973). *Counselling Homosexuals: A Study of Personal Needs and Public Attitudes.* (London: Bedford Square Press)

123. Bieber, I., Dain, H.J. Dince, P.R., Drellid, M.G., Grand, H.G., Gunlach, R.H., Kremer, M.W., Rifkin, A.H., Wilbur, C.B. and Bieber, T.B. (1962). *Homosexuality: a Psychoanalytic Study.* (New York: Basic Books)

124. Mayerson, P. and Lief, H.I. (1965). *Sexual Inversion,* 302 (J. Marmor, editor) (London: Basic Books)

125. Fox, B. and Di Scipio, W.J. (1968). An exploratory study in the treatment of homosexuality by combining principles from psychoanalytical theory and conditioning: theoretical and methodological considerations. *Brit. J. med. Psychol.,* **41,** 273

126. Feldman, M.P. (1966). Aversion therapy for sexual deviations: a critical review. *Psychol. Bull.,* **65,** 65

127. Gebhard, P.H. (1965). *Sex and Behaviour* (F.A. Beach, editor) (New York: Wiley)

128. MacCulloch, M.J. and Feldman, M.P. (1967). Aversion therapy in management of 43 homosexuals. *Brit. med. J.,* **2,** 594

129. Blitch, J.W. and Haynes, S.N. (1972). Multiple behavioural

techniques in a case of female homosexuality. *J. Behav. Ther. Exp. Psychiat.,* **3,** 319

130. McConaghy, N. and Barr, F.F. (1973). Classical, avoidance & backward conditioning treatments of homosexuality. *Brit. J. Psychiat.,* **122,** 151

# 4

# A Case Study: Homosexuality in the Netherlands

## R.W. Ramsay, P.M. Heringa and I. Boorsma

Why does this book include a chapter on homosexuality in the Netherlands? It is generally accepted that Holland is one of the few countries in the Western world in which homosexuals as a group are not victimised. Amsterdam is considered to be one of the 'gay' capitals of the world. Is it indeed true that Holland does not discriminate against homosexuals, and if that is so, how has this state of affairs come about? What happens when a country has no laws against homosexuality acts?

These topics will be discussed in this Chapter. Most people consider homosexuality to be a problem (hence this book). However, it depends on one's viewpoint what the problems are and what needs to be done about them. The jurist, the minister of religion, the psychiatrist, the police inspector, the employer, the parent of the homosexual, the homosexual himself, all see 'the problem' from different viewpoints and demand different action. In looking at homosexuality in Holland we shall briefly investigate the situation existing just over a decade ago, and then discuss recent developments, in the hope that we may answer some questions as to what happens when certain changes are made. In this way we hope to clear up some misconceptions, fears and biases, so that further progress can be made.

## JUDICIAL ASPECTS

Until the second half of the 16th century, when the Netherlands became an independent nation, the picture was more or less the same as that in the rest of Europe; accordingly nothing need to be said of this period. Between 1600 and 1730 probably little action was taken against homosexuals, and those that were arrested must have been tried behind closed doors. In 1730 there was a sudden outburst of activity against homosexuals which lasted for 2 years and in which 250 people were sent to trial and 57 were executed. Some of these were probably not homosexuals but political opponents of certain powerful persons; one man, Rudolf de Mepsche, was responsible for the torture and death of 22 of those arrested. In the years 1764—65 and in 1796—98 there were again upheavals. Some people argue that these corresponded with periods of socio—economic and political unrest, and were a result of the public working off their emotions against a minority group'.

After the annexation of the Netherlands by France, the Code Pénal of Napoleon was brought into effect in 1811; homosexual acts were no longer punishable. This remained in effect until 1813 when the Netherlands once more regained its independence. In 1886 a law was introduced making sexual acts with young people below the age of 16 punishable, and there was no distinction made between heterosexual and homosexual acts. There was thus complete legal equality. In 1911 this absence of discrimination was done away with. An article 248bis was proposed by a conservative Roman Catholic Minister of Justice, and passed in Parliament, against strong opposition. This made it punishable for a person over the age of 21 to have homosexual contact with someone under 21 years of age, while the legal age for heterosexual acts remained as before, namely 16 years. Homosexual acts between consenting adults over 21 remained legal. There was much criticism of article 248bis, mainly on the grounds that it was discriminatory, fostered blackmail, and that it could have adverse effects on young homosexuals: they would not be free to develop themselves, and situations could arise where a relationship between two young people could suddenly for a time become illegal when one partner reached the age of 21 and the other was still under age. The reasoning behind the instigation of this law was the fear that young persons in their teens could be seduced into a homosexual way of life.

During the Second World War when the Netherlands was occupied by German forces the Germans imposed their laws on homosexuality. During the occupation a large but unknown number of homosexuals were arrested and sent off to concentration camps; like the Jews, they had to wear a star, a lilac one in their case, and many were exterminated. The fact that more were not arrested was due to a number of reasons. Homosexuality is not like race, and can easily be hidden when necessary. During the war the minority who could not hide their homosexuality went underground to a large extent. Further, the Dutch police appeared to help in thwarting the efforts of the Germans in rounding up homosexuals. It is known (see later) that lists of homosexuals were kept by the police, but the German Commissioner-General for Welfare and Justice in 1941 complained that the results of attempts to activate the Dutch police into making large-scale arrests had been practically nil. Of course, after liberation, the previously existing laws were reinstated.

## THE CHURCHES

In the Netherlands at present one third of the population nominally is Roman Catholic, one third Protestant, and one third non-believers. The percentage of official non-believers is the highest in the Western world.

Of the Protestant churches, the most important aspect is the plurality of denominations. There are more than a dozen of importance, from Baptists who are tolerant through various gradations of Calvinisim to extremely orthodox fundamentalists. For more than a century now all denominations have had equal rights, and they have made use of this by obtaining their own schools, universities, hospitals, mental health clinics, etc. They have been establishing themselves in all walks of life, and for a long time now the religious-based political parties have held the balance of power in government. The denominational broadcasting organisations have until recently occupied more than half of the time on radio and television. The plurality of churches has remained a feature of Dutch life but there has been a shift from sectarian to oecumenical positions within the churches.

The changes in attitude towards homosexuality that have recently taken place are the more suprising because much of the taboo against homo-sexuality has been from a religious point of view, and the change of climate in the Dutch Reformed churches (the fundamentalist Calvinists) has been relatively larger and more rapid.

In the pre-war period the Roman Catholic church was strongly opposed to homosexuality, no doubt in the first place because of its being 'against nature'. An extreme but by no means atypical quotation is from a Roman Catholic monthly in 1935: 'If only this (i.e., the social wrongs of those days) extirpates the homosexuals then we will not have suffered it for nothing.' After this, the outraged men and fathers are urged to build concentration camps for authors of books that put homosexuality in a positive light, and also for those who review them favourably[2].

In 1950 the official Roman Catholic education centre proposed once again that the Netherlands adopt the English and German example of making homosexuality illegal. Later in the 1950's a study group was formed to look into the pastoral problems associated with homosexuality, and in 1958 a bureau was set up in Amsterdam to advise homosexuals on their problems.

## THE MEDICAL PROFESSION

The influence of Freud has been strong in labelling homosexuality as a neurosis, and in principle undesirable. Even if there is no legal sanction against being homosexual, psychiatrists and psychologists have exerted pressure against full acceptance of homosexuality in this country, as elsewhere. Until quite recently, seeking psychiatric help was actively discouraged from within homosexual circles.

In 1939 the Roman Catholic medical association held a congress on homosexuality and the chairman of the association, also director of a large mental hospital, in his opening address strongly attacked the increasing tolerance for homosexuality that was evolving. 'From more or less scientifically based opinions and theories about the nature, origins and spread of homosexuality, people have drawn misleading and destructive conclusions, mainly as a result of reckless and more and more impudent propaganda, and are busy poisoning the moral conscience of the population, with the effect that it is not an exaggeration to say that *the vice of homosexuality is increasing hand over fist*'. Further, 'older homosexuals are inclined to assault minors, and this is happening more and more frequently'. He then went on to give figures about the number of homosexuals registered in the files of the Amsterdam Vice Squad, 1.69% of the male population over 18 years, which then should work out to probably 3.5% in all. There was much more in a similar vein in his opening address but this brief excerpt gives the tenor of the argument[3].

Although the medical profession is as a whole conservative, not all of them were as bad as this. Of course, according to many stories, the advice of GPs to: 'just try it with a girl', or: 'it'll pass' prevailed till fairly recently. In the 1950's and 1960's psychiatric opinion was modified, and although the Freudian influence was and is still a force in this country, people such as Prof. van Emde Boas and Prof. Trimbos were regarding the problem in a broader social context, and there were study days and lectures organised for people working in the national health field and for ministers of religion.

## EARLY ORGANISATION

Around the turn of the century, there were the first signs of people occupying themselves, from a variety of motives, with the phenomenon of sexual inversion. Magnus Hirschfeld and others were active in Germany, and this filtered through into the Netherlands. In 1904 Dr. Aletrino wrote an extensive introduction for the Dutch version of Hirschfeld's book on homosexuality, and around this time the first brochures began to appear. It is possible that this scientific interest in Germany was too much too soon for the Netherlands because although there were reactions, but hardly what one would call a response from the public.

The most important figure in these times was Jhr. Mr. J.A. Schorer, a lawyer, who was open about his homosexuality. He actively opposed the passing of article 248bis in Parliament, but to no avail. He set up the Dutch counterpart of the Berlin-based W.H.K. (Scientific Humanitarian Committee), the aims of which were to disseminate unbiased information on homosexuality. In the 1917 annual report of the W.H.K. Schorer stated that he had sent a number of works dealing with homosexuality to the library of the Tweede Kamer (the House of Commons), with the idea that the members could do with some information on the subject. It was decided by the Tweede Kamer not to accept the gift. Schorer's reply to this decision is scorching[3].

At about the same time, the librarian of the University of Amsterdam refused to lend out scientific works dealing with homosexuality. Schorer soon changed this. He was active whenever he felt that there was something that should and could be done; due to his social standing (he belonged to the nobility) and financial independence he was able to continue his activities.

In the late 1930's there were the first signs of homosexuals organising themselves, chiefly amongst young socialists. A book, containing accounts of the homosexual way of life that could create understanding among the 'outsiders', was published in 1939: 'De Homosexueelen', compiled by Benno Stokvis[4]. The German invasion the following year cut short further progress: the journal 'Levensrecht' ('Right to Live') had to be discontinued after three issues, while the W.H.K. was also disbanded.

## THE COC

After the "underground" years of German occupation, in 1946 a society for homosexuals was set up in Amsterdam under the pseudonym of 'The Shakespeare Club', two years later the name was changed to Cultuur-en Ontspanningscentrum, COC (cultural and recreation centre). This anonymity, and the fact that everyone used only first names, is indicative of the position of the homosexual at that time: in fact, for a time their meetings were attended by plain-clothes policemen from the Vice Squad. The club was in the first instance meant as a place where members could come together, and the accent was on the forming of a group for protection and the exchange of information. Branches in other cities gradually appeared during the 1950's and 1960's. There are now ten of them.

The activities were inner-directed as there was little support from outside. Due mainly to the general change in public opinion, the churches, the medical profession, and other important influential bodies, the tendency in the 1950's and 1960's was towards more openness, and in 1964 the association was officially named the Nederlandse Vereniging van Homofielen COC (the Netherlands association of homophiles COC). At this stage a request for official recognition, in the form of the Royal Assent (Koninklijke goedkeuring), was refused. In the 1960's the association gave out more and more information about its activities to various public organisations, and members of the committee dared to use their own names in radio and television programmes.

## THE AWAKENING OF PUBLIC AWARENESS

The picture for the 1960's can best be given by describing the experiences of Ds. Klamer, the oecumenical radio pastor for the Netherlands[5]. Until the beginning of 1959 he was a minister of religion in a large town in the south of the country, and according to him, he never came across any problems of homosexuality. He was then appointed to his present position, and within a short space of time, was daily confronted with homosexuals who were in trouble — lonely, confused, and rejected by their church and family. He attributes this sudden upsurge of contacts to the fact that as a radio minister, he was not ostensibly attached to any one particular church. Because of this awareness of so many people in trouble, he prayed for homosexuals in one of his Sunday broadcasts. This brought an avalanche of responses by telephone and letter. There were grateful homosexuals; there were confused homosexuals who could not believe that he as a minister could do such a thing; there were confused colleagues, angry colleagues, and a wide range of response from non-homosexuals, some of whom accused him of being blasphemous and of not having read the Bible.

The experiences of Ds. Klamer show that at this time the subject of homosexuality was one that most people preferred not to discuss or to tolerate, and it took a brave man to bring it into the open. Another such man in the late 1950's was Prof. Trimbos. For a long time he gave regular radio talks on family life and sexuality, in the course of which he dealt with homosexuality in a matter-of-fact way in its natural contexts; as it was brought into the 'living-room,' it ceased to be a terrifying subject.

# RECENT DEVELOPMENTS

## Judicial

The legal sore point for homosexuals was art. 248bis which discriminated against homosexual contacts across a dividing-line at the age of 21. Mainly on the advice of a medical committee[6], and with little opposition, the law was changed back in 1971 to that extent in 1886.

Even though there had been no law against homosexual acts between consenting adults, the fact of being homosexual had been a reason for rejection for, or dismissal from service in the Armed Forces. In 1972 the COC issued a bulletin[7] dealing with homosexuality, the military, and fitness for service, and the discriminatory regulation was suddenly and with little publicity dropped at the end of 1973.

## The Churches

In 1960 the Catholic central association for public health set up a study day to discuss the social and psychiatric aspects of homosexuality. The report of this meeting appeared in print and represents a definite turning point in the attitude of the Roman Catholic church.

At about the same time a number of publications appeared from the Protestant churches, and the issue of one report, 'De Homosexuele Naaste' in 1961[8] was a catalyst in starting discussions. A new mentality was emerging in which there was a call for true Christian tolerance towards homosexuals. It was also decided by most parties that abstinence was not the only acceptable way of life.

The Roman Catholics and Protestants came together in an inter-denominational working group, Pastoral Help to Homosexuals, and in 1962 various contact groups were formed. A publication from the Nederlands Gesprekscentrum on homosexuality[9] tried to re-evaluate and re-interpret the Bible, and concluded that no one has to bear the personal guilt for his or her homosexual tendencies. Furthermore, sexuality was seen as a constructive strength in human relations, regardless of whether it is hetero-or homosexual. The homosexual can develop fully and find his or her right place in religion. Some of the co-authors of this report still wrestled with the problem of homosexuality being 'against nature' and there was certainly no unanimity in greater acceptance.

In the 1960's more and more information was sent out to ministers and the Roman Catholic priest Gottschalk set up a number of guidelines:[10]

(a) a stable relationship must never be broken;
(b) marriage as a solution for homosexuality must be rejected;[10]
(c) sexual abstinence is not to be seen as a natural thing for the homosexual, and is in fact exceptional;

(d) the minister must help the homosexual to build up a stable relationship;

(e) in giving guidance, attention should be given to faithfulness within a relationship.

In 1968 an interdenominational assembly of Roman Catholic and Protestant ministers found that although extensive information had been disseminated, most ministers still had problems: they felt that they were ill-equipped educationally and emotionally to offer help to homosexuals. One of the reasons was the lack of clearcut guidelines from above. As a result of this, a strong plea was sent to the governing bodies of the churches for more definite policies. Others stated that if the ministers in the field wait for guidance from the church leaders, they will wait forever, as the written policies follow long after what actuallyhappensin practice.

In another assembly in 1973 most of the churches expressed more openness and acceptance of homosexuals within the church, but there were still factions who stated that if some women who cannot find husbands can abstain from sexual contact, so can the homosexual. The Salvation Army is still strongly opposed to homosexuality and their policy, as stated to the Council of Churches, is one of rigid rejection i.e. a homosexual may not indulge in homosexual acts.

One big problem for the churches is that if homosexuals are freely admitted to the church, then it must also be possible for a homosexual to become a minister, and this is not quite acceptable to most people. There is one municipality in Holland which has accepted a homosexual as a minister, and he and his friend live in the rectory in complete openness.

A further complication of complete recognition of homosexuality would mean that relationships might be sanctified by the church. There are cases known of such homosexual 'weddings' but they are conducted in private (one instance, pictures of which reached the international press, seems to have been a matter of publicity). Straver warns against homosexuals trying to take over and mimic the heterosexual norms of getting married as a means of seeking social acceptance and security".

Most of the churches in the Netherlands are now much more open and tolerant, but there is still a great need for spiritual guidance for many homosexuals, and various ministers have organised contact groups where such people can come together and discuss their problems. There are at present 22 towns with one or more of such groups.

The Evangelical Broadcasting Company in 1973 produced two television programmes (as well as a series of radio programmes)on homosexuality; these caused an uproar. A psychiatrist and a psychologist(Van den Aardweg, see later) were interviewed to expound their views on homosexuality being a sin against God and a neurosis respectively, and then a number of 'ex-homosexuals' were interviewed to testify on how they had found cure and salvation through their religion. Such a programme, seen by millions of people, was deeply disturbing to many homosexuals, and parents and friends of homosexuals; there were reports of suicides, as a result of the programme. However, many of the other churches were forced to take a stand and express their (opposing) views in public.

**Medicine and Science**

The psychiatric views have also changed considerably over the last few years, and most psychiatrists now do not view homosexuality as *necessarily* being a neurosis which must be cured. Dr. Sengers has reviewed the Dutch literature on homosexuality in his dissertation[12]. He, in an earlier article[13], worked out the various phases and problems of the development of homosexual awareness in young people, and a study group of psychiatrists and psychologists who came together in 1968 to discuss homosexuality were favourably disposed to the idea of it not being necessarily a neurosis. However, they were not prepared to accept Dr. Sengers' article as a statement of policy for the group. Some did not agree with the proposal that, just as a young heterosexual should be helped to find sexual identity, the young person who is homosexually inclined should be helped and stimulated to develop in that direction.

In 1967, a dissertation[14] was presented by a psychologist, Van den Aardweg, arguing, on the basis of highly questionable material, that homosexuality is a neurosis and that as a consequence the homosexual's relationship is doomed to be meaningless because of his inability to love. (It is amusing that this was published as a book by someone who has made no secret of his own homosexuality, before or after.) This caused a flurry of articles in various newspapers, journals and magazines, but the publicity given him by the criticisms probably did him more harm than good. The newspaper with the largest circulation in the country has been open to Van den Aardweg's views, publishing among other items, the confessions of a man who had been 'cured' by him, with a lurid drawing of this person wearing a mask.

In a book[15] sponsored by the NVSH (Netherlands association for sexual reform) Prof. van Dantzig, one of the leading psychiatrists of the country, stated that 'where people accuse the psychiatrist and psychoanalyst of declaring, on inadequate evidence, all homosexuals neurotic, I can say that this accusation does not hold for a number of psychotherapists, among whom I count myself.' This he then qualifies by saying that, on the other hand, to hold that the homosexual development is just as natural as the heterosexual is just as untenable. The tone of the book is non—moralistic and non—partisan, and he leaves the question of whether a homosexual should seek treatment entirely to the individual. At the end of his book he expresses regret for the dearth of factual information on homosexuality, and the lack of guidance for the psychotherapist in helping homosexuals to live with their homosexuality.

A need for the use of aversion therapy to 'cure' homosexuals is not felt in Holland.

It is difficult to know what happens in the 'first line of defence', namely the contact which homosexuals and their parents have with their general practitioner. However, most GPs have little knowledge of the problems. Mainly through the efforts of Dr. Sengers, a number of consultation bureaux have been set up in the Netherlands to help young homosexuals in their struggle for sexual identity. There are also bureaux in various cities for homosexuals of all ages, but these will probably disappear in time. The NVSH (the association for sexual reform) in 1967 ceased to regard homosexuality as an illness and from then onwards has made no distinction between homosexuals and heterosexuals in its work of giving counsel to people with sexual problems. The staff of the bureaux for homosexuals, the Schorer Institute, are in conflict with themselves concerning their work. On the one hand they feel that there should be an organisation offering specialised help for the homosexual in trouble; on the other hand the very existence of such an organisation is a form of discrimination.

There have been some scientific studies in the last few years which have shed more light on homosexuality. We shall summarise here what we consider to be the relevant findings, not necessarily because they are peculiar to the Netherlands, but because they may be of interest but unavailable to readers outside this country. A Kinsey-like study of the incidence of homosexuality in the Netherlands[16] concluded that just under 5% of the population felt exclusively, mainly, or in some degree sexually attracted to someone of the same sex. About half of this percentage falls within the category 'in some degree'. The author warns that these figures may be on the low side.

Another study[17] showed that for the young homosexual, the process of becoming aware of his tendencies is a painful one. There seem to be two important periods in this process — the vague awareness of being 'different' from others, and the working through of this experience, and then the naming of these feelings as homosexuality. The main problem is the tension between the individual's feelings and the pressures of society towards the heterosexual way of life.

A study in 1970 of a number of young homosexuals and their relationship to their environment[18] found that about one quarter were open about their tendencies and about one third were not at all. Understandably, it was found that those who were open had little trouble in accepting themselves.

The higher social classes were more open than the lower, and where religion was important the person tended to be more closed. The period of feeling 'different' took about 2 years to crystallise into the awareness of being homosexual, which occurred at about 17 years of age. The discovery of being homosexual is a period of stress and conflict in which there is a fear of being rejected and being inferior. This is a period of loneliness and guilt, but more than half of the sample waited more than a year before talking to someone about it. Most often the first discussion was with a friend of the same age, seldom with the parents. The homosexual milieu played an important part in providing form and structure for their lives, where the usual social role of marriage and family is excluded. The parents provided little support; they were often not told, but came to know about it sooner or later. Many parents did not know what to do, and only one third could accept the knowledge without difficulty.

A study of personnel selection departments in a sample of commercial companies in 1971[19] showed that there is little blatant discrimination, however there is still enough under the surface to make it unwise in general for a homosexual to admit to his being so when applying for a job. Only 6% of the companies considered homosexuality to be a reason for discharging someone, and 59% had no objection to hiring a homosexual. However, more than half indicated that a homosexual could not expect promotion to a function of leadership in the firm. There was an indication that more tolerance was paired with more experience of having homosexuals in the company.

**Student Groups**
Student groups have in recent years been formed in various cities which have been active in trying to reach the churches, medical thinking, and public opinion. They have invited prominent people from various fields for discussions, and in Amsterdam they have set up a fraternity club where there is complete integration.

**The COC**
In the late 1960's the COC became more and more active in the dissemination of information, in organising study groups, and in providing counselling and discussion groups for individuals and their families.

In 1965 a foundation from within the COC was formed under the name Dialoog (dialogue). As the name implies, they wanted more contact with heterosexual circles and did not want to bury themselves in a sort of homosexual ghetto. There were also non-homosexuals on the committee. Between 1965 and 1967 a bi-monthly journal was produced, called

'Dialoog', which was also sold freely on bookstalls. As a protection to those who wanted to buy it, from the second year onwards only the title 'Dialoog' appeared on the outside cover and the subtitle — journal for homophilia and society — was shown on the inside. (The word homophilia was first coined in Holland in 1949, to refer to the sexual orientation rather than to use the term, homosexuality, which so strongly implies the sexual act.)

The work of the committee members of the foundation was divided into a number of sections — information, organising study weekends and evenings, documentation and the building up of a library, training of field workers, and counselling for individuals in personal or legal difficulties.

The function of the COC itself, however, remained to a large extent that of a safe refuge from a hostile outside world. This changed rapidly in early 1970 when, under pressure from a group of young activists, a new policy of integration was instigated. The name was changed to the Netherlands Association for Integration of Homosexuality COC.

There are a number of working groups involved with various projects. In the teaching profession there is still a strong discrimination against homosexuals, and the COC is planning an investigation. The group 'Orpheus', not originally started by the COC but now actively supported by them, is looking into the problems of marriage and homosexuality. In our culture there are strong pressures on people to get married, and those homosexuals who have submitted to these pressures, or those who discover after marriage that they have such tendencies, find themselves in great difficulties.

There is a group working on the relationship between homosexuals and the church, one dealing with publicity and contact with newspapers, weekly magazines, radio and television, one for contact with GPs, the military, labour unions, etc. One group is in contact with the Government and political parties in an attempt to bring about changes in the laws concerning relationships between individuals either heterosexual or homosexual, who are not married. A married couple enjoy certain privileges in income tax rebates, salaries, pension rights, the allocation of housing permits, inheritance rights, etc. On these points, a relationship that is not institutionalised, even if it is stable and of long standing, is at a disadvantage. The group for international contacts, striving not only for social reform for homosexuals but also for other policies such as equality for women, has found that its activities are not always welcome in other countries.

Special attention has been given to young people between the ages of 15 and 23 (which was particularly important before the discriminatory art. 248 bis was abolished), for example, to those who are not sure of their sexual orientation. Work groups and a number of clubs have been set up for this category.

The aims of the committee for 1974[20] go beyond tolerance for the homosexual in society. They demand emancipation and integration. By emancipation is meant the chance for each (homosexual) individual to develop in an optimal fashion. For true integration, so that different modes of living can exist side by side, fundamental changes in society will have to take place. The emphasis is not so much on sexual freedom but on a more general change wherever inequality exists. In this the COC is in step with other organisations pressing for social change, e.g. Woman's Lib. and MVM (man-woman-society). The COC wants to get away from the idea that the homosexual merely be tolerated, and that they meet only in ghetto-like protected places such as clubs, bars, and saunas. The strategies for achieving these aims are the circulation of information, and confrontation. To eradicate the aversion against homosexuality information is not enough, and it is necessary that people should be confronted with homosexuality in their direct environment. Non-homosexuals are encouraged to join the COC. For some time, groups of young homosexuals went out to dance together in 'straight' clubs, in order to promote integration. However this movement has died down.

Many of the present 7000 members of the COC are not in favour of the more aggressive policy of confrontation. On the other hand there are some people who think that the COC does not go far enough. Usually they wish the COC to play a role in a complete reorganisation of society. A typical fringe group is the Paarse September, a squad of lesbian girls who feel that being lesbian is a political choice which counteracts the oppression of the female.

As mentioned earlier, the COC applied in 1964 for Royal Assent, and this was refused. Another request in 1970 suffered the same fate, but in 1973 assent was finally given. The COC is now an officially recognised organisation in the Netherlands.

## Bars and Clubs

Even though some homosexuals are against the idea of separate places for meeting, many bars and clubs are set up or are known to be almost exclusively gay, places where the gay crowd can go and feel protected amongst their own kind. They are often semi-specialised into young, 'mixed', elegant, rough, etc.; a number of them are decorated in red velvet and imitation marble, some are stark and adorned with pictures of motorcycles. A recent development is their appearance in provincial towns; cities with a population over 100,000 already may feature 5 or more such clubs.

In Amsterdam, a city one-tenth the size of London, there are now approximately 30 clubs, some an attraction of long standing for tourists, particularly those from Germany and England, who often came, and still come to stay for a 'gay' weekend in Amsterdam. In 1965 a former mayor, who did not appreciate this reputation, announced steps to limit, and in the long run to reduce, the number of 'gay' bars; but after strong opposition his policy was rejected. The following year at The Hague measures were introduced which restricted the freedom of moving around of homosexuals in certain areas 'to protect them'. One could regard these and similar incidents at about the same time as a first wave of reaction against something which by now had come into the open.

## MINORITY GROUPS

So far mention has not been made of minority groups within or on the fringe of homosexuality. Society is strongly opprobrious of the paedophile, whether he be homo- or heterosexual, and homosexuals in general discriminate against the homosexual paedophile. This is understandable in that the non-paedophile homosexual wishes to avoid as much as possible the public image of a child-molester, but this attitude does nothing to alleviate the plight of the paedophile. Another group, the bisexual, married or unmarried, seems to suffer more than the exclusively homosexual. Those whose sexual preference swings backwards and forwards between homo- and heterosexuality fit into neither category. The homosexual comes to terms with the fact that he cannot get married and have a family. The bisexual cannot do this. Furthermore, the homosexual can, if he wishes, retreat into a world of homosexual friends and acquaintances; the bisexual is forced to switch constantly. Homosexuals often reject bisexuals on the grounds that they are greedy, wanting the best of both worlds.

Little has been heard of lesbian women, and although it is possible that there is relatively little interest amongst them to organise themselves and to raise their voices, it could indicate that, as women, they and their problems are not taken sufficiently seriously. They happen to be a minority within a minority group, and as such are liable to receive their share of the ill-feelings which so readily develop in such groups.

## THE MASS MEDIA

The press, radio, and television have played an important part in breaking the taboo against talking about the subject and in increasing the acceptance of homosexuals. In 1964 when the COC officially came to the surface, television gave it coverage and the chairman dropped his anonymity and appeared before the camera. A number of other homosexuals were interviewed, but in such a way that they could not be recognised. In later programmes others have not found it necessary to maintain their anonymity.

The press has on the whole treated the subject in a non-sensational and positive way. On Remembrance Day each year a ceremony is held for those who died in the Second World War. The Royal family and various organisations lay wreaths at the War Memorial in the centre of Amsterdam during an official ceremony. A few years ago some members of the Amsterdam association of young homosexuals wished to lay a wreath for all the homosexuals who had died in concentration camps, just as wreaths were being laid for the Jews. No official response was made to the request until after the closing date for applications had passed, and then they were told that it was too late. They nevertheless appeared at the ceremony, with a wreath, and when they stepped forward to lay the wreath, they were arrested. (They were released later that same day.) The press gave considerable coverage to this event; the next year permission to lay a wreath was granted.

A few weekly papers accept contact advertisements from homosexuals too. In one of them which has become renowned in this field, some of the advertisements are quite outspoken, as a few samples from one recent issue[21] will show: 'Homo, 37, masculine and slim, seeks slender, hairless, sexy guy, age up to 35'; 'Masculine bisexual boy, 28, seeks bisexual or homophile boy, without moustache, glasses or beard, to 24 years'; 'Attractive masochist fellow in tight jeans, 25, seeks dominant, sadist guy, preferably a lover of leather, jeans, uniforms, rubber, etc'. The daily papers are generally more conservative. A few years ago a woman journalist published a survey[22] of how she tried to phone through a clearly lesbian advertisement to all the national daily papers. Some accepted it outright, some were prepared to discuss the matter further, and some refused outright.

In the field of literature, the Dutch author Van het Reve, generally considered one of the two greatest living national writers, did much for homosexual emancipation by openly coming out with his homosexuality in his books from 1962 onwards, often in a rather drastic fashion. This led to protests, and even a heated argument in Parliament where some strong words were used against him. In 1966 he was indicted for blasphemy (picturing God as a donkey with whom the author cohabitates), but in 1968 he was acquitted by the Supreme Court, and subsequently awarded the 1970 State Prize for Literature. It would appear that Van het Reve has been instrumental in bringing about a degree of self-awareness and self-esteem in numerous homosexuals.

## PUBLIC OPINION

A survey of public opinion in 1966/67[23] showed that 10% of the sample, mainly older people, did not know what homosexuality was, and that the higher social classes and younger people were more tolerant of homosexuality. This tolerance is increasing, as shown by a comparison of two studies in which people were asked if homosexuals should be free to live their own way of life. The study published in 1969[16] showed that little more than half of the sample was in favour, and one third against. In 1970 the figures were 71% in favour and 22% against[11].

## DISCUSSION

The Netherlands is a country where there are no laws against homosexuality or homosexual acts, and where there is an increasing acceptance, understanding, and integration of homosexuals. This, possibly apart from some of the Scandinavian countries, is not to be found anywhere else in the Western world.

What conclusions can be drawn from this survey? In the first place, for those countries which operate laws against homosexuality and which do not wish to abolish such laws for fear that they will then be swamped by a lascivious outbreak of homosexuality, the experience in the Netherlands shows that the incidence of homosexuality is similar to that quoted by Kinsey in the U.S.A. where laws against homosexuality still exist in almost all States. Furthermore, rescinding art. 248bis did not lead to an explosion of homosexual contacts with minors. Thus, with or without laws the incidence of homosexuality seems to be stable. Each country could well count the cost in manhours of keeping a vice squad operative in an attempt to enforce their laws against homosexuality, plus the cost of mental health workers who have to try to help those oppressed by such laws. The Netherlands saves on this, and also on the human misery that such laws often bring.

For those who think that public opinion must change before any legal changes can take place, the experience in Holland shows that this need not be the case. In one survey, taken in 1966/67[23], it was found that most people were against adults having sexual relations either homo-or heterosexual, with young people younger than 20 years. Yet the law for heterosexual acts makes it illegal only for those under 16 yrs, and the article singling out homosexual acts was abolished in 1971, with little opposition, and thus no distinction was made any more between heterosexual and homosexual acts.

For those who think that abolishing discriminatory laws will solve all the homosexual's problems, the experience in the Netherlands indicates that this view is too simplistic. It is one step in the direction of saving the homosexual from much possible misery, but a great deal more needs to be done. Throughout our survey we have tried to show where and how problems still exist, and which problems have been successfully dealt with. The absence of discriminatory laws does not necessarily ensure freedom. In France the Code Pénal makes no distinction between homosexual and heterosexual acts; yet the Dutch homosexual enjoys much more freedom than his French counterpart.

Is the Netherlands a paradise for homosexuals? Many foreigners think so, and they may be right when they compare their own situation with that of the homosexual in Holland; however, it would not be right to call it a paradise. Social acceptance of homosexuals in the higher social classes in the large cities is well advanced; but the situation may not be quite so easy, for homosexuals in the lower social classes and outside the large cities. As has been mentioned, a homosexual applying for a job would as a rule be unwise to mention his sexual orientation.

In recent years there has been a change in the policy of the COC, away from the steady, careful build-up of acceptance for the homosexual, to a more forceful, aggressive confrontation. It will be of interest to see what now develops. Emancipation may be more rapid, but there is the possibility of a backlash. The sight of homosexual couples ostentatiously kissing in public, dancing together in previously exclusively heterosexual places, and parading in public with banners, may backfire and create more opposition than it breaks down. Furthermore, if homosexuals achieve true integration so that their bars and clubs cease to exist, the chances of homosexuals meeting each other will be drastically reduced. If there are no recognised meeting places the young homosexual will be in a worse position than his heterosexual counterpart. Young people in general have difficulty in meeting each other and in finding a partner, but the statistics of the incidence of homosexuality indicate that the young homosexual would be worse off than the young heterosexual. There will probably never be true integration in that homosexual bars and clubs will cease to exist.

What makes Holland a special case? It is often ascribed to a sort of national tolerance. This we believe to be a myth, and a dangerous myth at that. If it is accepted, then other countries could easily shrug off all efforts to change, with the attitude that 'it can happen in Holland because of their tradition of tolerance; we have no such tradition so it's no use trying'. Our contention is that, firstly, tolerance is not a unitary trait, as Hartshorne & May in their famous studies noted that traits like honesty are not unitary. Secondly, tolerance does not come naturally to the Dutch; if an amount of moderation seems to be typical of most of them, this is a matter of behaviour rather than genesis of opinions anyway. Thirdly, it all seems to us to be rather a certain lack in tolerance, at least in public: although people may dislike or detest specific groups or individuals, but they will not easily unite to take action. Due to the multi-faceted aspect of contemporary Dutch society, private fanaticism has little chance of developing into a large scale crusade.

Why then has acceptance advanced so far in this country? We cannot answer that question, but we contend that the acceptance has been won by steady work by a number of people over a long period of time. There has been no revolution that we can point to and say, 'From that event onwards, things changed.' Changes in the climate of opinion do not just happen; they have to be worked at and won against passive, sometimes active, resistance; such advances will remain fragile for quite some time. There were a few homosexuals who dared to come into the open and to face persecution. There were also a number of non-homosexuals who felt strongly enough about the social injustices confronting homosexuals that they were prepared to calmly and deliberately propose different approaches. Later, more people could then move further. But any man or woman may be able to even single-handedly tilt the Galton board which represents the formation of public opinion.

The foregoing has taken place in what was 40 years ago a deeply conservative and stable society. But a crisis and a war have shaken it, and 'things were not going to be the same again'. In all sorts of detail this has come true. Ideas on the authority of the churches, the role of the wife, sex before marriage, contraception and abortion, have changed drastically and as rapidly as in any other Western country, and this development could easily take a change of mind on homosexuality in its stride.

At the same time, a city such as Amsterdam, not too inhumanly large, yet not too provincially small with a harbour and with a red-light district, with its many artists, journalists, students, and foreigners, may have provided the very milieu in which more and more homosexuals could organise a background against which they could be themselves, and where they could gain the self-esteem which would eventually enable some of them to stick out their necks and try the outside world for what it is worth.

## REFERENCES

1. Emde Boas, C. van (1965). De positie van de homoseksueel in Nederland. *De Gids,* 1 & 2, 15
2. Sassen, A. (1935). Lob der Lächerlichen Affen. *De Nieuwe Gemeenschap,* **2**, 117
3. Rogier, J. (1966). Homoseksuele emancipatie. *Dialoog,* **5**, 173

4. Stokvis, B. (1939). *De Homosexueelen.* De Tijdstroom, Lochem
5. Klamer, A. — personal communication
6. Advies van de gezondheidsraad. . . In; *Homofilie: informatie, onderzoek en herwaardering.* DieMap 19, De Horstink, Amersfoort, 1970, 83
7. *Homoseksualiteit, de krijgsmacht en de militaire keuring.* (COC, Amsterdam,) (1972)
8. *De Homoseksuele Naaste* (1961). Bosch and Keuning, Baarn
9. *Homosexualiteit* (1966). Nederlands Gesprekscentrum, 31, Kok, Kampen, etc.
10. Sengers, W.J. (1968). *Gewoon hetselfde?* Paul Brand, Hilversum
11. Straver, C.J: (1972). *Homofilie in Nederland,* Intermediair, 27 and 28
12. Sengers, W.J. (1969) *Homoseksualiteit als Klacht.* Paul Brand, Bussum,
13. Sengers, W.J. (1968). Voorstellen over de opvang van homofiele minderjarigen. Maandblad voor Geestelijke Volksgezondheid, 7 & 8
14. Aardweg, G.J.M. van den (1967). *Homofilie, neurose en dwangzelf-beklag.* Polak and Van Gennep, *Amsterdam.*
15. Dantzig, A. van (1969). *Homoseksualiteit bij de man.* NVSH, 's-Gravenhage
16. *Sex in Nederland* (1969. (Het Spectrum, Utrecht)
17. Sanders, G.J.E.M. (1968). *De zelfbeleving als uitdagingssituatie.* Instituut voor Sociale Psychologie, Groningen
18. Moerings, M. (1970). Homofiele jongeren in relatie tot hun omgeving. *Nederlands Institut voor Sociaal Sexuologisch Onderzoek,* **3,** Zeist
19. Manschot, B. (1971). *Homosesexualiteit: een onderzoek naar problemen voor homosexuelen in het bedrijfsleven.* (Stichting tot Bevordering Sociaal Onderzoek Minderheden, Amsterdam)
20. Sek 10 (1973). COC, Amsterdam
21. Vrij Nederland, 5 January, 1974
22. Mijs, J. (1970). Het Parool
23. Meilof-Oonk, S. (1969) *Meningen over homosexualiteit.* (Stichting tot Bevordering Sociaal Onderzoek Minderheden, Amsterdam)

# 5

# Homosexuality — Some Social and Legal Aspects

## Antony Grey

Homosexuality is commonly and often somewhat thoughtlessly regarded as a 'problem'. And it undoubtedly does constitute a problem to many of those affected by it, whether they are homosexual themselves, or are among those trying to help other people who are. Having been in the first category all my life, and in the second for the past 16 years, I have had a greater opportunity than most people, perhaps, of wondering what precisely the 'problem' consists of. Certainly we live today in times of rapidly shifting social attitudes; and attitudes towards homosexuality have been no exception: the past 20 years have been ones of transformation scenes and shifting battlegrounds where the problem (or, as I prefer to call it, the question) of homosexuality is concerned.

First of all, it would be as well to dispose of the fallacy that there is on the one hand an inside 'subjective' view of homosexuality as seen by homosexuals themselves, and on the other hand an outside 'objective' view of it as seen by the non-homosexual, and that never can the twain meet. Such a belief is not only erroneous: it frequently and perniciously implies that the 'objective' view is, in some unexplained way, more 'authentic' than the 'subjective' one. But a moment's reflection will convince any reasonably impartial person that this is not so. Indeed, a fairly strong case can be made — and is made, by those campaigning in the homophile movement — that the subjective, 'inside' view is far more authentic and realistic than any outside one can ever be. Without plunging too deeply into abstract philosophical or metaphysical considerations, I would venture to suggest that the subjective/objective view of the world propounded by most Western scientists, while it is all very well when considering    inanimate objects, is a far less satisfactory tool for understanding human beings, their emotions and behaviour. We are all of us, whether the viewer or the viewed, approaching one another from our own distinctive and uniquely individual standpoints, and our opinions are bound to be modified by this obvious fact. So surely there is no completely 'objective' view of homosexuality any more than of any other psychological or emotional phenomenon. The point I am trying to make is that one cannot meaningfully consider one half of the equation without the other, and that homosexuality cannot usefully be considered without also considering the larger society in which it exists and of which it forms a part.

The Wolfenden Report[1] — that towering landmark in the fight towards a more dispassionate and common sense view of homosexuality — was itself a valiant attempt to apply a more balanced and less prejudiced standard to the subject. But it now seems curiously dated in some respects. It is still, however, one of the best introductions to the topic, and its disposal of the notion that homosexuality is a 'disease' has not to my knowledge ever been effectively answered, even by those who still maintain the contrary. As the committee pointed out (in paras. 26-29 of their report), none of the prerequisite criteria for the classification of a condition as a disease exist universally even amongst those homosexuals known to the medical profession (themselves admittedly a minority); while 'even if it could be established that homosexuality were a disease, it is clear that many individuals, however their state is reached, present social rather than medical problems' (para. 31). Furthermore, the misclassification of homosexuality as illness carries with it moral consequences which are as unwelcome to the critic as to homosexuals themselves — the implication, namely, that 'the sufferer cannot help it and therefore carries a diminished responsibility for his actions'. The Wolfenden Committee commendably refused to accept this view, holding correctly that 'there are no *prima facie* grounds for supposing that because a particular person's sexual propensity happens to lie in the direction of persons of his own or her own sex it is any less controllable than that of those whose propensity is for persons of the opposite sex' (para. 32). This assertion of the homosexual's equality of moral responsibility with his or her heterosexual brother and sister is an essential ingredient in a correct understanding of their respective situations and in creating the self-respect which every human being has to have in order to behave responsibly.

Condemnatory attitudes to homosexuality have evolved during the past thousand years from the notion that such behaviour is unnatural, through the religious concept of its being in all circumstances sinful, to which the

State (in the reign of Henry VIII) added the corollary that it was an especially wicked crime, and finally to the apparently more charitable view of it as an illness. But this latter view is in fact just as denigrating of the homosexual as any of the others; and most of the homosexuals with whom I have discussed this have forcefully expressed the view that if they had to choose, they would prefer to be treated as responsible criminals rather than as irresponsible sick people — which they are not.

# HOMOSEXUALITY—SOME SOCIAL AND LEGAL ASPECTS

British law, not merely about homoseuxality but about sexual behaviour generally, still contains many curious and out-of-date anomalies. Until 1967 its treatment of the male homosexual was especially harsh, and even after the reforms of that year men who behave homosexually remain under a number of legal disabilities which do not apply to heterosexuality or to lesbianism (sexual expression between women has never attracted the law's attention in the same way that such behaviour between men has done, although social pressures make it little if any easier for lesbians to be open about their orientation). Henry VIII's statute of 1533 made 'the abominable and detestable crime of buggery not fit to be mentioned among Christians' punishable with death—a penalty which survived until 1828 and was not infrequently inflicted up to the early nineteenth century. But anal intercourse is not a specifically homosexual activity: it can be (and, researchers tell us, frequently is) practised between men and women; and, strangely, it still remains punishable with up to life imprisonment in such circumstances even between a consenting husband and wife, although since 1967 it has no longer been a criminal offence in England and Wales when done in private between two consenting men aged over 21.

In 1885, specifically homosexual behaviour as such was for the first time made a crime by the notorious 'Labouchere Amendment' (named after the member of Parliament who proposed it), inserted into a Bill which was mainly concerned with prostitution; this made it an offence, punishable with up to 2 years' imprisonment, for a man to commit an act of 'gross indecency' with another man, whether in public or in private. Despite prophetic protests that such a law would become a blackmailers' charter, it remained the law of the land for 82 years, spreading a trail of misery and suicide in its wake, and still applies to male homosexual behaviour which is not 'in private' as defined by the Sexual Offences Act 1967 (i.e. where more than 2 persons take part or are present). As the courts have decided that physical contact is not necessary to constitute an act of gross indecency—suggestive postures being sufficient—it will be seen that this law has had far-reaching effects. (I have even heard of cases where the police stoutly maintained that two men kissing were committing 'gross indecency'.) Certainly it rendered criminal all forms of erotic contact between men of any age, whether consenting or not, whether in a public place or not, and whether observed or not.

It was the indiscriminate application of this law, under which some police forces hunted down known homosexuals as if they were dangerous criminals, which ultimately led to the broadly-based public campaign for reform which first secured the appointment of the Wolfenden Committee in 1954 and then, 10 years after the publication of the Wolfenden Report in 1957, achieved the reforms of the Sexual Offences Act 1967. For 5 of these 10 years I was Secretary of the Homosexual Law Reform Society, and so learned much about the law's injustice at first hand.

The 1967 Act, while implementing the Wolfenden Committee's main recommendation 'that homosexual behaviour between consenting adults should no longer be a criminal offence' (at least so far as England and Wales were concerned—Scotland and Northern Ireland are excluded from the Act), did so in an essentially negative fashion and was not as liberal as the Wolfenden Report itself. While the reform remove the private homosexual behaviour of two consenting men aged over 21 from the list of crimes, it did not put male homosexuality legally on a par with either lesbianism or extramarital heterosexual activity. Thus it remains an offence for more than two men (but not for more than two women, or for a mixed group consisting of a man and two or more women) to engage in mutual sexual activity, even if on a private premises and with the consent of all concerned: homosexual acts between two consenting adult men become criminal even if there is a non-participating spectator. These restrictions stem from lurid fantasies aired in Parliamentary debates on the reform Bill—notably by elderly law lords who recollected cases they had tried involving 'buggers' clubs' (they seemed to imagine that every bar patronised by homosexual men has an orgy room!). It is still a crime, punishable with up to 5 years' imprisonment for the older man and 2 years for the younger, if there is a homosexual contact between a man aged over 21 and a youth below that age—although the legal age of adulthood is now 18, and 16 is the age at which a girl can legally consent to heterosexual or lesbian intercourse without exposing her partner to the risk of indecent assault.

These two major shortcomings of the 1967 Act mean that even the reformed law remains a blackmailers' charter in some respects, and the attitude of the authorities towards homosexuality is still by and large unenlightened and repressive. It has been apparent in some recent

obscenity prosecutions, for instance—such as those c
*International Times*—that the encouragement or facilitati
sexual behaviour was seen by the prosecution as being far mc
and immoral than promoting heterosexual behaviour. Ot
natory provisions remain in penalties (which are higher fo
sexual crimes than for equivalent heterosexual offences) and ...
continuing illegality of homosexual acts even between consenting men
aged over 21 if they are members of the armed services or the merchant
navy, or if the acts occur in Scotland or Northern Ireland.

Besides the laws referring specifically to homosexual behaviour, there
are many other provisions, both national and local, under which homosexual behaviour can be prosecuted. Section 32 of the Sexual Offences Act
1956, which makes it an offence for a man 'persistently to solicit or
importune in a public place for immoral purposes', is one of the most
widely used. Originally introduced to deal with female prostitutes' touts or
'bullies', it has throughout most of this century been applied almost
exclusively against male homosexuals seeking a partner, and until 1967
there was no right for the defendant to opt for a jury trial if charged with
this offence, although it could result in his imprisonment. Used in
conjunction with local indecency bye-laws and the threat of a gross
indecency charge if the accused proved recalcitrant, it has therefore been
a comparatively easy matter to secure 'guilty' pleas to Section 32 charges
in circumstances where no evidence in addition to that of the arresting
police is required. For these and other reasons, recent moves to reform
this area of the law are to be welcomed. *Agent provocateur* tactics are
universally and rightly disliked, and the best way to eliminate the
temptation to use them would seem to be to alter laws which make them
possible, by providing that when such charges are brought an offended
member of the public is produced to give evidence of annoyance.

Since 1967, the need for wider reforms of the laws relating to sex
generally, and not just those affecting homosexuality, has become more
generally recognised. The Sexual Law Reform Society's working party (of
which I am secretary) will be reporting soon to this effect, basing its
recommendations on the principle that the only socially valid reasons for
which the law should be permitted to curtail the citizen's freedom of
sexual expressions are: (1) where there is not true consent; (2) where there
is not full responsibility, by reason either of age or condition, on the part
of one or more of those engaging in the activity in question; and (3) where
offence is caused to identifiable members of the public.

Obviously it will take some time to educate public and Parliamentary
opinion to accept the full implications of this philosophy and translate it
into law. Meanwhile, other useful initiatives—such as the Scottish

Minorities Group's draft Bill to reform the Scottish law—have been taken and are deserving of support.

How do British legal and social attitudes to homosexuality compare with those of other Western countries? It would be idle to pretend that we are either the most progressive or the most backward of countries in our collective national response to the gay minority. It is instructive to observe that a non-punitive legal system is by no means always accompanied by enlightened social attitudes. The criminal codes of most Western European countries either ignore homosexuality completely or have fewer punishable offences connected with it than we do, and frequently a lower age of consent than ours; nevertheless, in some of the countries which inherited the Code Napoleon—and notably in predominantly Catholic societies such as France, Italy and Spain—homosexuals are at best ignored and at worst despised: they do not have even the imperfect degree of social acceptance or the increasingly open organisations which now exist in Britain.

Although the French homophile association, *Arcadie,* claims 15 000 members in metropolitan and overseas France, it has only within the past six months (through holding an impressive international congress to celebrate its 20th birthday) succeeded in achieving significant recognition in the press and on television. French homosexuals tend to be more secretive and socially stifled than their British brethren nowadays are. In Spain, known homosexuals are liable to summary arrest and incarceration as "vagabonds". In Italy, although homosexuality—or at any rate bisexuality—would appear to the observant tourist to be common, there is little public discussion of the topic and no organisation catering for homosexuals.

It is in northern Europe that the social as well as the legal emancipation of homosexuals has proceeded furthest. Holland, that traditionally minded yet strongly libertarian nation, has extended toleration of homosexuality to a high level of social acceptance which makes it more possible for Dutch homosexuals than for most others to live open yet socially integrated lives. The Dutch homosexual organisation COC* has during its 25 years' existence evolved from a semi-secret discussion group through a more open yet introverted recreational club with its headquarters (including a bar and dancefloor) in Amsterdam and branches in many provincial towns, into a primarily outward-looking social service organisation whose educational and counselling work is closely integrated with that of the wider national marriage guidance, family planning and sex education agencies. Recently COC achieved the public recognition conferred by the grant of a royal charter—roughly equivalent to

* Cultuur-en Ontspanningscentrum (Cultural and Recreational Centre)

charitable status in Britain—which will entitle it to receive grants from state funds. All this is accepted with equanimity by the Dutch public, whose reaction to the existence and needs of the young homosexual also appears to be much calmer and more rational than is the case here. Following a comprehensive report by a Goverment committee of health experts, Dutch law was recently altered to make homosexual relations legal for anyone aged over 16; there was little Parliamentary opposition to this move, which was sponsored by the Government.

Scandinavia is also traditionally tolerant—legally and also socially. Denmark and Sweden have had liberal laws since the 1940s. Norway recently abolished legal penalities against consenting homosexual behaviour following a short, successful campaign by a reforming group. West German law has also been recently reformed. There, however, there had been a prohibitory law for upwards of a century, and social attitudes are still less generally accepting of homosexual behaviour.

The United States are possibly the home of both the most widespread 'homophobia' and also of the most militant gay liberationist activities. These conflicting attitudes stem from contrasting strands in the complex American tradition: on the one hand, the puritanical heritage of the Pilgrim Fathers which resulted in one of the most comprehensively moralistic legal codes inflicted upon a Western community; on the other, the strong attachment to civil liberties and minority rights which has characterised the Republic's history. The result is a plethora of extraordinarily detailed State laws against almost every conceivable variety of sexual behaviour (heterosexual as well as homosexual) outside marriage which have only very recently begun to be expunged from the criminal code—as yet, only seven of the 50 States (Connecticut, Colorado, Delaware, Hawaii, Illinois, Ohio and Oregon) have repealed their anti-sodomy statutes—and an increasingly vocal and widespread gay rights movement, dating back some quarter of a century in its origins but much more militant and radical during the past decade. Despite the law, homosexual organisation, both political and social, is in many ways more widespread and open than in Britain—there appears to be a more cohesive self-awareness on the part of American homosexuals, some manifestations of which, such as the rapidly growing Metropolitan Community Churches, are peculiarly American. There is also, in some quarters, much more strident homophobia. Perhaps it is not altogether surprising that in a country where psychoanalysis has such a strong hold on the middle-class imagination, the concept of homosexuality as a sickness is proving hard to dislodge, despite the massive data on incidence and characteristics accumulated during the past 25 years by the Kinsey Institute for Sex Research.

As significant as the Wolfenden Report, and perhaps even more so in the long run, was Kinsey's massive study of *Sexual Behaviour in the Human Male*[2], published in 1948, which made the public aware for the first time of the widespread incidence of homosexual feelings and behaviour in the population at large. As is well known, Kinsey found that over one-third of his male sample had had at least one homosexual experience, that 10% of them were predominantly or exclusively homosexual for a significant period of their lives, and that 4% were exclusively homosexual throughout their lives. 'The homosexual', he concluded, 'has been a significant part of human sexual activity ever since the dawn of history, primarily because it is an expression of capacities that are basic in the human animal'. Kinsey also postulated the concept of the sexual spectrum: he pointed out that in most human beings homosexuality and heterosexuality are not 'all or nothing' states, but that there is a spectrum of feeling and sexual activity ranging from the exclusively heterosexual at one extreme to the exclusively homosexual at the other extreme; and that the majority of people are somewhere in the middle, most of them somewhat more towards the heterosexual end than the homosexual end. This concept of the spectrum is immensely valuable in emphasising the unity of humanity's sexuality, and in disposing of the notion that people who have homosexual or bisexual feelings are in any important sense members of a different species to heterosexuals.

In some ways, Kinsey's findings (which reinforced from a biological standpoint the psychological theories which Sigmund Freud had enunciated earlier in the century) have moved American and Western European sociological thinking towards a more realistic appraisal, not only of homosexuality but of sexuality as a whole. But in these largely 'white Anglo-Saxon protestant' societies, which still contain — even in today's so called (and in my view misnamed) 'permissive society' — some quite virulent pockets of anti-sexual phobia, the movement towards a recognition that the sexual problem is universal does not necessarily simplify it in a social sense, it merely extends it. The need for more adequate and comprehensive sex education (a battle which still has to be hard fought if it is to be successfully won) and the popularity of magazines such as *Forum*, with their mass readership of men and women who obviously still find it difficult to accept a guilt-free and pleasurable attitude to sex, illustrate how much remains to be done in order to remove the twin blights of fear and ignorance. We are not, in fact, dealing with a homosexual problem in the sense that there is no equivalent heterosexual problem; it is only too clear that there are no problem-free heterosexuals any more than there are problem-free human beings. We all live in a common human sexual dilemma; and it is only by mutual acceptance of this fact that we shall begin to lighten the difficulties which so many people feel about sex and emotional relationships.

And while this common human dilemma is often focussed upon sex, it is by no means exclusively sexual. On the contrary, it involves the total personality and concerns the deepest complexities of being human: the search for peace and serenity which most individuals find so elusive amidst the incessant clamour of physical and spiritual desire, and the fears of loneliness which beset each one of us. The urge to mate, the need for a complementary partner, is at the root of our deepest instincts. So are the paradoxes of love and of selfishness.

All these things are fundamentally the same for the homosexual person as for the heterosexual. And I believe that it is necessary to stress this fundamental fact because of the old fashioned views, still unhappily adhered to in some quarters, which have dismissed all homosexuality as neurotic or pathological. In saying this I do not wish to beg the question of the aetiology of homosexuality, but I think it is important to approach this question from a balanced standpoint. While it is interesting and important, as well as useful, to find out what may be the precipitating causes of homosexuality as well as of heterosexuality in different individuals, the really essential question to ask is not 'why are some people homosexual and not heterosexual,' but: 'what is the nature of human sexuality and the sexual drive?' If research concentrated on the forces — whether these be biological, endocrinological or emotional — which condition human sexual drives in all people, and not just in those with a particular sexual propensity, it could be that we should arrive at some of the relevant answers much more quickly. There is no doubt that the really profound questions and answers involve the entire human personality and the relationships of individuals to society.

It is important to stress this when talking about the *social* aspects of homosexuality, because what is involved are the interrelationships of society as a whole — that is, of its homosexual, its bisexual and its heterosexual members respectively with each other as social groups and with one another as individuals. In some aspects homosexuality can be viewed as a minority problem; but this is largely because an ignorant majority has historically reacted towards it with prejudice heavily tinged with emotion (and perhaps more heavily so than in relation to other questions, because of the sexual component), seeking to exorcise the strange and the different, which the more extreme regard with repugnance. But to view homosexuality as nothing else but a minority problem is to approach it superficially. It is, as I have stressed, a question involving the whole of society, because in order to ameliorate its problematic aspects the whole of society will have to change.

This, it should be said at once, is one of the chief merits of the approach adopted by the Gay Liberation Front, both and in the USA. Leaving aside the political and economic assumptions underlying their 'radical' critique, they must be acknowledged to have brought valuable, indeed indispensible, insights to the consideration of homosexuality and of the homophile movement.

The latter is relatively new in Britain but considerably older in the USA and in Europe. Although since the 1880s various voices in England, some of whom (such as Edward Carpenter) were homosexual but not openly so, while others (like Havelock Ellis) were not themselves homosexual but had been led by their scientific studies to see the need for reappraisal, had combined to advocate legal reforms and a new approach to homosexuality and social attitudes to it, and a modern public movement emerged in the late 1950s which successfully campaigned for the law reforms achieved in 1967, it is only in the past few years that homosexuals themselves have openly organised in order to assert that 'Gay is Good' and to challenge ingrained public assumptions about themselves.

This slogan, and the demand for equal civil rights and social acceptance on the part of homosexuals which it betokens, is American in origin, although not necessarily the worse for that. While there may be a stronger ingrained consciousness in the USA, stemming from American history, of the claims of all minority groups to parity of treatment within the community, it is not before time that British homosexuals are also developing this consciousness. American homophile organisations have existed openly since the early 1950s and covertly before that; while in the Netherlands the COC (Cultural and Recreational Centre) — the doyen of European homophile organisations — was founded in 1946, largely by Dutch Jewish homosexuals in the wake of the end of Nazi oppression and optimism generated by the United Nations Declaration of Human Rights.

In the pre-1967 law reform campaigning period, the Homosexual Law Reform Society (founded in 1958) gathered to itself a wide range of supporters, many of whom were of course homosexual, but a great many others of whom were not. Its list of sponsors ranged from Archbishops and Bishops of the Church of England and dignitaries of other Churches to leading scientists, artists, lawyers, doctors and people from other walks of public life who may have diverged quite violently in many of their opinions about homosexuality — whether or not (for instance), it was a desirable trait or otherwise, a sickness, or a sin, or neither. They were, however united in the conviction that the criminal punishment of whatever sexual behaviour consenting adults chose to indulge in together in private did more individual and social harm than good, and was totally unjustified and against the public interest. In their battle they were of course powerfully reinforced by the arguments put forward by the Wolfenden Committee. But the Homosexual Law Reform Society had no 'philosophy of homosexuality' as such. Neither had its social arm, the Albany Trust, a registered charity set up in 1958 to promote psychological health.

From its earliest days, the Albany Trust has been the respository of an unceasing stream of requests for help and advice, not only from homosexuals of both sexes and all ages, but from many other people perplexed and distressed by their sexual natures or by episodes or relationships in their sexual lives which they feel unable to cope with unaided. Confronted with these inroads from the sea of human misery, with which their resources to cope are totally inadequate, the Trustees have adopted a policy of seeking out reliable and experienced help in all the various spheres and professions dealing with human needs and relationships — whether medical, physical, emotional, spiritual, or psychological, and endeavouring to put those needing such aid into touch with it. The criterion of help regarded by the Trust as reliable is a humane and non-judgmental approach to the fact of homosexuality or other socio-sexual difficulties, and acceptance of these as simply one facet (and not necessarily the most important) of a personality which may be desirable or otherwise in many different ways, and which may need to be helped in some respects other than those directly impinging upon sexuality. Needless to say, the Trust recognises that all help, to be effective, must be in tune with the inner needs and desires of the individual concerned.

If this 'eclectic' approach distinguishes the Albany Trust from the more militant and partisan (using these terms in a non-pejorative sense) attitudes of the various homophile organisations, the Trust is no less aware or sympathetic than they are towards the need of homosexuals for wise counselling and help. Indeed, we recognise that, while this need is a universal one, it is often especially acute for 'gays'. But it does seem to me, in the light of my 16-years' work in the field, that an agency which has slowly built up the links which the Trust has done with the various non-homosexual professional people and community services has its own special contribution to make both to their work and to that of the homophile movement. The Albany Trust, therefore, concentrates on building up and strengthening its professional and social agency links, so that it can ensure competent help from them for its and their homosexual, bisexual and other clients.

The latters' needs of course vary. A minority may need medical, psychological or spiritual help — not because their homosexuality is 'wrong' or 'sick', but because they themselves feel that this is so, or are otherwise confused. The majority, however, are in *social* need, being lonely through isolation from fellow homosexuals, or demoralised because of the ignorant or hostile attitudes of non-homosexuals towards them. For these, help in socialising themselves is vital; not necessarily by throwing them willy-nilly into situations where immediate sexual activity or emotional relationships follow, but by generally helping them to go outwards to meet and relate to other sympathetic and congenial people. (Once again it should be emphasised that neither the sexual nor even the amorous aspects of homosexuality are the whole of the picture. While one of course hopes that the lonely gay person will succeed in cultivating successful and happy sexual and emotional relationships, these can often be byproducts of more generalised socialising activity of which the self-consciously isolated personality has become incapable and to which he must be gently and unhurriedly acclimatised.)

In this connection, the efforts of a pioneer agency for young homosexuals and their parents deserve mention. Work in this area is fraught with difficulties, not only because of the legal situation which still makes all homosexual contact for males aged under 21 criminal, but because of the prejudices of so many adults — not only parents but also teachers, youth welfare workers, etc. These difficulties have not deterred Mrs. Rose Robertson from setting up and developing Parents Enquiry as a means of helping homosexual children to cope with their family situations and of helping their parents to help them instead of rejecting them. While this work is still on a small scale, it is already performing a valuable function both educationally and therapeutically. It may and has been asked whether to inculcate such family tolerance is not encouraging what might otherwise be a temporary and transient homosexual phase to become permanent. This, as I hope my earlier observations have demonstrated, is a misreading of the situation. Of course, each individual is at a different point of the sexual spectrum; nor may any of us (whether teenagers or adults) remain exactly at the point where we now are. But to reduce family tensions and young peoples' fears by taking homosexual feelings and relationships seriously is more likely to produce a flexible and realistic attitude to each person's situation than otherwise; and to generate a wider acceptance of the fact that a homosexual or a bisexual orientation is in no way worse, morally or socially, than a heterosexual one can only be socially beneficial because it expresses a deep truth. It is never too early to inculcate the lesson that the degree of sincerity with which anyone lives, both in relation to themselves and to other people, is immeasurably more important to their ultimate happiness than the mere fact of their sexual preference.

For older homosexual and bisexual people there are an increasing number of homophile helping agencies and groups. Friend, the befriending agency originally set up by members of the Campaign for Homosexual

Equality, is now 2 years old and is still growing, with several groups operative in London and the provinces. Another agency, more GLF orientated, is Icebreakers. Both of these offer the befriending support of avowedly homosexual people to their distressed brothers and sisters. All these agencies (including the Albany Trust) would be the first to recognise that what they are currently providing is inadequate, as are their resources: this makes it all the more essential that they should strive to develop co-operative links of mutual friendship rather than indulge in any destructive attitudes of rivalry towards one another.

To approach the homophile movement through counselling may seem to be putting the cart before the horse. But I do not believe this to be the case. For counselling and individual help are the most universal needs revealed by the work of all homophile groups. It is now time for a brief account of some of these.

Like many other causes, that represented by the various homosexual organisations now existing in Britain displays a variety of emphases, attitudes and personalities. The homophile movement, in common with other facets of politics and of social work, ranges from 'radical left' to 'reformist right', providing a number of different outlets for committed individuals of varying temperaments.

On the extreme left of the spectrum is the Gay Liberation Front. In its early days, with a big London weekly meeting involving several hundred men and women, it could properly be regarded as a cohesive and growing movement, but latterly it has evolved into a number of smaller, autonomous groups active not only in London but also in other parts of the country. While these vary somewhat in their ideologies and strategy they can all correctly be described as revolutionary in a social sense, demanding as they do the reconstruction of society, and in particular the dissolution of the nuclear family, as a prelude to ending the 'oppression' of homosexuals. They are consciously engaged in sexual politics of an extreme and frequently Marxist (or neo-Marxist) tinge. A most useful service is performed, not only for them but for everyone interested in the homophile movement, by the Leeds GLF which produces several times a year a Broadsheet, listing all the homophile groups throughout the country known to the compilers, frequently with up-to-date news of their activities.

At the other extreme of the homophile movement is CHE, the Campaign for Homosexual Equality, which claims well over 3000 members and some 80 local groups and which has a highly structured organisation, including an annual conference, a quarterly national council and a national executive committee. 'Reformist' in attitude, CHE has evolved from a North Western Homosexual Law Reform Committee, founded a decade ago by Allan Horsfall, a Lancashire Labour councillor who later became CHE's first Chairman, in local support of the Homosexual Law Reform Society's work. After the 1967 Sexual Offences Act was passed, the North Western Homosexual Law Reform Committee became first the Committee and then the Campaign for Homosexual Equality, basing its programme on the need for further law reform so as to remove remaining legal discrimination against homosexuals, and also on the need to fight continuing social discrimination. Its efforts to promote non-profit-making, openly homosexual social clubs in various English towns along the lines of COC's famous Amsterdam clubhouse have not, so far, met with success (the resources and public backing needed for such an enterprise would be considerable), nor has the law as yet been further reformed; but the very fact of CHE's existence has given great help and encouragement to many thousands of homosexuals. Latterly, CHE has been concentrating upon an educational campaign, aimed at drawing the attention of schools to the needs of homosexual pupils. This has, not altogether surprisingly, been received by some teachers rather negatively, but perseverance may well yield worthwhile results. A most powerful ally in this respect has been the National Union of Students, which at its 1973 Annual Conference passed a comprehensive resolution condemning educational and social discrimination against homosexuals and pledging the NUS itself to campaign on their behalf and to support the setting up of 'Gaysocs' in Universities and other Colleges of Further Education. This first active involvement of a major national non-homosexual organisation in the promotion of a fairer deal for homosexual people has been of great encouragement to everyone concerned with the question.

Results of campaigns such as these are bound to be slow at first. But it is much to the credit of those individual members of CHE, of GLF and of other homophile groups who are actively involving themselves in this way that they are prepared to face up to public ignorance and prejudice as they are doing; by no means always without considerable personal risks to their careers and personal relationships with their families and others who do not know them to be 'gay'. The mere fact that such risks are still involved in letting it be known that one is homosexual or bisexual emphasises the urgent need for what they are doing.

Active campaigning is, however, only carried out by a minority of any homophile organisation's members. Most of those who join one of the groups are primarily interested in the social and recreational opportunities provided by their existence. For an exhaustive list of the homophile organisations, the reader is referred to Gay News (published fortnightly from 62A Chiswick High Road, London W41 SY, price 15p.) or to the Leeds GLF Broadsheet previously mentioned (obtainable from Gay Liberation Leeds, 153 Woodhouse Lane, Leeds LS2 9JT). It is only possible here to refer briefly to some of the other larger groups which exist in addition to GLF and CHE.

In Scotland, the Scottish Minorities Group has achieved some remarkable progress in its relatively few years of life. With some initial help from the Albany Trust, good working relationships were established at an early stage with the Care and Counselling Unit of the Church of Scotland. This was of especial significance because of that Church's original opposition to the Wolfenden recommendations, an opposition recently reversed. The law in Scotland, however, remains formally as it was in England before 1967, although the Scottish Law Officers have recently assured SMG that it is not public policy to prosecute consenting adults for their private behaviour. SMG has recently drafted its own law reform Bill for Scotland, going further in some respects than does the present English law, but they have not so far found a parliamentary sponsor, and it may be that law reform in Scotland (and in Northern Ireland) will have to await the more comprehensive revision of English and United Kingdom law relating to sexual behaviour foreshadowed by the report which has been drafted by a working party of the Sexual Law Reform Society (the successor to the Homosexual Law Reform Society). SMG, in addition to its law reforming vigour, has held some useful public seminars and established regular social meetings in Edinburgh, Glasgow and other Scottish towns. It is already a significant influence north of the Border.

In England, there are, in addition to CHE and other smaller primarily social groups (such as St. Katharine's) or groups catering for special interests (e.g. The Jewish Homophile Liaison Group), all of which are predominantly male, several homophile organisations catering primarily for women. The earliest of these, Arena Three, began as a magazine in 1963 and subsequently developed social groups in various parts of the country. A second primarily social group, Kenric, exists in London and a third, Sappho, is (like Arena Three) national with a monthly magazine as well as regular meetings.

As a result of a conference convened at York in 1970 by the Albany Trust and the Yorkshire Council of Social Service, a working party of the various groups then existing drew up a constitution for a National Federation of Homophile Organisations, which came into being in the autumn of 1971. Originally intended to be an umbrella for the various homophile groups, NFHO was never comprehensive because the GLF did not join, and was weakened in the summer of 1973 by the withdrawal of CHE and SMG who, for reasons never made entirely clear to the NFHO's executive committee, were not willing to remain within the framework which they themselves had helped to create. Nonetheless, it is to be hoped that breaches within the homophile movement — whether caused by structures or by personalities — will be overcome in the best interests of the millions of homosexual and bisexual people who are not members of any homophile organisation, but who can only stand to lose by feuds and divisions amongst the people who actively set out to champion their cause.

Those of us who work in any sector of the homophile cause are only too wearisomely familiar with the main aspects of the homosexual 'problem'. The obvious question to be asked is why should it be a problem at all? Ultimately it is not homosexuals themselves, but the rest of society, which makes it so. Sex is not the single most significant aspect of most peoples personalities (though of course there are some homosexuals — and some heterosexuals as well — who are obsessed by it). What all human beings seek is the freedom to live and to love freely as they choose and as happily as they can; surely not an unreasonable aspiration. For the homosexual, in society as its present laws and conventions are structured, this is frequently harder than for the heterosexual. Yet homosexual love and successful homosexual love-relationships are not hard to observe around us in the community — at any rate to those whose eyes are open.

What is distressing is the amount of hypocrisy and self deception involved, among both the majority and the minority. Homosexuals are enmeshed, despite themselves, in a pernicious form of 'double blind' whereby — unless they are brave enough or lucky enough to have managed to 'come out' without adverse effects upon their personal and working lives — they are forced to conceal their homosexuality from most of their non-homosexual acquaintances and are then denounced as hypocrites if it is inadvertently revealed. Prejudice and discrimination against homosexuals in the home, in education, in employment and in social relations is still the rule rather than the exception; as one of the leaders of the American homophile movement, Dr. Franklin Kameny, has written: 'The homosexual is faced at every turn with a relentless barrage of assaults upon his self-esteem and his dignity . . . (which) add up to a concentrated and rather virulent dose of psychological poison[3]. It is small wonder that the response of some homosexual people to this situation is to take refuge in over-compensatory arrogance, in self-deception, or even in self-hatred, or in some other neurotic manifestation of social pathology, such as alcoholism: the wonder, in prevailing circumstances, is not that there are so many damaged and neurotic homosexual personalities, but that there are so few.

The helping professions, notably the Churches, medicine, psychiatry and social work have a bounden duty to take the lead in reducing the historic injustices heaped upon the homosexual. A start has been made; in the 16 years since the Wolfenden Report appeared, all these institutions have markedly changed their own traditional attitudes. But many members of them are still far from accepting the homosexual or bisexual man or woman as a human being who is simply equal but different. When such a happy state of understanding and tolerance has been reached, the resulting benefits to the community as a whole will be enormous. We shall have achieved a state in which we can approach our own and others' sexuality without fear or bias, and value a man or a woman not for *whom* they love but for how *loving* they are.

## REFERENCES
1. *Report of the Departmental Committee on Homosexual Offences and Prostitution.* (1957). (HMSO, Cmnd. 247)
2. Kinsey, Pomeroy and Martin (1948). *Sexual Behaviour in the Human Male.* (Philadelphia and London: Saunders)
3. Kameny F. (1969): "Gay is Good". In, *The Same Sex.* (Weltge, editor) (Philadelphia: Pilgrim Press)

**For Further Reading**
Albany Trust: *Homosexuality — some questions and answers*
Wainwright Churchill: *Homosexual Behaviour Among Males.* (Hawthorn Books Inc.)
L. Crompton: *Homosexuality and the Sickness Theory.* (Albany Trust)
Gay Liberation Front: *Manifesto*
Peter Righton (ed): *Counselling Homosexuals.* (Bedford Square Press)

# 6

# Homosexuality and the Law

## N.H. Fairbairn

In an ideal society, law would probably be unnecessary, since the concept of an ideal society involves the assumption that the aspirations and activities of the members of the society will never be in conflict or in contradiction. The fact that they inevitably are regularly in contradiction, not only demonstrates the absurdity of the concept of a society so different from the world as we know it, but it also explains the necessity for the law. All laws are concerned with the status, rights, duties, and powers of the individual—what is loosely called 'the freeedom of the individual'. And the law becomes necessary only when the rights or freedoms, of one individual come into conflict with the rights or freedoms of others—either individually or as a group. The law is created to adjust those competing freedoms. Indeed, it is frequently and often deliberately overlooked by those who seek reform of the law in one particular direction or another, that the 'right' sought can be exercised *in vacuo* whereas the exercise of almost all 'rights' impinges upon the ability of others to exercise their rights.

This conflict between competing rights whether active or passive rights, may take place instantly or vicariously. The law therefore has to protect or balance, as society wishes it, not only freedoms which are in inevitable competition with one another, but also freedoms which may have a distant effect on the rights of others, or of society. The proper scope of this second aspect of the law's duty is more difficult for the legislators to anticipate correctly because it varies from time to time in society and is often  matter of conflicting opinion. Since it is difficult to assess or measure accurately, it is more easy for a tilted reformer to ridicule or hold null.But the law is very concerned with the secondary effect of private behaviour on other rights, and it is for this reason that it puts many limitations on the freedom of individuals, even in the privacy of their own homes. That even in the confines of privacy the exercise of certain rights may be held to have a secondary effect, is demonstrated by the case of the Law of Homosexuality in Germany. Article 175 of the German Legal Code makes sodomy an offence punishable by imprisonment. Article 8 of the European Convention of Human Rights guarantees, as one of those rights, the sanctity of private life. But attempts by reformers in Germany to have Article 175 declared a violation of Article 8 of the European Convention of Human Rights have been held to be manifestly ill-founded, because of the secondary effects of such conduct. Thus, under Article 8, a high contracting party is permitted to punish homosexual acts in private since the right to respect for private and family life may, in a democractic society, be subject to interference in accordance with the law of that party for the protection of health and morals. In approaching, therefore, any discussion of the rights or wrongs of the law as it applies to persons in private, it must be remembered that the law is concerned not only with immediate conduct and its effect, but with the secondary effect which conduct in private may have.

Now, while in matters of civil law the individuals are left to fight it out between themselves when their rights compete, in the criminal law the power is reserved for the state on behalf of society to declare and prosecute as criminal what it considers, as the guardian of society, to be contrary to the interest of society. There are, of course, many forms of conduct which are deviant but which the state holds nevertheless to be harmless because such conduct does not affect the interests of anybody else. The practice of homosexuality is deviant and psychopathological in origin, a fact which is denied only by those 'for whom hope creates of itself the thing it contemplates'. Its origin and consequent manifestation emanates from the relationship of the child with its father or mother—a relationship which may be echoed or magnified, modified or snuffed, by aspects of the community in which the child grows up, and by other experiences. Since the sexual drive is overriding, and since the law is particularly concerned with the rights of the child and the family, it is naïve to approach the duty of the law from the point of view that 'what I do in my own house is nothing to do with anyone else'. But there does remain the important question, which is in many societies a subject of bitter debate, as to whether homosexual acts between males in private have an effect on the rights of other members of society who are not parties to the particular act, to such an extent that society should receive the protection of the criminal law; in other words, should such activity be forbidden or permitted? If forbidden, it must be treated as criminal since the law has no other sanction.

Homosexual acts between males in public, or in private, have been held to be criminal in varying degrees by societies and nations throughout the ages. The law in communities has differed widely from time to time and from place to place. There are many societies in which homosexuality as a phenomenon, amongst male or female, is unknown, unsought, and unpractised, and has never been known—such as in Nigeria, certainly until very recently. In such societies, where it is known and practised, its extent and practice differ widely from time to time and amongst different sections of the community. It is sometimes argued that a society that holds such acts to be criminal is uncivilised and one that does not is enlightened. However, the state of the law is more often an indication of the extent and practice of the deviancy than of an attitude of society to it.

Today, homosexual acts of almost any kind between males in public are held to be criminal in the majority of nations, and the silence of the law in the remaining nations is more often due to the absence of the problem rather than the tolerance of such public behaviour. But most Western societies which previously held homosexual acts in private between males to be criminal have reformed the law on this matter since the Second World War. The German Invasion of many European countries suspended the law of the occupied countries for 5 years, as had the Napoleonic Invasions before it. And the reform or the renaissance of the system of law at the time of liberation is one of the unintended, or incidental benefits, of war. For laws are made for the benefit of society as society judges its good from time to time. The opportunity to begin afresh is rare, and results usually from terrible political trauma such as war or revolution. Normally, the law is in favour of its established principles and its *status quo* until it can be shown that the need and rights of the community require a change. Hence the national resistance to reform. Such is the story of the reform of the law of male homosexual practice in private in England and Wales. The Sexual Offences Act of 1956, Section 12, makes it a felony for a person to commit buggery with another person, or with an animal. Section 13 makes it a felony for a man to commit an act of gross indecency with another man in public, or in private. This Act of Parliament, codified and brought up to date, was the Law of England on a wide number of sexual offences all others of which were concerned with heterosexual acts against women of tender age. 11 years later, the Sexual Offences Act of 1967 made major amendments to the law of England and Wales relating to homosexual acts between males in private.

The reform began seriously with the setting up on August 24th 1954 of the Wolfenden Committee. This arose because there had been a very large increase in the number of prosecutions of males for private homosexual acts in England. The Committee reported in September 1957 and a debate occurred on December 5th 1967 in the House of Lords. At that time, the Lord Chancellor said, 'The Government does not think that the general sense of the community was with the committee in their recommendations'. In the House of Commons, a debate occurred nearly a year later on November 26th 1958 when the Home Secretary asked this pertinent question: 'If we were drawing up a code for the first colonists of the moon, should we make this kind of offence a criminal offence?'. Nearly ten years later, the Sexual Offences Act under the steering head of Leo Abse, MP, became law. Sub-Section One provided 'Notwithstanding any statutory or common law provision but subject to the provisions of the next following section, a homosexual act in private will not be an offence provided the parties consent thereto and have attained the age of 21 years'. And Sub-Section Seven provides: 'That a man shall be treated as doing a homosexual act if, and only if, he commits buggery with another man or commits an act of gross indecency with another man, or is a party to the commission by a man of such an act'. Thus, in the absence of war, this reform took the classic route — injustice, pressure, resistance, debated and reluctant acquiescence. And Parliament decided, balancing the rights of a homosexual to exercise the overriding urge of sexual expression, and the rights of the community to be free from homosexual assault or justified fear of it, that such conduct should not be treated as criminal.

Now, while England acted in the classic method of reform and looked at matters afresh, Scotland, her neighbour, has not. In Scotland, homosexual acts in private can still be prosecuted at common law in the Sheriff Court by summary or solemn procedure, or in the High Court at common law, or in either court under Section Eleven of the Criminal Law Amendment Act of 1885 which states, under the heading of Outrages on Decency: 'Any male person who in public or private commits, or is a party to the commission of, or procures or attempts to procure the commission of by any male person an act of gross indecency with another male person shall be guilty of a misdemeanour and being convicted thereof shall be liable at the discretion of the court to be imprisoned for any term not exceeding two years'. At first, it might be assumed that the puritan and presbyterian character of Scotland were responsible for the distinction in the reforms of the two countries. But that is not so. On almost all matters, the law of Scotland has always been much more liberal than the law of England, and the reason that the law of England required reform was because under their system, a growing number of random, selective, and often seedy and spiteful prosecutions of homosexual activities between consenting adult males in complete privacy were being presented and prosecuted by the police. Manifest injustice produced inevitable and just reform as it often does. But in Scotland no such prosecutions occur. Homosexual acts in private are unmolested by the law, and more important than that, the prosecutor in Scotland is either the Procurator-Fiscal in the Sheriff Court or the Lord Advocate in the High Court, each of whom is independent of the police and is able to take a more detached and less emotional view of the circumstances of each case. Section Eleven, like other Sections of the Act, has fallen into somnolent dissuetude which is frequently a better system of reform since it raises no clamour and arouses no passion and allows the practice of the law to adjust naturally to the habits of society. Indeed, the Lord Advocate has given an assurance that the law will be applied in that way. And were that assurance not enough, the records of the Courts speak for themselves. In 1877, before the passing of the Act, two soldiers in Oban were sentenced to 12 months imprisonment for a homosexual act in public and in 1879 a man was sentenced to 15 years for a homosexual assault on a boy of 9; in 1884 a man was sentenced to 8 years for a homosexual assault on a boy of 11; in 1895 a man was sentenced to 5 years for a homosexual assault on a boy of 6. There is no case recorded in Scotland of a prosecution of consenting adults in private—only in public acts, and those against boys of tender age, have been prosecuted in the last 100 years. Two cases in quasi private perhaps demonstrate the attitude to the homosexual in private in Scotland; in 1933 two consenting adults in a urinal received sentences of only 1 and 2 months, and in 1936 a man of 71 and a boy of 21 committing buggery in a lane, received sentences of 8 and 18 months respectively. The tolerance of homosexual acts in private between consenting adults has been the practice of the law of Scotland for 100 years, and it is now the statutory law of England where the prosecution of such offences had previously been the habit of the law.

This tolerance is both enlightened and sensitive, but it is also perhaps reluctant, and it is important to notice the exceptional position of homosexuality in the law, for no other activity tolerated in private attracts such strict control in public. Even the most liberal nation sets strict limits on age and privacy. Throughout the world, acts with persons under age are severely punished because consent may be obtained from the young under the cloak of friendship, and may be given from fear of rejecting the will of an adult. For this reason the law protects equally severely the young male and the young female from adult sexual advances. It is sometimes argued, however, that it is discriminating against the homosexual to make the age of consent higher for girls than for boys. But homosexuality and hetero-sexuality are not equivalent phenomena or activities. It is normal for the female to be sexually orientated to the male, and the female develops the innate ability to reject the advance of a male which the male lacks. Where deviant behaviour is tolerated, it is important to ensure that the sexual orientation of the younger partner is mature and that consent is genuinely forthcoming. It is interesting to note that where they are dealt with in the legal code of nations, whether tolerated in private or not, homosexual acts between males are generally classed amongst outrages against decency, and in most systems with outrages and assaults upon the female person. The Sexual Offences Act of 1956 which governed the law of England until its reform summarises the law relating to sexual crimes, abduction, procuration and prostitution of women and kindred offences, and it includes intercourse by force, intercourse with girls under 16, intercourse with defectives, incest, sexual assaults, abduction, prostitution, procuration, solicitation, and the suppression of brothels. The restrictions and principal restraints which are put upon heterosexual behaviour in that Act, are equally struck at by the liberal 1967 Act with regard to male homosexual conduct. The law is anxious to ensure that any sexual act with a young person is one which is genuinely consented to.

If adults can consent in private, what is an act of gross indecency in public? The Turkish Legal Code describes it as a lewd act which causes public annoyance, and that probably is as good a definition as any. But one may ask 'If heterosexuals can kiss each other in public without committing an act of gross indecency why should not homosexuals?'. The answer is quite simple. All nations forbid the manifestation of deviant conduct in public. It is both false and illogical to try to equate heterosexual and homosexual conduct, or to suggest that the homosexual has the same 'rights' as the heterosexual. For these two phenomena, though both expressions of sexual activity, have different origins and different goals, the only thing they probably have in common is the strength and ferocity of the drive. Any attempt to equate the 'rights' of the homosexual to the 'rights' of the heterosexual overlooks the deeply felt fears and aggressions from which homosexuality springs, and would be likely to antagonise and offend the community, whose support is essential for any tolerance and reform. The law is concerned that each person should be able to exercise the maximum of freedom in safety with the interests of others. Therefore so long as the homosexual can exercise his sexual rights in private the law properly allows him to do so, but any attempt to make the homosexual a competitor with the heterosexual for equality or ascendancy of rights would result in a grave entrenchment of the law in any community in which it was tried. It is to be hoped that the tolerance of the law will be matched by the tolerance of the community and will thus remove the feeling of frustration and persecution which are the sources of challenge and conflict, and which it is the purpose of the law to resolve.

# 7

# Homosexuality and the Church

## K. Boyd

The Christian Church no longer keeps the conscience of the West. During the last few centuries much of that task has been taken over by such secular agencies as the Press, Parliament, Schools, Universities, the Professions and many different voluntary and statutory bodies concerned with the common good. At the same time the part played by private judgement in the determination of matters of belief and conduct has greatly increased. The Church, whose membership now represents a much smaller proportion of the population than in the past, thus can no longer expect its teaching on religion and morals to command widespread attention. As a consequence of this, any discussion in the present context of the Church's attitude to homosexuality may seem superfluous, or at best peripheral to the real needs of contemporary society.

Against this conclusion, however, the following four considerations must be set. Firstly, the church's attitude to homosexuality requires some attention because in historical terms the Church has played an important and perhaps a decisive part in the formation of contemporary public opinion on the subject. Anyone who is concerned with difficult psychological or sociological problems cannot afford to ignore the question of how these problems arose, nor the question of how those ultimately affected by such problems are to come to terms with their personal and social past. For this historical reason alone the Church's attitude to homosexuality cannot be regarded simply as a peripheral matter.

However the Church's attitude to homosexuality also requires attention for a second reason. The Churches may at present be in a state of institutional decline. But this is more apparent in the European than in the world-wide context, and there is little reason to suppose that the present trend, which owes a great deal to a particular set of historical circumstances, will continue. The Western Church's loss of influence stems in no small measure from a secularisation of human hopes consequent upon the rising expectations of industrial society and scientific culture. Many people, including many Christians and certainly the present writer, may dislike the prospect of a 'return to religion' based on the rejection of these rising material standards. These developments, after all, have greatly improved the health and welfare of very many human beings; and very many others remain desperately in need of them. But disenchantment with the achievements no less than with the failures of secularised society is far from impossible in the long view of human history. And if this possibility is realised, on however individualistic a basis, it is likely that the Church's attitudes to question of belief and behaviour will play no little part in the formation of new social attitudes and public policies.

A third reason for paying some attention in the present context to the Church's attitude is less speculative. Statistics concerning church membership or religious orthodoxy may be misleading. For they may obscure the fact that a substantial proportion of the population continue, however occasionally, to find ways of articulating their self-understanding within the language and practices of the institutional Churches. And since a proportion of those who do so are homosexuals, it follows that a proportion of professional relationships with homosexuals are relationships with Christian homosexuals. Under these circumstances a counsellor or therapist may wish that his Catholic or Evangelical homosexual client would abandon beliefs which seem to frustrate the goals of therapy. Yet he cannot ignore the possibility that these goals may be no less endangered by the psychological consequences of such a desired deconversion itself. Only if the counsellor or therapist is able to offer an alternative form of self-understanding and an alternative supportive community could such dangers be avoided, even in theory. And even if the theoretical and practical problems involved could be overcome — which seems unlikely — it would hardly be consonant with the counsellor's or therapist's professional neutrality to make such an offer. This being the case the professional relationship with a homosexual who is in some sense Christian would seem to demand respect for and understanding of the way in which that client chooses to articulate his self-understanding. If the language which the client chooses then still appears to the counsellor or therapist to be positively unhelpful, his task would seem to involve questioning it in ways which connect rather than conflict with the client's self-understanding.

But if it is important for professional and therapeutic reasons that the Christian attitude to homosexuality should be widely understood, it is no less important for social reasons. If a certain proportion of the much larger homosexual population who need no therapy are Christians, then society should do everything possible to allow these Chistian homosexuals to come to terms with their condition and with their religion. Optimistic heterosexual social engineers may think differently: but neither Christianity nor homosexuality is a temporary phenomenon. The full implications of this have only very recently dawned on many Christians, and this has not happened without a great deal of social pressure from outside the Church. But under this pressure the Church has begun to rethink its attitude to homosexuality, and this rethinking has proved beneficial to homosexuals and Christians alike. It may not continue, however, and there may even be a backlash, unless those who are concerned with the question of homosexuality also continue to be concerned with such organisations as the Churches, within which many people still find ways of explaining who they really are.

These then are four reasons why the Church's attitude to homosexuality may seem worthy of serious consideration in the present context. But it is of course an oversimplification to talk of the Church's attitude. Different Churches and different Christians have held and hold different views about homosexuality. What follows therefore is an attempt to trace the development of those views and to understand some of their implications. The discussion is in 6 sections which deal, respectively, with: (1) The Judaeo-Christian Scriptures; (2) The Catholic Tradition; (3) The Reaction to Enlightenment; (4) Attitudes to the Law; (5) Contemporary Theological Rethinking; and (6) Pastoral Implications.

## The Judaeo—Christian Scriptures

One of the tasks of Christian theology is that of making the present meaningful through the creative reinterpretation of the past in terms of the transcendent. There are perhaps few aspects of Christian teaching in which this task has been more constructively carried out in recent years than in relation to the Scriptural view of homosexuality, the sometime sin of Sodom. Inevitably, Christian teaching is rooted in the Scriptures of the Old and New Testaments. But whereas prior to a hundred or so years ago priests and ministers were able to cite these Scriptures with a fine disregard for questions of context, consistency and composition, the modern period has brought to the Bible a form of critical scholarship which makes such cavalier treatment, if not impossible, then at least much more difficult. Most students in training for the ministries of the major denominations are at some point in their careers exposed to this scholarship, and even if they choose to forget or to suppress what they have been taught, the existence of an increasingly educated laity, who learn about such scholarship in schools, colleges and popular books about religion, makes it daily more difficult for the average clergyman to avoid the issues involved.

The conclusions of this Biblical criticism concerning the Scriptural view of homosexuality have been dramatic. The crucial work on this subject was done in the early 1950's by the Anglican clergyman D.S. Bailey. Before the public controversy which led to the Wolfenden Commission had broken, Bailey realised that his Church's attitude to homosexuality required revision, especially in relation to the law and to pastoral care. And having persuaded the Church of England's Moral Welfare Council to set up an interdisciplinary group to study these questions, he undertook, at that group's request, an investigation of the Biblical and historical aspects of the problem'. His conclusions concerning the Scriptural view of homosexuality may be briefly summarised.

Bailey found that Biblical references to homosexuality were few and far between. In the Old Testament, apart from the story of Sodom, to which we shall return in a moment, he found only two short passages which in his opinion definitely referred to homosexual acts. These two passages (Leviticus ch. 18 v. 22 and ch. 20 v. 13) condemned homosexual acts between males, and the second prescribed the death penalty. The exact date and purpose of the legal code to which they belonged however was uncertain, and they gave little clue to the incidence of homosexual acts or of their punishment among the ancient Hebrews. Nor, in Bailey's opinion, was there sufficient extra-Biblical evidence to substantiate the suggestion, which the authors of Leviticus may have wished to imply, that their Middle Eastern neighbours were particularly tolerant of homosexuality. Other Old Testament passages investigated by Bailey on the ground that their language either in the original or in translation had at some time suggested a reference to homosexual acts, were even less revealing. Even supposing that they did refer to homosexuality, which was unlikely, they added nothing very significant to the passages from Leviticus; and overall there was little or no evidence for the assertion, sometimes made by scholars, that the Old Testament singled out homosexual acts for more severe criticism than other sexual offences.

But the locus classicus of Old Testament teaching on homosexuality had always been the story of Sodom, and it was primarily in this connection that Bailey's researches were most interesting. The story, contained in Genesis ch. 19 vv. 4-11, tells of how the men of Sodom demanded that Lot should bring out his two angelic visitors 'that we may know them'. In view of the consequent destruction of Sodom and Gomorrah, and in view of their interpretation of the Hebrew word for 'know', most ecclesiastical authorities had assumed that the men of Sodom were punished by God for their desire for homosexual relations with Lot's visitors. But careful investigation of this and other Old Testament texts in which the relevant Hebrew word for 'know' appeared, led Bailey to conclude that the homosexual interpretation was highly tenuous, and that this passage, like some other similar Old Testament stories, in fact referred to an offence against hospitality. The destruction of Sodom and Gomorrah, a historical event whose cataclysmic proportions assumed great significance for subsequent generations, was certainly referred to by later Old Testament and Apocryphal writers. It was however referred to as a punishment, not for the homosexual proclivities of the Sodomites, but for their inhospitality, meanness, arrogance and general wickedness. The first suggestion that the sin of Sodom might have any homosexual connotations did not in fact appear, Bailey discovered, until about the beginning of the second century B.C. And when it did appear, it was found to be the product of patriotic Palestinian Jews who had reinterpreted the story in the light of their own contempt for contemporary Hellenistic culture, a culture which in their eyes was forever associated with homosexual practices and paederasty in particular.

Not all Jews were so zealous however, and the homosexual interpretation was not yet to be accepted by mainstream Judaism. But it did appeal to many of the early Christians, whose eschatological perspectives made them just as suspicious of the corruptions of antiquity as the patriotic Jews had been. Yet even the Christians were slow to confirm the homosexual interpretation of the Sodom story. Examining the New Testament evidence, Bailey found only three or four definite references to homosexual practices. These references (Romans ch. 1 vv. 26 and 27, 1 Corinthians ch. 6 vv. 9 and 10, and 1 Timothy ch. 1 vv. 9 and 10) mentioned homosexual acts as examples of contemporary idolatrous and sinful practices, illustrating an orientation towards worldliness which Christians were not to share. But these passages did not mention Sodom, and even when the story was mentioned and given a sexual interpretation, as in the late New Testament Epistle of Jude (vv. 6-7) and Second Peter (ch. 2 vv. 4 and 6-8) this interpretation was probably more heterosexual than homosexual.

The homosexual interpretation of the Sodom story however made some progress during the first two Christian centuries, and when Bailey went on to examine the writings of the Fathers of the Church he found abundant evidence that such influential figures as Clement of Alexandria, John

Chrysostom and Augustine were clearly of the opinion that sodomy was the particular sin of the Sodomites. With a few notable exceptions, including perhaps Calvin, subsequent theologians and church leaders were to adhere to this opinion, and in identifying homosexual acts with such a notable example of Divine retribution, were to put the question of their morality — which otherwise would have turned upon the passages from Leviticus and the Epistles — beyond question.

In general then Bailey found that the popular, and indeed the scholarly view, that the Old and New Testaments regarded homosexual practices with a special abhorrence, was ill-founded. The Scriptures indeed proved to have very little to say on the subject. As commonly happens in discussions of the sexual attitudes and behaviour of earlier generations, it seems that assertions had been made and repeated on the basis of highly unreliable and unsatisfactory historical foundations. On the other hand however, such Biblical evidence as there was did not betoken either approval or tolerance of homosexual acts. Any suggestion that such might be implied from, for example, the Old Testament's description of David and Jonathan's friendship was firmly rejected by Bailey. His argument that there was no possible evidence for putting a narrowly homosexual construction upon this relationship, whose nature (*vide* 1 Samuel ch. 20 and 2 Samuel ch. 1) was far from clear was not however as convincing as his treatment of the Sodom story.

One further case, which Bailey did not deal with, but which has sometimes been seen as a possible example of homosexuality being tolerated in the Scriptures, is of course that of Jesus himself. The notion that Jesus might have been a homosexual is an old one: Christopher Marlowe, the sixteenth century dramatist, suggested rather disapprovingly that Jesus was not only a homosexual but also a bastard . And in the contemporary moral climate the former suggestion has been repeated rather less disapprovingly and in more respectable theological circles. But it is difficult to see how this might be substantiated. It seems to derive from Jesus' unmarried state and from the gospel reference (John ch. 13 v. 23) to one of the disciples 'whom Jesus loved' leaning on his breast. That this could bear a homosexual interpretation is possible, but the oriental context makes it far from certain. Like the suggestion that Mary Magdalene might have been Jesus' mistress, and many other notions about Jesus, it must remain in the realm of pure speculation.

This then is about all that can be said about the Scriptural foundations of Christian teaching on homosexuality. Bailey's conclusions have not, since he reached them, suffered any serious contradiction, and they are generally in line with those of other modern authorities. Leading Continental Old Testament scholars, such as G. von Rad[3], and theologians, such as H. Thielicke[4] also doubt the homosexual interpretation of the Sodom story, while the latter builds his theological assessment of the question on an interpretation of the relevant New Testament passages similar to that of Bailey. Even a Conservative Evangelical writer[5] who wishes to retain the older view of the Sodomites is careful to attribute their city's downfall more to its materialism and godlessness in general than to the specifically homosexual vices of its inhabitants. Nevertheless, while this reinterpretation of the Sodom story has removed from the scene what was formerly the most emotionally powerful Biblical text, it is undeniable that the Scriptures as a whole still assume the sinfulness of homosexual acts. The outstanding theological question therefore is that of in what this sinfulness consists.

As Western Christianity developed, the sinfulness of homosexual acts was seen to consist primarily in their intemperate and unnatural nature. On the one hand, a deepening respect for rationality led to an abhorrence of irrational or intemperate behaviour, of which unchecked lust was a type. On the other, a growing sense that the orderliness of Creation could be understood, at least in part and imperfectly, led to the opinion that unnatural behaviour was insulting or injurious to the Creator. That homosexual acts were sinful in both of these ways was clear to the Fathers of the Church, and in the influential writings of Thomas Aquinas, the thirteenth century theologian[1], this view received its definitive and normative expression. Briefly, Aquinas taught that, by reason of its irrational and intemperate nature, lust in all its forms was a vice contrary to temperance, but that unnatural vice was more sinful than such forms of lust as adultery, seduction or rape. These forms injured only other  persons: but unnatural vice injured God himself by breaking the Divine laws of sexual behaviour. According to these laws and to the ideal of rationality, sexual activity was intended as a means towards the sole end of procreation. The four forms of unnatural vice, of which the most serious was bestiality, followed in turn by sodomy, other homosexual venereal acts, and masturbation, thus included every kind of homosexual act. Homosexual contact or touch, however, was not itself sinful, provided lust was not its motive.

Aquinas' rational attitude to homosexual acts, which ultimately rested on Scripture (including the homosexual interpretation of the Sodom story) does not of course provide us with a full account of why the Church and churchmen considered such acts to be sinful. Other and less temperate Christian thinkers revealed a sort of high distaste for homosexual acts which must make them suspect to the post-Freudian mind. Aquinas however had provided reasonable arguments, which in the context of his time seemed plausible, and which continued to be plausible long after the

thirteenth century. The intemperate nature of lust and the unnatural
nature of sexual acts undirected towards procreation continued to
establish the sinfulness of homosexual practices. But when the questioning spirit of the Renaissance and the purifying spirit of the
Reformation began to break up the unity of mediaeval life and thought,
the arguments of such theologians as Aquinas were undermined.Outside
the Church there had come into existence a new sphere of autonomous
secular thinking. Within its divided framework there now existed a
Protestant theology which respected the Catholic tradition much less than
it respected Scripture. On such less radical wings of Protestantism as the
Anglican and Lutheran Churches attempts of course were made to retain,
in an attenuated form, something of the traditional natural theology. But
for the most part, the increasing separation of the religious and secular
spheres and the expansion of the latter, meant that many theological
arguments which had seemed obvious in the Middle Ages were no longer
plausible. Many of these arguments were now live options only within the
circle of faith and language of the Roman Catholic Church, which despite
its losses remained large enough to generate its own system of plausi-
bilities. Outside that circle, Reformers such as Calvin roughly repudiated
such aspects of the traditional treatment of homosexuality as Aquinas'
method of grading sins in order of seriousness. Calvin, it is true, believed
that some sins were graver than others, but he also believed that any
attempt to enumerate them in detail was impossible. For Scripture taught
that sins were too many to be counted, and the traditional distinction
between mortal and venial sins simply obscured the fact that all of them
were deadly [6].

Yet despite their repudiation of traditional opinions it is difficult to
escape the impression that in their own minds the Reformers continued to
grade sins in order of seriousness, and that with the possible exception of
Luther and certain radicals, they put sexual sins rather high on their
private lists. It would of course have been surprising if this had not been
the case, for apparent discontinuities in history are rarely as discontinuous
as they appear in retrospect. But while the Reformers and their successors
often accepted the conclusions of the very arguments they repudiated,
their repudiation of these arguments eventually made it difficult for them
to defend the conclusions. After the Enlightenment, and the rise of the
natural and social sciences, when the traditional ways of understanding
both rationality and human nature were thrown into the intellectual
melting-pot, the assertions of Protestant theologians on such subjects as
sexuality lacked the support of any very rigorous theological arguments.
Such arguments as there were consisted either in very general appeals to
Scripture — the mere mention of Sodom was enough to stop an

argument — or in equally general appeals to popular notions of what was natural. But on the whole arguments were not required, since on the plane of popular discussion if not always on that of popular behaviour, the Church's assertions were in broad agreement with the consensus of public opinion. The question of homosexuality was thus scarcely mentioned by those nineteenth century Protestant theologians who undertook the task of interpreting Christian ethics. But when popular notions of what was natural began to be questioned by natural and social scientists, and when popular interpretations of what Scripture meant began to be questioned by biblical critics, Protestant theologians and churchmen found their traditional stance undermined. Understandably enough they were confused: and while some were reduced to emotional reactions, others remained silent in the hope that the problem would go away. Their position was made no easier by the uneasy feeling that criticism of any particular Christian teaching was criticism of the whole, and this induced a defensive mood. Catholic theologians, on the other hand, had preserved many of the traditional theological arguments. Together with Conservative Evangelicals (who rejected biblical criticism) they were in no position to persuade the unconverted of the truth of their teachings on sexuality. But in Protestant countries, at least, they were for the time being in the militant mood of a once persecuted minority which now saw its chance to convert the unconverted. Over against an increasingly agnostic Protestantism, they offered the eternal verities of a great tradition, whose particular verities it was unwise to question.

At the present time the attitudes just described are still in many respects those of many Protestants and Catholics. In the case of Catholicism of course, moral theology has in some respects moved on from the Middle Ages: on some related matters, such as for example, the legitimate contraceptive use of the rhythm method, the position has certainly changed: what Augustine condemned is now permitted. But on the whole continuity is more apparent than change; and this is particularly true in relation to homosexuality. The orthodox Catholic view today, as expressed for example by E.F. Healy in *Medical Ethics* (1956)[7], is still basically that of Aquinas. Even within the Anglican tradition the arguments of mediaeval moral theology continue to have currency. The group mentioned above, which initiated Bailey's Scriptural and historical investigations, were far from being prepared to jettison the traditional interpretation of the sinfulness of homosexual acts. In their report, *Sexual Offenders and Social Punishment* (1956)[3], which Bailey edited, they argued that sexual intercourse was legitimate only within a marriage relationship which did not exclude the conceptional as well as the relational purposes of intercourse. This formula left room for contraception within a marriage relationship, since it was argued that every single act of coitus need not be directed towards procreation; and of course the variety of forms of permissible contraception was wider than that allowed by orthodox Catholics. But the purpose of the formula, which was to deny legitimacy to sexual intercourse outside the context of a marriage relationship, the overall aim of which was procreation, clearly ruled homosexual intercourse out of court. It was, the group argued, not only an aberration from the norm, but also a sin, since the norm was divinely ordained. In this respect therefore the traditional position was maintained, as it was in the concession that homosexual affection and caresses were permissible if their motive was innocent, if that is to say they had no narrowly sexual intention. Not even when the group went on to develop the traditional distinction between objective morality and moral culpability was any radical change apparent. They argued that a homosexual, who had fully investigated the moral question and was nevertheless convinced that homosexual acts were not sinful but right for him, might just possibly be regarded as in a state of invincible ignorance: he might in other words be objectively sinful without being morally culpable. But the group was quick to point out that such cases were few and that their existence should never be seen as an encouragement to objectively sinful behaviour. This particular Anglican view of the 1950's was thus in the end not so very different from that of mediaeval Catholicism.

As has already been indicated, the arguments of modern Protestants about the sinfulness of homosexuality have been much more deeply undermined by the findings of the natural and social sciences than have those of the Church's Catholic wing. But the relative receptiveness of Protestantism to new learning is its strength as well as its weakness, and in the present century some Protestants have attempted to rethink their attitude to homosexuality in a manner which is both creative and constructive. This process of rethinking has taken place in at least two stages, the first earlier in the century, the second much more recently.

Characteristic of the first stage was the writer Hugh Northcote, whose *Christianity and Sex Problems*[9], first published in 1906, represented an honest attempt to come to terms with the research of such writers as Geddes and Thomson, Krafft-Ebbing and Havelock Ellis. Northcote was particuarly concerned with the then current theory that some cases of homosexuality were caused by hereditary factors, precipitated after a latent period by some traumatic childhood or adolescent experience. This theory undermined the traditional Christian assumption that the individual might be held responsible for his homosexual inclinations. But Northcote accepted it, as he did the probability that suppression of these inclinations might cause actual physical harm to congenital homosexuals.

What he could not accept however, was the conclusion to which this led some contemporary scientists, namely that the law should no longer prohibit the homosexual cohabitation of consenting adults.

Now the reasons which Northcote gave for not accepting this conclusion are interesting in so far as they help to point out the nature of the confusion felt by many modern Christians in dealing with the subject of homosexuality. His disagreement was in the first place grounded, as might be expected, in Scripture. The Bible, he could not but conclude, condemned homosexual behaviour: for whatever might be said about David and Jonathan, Sodom was always in the background. Yet after saying this Northcote inserted a qualification: the Bible, he suggested, might not in the end be the final court of appeal for a broad-minded modern religious scientist. This caveat was perhaps characteristic of the liberal Protestant temper of his time. But so too was his veneration for science, and the evolutionary mould in which his arguments were cast. Homosexual acts, he claimed, were not merely unprocreative but also regressive as far as moral and social evolution was concerned. Mankind's original suspicion of homosexuality had evolved into outright opposition, so strong that even homosexuals themselves instinctively disapproved of their own inclinations, and it was in society's interest to strengthen this disapproval. True, some societies had tolerated homosexual behaviour, perhaps as a contraceptive expedient: but when toleration lasted too long such societies became unhealthy and regressive. Although contemporary evidence of the results of legal toleration was ambiguous, there was always some danger that toleration might increase the incidence of homosexual acts among or involving consenting adults who were not congenitally homosexual. Society also in Northcote's view had an interest in the aesthetic side of the question, for homosexual acts were not only regressive but also objectively disgusting. And even if after taking all these considerations into account society was still prepared to tolerate the homosexual cohabitation of consenting adults, Northcote did not see how this could be arranged: for it would be difficult if not impossible to find any way of regulating such unions, since they lacked definitive sexual rights and the procreative function.

With these arguments—most of which still seem cogent criticisms of homosexual behaviour to many Christians and others—Northcote opposed removing the legal ban. At the same time however he argued that the penalties for homosexual behaviour should be extensively revised. The law, he believed, ought to recognise the existence of congenital homosexuality. And society as a whole ought not to condemn but to honour true inverts whose relationship was conducted on a spiritual plane. As did the Catholics he contended for toleration of intense, but not narrowly sexual homosexual affection and even caresses, so long as they did not descend to the venereal level. If they did so descend, the law, he believed, could not stand idly by, but when this resulted from the failure to reach a desired spiritual ideal, the legal penality should be as light as possible. Severe punishment should be reserved only for when non-congenital homosexuals or the grosser aspects of homosexuality were involved.

Northcote's treatment of homosexuality then illustrates two important aspects of the development of modern Protestant thought on the subject. The first of these is its dependence on current scientific myths and opinions. Northcote's use of biological theories about the causation of homosexuality, and his reliance upon the notion of social evolution illustrate this. Although he does not say as much, he implicitly acknowledges the possibility of further illumination from secular thinking as well as from Scripture and Tradition: and of course Scripture and Tradition will themselves have to be interpreted in the light of scientific critical enquiry. Northcote's arguments are thus open-ended, and allow for the possibility of development through further scientific investigation.

The second point to be noted here is the dependence of modern Protestant thought upon contemporary cultural attitudes to sexuality. Northcote's opposition to legislative change illustrates this. His opposition seems to rest on the belief that homosexual acts are wrong not so much because they are homosexual as because they are unregulated sexual acts. But while the social regulation of sexual behaviour is universal, the particular forms of regulation implied in Northcote's approach are not. His talk of definitive sexual rights, together with his evaluation of the passionate at the expense of the sensuous aspects of sexuality, suggest a transfer into the homosexual sphere of attitudes to physical virginity which were inextricably interwoven not just with the Christian tradition but also with nineteenth century middle class patterns of behaviour. These patterns however changing even as Northcote wrote; and today they are much criticised because of their association with property and inheritance. In contemporary Western society, marriage has become a compact between individuals rather than a transaction between families, and the premarital loss of physical virginity is now much less frequently regarded in terms of spoilt goods. As a consequence, heterosexual intercourse is now regarded in terms more of relationships than of rights. Thus while there are many other popular reasons for objecting to homosexual acts, objections based on the transference from the heterosexual sphere of notions about physical virginity have lost a great deal of their force.

Northcote's arguments thus show how modern Protestant thought about homosexuality is dependent on the one hand upon current scientific myths and theories, and on the other upon contemporary cultural attitudes to and patterns of sexual behaviour. Modern Protestant thought about homosexuality therefore is in principle at least extremely open-ended. Just how open-ended it is, can be seen by comparing two popular Christian books about sex which appeared in the succeeding decades. Following Northcote, mention of homosexuality as such became permissible and the Presbyterian minister A. Herbert Gray dealt with the subject in passing in his *Men, Women and God* (1923)". Gray's treatment of the subject largely consisted in warning young people that homosexuality was always a perversion, regressive and fraught with psychological dangers. In particular he warned young women that an innocent 'G.P..' (grande passion) should not be allowed to develop into an unhealthy homosexual relationship. But his advice on how to deal with homosexual inclinations — plenty of exercise, cold baths and prayer — was in fact little different from that of the average Victorian pulpit allusion to nameless sins. In contrast to this, *The Mastery of Sex through Psychology and Religion* (1931 and still being reprinted in the late 1950s)" by the Methodist minister, Leslie D. Weatherhead, was a more serious attempt to take psychological insights into account. Weatherhead distinguished between innate and acquired homosexuality: the former, he wrote, was something the psychiatrist could do little about: but although the patient might never be cured, the knowledge that his condition was not a vice might alleviate his mental anguish. Acquired homosexuality on the other hand was something the psychiatrist could do something about. In some cases at least, the abandonment of sexual repression and the development of a deeper level of self-awareness, as well as hypnosis and other psychological or religious methods, could lead to a cure for homosexuality. Weatherhead's position, which was, roughly, that good psychology and good religion were the same, thus again illustrates both the dependence of modern Protestant thinking on contemporary scientific views and the open-endedness of that thinking.

But although Weatherhead's position exemplifies the way in which the open-ended nature of modern Protestant thinking has developed, it also exemplifies the way in which modern Protestant thinking has maintained continuity with its past. This can be seen by observing how, in Weatherhead's account, the overt stigma of homosexual sinfulness is replaced by the covert stigma of homosexual sickness or at best homosexual immaturity. Thus the mediaeval conclusions were in some sense retained; and it is perhaps as a consquence of this that such views, once considered ultra-liberal, have come to be accepted by a wide variety of Protestants. Even as orthodox a theologian as Karl Barth[12], and even

Catholic writers[7][13], can make use of the language of pathology alongside that of traditional theology in order to condemn homosexual behaviour.

Until recently Weatherhead's position could have been considered modern Protestantism's last word on the subject. For although Protestant thought is open-ended, it is not so open-ended as to regard all forms of sexual behaviour as equally acceptable. It has after all been assumed to be part of the task of Churches and theology to reflect on human behaviour in a discriminating fashion, to say 'yes' to some activities and 'no' to others. Thus as long as Protestant thinkers found that secular scientists and therapists considered homosexuals to be unhealthy or immature, and as long as homosexuals themselves did not challenge this view, there was little reason to reconsider the Church's basic position.

## ATTITUDES TO THE LAW

The only point at which there did seem some reason to question rather than to reinterpret the Church's basic position was, as Northcote had suggested, in relation to the law. But this question did not become urgent — in terms that is of British public opinion — until the 1950's, when the Churches made submissions to the Wolfenden Committee and reacted to its findings.

In this context the question of the history of the Church's attitude to laws concerning homosexuality was another subject which D.S. Bailey and his colleagues greatly clarified. In Bailey's view the Church's record in this field had been widely misinterpreted, not only by popular writers but also by scholars such as Havelock Ellis. It had been repeatedly asserted that throughout history the Church had been obsessed with homosexuality and had been a prime persecutor of homosexuals. But the context from which these assertions derived had been the highly polemical atmosphere of much eighteenth and nineteenth century historical and anthropological scholarship. In that period many advanced thinkers had seen themselves, with some but not much justification, as latter day Galileos, and the Church as the great enemy of free enquiry. Since many of these scholars were conscious unbelievers in what was at least outwardly a religious age, they had often tended towards gullible extrapolation when they came across any evidence of ecclesiastical obscurantism or inhumanity. It was necessary therefore for some of their assumptions to be questioned, and this was what Bailey set out to do.

Bailey did this by examining ecclesiastical legislation and pastoral practice in the Patristic and Mediaeval periods. From his examination of ecclesiastical legislation it emerged that Christianity had not been the inventor of laws against homosexual practices. Although the symbolism of

Sodom added colour to the Church's condemnation of such practices, it was clear enough that homosexual acts between adults as well as with minors had been punishable, if not always punished, under the pre-Christian Roman Law. What the establishment of Christianity as the religion of the Roman Empire had led to had been the reinforcement of legal sanctions, so much so indeed that by the end of the fourth century A.D. the penalties for sodomy included death by burning. But it was very uncertain how far such extreme penalties were ever exacted, since as Bailey's research revealed, the primary purpose of these Christian law-makers and later of the legislative efforts of Justinian, the sixth century Christian Emperor, was to produce repentance reformation and re-habilitation among sinners through the much less extreme discipline of the Church. Only if this failed was the obdurate sinner to be handed over to the full rigours of the civil law. A further point also had to be taken into consideration: this was that the fourth century severities may have been part of an effort to reduce the incidence of homosexual prostitution, while Justinian's legislation was probably occasioned by contemporary natural disasters reminiscent of the fate of Sodom and Gomorrah. Yet while that much could be historically established, it was very difficult, Bailey discovered, to find substantial historical evidence for any very widespread persecution of homosexuals by means of these laws.

A similar absence of evidence for ecclesiastical obsession with and persecution of homosexuals emerged from Bailey's examination of the enactments of Pre-Reformation Church Councils and Synods. These bodies did of course sometimes condemn sodomy, as they condemned most other obvious sins: but the number of enactments specifically concerning it were few and far between, less than 100 in a 1000 year period; and the Church's overall aim continued to be rehabilitation through repentance, rather than punishment or persecution. The rules laid down to direct mediaeval confessors were admittedly very detailed in relation to the specific forms of penance required for the specific forms of male or female homosexual acts. But they were also very detailed in relation to other sins as well; and the fact that these rulebooks for confessors contained long lists of specific sins did not necessarily mean that these sins were frequently committed. Yet the assumption that 'ought not' implied 'was frequently' seemed to have lain behind much that had been written about the church's attitude to homosexuality. This assumption, similar to that which historians used to make about police statistics and the actual incidence of crimes, had thus produced, in Bailey's view, conclusions which were unreliable, misleading and often uncritically repeated. Clearly it was undeniable that some homosexuals, both in the Middle Ages and afterwards, had suffered the extreme penalty of the law; and clearly ecclesiastical opinion had helped to sustain the climate of public opinion in which this was possible. But equally clearly the Church, which was in many ways coterminous with society, could not alone be blamed. Nor was it plausible, assuming the proportion of homosexuals in the population to be no less than at present (although this assumption cannot be proved) to argue that the Church had singled them out for persecution.

The lack of differentiation between Church and society then had clearly confused the issue of the Church's historical record on the question of homosexuality and the law. But in the context of the Churches' mid-twentieth century discussion of this subject, the position was much clearer. In Britain at least, Church and State and the Churches and society were no longer coterminous: days when the ecclesiastical establishment could call upon the civil establishment to enforce its wishes were gone. When the Wolfenden Committee recommended that homosexual acts between consenting adult males should be removed from the sphere of the criminal law, therefore, the Churches by themselves had little hope of resisting this proposal. Nor for that matter did most of them want to. Bailey and his colleagues for example, observed that since such sinful and anti-social activities as prostitution, adultery, illegitimate parenthood and even female homosexuality were no longer punished by law, the continued legal ban on the homosexual acts of consenting adult males was obviously anomalous and anachronistic. For such reasons therefore the official representatives of the Church of England accepted the recommendations of the Wolfenden Report, as did those of the Roman Catholic and all but one of the other major Churches in Britain.

The one exception was the Church of Scotland. Both in 1958 and again in 1967 its General Assembly rejected the advice of its own specialist sub-committees, and refused to accept the conclusions of the Wolfenden Report. Its reasons for doing this were reminscent in many ways of Northcote's arguments, except that they were much less clearly expressed. But fundamentally the arguments of the Church of Scotland were those it normally used when any change in the law relating to sex or marriage was proposed. These were, first, that the law of a Christian country should reflect the general conclusions of Christian ethics, and second, that the proposed change was contrary to the consensus of public opinion.

On the second of these points the Church of Scotland may well have been correct. Its General Assembly was and is a body which represents a wide cross-section of Scottish opinion, and certainly many Scottish Members of Parliament were, for their own reasons, of a similar mind. Thus although the Wolfenden proposals were adopted by Parliament in 1967 the new law did not extend to Scotland. Curiously enough however, immediately after this the General Assembly reversed its position, and recommended in 1968 that the Scottish law should be brought into line with that of England. Part of the reason for this dramatic about-turn was no doubt the fact that the composition of the Assembly and of its committees changes from year to year. But it also had a good deal to do with the fact that a homosexual counselling service set up by the Church was simply not used by homosexuals after the 1967's Assembly's declaration that homosexual practices were unclean and decadent[14].

Whatever the reasons for this change in heart of the Scottish Church the position reached in 1968 has been adhered to since then, and a number of leading Scottish churchmen have been closely identified with the campaign for legal reform conducted by the homosexual Scottish Minorities Group. This does not of course mean that the Church of Scotland has ceased to regard homosexual acts as sinful: its representatives are often quick to point out that it does not 'condone' such practices. But by its involvement in the legal and pastoral aspects of the question it is being weaned away from the denunciatory attitudes of the past. In this situation, perhaps because it is a Protestant Church, there is a noticeable absence of the sort of theological language which might legitimate the Church's growing sympathy with homosexuals in terms acceptable to more Catholic thinkers. But this is part of the more general problem of theological articulation in the present age; and if this growing sympathy genuinely reflects a changing mood in Church and society alike, ways of articulating it more adequately may eventually be found.

## CONTEMPORARY THEOLOGICAL RETHINKING

During the last 10-15 years there have been a number of attempts to find theologically adequate ways of articulating the Church's sympathy with homosexuals. Both Protestant and Catholic writers have been involved, and in Britain a notable contribution was made by some members of the Society of Friends in *Towards a Quaker View of Sex* (1963)[5]. Much of the relevant literature has been reviewed by the American Methodist minister, H. Kimball-Jones, in his *Towards a Christian Understanding of the Homosexual* (1967)[16], which itself breaks some new ground.

Two major theologians who have given their attention to this subject are H. Thielicke and N. Pittenger. Thielicke, in *The Ethics of Sex* (1964) takes the view that the homosexual condition is a manifestation of that disorder on the human plane which reflects disorder in the relationship between man and God. As such it is a phenomenon like disease or pain which should be neither condemned nor idolised, but regarded as something with a questionable potential. Given this condition Thielicke believes that the homosexual has the possibility of relating to other men in an ethically responsible way. He is very guarded about how far this allows the further possibility of directly sexual relationships between homosexuals, and he stresses the magnitude of the difficulties confronting a homosexual who wishes both to express himself sexually and to be responsible ethically. But, although he points to sublimation as an alternative, Thielicke does not in the end entirely close the door on the possibility that physical homosexual relations between consenting adults may be conducted in a way which is acceptable to Christian ethics.

Thielicke's argument then represents a significant piece of theological rethinking. But although it reflects a genuine pastoral concern sadly lacking in the writings of many other theologians, it still somehow manages to convey the impression that Thielicke is, essentially, making concessions. To many homosexuals therefore his approach must probably seem paternalistic and slightly patronising, while to many conservative theologians, it must seem yet another example of the Christian deferring to his faith's cultured despisers.

*Time for Consent* (1967)[17] by the Cambridge theologian N. Pittenger, avoids these criticisms by a much more openly revisionist approach to theology and a much more open attitude towards homosexuals. Pittenger makes no pretence of defending the traditional view, and frankly admits that what is now known about homosexuality must change the Christian attitude to it. But this change, he believes, may well be the work of the Holy Spirit. The theological perspective in which Pittenger wishes to discuss homosexuality is based on the belief that man is created to be and is a lover, that as a lover man is frustrated and liable to distortion, and that as such man can be released to love as he is meant to love. This threefold belief, which is essentially nothing other than a restatement of the classical doctrines of Creation, Sin and Redemption, enables Pittenger to point out that the sinfulness of a sexual or any other act is determined not by its external aspects, but by its inner spirit and by the element of intentionality. All human beings of course are sinners in so far as all human loving can be twisted, distorted and frustrated, but in so far as human loving moves in the direction of its ultimate aim, which is the fulfillment of man's unfulfilled capacity for love in loving union with God through the love of God's creatures, the human aim is on the way to being realised. In Pittenger's view homosexual acts can be examples of this kind of loving, and he believes that many homosexual partners, like many married couples, aim at that permanence which characterises the partial but dynamic realisation of the human goal. For these reasons he argues on the one hand for a much franker acceptance of homosexuals within the Church, while on the other he proposes an ethic for homosexuals. In the latter Pittenger suggests that no one should assume that he is a homosexual without thoroughly questioning this, but that if he is a homosexual he should accept his condition without shame and be as good a homosexual as he can be, in the knowledge of God's love for him. Pittenger's homosexual ethic involves the further component of responsibility, which implies that homosexuals should be as careful as heterosexuals not to express their sexuality in ways which do not fulfill the goals of their humanity; and it asks the homosexual to develop close non-sexual as well as sexual relationships. If then the homosexual wishes to love another homosexual, he must decide for himself whether or not his desire is for mutuality and genuine affection, just as an ethically responsible heterosexual must. Pittenger believes that such an ethic is possible, because it is what very many homosexuals desire, despite the accumulated distortions of centuries of furtiveness.

Pittenger's views, it must be emphasised, are not those of many contemporary Christians, but they so faithfully reproduce in the modern context so many of Christianity's most profound insights that they cannot but be judged deeply Christian. As part of a general move in Western Christianity away from that traditional approach to sexuality whose banal and bourgeois spirit reminded the great Eastern theologian N. Berdyaev of nothing more than treatises on cattle breeding[18] it ought to be welcomed by Christian homosexuals and heterosexuals alike. But although it has been welcomed by some, it remains to be seen how far the middle ground of Christian believers will accept this new direction.

## PASTORAL IMPLICATIONS

The present uncertainty about the attitude to homosexuality of the Christian middle ground makes the question of the pastoral implications of the foregoing discussion a difficult one. In the narrow context of the counselling relationship the homosexual is probably more likely than hitherto to find the Christian priest or minister a sympathetic listener. That this is true of Catholics as well as Protestants is amply evidenced in a recent pamphlet by Fr. Michael Hollings on *The Pastoral Care of Homosexuals* (1972)[19]. But the homosexual cannot be sure of finding this, since many clergymen, however hard they may try to conceal this, are ill at ease with the subject. In the absence of any research on this point however, it is difficult to know just what the position in fact is, and informal soundings made by the present writer suggest that even those clergymen who have been deeply involved in the counselling of homosexuals have little more than local knowledge of the situation. The recent constitution of an organisation (Reach[20]) set up specifically for Christian homosexuals and other Christians concerned with the subject may however help to make matters somewhat clearer. But it is unlikely that this will happen unless many more homosexuals than at present identify themselves as such. And while those who have done so are to be applauded for their courage, perhaps only homosexuals themselves have the right to challenge the many others who choose, in the present climate, to preserve their anonymity.

Under these circumstances the homosexual who wishes for Christian counselling faces a difficult problem. Nor is he necessarily any more likely to find what he wants from a secular counsellor, whose professional training, by virtue of those of its very qualities which may prevent him from being overtly directive, may also prevent him from engaging his client on the deeper levels of spirituality. One way out of this difficulty of course is by making the observation that counselling is only a very small part of the pastoral function of the Church. The Church's true pastoral function lies in the interdependence of each of its members upon one another, through the common recognition of each other as God's sinful and redeemed creatures. How far this function is actually exercised is of course another question, but the various homosexual organisations, however unrepresentative they may be of homosexuals as a whole, have at least the right to require the Church to live up to its ideals, and insofar as some of these organisations are in fact doing this, the present situation is rather more open than it was.

The openness of the present situation however also raises difficulties for the Christian pastor or church member, since Christian homosexuals themselves interpret their condition very differently. The Christian Gay Liberationist is in a very different situation to the homosexual Conservative Evangelical. But the pastoral problems such differences occasion are not confined to the homosexual context, and can be resolved only through a deepening of spiritual awareness among Christians of all persuasions.

In conclusion then it can be said that while in practice the Church often fails to be the sort of accepting community in which a homosexual may find ways of coming to terms with the difficulties and opportunities of his nature, it does at least claim to aim to be a community of this sort. The Christian recognition of man as a sinful yet redeemed creature, as a lover frustrated yet set free, implies a community in which the homosexual, the celibate, the unmarried, and those who are married but childless, as well as widows, widowers and those who are divorced, each has in his or her own way a possibility, equal to that of married parents, of self-transcendence through loving, since in each case the ultimate goal of all these kinds of loving is the same God. In principle such a community neither idolises the conventional family nor regards it as the root of all evil; and thus it offers a way of overcoming the fears and suspicions often betrayed by groups which speak on behalf of sectional interests. No doubt such groups may be necessary for the achievement of limited political objectives. But in the long run it is intolerable that those whose relational potential is realised in one way should feel threatened by those whose relational potential is realised in another. If the Church's ideal offers a way of resolving this conflict, even if only in principle, then Christians and unbelievers alike have some responsibility for finding ways of implementing it. For insofar as they do not, many homosexuals seem condemned to an unending alternation between furtiveness and compulsive self-importance.

## REFERENCES

1  Bailey, D.S. (1955). *Homosexuality and the Western Christian Tradition*, (London: Longmans) *passim*.
2. *Vide:* Thomas, K. (1971). *Religion and the Decline of Magic*, 198 (London: Penguin Edtn. 1973)
3. von Rad, G. (1972). *Genesis*, 218 (London: S.C.M. Press)
4. Thielicke, H. (1964). *The Ethics of Sex*, 273 (London: James Clarke)
5. Scorer, C.G. (1966). *The Bible and Sex Ethics Today*, 121 (London: Tyndale Press)
6. Calvin, J. (1559). *Institutes of the Christian Religion*, (London: S.C.M. Press 1960 Edtn.): iv:xii:4; iii:iv:16; ii:viii:58.
   *Vide* also (1554). *Commentary on Genesis*, 497 (London: Banner of Truth Trust 1965 Edtn.)
7. Healey, E.F. (1956). *Medical Ethics*, 292 (Chicago: Loyola University Press)
8. Bailey, D.S. (Ed.) (1956). *Sexual Offenders and Social Punishment*, (London: Church Information Board) *passim*.
9. Northcote, H. (1906). *Christianity and Sex Problems*, 284 (Philadelphia: F.A. Davis 2nd 1923 Edtn.)
10. Gray, A.H. (1923). *Men, Women and God*, (London: S.C.M. Press) *passim*.
11. Weatherhead, L.D. (1931). *The Mastery of Sex through Psychology and Religion* London (S.C.M. Press 1959 Edtn.) pp. 122ff.
12. Barth, K. (1961). *Church Dogmatics III, 4*, p. 166 (Edinburgh : T. and T. Clark)
13. Häring, B. (1972). *Medical Ethics*, 184 (Slough : St. Paul Publications)
14. Church of Scotland (1958). *Reports to the General Assembly*, 416 (1967). *Reports to the General Assembly*, 511 (1968). *Reports to the General Assembly*, 391

15. Friends (1963). *Towards a Quaker View of Sex* (London : Friends Home Service Committee)

16. Kimball-Jones, H. (1967). *Towards a Christian Understanding of the Homosexual.* (London : S.C.M. Press)

17. Pittenger, N. (1967). *Time for Consent* (London : S.C.M. Press enlarged 1970 Edtn.)

18. Berdyaev, N. (1937). *The Destiny of Man,* 233 (London : Geoffrey Bles)

19. Hollings, M. (1972). *The Pastoral Care of Homosexuals* (Southend-on-Sea : Mayhew McCrimmon)

20. Reach, 27 Blackfriars Road, Salford, Lancashire, M3 7AQ

# 8

# Homosexuality and Venereal Disease

## A. J. King

## INTRODUCTORY REMARKS

The fact that homosexual practices can result in transmission of venereal disease has been known from time immemorial, but until recent years it has not been possible to form any reliable estimate of the extent of the problem. The public attitude of disgust and condemnation of these practices was such that most homosexuals were unwilling to disclose the sources of their infection, even to physicians whose advice they sought in the strictest confidence. It is said that homosexuals are usually able to recognise each other, presumably by minor peculiarities of appearance, habits and mannerisms; but the clinician has to be exceptionally experienced to acquire such knowledge. He recognises the effeminate individual and he may suspect inversion from tendencies in dress or hair styles, or from the use of perfumes or cosmetics. However, it is probably true that it is not usually possible to detect homosexual tendencies from a short interview and medical examination. Many male homosexuals are wholly masculine in appearance and behaviour. Clearly, the sites of infection may point to the probability of homosexual contact but this, too, can be misleading. For instance, the most infectious lesions of syphilis, the *condylomata lata* or syphilitic moist papules of the secondary stage, are found most commonly around the anus. They arise from blood-borne infection and not from direct contact; but if one or only a few are present they may be the only surface lesions of secondary syphilis and they are easily mistaken for primary lesions.

The hazards of venereal disease resulting from homosexual practices seem to be almost exclusive to males. Lesbians seem to run no special risks although, of course, infection is occasionally acquired by contact between two females. Webster[1] stated that male-to-male contact accounted for 25.4% of cases of venereal disease in men in the United States in 1968. Female-to-female contact accounted for only 1.6% of cases in women in the same year.

The discussion which follows is limited to the problem as it affects males, since the problem among females is believed to be small and has never really received detailed consideration.

The fact that homosexuals tend to keep together and to have clubs and associations has led to the suggestion that the diseases they communicate to each other are unlikely to spread to the general community, because the circle of exposure is closed. This is probably untrue. Some homosexuals practice both kinds of sexual activity and some promiscuous people who are not truly homosexual indulge in these practices for stimulation of a jaded sexual appetite. There are some who undertake homosexual activity for gain, but take their pleasures heterosexually.

It is important for the physician to know whether men suffering from venereal disease are homosexual because some of them require help with considerable problems other than the fact of infection, and because of the importance of persuading the patients to urge their infectious contacts to seek medical advice and so prevent further spread of infection. Fortunately there has been some change in public attitude to this problem in recent years, particularly since the Wolfenden Report of 1957 and the changes in the law that followed. Condemnation is less virulent and homosexuals who seek advice are much more ready to disclose their situation. There seems no doubt that estimates of the size of the problem have become increasingly more accurate during the past 25 years although the figures presented are more likely to be under- than over-estimated.

**The Extent of the Problem**

Harkness[2](1948) was one of the first to draw attention to the importance of homosexual practice in the spread of venereal disease. He described his experience with cases of anorectal gonorrhoea at St. Peter's Hospital and in practice, in London. Recent evidence of the high incidence of syphilis among practicing homosexuals has perhaps received special attention because of the low incidence of syphilis in the population generally. It may be that homosexuals have always been particularly liable to syphilitic infection because Harkness found that 60 (35%) of 168 men suffering from gonococcal proctitis had positive serological tests for syphilis.

Jefferiss[3](1956) reported that 8.4% of 1,000 male patients with gonorrhoea or early syphilis attending St. Mary's Hospital in London in 1954 admitted a recent homosexual contact. Nicol[4] (1960) found that 31% of patients attending St. Thomas's and St. Bartholomew's Hospitals with early syphilis in 1959 were homosexual. Of 37 homosexual patients with early syphilis, 12 admitted to being the active and 18 the passive partners. 7 practiced both forms of activity.

Mascall (1961) at St. Peter's and St. Paul's Hospital in the West End of London, reported that 53 (79%) of 67 men with early syphilis had acquired it by homosexual contact. Laird[6] (1962) in Manchester, found that in the period 1957 to 1961 17 (27.6%) of 62 male patients with early syphilis had acquired it homosexually.

Attention has often been drawn to the fact that some, and perhaps many, homosexuals are not aware that they run considerable risks of contracting venereal disease. They may then present to proctologists for advice when they have symptoms. The need for awareness of this problem in rectal clinics has been emphasised by Hollings[7] (1961) who described 65 cases of anorectal syphilis seen at St. Mark's Hospital in London between 1932 and 1960. Jefferiss[8] (1966), again at St. Mary's Hospital, reported that of 113 men suffering from infectious syphilis in 1961, 81 (72%) admitted homosexual exposure and were believed to have contracted the disease in this way. In the first 3 months of 1965, of a total of 1997 new male patients, 281 (14%) admitted homosexual contact. Of 50 cases of early syphilis, 31 (62%) and of 604 cases of gonorrhoea, 89 (14.7%) had resulted from homosexual contact.

Fluker[9] (1966) reported from the West London Hospital that in the first quarter of 1965 30 (73.2%) of the 41 men found to be suffering with infectious syphilis were homosexuals. The equivalent figures for gonorrhoea were 60 (19.3%) of 311 cases. At the West London Hospital there has been an active campaign since 1963 to encourage homosexuals to attend the department of venereology. Waugh[10] has recently described a prospective study of all patients attending that department with untreated early acquired syphilis in the 2 years January 1st 1970, to December 31st 1971. During the study 3400 new male homosexual patients were seen of whom 1337 had gonorrhoea, in the urethra in 630 cases and in the rectum in 707, and 190 had early syphilis. Of the latter, 172 described themselves as exclusively homosexual; 35 (20.4%) were exclusively active participants, 62 (36%) were usually passive and 75 (43.6%) adopted both roles. 18 of the patients described themselves as bisexual but had contracted syphilis as the result of homosexual contacts. The 190 cases of early syphilis acquired by homosexual contact amounted to 84.1% of the 226 cases of early syphilis in men treated during that period. 23 of the 172 men who were exclusively homosexual had acquired the infection abroad. Woodcock[11] (1971) at St. Mary's Hospital, stated that 68.5% of patients with early syphilis were either homosexual or bisexual. Oriel[12] (1971) found that in a period of 9 months 27 (6%) of the white homosexuals attending the V.D. department at St. Thomas's Hospital, London, had primary syphilis.

Some facts and figures have been given from Europe. Hartmann[13] (1955) in Copenhagen stated that ⅓ of men in that city found to be syphilis contacts were homosexuals and some of them were male prostitutes. Schuppli[14] (1962) stated that from 12 to 15% of cases of early syphilis in Zurich had been acquired homosexually. According to Schmidt, Hauge and Schønning[15] (1963) 13 (25%) of males attending the Rudolph Bergh Hospital in Copenhagen in 1961 were homosexuals. In Holland, Bijkerk[16] (1970) found that of 224 indigenous men with early syphilis attending up to 1967, 84 (38%) had acquired the infection homosexually. Racz[17] (1970) stated that the percentage of known male homosexuals among syphilitic patients in Budapest increased from 0 to 32% between 1965 and 1969. Presumably this was a matter of more careful enquiry and identification rather than a genuine increase in patients of this type. Ekström[18] (1970) stated that 12 of 100 males aged from 14 to 19 years reporting for treatment of venereal disease in Copenhagen had engaged in homosexual relations, most of them with more than 10 different partners. Laugier *et al.*[19] (1971) found that 11.9% of all patients, male and female, seen at the University clinic in Geneva were male homosexuals. They considered homosexuality to be more important than prostitution in the spread of syphilis in that city.

The most recent and most complete survey of this problem is a report[20] by the British Cooperative Clinical Group of the Medical Society for the Study of Venereal Diseases (1973). The study refers to the year 1971 and information was obtained from 176 V.D. clinics of which most were in England and the remainder in Scotland (13) and Wales (11).

TABLE 1    SYPHILIS

| Cooperative Clinical Group Investigation 1971. All Cases. | National Total | Included in Study | Per cent in Study |
|---|---|---|---|
| Primary and Secondary Syphilis | | | |
| ENGLAND | 921 | 830 | 90.1 |
| WALES | 42 | 42 | 100.0 |
| SCOTLAND | 54 | 52 | 96.3 |
| Total | 1017 | 924 | 90.9 |

Table 1 deals with the subject of primary and secondary syphilis in the year under review and shows the extent of the information supplied by the participants. 90.1% of the cases seen in English clinics, 100% of those in Wales and 96.3% of those in Scotland were included.

TABLE 2   GONORRHOEA

| Cooperative Clinical Group Investigation 1971. All Cases. | National Total | Included in Study | Per cent in Study |
|---|---|---|---|
| Gonorrhoea | | | |
| ENGLAND | 37,905 | 32,328 | 85.3 |
| WALES | 1,126 | 1,092 | 97.0 |
| SCOTLAND | 3,077 | 2,822 | 91.7 |
| Total | 42,108 | 36,242 | 86.1 |

Table 8.2 shows the equivalent figures for gonorrhoea, namely 85% for England, 97% for Wales and nearly 92% for Scotland.

TABLE 3      EARLY SYPHILIS

| Heterosexual and Homosexual Infections | Total | Penile Heterosexual | Penile Homosexual | Ano-Rectal | Total Homosexual No. | Per cent |
|---|---|---|---|---|---|---|
| ENGLAND | 830 | 449 | 168 | 213 | 381 | 45.9 |
| WALES | 42 | 38 | 1 | 3 | 4 | 9.5 |
| SCOTLAND | 52 | 45 | 3 | 4 | 7 | 13.5 |
| Total | 924 | 532 | 172 | 220 | 392 | 42.4 |

Returning to early syphilis, the evidence was that 46% of the infections in England were homosexually acquired, 9.5% in Wales and 13.5% in Scotland. The fact of the unwillingness of some patients to admit to homosexual activity has been discussed. It may or may not be true that they are less willing to make this disclosure in Wales, Scotland and in the English provinces than in London. It is probably true that many homosexuals seek private treatment if they are able to afford it.

The figures in Table 3 show that in Great Britain, unlike many other countries, infectious syphilis has been a small problem in recent years. It seems to be true that it might almost have reached vanishing point but for homosexual activity.

TABLE 4   GONORRHOEA

| Country | Total Infections | Penile Heterosexual | Penile Homosexual | Ano-Rectal | Total Homosexual No. | Per cent |
|---|---|---|---|---|---|---|
| ENGLAND | 32328 | 28938 | 1843 | 1547 | 3390 | 10.5 |
| WALES | 1092 | 1048 | 31 | 13 | 44 | 4.0 |
| SCOTLAND | 2822 | 2707 | 71 | 44 | 115 | 4.1 |
| Total | 36242 | 32693 | 1945 | 1604 | 3549 | 9.8 |

The collected figures for homosexually acquired gonorrhoea are shown in Table 4. The known cases, amounting to 3549, are by no means few but they are vastly outnumbered by those presumed to result from heterosexual activity. The figures for the 3 countries are shown. The combined percentage is 9.8.

**Geographical Distribution**

Like venereal disease in general, homosexually acquired venereal disease is a problem of urban areas and particularly big cities. There is evidence, however, that the distribution of these cases is uneven. Some details will be given of the large numbers of these cases found in the West End of London. On the other hand, King[21] (1962) at the London Hospital in the East End of London, found that of 35 men with infectious syphilis in 1961, only 5 (14%) admitted homosexual contact and were believed to have contracted the disease in this way. He thought it unlikely that there were fewer homosexuals in East London. The likely explanation was that they sought each other's company and their meeting places were in the West End. They probably sought advice at West End clinics where their friends might have attended for treatment and where perhaps other patients might be more tolerant of their idiosyncrasies. The Cooperative Group Report goes into this matter in considerable detail.

TABLE 5 SYPHILIS ACCORDING TO POPULATION

| Population | Total Infections | Total Homosexual | |
|---|---|---|---|
| | | No. | Per cent |
| 50 000 or less | 21 | 2 | 9.5 |
| 50 000-100 000 | 70 | 20 | 28.6 |
| 100 000-500 000 | 171 | 52 | 30.4 |
| 500 000 or more | 101 | 17 | 16.8 |
| London | 467 | 290 | 62.1 |
| Total | 830 | 381 | 45.9 |

In Table 8.5 the early syphilitic infections in England are related to the size of the towns and cities in which they occurred. As might be expected the number of infections declared to be homosexually acquired increased with the size of the population group and reached its peak in London. However, the figures for towns of 500 000 or more are relatively low—an anomaly for which there is no obvious explanation.

Table 8.6 shows the figures of infectious syphilis for London in more detail. It can be seen that the problem is mostly concentrated in 5 clinics in the West End, namely at the Middlesex Hospital, St. George's, St. Mary's, the West London and the Westminster. One quarter of the clinics in London saw more than 80% of the infections acquired homosexually.

TABLE 6 HOMOSEXUAL SYPHILIS
Concentration in West End of London

| | Clinics | Total Cases | Total Homosexual No. | Per cent |
|---|---|---|---|---|
| Total for London | 20 | 467 | 290 | 62.1 |
| West End Clinics | 5 | 322 | 236 | 73.3 |
| Other Clinics | 15 | 145 | 54 | 37.2 |
| Per cent West End Clinics | 25.0 | 69.0 | 81.4 | |

Table 8.7 shows the distribution of the total cases of gonorrhoea and those homosexually acquired according to populations. The same pattern appears as for syphilis with the same unexplained anomaly in respect of towns and cities of 500 000 inhabitants or more.

TABLE 7 GONORRHOEA ACCORDING TO POPULATION

| Population | Total Homosexual Infections | No. | Per cent |
|---|---|---|---|
| 50 000 or less | 1 102 | 57 | 5.2 |
| 50 000-100 000 | 3379 | 168 | 5.0 |
| 100 000-500 000 | 8852 | 495 | 5.6 |
| 500 000 or more | 6590 | 202 | 3.1 |
| London | 12405 | 2468 | 19.9 |
| Total | 32 328 | 3390 | 10.5 |

TABLE 8 HOMOSEXUAL GONORRHOEA
Concentration in West End of London

| | Clinics | Total Cases | Total Homosexual No. | Per cent |
|---|---|---|---|---|
| Total for London | 20 | 12405 | 2468 | 19.9 |
| West End Clinics | 5 | 7582 | 2095 | 27.6 |
| Other London Clinics | 15 | 4823 | 373 | 7.7 |
| Per cent West End Clinics | 25.0 | 61.1 | 84.9 | |

In Table 8.8 dealing with gonorrhoeal infection in London, the same concentration of homosexually acquired disease in 5 West End clinics is again evident.

## THE PATIENTS

As regards occupation, Jefferiss[3] in 1956 found among his homosexual patients those who described themselves as clerks, shop assistants, waiters and men employed in 'artistic' activities. Waugh's[10] findings were similar but with the addition of hairdressers and air stewards. 14% were professional men including churchmen, lawyers and doctors but school teachers and social workers were also included. Nevertheless, in both series unskilled, indoor workers formed the largest groups. Ages varied from 15 to 60 with a mean of 29.5 years.

Racz[7] in Budapest found that of his 496 male homosexual patients, 16% were in the catering industry; 12% were industrial workers and in this group the number of unskilled workers was nearly as high as that of skilled workers. However, it seemed that some homosexual prostitutes chose the designation of unskilled worker as a cover and these people wore good clothes which seemed unsuitable to the occupation they claimed. Their attitude and fastidious behaviour were also out of character. The number of theatre personnel was considerable and there was a large proportion of medical workers, not only male nurses and surgeon-assistants, but also many physicians. The percentage of travellers and transport workers was also high. 74 of the patients were married.

According to Willcox[22] (1970), at St. Mary's Hospital, homosexual practices were most common amongst patients born in the United Kingdom. They seemed to be less frequent among immigrants in general and least of all among West Indians. However, he[23] did find some homosexuals among West Indians.

Pedder[24] (1970) examined 40 patients referred from a V.D. clinic in London for psychiatric examination. There were 14 men with personality disorders, of whom 12 were homosexuals. In general these patients did not want or did not pursue the offer of psychiatric help. Wells and Schofield[25] (1972) in Glasgow administered the Eysenck Personality Inventory to 109 homosexual men successively presenting for treatment at special clinics for sexually transmitted diseases. It was found that the 'active'-'passive' classification based on symptoms and clinical signs yielded no distinguishable groups. Homosexuals attending special clinics as a group scored lower for extroversion than heterosexual males but, like them, were significantly more neurotic than the general population.

## THE DISEASES

### Syphilis

The lesions of infectious syphilis are highly variable wherever they occur but there is nothing characteristic, other than the site, about primary or secondary lesions found in the ano-rectal region. The important thing is to be aware of the possibility, to have what the Americans call 'a high index of suspicion', and to take the necessary steps to exclude this diagnosis with any doubtful lesion on the genitalia, in the ano-rectal region and, for that matter, elsewhere on the surface. The most satisfactory method of diagnosis is by dark-ground microscopy. Serum from an anal lesion should be taken before proctoscopy because the lubricant may invalidate the specimen. It is not always easy to distinguish *Treponema pallidum* from other spirochaetes which may be present in the area and an expert opinion is desirable. Serological tests are also essential. The ordinary reagin tests may be negative in the first 7-10 days after the appearance of the syphilitic chancre and if the tests are negative they should be repeated after a short interval. Positive results of these tests should always be confirmed by a specific test such as Fluorescent Antibody Test (F.T.A. Absorbed) which becomes positive very early in the course of primary syphilis.

A syphilitic chancre in the ano-rectal region may have to be diagnosed from an anal fissure, a thrombosed external pile, lesions due to Herpes virus Type 2, a squamous-cell carcinoma or Bowen's disease which is an intra-epithelial carcinoma which may precede the latter. Bowen's disease appears as an elevated irregular plaque covered with scales and it may present unchanged for several years. Biopsy may be required.

### Gonorrhoea

*Symptoms*

Ano-rectal gonorrhoea may be present without symptoms or perianal warts may be found. The warts are due to an associated viral infection and not to gonorrhoea. The term 'gonorrhoeal warts' is a misnomer. Perianal warts are often found with passive homosexuals but not every patient with warts round his anus is homosexual.

Occasionally gonococcal proctitis presents acutely with burning pain in the ano-rectum, tenesmus, pain on defaecation and blood and mucus in the stools. In less acute cases the patient may complain of moisture or irritation round the anus.

Complicating conditions such as perianal abscess, ischiorectal abscess or anal fissure occur only rarely.

These symptoms are summarised in Table 9

TABLE 9 ANO-RECTAL GONORRHOEA—SYMPTOMS

| (1) | No symptoms. |
|---|---|
| (2) | Perianal warts. |
| (3) | Acute onset (occasionally)—<br>Burning pain in ano-rectum.<br>Tenesmus. Pain on defaecation.<br>Blood and mucus in stools. |
| (4) | Less acute—<br>Moisture or irritation around anus. |
| (5) | Rare—<br>Associated perianal abscess,<br>ischiorectal abscess or, anal fissure. |

*Signs*—On proctoscopy the rectal wall is inflamed, oedamatous and bleeds easily. Pus or mucopus is usually evident on the surface of the mucosa. There may be streaks of pus. or mucopus in the columns of Morgagni. The mucous membrane may be infiltrated or eroded.

The signs are summarised in Table 10

TABLE 10 ANO-RECTAL GONORRHOEA—SIGNS

| | Detected on proctoscopy:- |
|---|---|
| (1) | Redness and oedema of rectal wall.<br>Bleeds easily. |
| (2) | Streaks of pus or mucopus, usually evident on<br>rectal wall and in columns of Morgagni. |
| (3) | May be infiltration or erosion of<br>mucous membrane. |

*Diagnosis*—This is clinched by identifying the organism in direct smear and culture. A selective medium (Thayer-Martin)[26,27] is available for this purpose. It incorporates antibacterial agents which inhibit normal inhabitants of the ano-rectum but not the gonococcus. The preparations concerned are vancomycin, which inhibits many Gram-positive organisms, sodium colistimethate, which inhibits many Gram-negative contaminants, but not *B. Proteus,* and nystatin which is effective against yeast-like organisms.

## Other Diseases
### Lymphogranuloma venereum
This is a disease of tropical and sub-tropical countries but it is found in

temperate climates and occurs occasionally in Great Britain. The ano-rectal complications occur after the lapse of years. They are more common in women than in men, probably as the result of direct spread of the infective process from the vagina to the rectum. Grace and Henry[28] (1940), who studied many cases at the New York Hospital, believed that ano-rectal involvement in males was commonly acquired by deposit of the causative organism, now regarded as a member of the *Chlamydia* group, upon the perianal region or the wall of the anal canal or rectum. It was, in fact, a hazard of homosexual practices. This view has been supported by Greaves[29] (1963).

The earliest symptom of the condition is bleeding from the anus, followed by purulent anal discharge. Proctoscopy may reveal proctitis, rectal ulceration or rectal stricture, or a combination of these findings. In late neglected cases there may be severe procto-colitis resembling ulcerative colitis. Fistula-in-ano, peri-rectal abcesses, recto-vesical and recto-vaginal fistulae may develop; tumour-like swellings may sometimes be seen at the anal orifice. Stricture formation is likely to cause rectal discharge and bleeding, associated with constipation. Later, complete obstruction may occur. Malignant changes have been described as a sequela.

*Diagnosis*—With late manifestations of lymphogranuloma venereum it is not usually possible to isolate the causative organism and reliance has to be placed on clinical appearances and accessory tests. The *Frei test* is an intradermal technique employing an antigen made from the causative organism grown in the yolk sacs of developing chick embryos. The test is performed by injecting 0.1 ml of such an antigen intradermally, usually in to the skin of one forearm, and 0.1 ml of control material made from normal yolk, into the other forearm. The test is read at 48 and 72 hours; the control should give no reaction. If the test is positive, a raised, red papule, at least 6 mm across and surrounded by a variable area of erythema, appears at the site of injection of the antigen. The positive intradermal test is obtained at varying intervals after the time of infection, but a positive result is to be expected with a late manifestation. Once reactivity is established it may persist for many years and perhaps for life.

The same specific antigen is used for a *complement-fixation test* on blood serum, and it is generally agreed that this is a more sensitive and reliable test than the intradermal reaction. There is cross-reaction with the organism of psittacosis, and an antigen made from that organism will give equally satisfactory results. The test is reported quantitatively, and a positive result in dilutions of the serum to 1 in 16 or above is usually taken to indicate the presence of active or recent infection with the organism.

There is often an alteration in the serum proteins in cases of lympho-granuloma venereum. This usually takes the form of hyper-proteinaemia with increase in the globulin fraction but normal or reduced albumen, giving reversal of the albumen-globulin ratio. Sonck[30] found an early rise in the level of immunoglobulins, especially IgA, in patients infected with the disease. This persisted with active infection and could be used to determine the efficacy of treatment over the longer term. The erythrocyte sedimentation rate is usually raised when active lesions of the disease are present.

*Perianal Warts*

These are, of course, infective epidermal tumours caused by a virus. Various types are described according to their morphological appearances. Those occurring on the genitalia and most of those occurring in the perianal area are hyperplastic pedunculated structures of the pointed or 'acuminate' type. Sexual transmission has not been proved although clinical experience suggests that it occurs. It often happens that sexual partners of these patients have no warts and it may be that some of them are asymptomatic carriers of the virus. On the other hand, the incubation periods seem to be long, according to Oriel[31] from 3 weeks to 8 months with an average of 2.8 months, so that sexual partners may have been examined before their warts develop. The experience is that perianal warts are more common in homosexual men who practice the passive role than in other men. Oriel[32] examined 72 men with anal warts attending a V.D. clinic. Sixty were practicing homosexuals and all of these admitted to anal coitus during the year before the warts appeared. Thus, it may be said that the presence of perianal warts should make the clinician consider the possibility of homosexual practice but it should not be regarded as pathognomonic.

*'Non-Specific' Genital Infection*

This condition, of which the cause has not been determined, is commonly manifested as a form of urethritis in the secretions from which no gonococci can be found. In the absence of a known specific cause the diagnosis is based on clinical appearances with the presence of an excess of polymorphonuclear leucocytes and no specific organisms in the secretions. The characteristic urethritis effects male homosexuals who adopt the active role and apparently they contract it as the result of anal intercourse. The signs of proctitis presumed to be due to this condition may be indeterminate but often there is clinical evidence of localised inflammation and mucopus on the surface of the anal canal and rectum with an excess of polymorphonuclear leucocytes on microscopical examination. A possible cause, an organism of the *Chlamydia* group (Sub-group A) sometimes called TRIC agent, has been isolated in a proportion of cases from the sites of each of the various manifestations of this disease, including the rectum in women. Whether it can be found in the ano-rectum in passive male homosexuals has not yet been determined.

The other sexually transmitted diseases do not present special features where homosexuals are involved. However, some recent reports have suggested that homosexual practices among men may be associated with an unusually high incidence of Australia (Hepatitis-Associated) antigen in the blood. Jeffries, *et al.*[33] tested for this antigen 1650 patients attending the venereal disease department of St. Mary's Hospital in London. They found 23 positive results (1.39%) which was more than 10 times the rate noted by others among blood donors in the UK and the USA. The highest rates were found among European male homosexual patients (11 out of 282 or 3.9%) and non-European heterosexual patients (8 out of 259 or 3.1%). The fact of a high incidence of Australia antigen among promiscuous people but especially practicing male homosexuals has been confirmed by Heathcote & Sherlock[34] and Fulford *et al.*[35].

## TREATMENT

### Syphilis

The treatment of early syphilis by modern methods is, of course, equally effective whether the initial lesion involves the ano-rectum or elsewhere. The matter does not require detailed consideration here but the methods in common use are shown in Table 11

TABLE 11    TREATMENT OF EARLY SYPHILIS

| | |
|---|---|
| (1) | Procaine penicillin (watery suspension). Single intramuscular injections of 600 000 units—daily for 10 days. |
| (2) | Procaine penicillin in oil with 2% aluminium monostearate (PAM). Intramuscular injections of 600 000 units daily or every 2-3 days. 10 injections. |
| (3) | Benzathine penicillin. Single intramuscular injection of 2.4 mega units or 2 injections of 1.2 mega units given at the same time. |

### Gonorrhoea

Treatment as for genital infection does usually prove effective. Some standard methods of treatment are shown in Table 12.

However, methods of treatment of gonorrhoea need constantly to be reviewed and adjustments are often required because of changing

TABLE 12    TREATMENT OF GONORRHOEA

| | |
|---|---|
| (1) | Procaine Penicillin (watery suspension). Single intramuscular injection of 2.4 mega units. |
| (2) | Ampicillin 1 g orally, together with probencid 1 g orally, given at the same time. |
| (3) | Fortified procaine penicillin. (3 mega units of aqueous procaine penicillin and 1 mega unit of crystalline penicillin G. given intramuscularly) with or without probenecid. |

sensitivity of the organism. Some doubts have been expressed as to the possibility of failure in cases of gonococcal proctitis, because of the production of penicillinase in the lower bowel or for other reasons. Scott and Stone[36] (1966) described 13 failures (43%) of treatment of 30 male patients with rectal gonorrhoea. They believed that the standard of dosage of penicillin at that time (600 000 units) was inadequate and increased the dosage to 2.5 mega units of Triplopen in these cases. Triplopen is a mixture of benethamine penicillin, 475 mg, procaine penicillin, 250 mg, and sodium penicillin, 300 mg in each single dose. Evans[37] (1966) treated 83 men suffering from gonococcal proctitis each with a single injection of 600 000 units of procaine penicillin. There were 17 failures (20.5%). He also treated 132 men suffering from gonococcal urethritis who stated that the infection was acquired homosexually, giving the same dose of procaine penicillin to each. There was thirteen failures (9.9%) and this failure rate was similar to that for all men with gonococcal urethritis treated with this dosage. As noted, it was less than half the failure rate in cases of proctitis. Fluker and Hewitt[38] reported failure of treatment in the cases of 26 of 96 patients (27.1%) suffering from rectal gonorrhoea, each of whom had been treated with a single injection of 1.8 mega units of procaine penicillin. In a similar group of 90 patients each treated with a single intramuscular injection of 2 g of kanamycin the proportion of failures was less, amounting to 14 (15.5%). Kanamycin is an effective remedy for gonorrhoea, but it has toxic effects and is unsuitable for the treatment of elderly patients or those with renal disease or impairment of hearing. Waugh[39] (1971) used cotrimoxazole, the combination of trimethoprim and sulphamethoxazole, 2 tablets night and morning for 7 days, in the treatment of 66 cases of gonococcal proctitis in men; he reported failure in 8 cases (12.1%). Holder *et al.*[40] (1972) claimed success in 14 of 15 cases of rectal gonorrhoea treated with single intramuscular injections each of 4 g of spectinomycin hydrochloride (Actinospectacin or Trobicin). This antibiotic was introduced some years ago and found to be effective and non-toxic. It was not generally adopted because it was expensive but now seems to be finding favour because penicillin is losing some of its efficacy in some parts of the world.

Briefly, then, the evidence is that larger doses of penicillin are required in the treatment of some cases of gonorrhoeal proctitis than of urogenital gonorrhoea. Kanamycin, cotrimoxazole and spectinomycin are known to be effective. Careful tests for cure are required and these should include cultures on a selective medium.

## Lymphogranuloma venereum

Treatment of this disease in its later stages presents difficulties and is less than satisfactory. It is customary to give sulphonamides because they appear to be effective in the early stages. It is best to give a soluble sulphonamide, such as sulphadimidine, and dosage may be 5 g daily in divided doses for 2 or 3 weeks. Alternatively, cotrimoxazole may be given in the dosage of 2 tablets twice a day for 10 days or more. Clinical improvement has been claimed from the treatment of the ano-rectal syndrome with sulphonamides but the beneficial effect may well be due to control of secondary infection. The same observation applies to the use of broad-spectrum antibiotics such as tetracycline which has been given in a dosage of 1 g every 6 hours by mouth for 7 days, or 500 mg| every 6 hours for 10 days. If response is indifferent it may be worth while to repeat the course after an inverval of 7 days without treatment.

Saad, De Gouvleia and Da Silva[40] (1962) used corticosteroids (pre-dnisolone, triamcinolone or dexamethasone) by mouth in the treatment of late cases of lymphogranuloma venereum, alone or in conjunction with sulphonamides or antibiotics. They noted improvement in some cases with diminution of anal discharge, relief of rectal and intestinal pain and lessening of constipation.

Surgical intervention is required in some cases, but should only be undertaken after adequate treatment with antibiotics. Patients with the ano-rectal syndrome may need regular dilatation of rectal strictures with bougies. Perianal and perirectal abscesses may require drainage. If the rectal obstruction is complete, colostomy may be necessary; in certain cases this may be followed by abdomino-perineal resection of the rectum, particularly when multiple perianal fistulae are present.

## Perianal warts

These require local treatment. If they are large cauliflower-like masses or if they are situated internally they should be destroyed by electro-cautery under anaesthaesia. For smaller warts the local application of podophyllin, 25% in spirit, or of saturated solution of trichloracetic acid is likely to be effective. Both preparations are damaging to normal skin which should be protected by petroleum jelly. Several applications may be required. Sometimes the warts recur but they respond well to further treatment along the same lines.

### 'Non-Specific' Proctitis
This condition usually responds well to tetracycline or oxytetracycline by mouth—250 mg every 6 hours for 2-3 weeks. Local treatment is unnecessary. Response to treatment should be checked by microscopical tests.

Thus, the venereal diseases constitute a considerable problem to practicing male homosexuals. Their detection requires a measure of awareness of the possibilities when the manifestations are seen elsewhere than in a V.D. clinic, as they often are. The patients themselves are often anxious troubled people who require sympathetic handling and all possible support.

## REFERENCES
1. Webster, B. (1970). Venereal Disease Control in the United States of America. *Brit. J. vener. Dis.,* **46,** 406
2. Harkness, A.H. (1948). Anorectal Gonorrhoea. *Proc. R. Soc. Med.,* **41,** 476
3. Jefferiss, F.J.G. (1956). Venereal Disease and the Homosexual. *Brit. J. vener. Dis.,* **32,** 17
4. Nicol, C.S. (1960). Homosexuality and Venereal Disease. *Practitioner,* **184,** 345
5. Mascall, N. (1961). Resurgence of V.D. *Brit. med. J.,* **1,** 899
6. Laird, S.M. (1962). Present Pattern of Early Syphilis in the Manchester Region. III. Homosexual Infections *Brit. J. vener. Dis.,* **38,** 82
7. Hollings, R.M. (1961). Syphilitic Ulcers of the Anus. *Proc. R. Soc. Med.,* **54,** 730
8. Jefferiss, F.J.G. (1966). Homosexually Acquired Venereal Diseases. *Brit. J. vener. Dis.,* **42,** 46
9. Fluker, J.L. (1966). Recent Trends in Homosexuality in West London. *Brit. J. vener. Dis.,* **42,** 48
10. Waugh, M.A. (1972). Studies on the Recent Epidemiology of Early Syphilis in West London. *Brit. J. vener. Dis.,* **48,** 534
11. Woodcock, K.R. (1971). Re-Appraising the Effect on Incubating Syphilis of Treatment for Gonorrhoea. *Brit. J. vener. Dis.,* **47,** 95
12. Oriel, J.D. (1971). Anal Warts and Anal Coitus. *Brit. vener. Dis.,* **47,** 373
13. Hartmann, G. (1955). An Epidemiological Study of the Import of

Syphilis into, Diffusion within and Export from a Major Seaport. Copenhagen. *WHO/VDT 137.* WHO Geneva

14. Schuppli, R. (1962). Über die Bekämpfung der Syphilis bei Homosexuellen. *Dermatologica (Basel),* **124,** 155

15. Schmidt, H., Hauge, L. and Schønning, L. (1963). Incidence of Homosexuals among Syphilitics. *Brit. J. vener. Dis.,* **39,** 264

16. Bijkerk, H. (1970). Incidence of Venereal Disease in the Netherlands. *Brit. J. vener. Dis.,* **46,** 247

17. Racz, I. (1970). Homosexuality among Syphilitic Patients. *Brit. J. vener. Dis.,* **46,** 117

18. Ekström, K. (1970). Patterns of Sexual Behaviour in Relation to Venereal Disease. *Brit. J. vener. Dis.,* **46,** 93

19. Laugier, P., Hunziker, N., Orusco, M., Brun, R., Grand, M.-L., Maillard, C., Bauquis, R. and Posternak, F. (1971). La Syphilis à Genéve au cours des deux dernieres années. Epidémiologie, Sérologie et Traitement. *Praxis (Bern),* **60,** 1628

20. British Co-operative Clinical Group (1973). Homosexuality and Venereal Disease in the United Kingdom. (Compiled by R.R. Willcox). *Brit. J. vener. Dis.,* **49,** 329

21. King, A.J. (1962). The Complications of Homosexuality (Introduction). *Proc. R. Soc. Med.,* **55,** 869

22. Willcox, R.R. (1970). Immigration and Venereal Disease in England and Wales. *Brit. J. vener. Dis.,* **46,** 412

23. Willcox, R.R. (1966). Immigration and venereal Disease in Great Britain. *Brit. J. vener. Dis.,* **42,** 225 V

24. Pedder, J.R. (1970). Psychiatric Referral of Patients in a V.D. Clinic. *Brit. J. vener. Dis.,* **46,** 54

25. Wells, B.W.P. and Schofield, C.B.S. (1972). Personality Characteristics of Homosexual Men suffering from Sexually Transmitted Diseases. *Brit. J. vener. Dis.,* **48,** 75

26. Thayer, J.D. and Martin, J.E. (Jr.) (1964). A Selective Medium for the cultivation of N. Gonorrhoeae and N. Meningitidis. *Publ. Hlth. Rep. (Wash.),* **79,** 49

27. Thayer, J.D. and Martin, J.E. (Jr.) (1966). Improved Medium Selective for Cultivation of N. Gonorrhoeae and N. Meningitidis. *Publ. Hlth. Rep. (Wash.),* **81,** 559

28. Grace, A.W. and Henry, G.W. (1940). The Mode of Acquisition of Lymphogranuloma Venereum of the Anorectal Type. *N.Y. State J. Med.,* **40,** 285

29. Greaves, A.B. (1963). The Frequency of Lymphogranuloma Venereum in Persons with Perirectal Abscesses, Fistulae in Ano, or Both with Particular Reference to the Relationship between

Perirectal Abscesses of Lymphogranulomatous origin in the Male and Inversion. *Bull, Wld. Hlth. Org.,* **29,** 797

30.  Sonck, C.E. (1972). Lymphogranuloma Inguinale. Klinische, epidemiologische und immunologische Aspekte. *Hautarzt,* **23,** 280

31.  Oriel, J.D. (1971). Natural History of Genital Warts. *Brit. J. vener. Dis.,* **47,** 1

32.  Oriel, J.D. (1971). Anal Warts and Anal Coitus *Brit. J. vener. Dis.,* **47,** 373

33.  Jeffries, D.J., James, W.H., Jefferiss, F.J.G., MacLeod, K.G. and Willcox, R.R. (1973). Australia (Hepatitis-Associated) Antigen in Patients attending a Venereal Disease Clinic. *Brit. med. J.,* **2,** 455

34.  Heathcote, J. and Sherlock, S. (1973). Spread of Acute Type-B. Hepatitis in London. *Lancet,* **i,** 1468

35.  Fulford, K.W.M., Dane, D.S., Catterall, R.D., Woof, R. and Denning, J.V. (1973). Australia Antigen and Antibody among Patients attending a Clinic for Sexually Transmitted Diseases. *Lancet,* **i,** 1470

36.  Scott, J. and Stone, A.H. (1966). Diagnosis of Rectal Gonorrhoea in Both Sexes using a Selective Culture Medium. *Brit. J. vener. Dis.,* **42,** 103

37.  Evans, A.J. (1966). Relapse of Gonorrhoea After Treatment with Pencillin or Streptomycin. *Brit. J. vener. Dis.,* **42,** 251

38.  Fluker J.L. and Hewitt, A. Boulton (1970). Kanamycin in the Treatment of Rectal Gonorrhoea. *Brit. J. vener. Dis.,* **46,** 454

39.  Waugh, M.A. (1971). Trimethoprim-Sulphamethoxazole (Septrin) in the Treatment of Rectal Gonorrhoea. *Brit. J. vener. Dis.,* **47,** 34

40.  Holder, W.R., Roberts, D.P., Duncan, W.C. and Knox, J.M. (1972). Spectinomycin Hydrochloride in the Treatment of Gonorrhoea in Homosexual Men. *Brit. J. vener. Dis.,* **48,** 274

41.  Saad, E.A., De Gouveia, O.F. and Da Silva, J.R. (1962). Treatment of lymphogranuloma venereum of the Anus Rectum and Colon with Glucocorticoids. *Amer. J. trop. Med. and Hyg.,* **11,** 108

# 9

# The Population Explosion and the Status of the Homosexual in Society

John A. Loraine*, Iain Chew+ and Tim Dyer+

1974 is a year which sees our planet beleaguered and beset with problems. The difficulties which mankind faces are of two types. The first category is global, and here the population crisis and the depletion of the earth's finite resources, as exemplified by current energy shortages, are the transcendent themes. The second category is personal, and within this area homosexuality, because of its relatively high incidence, its emotive overtones and its propensity to evoke bigotry and predjudice is undoubtedly an issue of considerable significance.

This chapter has two main sections. The first looks briefly at the world dilemma of overpopulation. Heterosexuality is its primary cause; yet it affects all world citizens whether they be homosexual or heterosexual in their orientation. The second section of the chapter is concerned with the difficulties encountered by the homosexual in society, and with popular misconceptions which still surround the condition.

The entire emphasis of this chapter is generalist rather than specialist, and it is intended for non-medical as well as for medical readers. As far as is possible, consideration is not given to topics dealt with elsewhere in this book.

*MRC External Scientific Staff, Department of Community Medicine, University of Edinburgh.
Chairman, Doctors and Overpopulation Group.
+Final year medical student, University of Edinburgh.

## OVERPOPULATION, THE SUPREME MALADY OF HETEROSEXUALITY

1974 was designated World Population Year by the United Nations Organisation. Its culmination was the World Population Conference held in Bucharest, Rumania from August 19th-30th. The conference was unique, for it was the first occasion on which population, the most politically charged issue of the last third of the 20th century, was brought into the arena of public debate. As at the Environmental Conference in Stockholm in 1972 Governmental representatives were present in Bucharest. In addition a large and highly disparate group of non-Governmental representatives attended and participated in the so-called 'Tribune' running *pari passu* with the inter-Governmental meetings.

Politicians faced a daunting task in Bucharest for by any standards the planet is grossly overpopulated[4] . By mid-1973 the world population stood at 3780 million[5]. it was growing at a rate of 2% per annum and was likely to double in a mere 35 years. At current rates of growth world population will reach 5000 million by 1985, and by the first decade of the 21st century we shall be attempting to support not far short of 8000 million people, more than double the figure of today.

In addition to being grossly overpopulated the world demonstrates an acute imbalance in its distribution of numbers. The great preponderance of people — over 70% at present and increasing relatively with the passage of time — occupy the Third World countries of Asia, Africa and Latin America. Between 1972 and 1973 Asians increased by 50 million, Africans by 10 million and Latin Americans by 8 million. Throughout the Third World the vast majority of the inhabitants are poor, underfed or downright starving[6]. More than 30% are unemployed[7]; vast numbers are underemployed. Health, medical and welfare services are grossly inadequate[8]. Illiteracy is on the increase, and a recent survey conducted by UNESCO reported that the number of illiterates in the world increased by 50 million between 1960 and 1970, the great majority of these illiterates being resident in the Third World.

Many countries of the Third World are highly male dominated and the male libido remains a prized possession. Admiration for it reaches it apogee in the Latin American *machismo,* the symbol of virility, but it is by no means denigrated elsewhere. Women continue to be regarded as second class citizens and have few opportunities to find fulfillment in careers other than marriage and childbearing. It is therefore not surprising that there is a huge excess of youth in the third World and that this constitutes a millstone round its neck. Indeed in many areas of the region over 40% of the population is under 15 years of age as compared with 30%

in North America and 25% in Europe. Amongst such young people the capacity for reproduction is enormous. Family planning programmes in the Third World with the notable exception of the People's Republic of China have either failed completely or have presented a lack-lustre image[2, 9, 10]. Furthermore, in many of the poor countries of the Third World abortion laws remain illiberal with the result that this highly effective form of birth control is denied to those most in need of it.

In the developed world procreative activity slowed between 1972 and 1973. In the USA the crude birth rate stood at 15.6 per 1000, and the annual rate of population growth was only 0.8%. Not even during the Great Economic Depression of the 1930s before the introduction of the Rooseveltian New Deal had the birth rate been so low, and even in 1936 it stood at 18 per 1000. In many other Western countries a similar trend was apparent, and in the Federal Republic of Germany, the German Democratic Republic, Luxembourg, Malta and the city states of East and West Berlin, death rates exceeded birth rates with the result that, if present trends continued, these areas will eventually suffer a net decline in population.

Heterosexual activities in Britain continued to give cause for anxiety. The UK, with a population density of 228 persons per square kilometre, remained the ninth most densely populated nation on earth, after Bangladesh, Taiwan, the Netherlands, Belgium, South Korea, Federal Germany, Japan and the Lebanon. But if England and Wales is considered as a separate geographical entity the situation was even less favourable. For this area with a population density of 323 persons per square kilometre is now third equal with the Netherlands in the over-populated league of nations, its population density being exceeded only by those of the newly established state of Bangladesh and of Taiwan.

However, there were some bright spots in the population scenario in Britain[9]. One of the most outstanding was the city of Sheffield. There during 1972/ 73 deaths exceeded births, the figure for the former being 6727 and the latter 6100. According to the Medical Officer of Health of that city, Dr Clifford Shaw, this highly significant result was obtained by the abolition of prescription charges for contraceptives, by increased education in the general field of population control and by ·a large expansion in local family planning services.

In late 1973 the Conservative Government appointed a Minister for Population Affairs in the person of Mr James Prior. Following the defeat of the Conservatives at the polls in February 1974 the incoming Labour adminstration appointed Lord Shepherd, Lord Privy Seal and Leader of the House of Lords, to this most important post. It behoves us to wish the new Population Minister well. For there can be no question that many of

Britain's formidable problems would be eased if numbers in these islands were smaller. Only by the introduction of a rational and effective population policy such as that outlined in a recent report [4] will such a desirable result be achieved.

## SOME SOCIO-MEDICAL ASPECTS OF HOMOSEXUALITY

### General Considerations

Homosexuals have been classified according to sexual roles, sexual preferences and sexual types. Any strict classification is obviously of limited value due to the complexity and diversity of human behaviour. Thus 'passive' and 'active' homosexuals have been described[12] even although sexual roles vary with any particular relationship and with different partners. Terman and Miles[13] used masculinity—femininity test scores and data obtained through interviews to compare 'active and 'passive' male homosexuals. They then compared both types of homosexuals with selected groups of heterosexual men and women and found that the femininity scores of the 'passive' homosexuals correlated with those of the female heterosexuals. Furthermore, they noted a correlation between the masculinity scores of the 'active' male homosexuals and the male heterosexuals. These observations suggest that a definite gender identity may exist in homosexuality leading to a gender role performance. On the other hand, there are reasons to believe that a classification based purely on sexual roles is inadequate because other factors such as ageing may play a part in determining whether the role of the individual is 'active' or 'passive'.

Kinsey and his associates[14,15] classified their sample according to overt sexual acts. The sample ranged from the exclusive homosexual through the facultative homosexual to the exclusive heterosexual. Such a classification has the disadvantage of suggesting that homosexuality is an 'all or none' phenomenon and fails to take into account that an individual does not necessarily become an exclusive homosexual merely by having a number of homosexual episodes in the course of his life.

Prototypes of the homosexual are rife. Effeminate male homosexuals are frequently described as are aggressive, so-called 'butch' lesbians[16,17]. The suggestions have been made firstly that such type-casting is a manifestation of the social milieu and conditioning, and secondly that it is the attitudes of society which drive the male homosexual to appear effeminate and the lesbian to assume aggressive and apparently dominant characteristics.

Indeed homosexuals are just as variable as heterosexuals in their attitudes, their ways of life and their orientation to society. Accordingly, no classification of homosexuals will be entirely satisfactory, for the condition is not one which readily lends itself to compartmentalisation.

Historically homosexuality dates back to Old Testament days, and the trials and tribulations visited on the homosexual throughout the ages are legion. Also there have been incessant wrangles about the aetiology of the condition[17-20] and in particular as to whether it is an inborn propensity or an acquired trait. These topics are dealt with elsewhere in this book.

## The social problem of homosexuality

Virtually everywhere society is dominated by men and is orientated towards heterosexuality. Gender identity and gender roles remain of great importance. Money and Ehrhardt[21] define gender identity as the sameness, unity and persistence of one's individuality as a male or a female in greater or lesser degree, the identity being expressed particularly in the facets of self-awareness and behaviour. They regard gender identity as the private experience of gender role and gender role as the public expression of gender identity.

On the basis of her studies on male and female roles in various groups of people Mead[22,23] has concluded that masculinity and femininity are arbitrary terms determined by any particular society. Karlen[24] has described the major masculine traits in present day Western society as aggression and competitiveness; he regards the main feminine traits as passivity and complacence. Mead considered that sex-role distinctions were basic to the organisation of society. She emphasised that every society had its norms and rules and noted that infringement of generally accepted social customs usually penalised the individual concerned. More recently Hoffman[16] has investigated sexual taboos in more detail, and has put forward the viewpoint that sexual norms are necessary for the smooth functioning of any society.

The man in the street still regards homosexuality as deviant and somehow wrong. This is largely because he is incapable of fitting it into his concept of normal sexual behaviour. Most people fear the unknown, for example they are generally afraid to die, and before homosexuality can be accepted by society a considerable degree of popular education will be required.

In the past homosexuality has been equated with evil and debauchery. Discrimination against homosexuals is still rampant although such discrimination is now more subtle than in days of yore. Often the problem of homosexual orientation first manifests itself within the family setting. A child recognises that his sexual aspirations are different from those of his brothers and sisters and finds it difficult to adapt to this situation. As a result an anxiety state and even grosser forms of mental illness may supervene.

Sexual experimentation is at its peak during adolescence. Then 'dating' of the opposite sex is the accepted pattern of activity, and the homosexual may discover that he does not share this *modus vivendi*. Often his parents do not help him or her because they are prisoners of their past and are tied to the conventional wisdom of society. In the offspring feelings of alienation are produced. Insecurity, loneliness and inadequacy are experienced; these feelings may become so severe that depression ensues and there may even be suicidal attempts[25].

There is still great fear of being suspected of a homosexual orientation[26,27]. The reason for such fear is easy to comprehend as homosexuality still remains a taboo in our society and conflicts with 'normal' social and cultural values. Fears of this type in the young homosexual can often be dispelled by psychiatric counselling and by providing the information that homosexuality is not an 'all-or-none' situation, homosexual episodes forming merely a segment of an existence which may become predominantly heterosexual in its orientation.

Many homosexuals, overwhelmed by the conformism of society, are prepared to erect a facade and to live an apparently 'normal' existence for social and economic reasons. Such individuals may marry and even have children; if they remain single they may occasionally 'date' members of the opposite sex. Many of the homosexuals who opt for marriage indulge in clandestine homosexual acts behind the heterosexual front. However, for obvious reasons the number of true homosexuals masquerading as heterosexuals is very difficult to determine.

To the homosexual conventional society must appear prejudiced, bigoted and inflexible. It inflicts on the homosexual a sustained trauma which for many is exceedingly difficult to bear. How can we wonder, therefore, that some homosexuals become exquisitely sensitive and chary of making normal human relationships for fear of non-acceptance? How can we wonder that other homosexuals compensate for their feelings of inferiority and inadequacy by showing to others a brazen and sometimes highly abrasive front?

## Male and female homosexuality in a male-dominated society

Throughout the developed world and in most of the underdeveloped countries the male is dominant and reigns supreme. In Western societies male homosexuality is frequently perceived as a threat to masculinity; the male homosexual is regarded as 'inferior', and his status approximates to that of a woman. However, with increasing and very welcome female emancipation the traditionally aggressive male role may now gradually become anachronistic[24]. Masculinity and lascivious pursuits indulged in by males may come to be accepted much less readily, and the emphasis of society towards male and female relationships may become more egalitarian in nature. Such a change in emphasis could well ease the path for the male homosexual.

Persecution of lesbians by society has never been as acute as has been the case for male homosexuals. Lesbians are fewer in number; they are tolerated better; they pose no threat; they are often regarded as eccentrics and objects of pity rather than targets for opprobrium. A male chauvinist — and there are still many in society — cannot comprehend how a relationship between two women could ever be as satisfying as his own heterosexual indulgences. Thus the masculine superego is protected and the conventional wisdom remains content.

Yet there exists in the world a group of people where the mores of society are quite different. This is the Tchambuli tribe of New Guinea[22]. Here the men are vain, emotional, dependent and flighty — just the description often applied to women by male chauvinists in Western societies. On the other hand, the Tchambuli females are aggressive, efficient and businesslike; they dominate their men folk and keep them under control. The studies in the Tchambuli tribe conducted by Mead[24] indicate that gender roles can to a great extent be learned and that masculinity and femininity are not necessarily related to dominance on the one hand and passivity on the other.

**Popular misconceptions about homosexuality**
Many of the public remain disgusted by the whole concept of homosexuality. To them it is unnatural, unorthodox and totally incomprehensible. And until quite recently figures in public life have done little to dispel such subjective and inappropriate emotions. Indeed in Britain less than two decades ago one of the then Conservative Government's Home Secretaries, Lord Kilmuir, took a certain relish in designating himself 'the hammer of the homosexuals' and was continuously denouncing the evils of 'sodomite societies' and 'buggery clubs'[28]. Fortunately, nowadays, the conventional wisdom has become less vociferous in its condemnation of the homosexual. Yet intransigence on the issue persists for, as mentioned previously, within the narrow conceptual horizon of the conformists, there is no room for the thought that a proportion of men and women actually prefer homosexual to heterosexual relationships and that they will persist in such activities in spite of the most strident calls to sexual orthodoxy. Indeed the conventional wisdom of society often seems incapable of judging a man or woman by parameters other than his sex life. Nor does it apparently ever contemplate the contributions to civilisation of avowed homosexuals such

as Leonardo da Vinci, Oscar Wilde, John Maynard Keynes and Ivor Novello.

Homosexuality is often confused with paedophilia. Yet there is no objective evidence to suggest that homosexuals are more likely to seduce young children than are heterosexuals[28-30]. This was an important point made in the Wolfenden Report of 1957. When homosexuals *do* attempt to seduce children it seems probable that the degree of violence used is less than that displayed by heterosexuals. Gibbens and Prince[31], in their study on sexual offences committed on children, point out that many of the latter were active participants in their seduction, being both sensuous and unduly precocious. Accordingly, the generally held belief in the naivety and innocence of the child subjected to seduction is probably unduly simplistic.

Many adults are uneasy in the presence of known or obvious homo-sexuals because they fear they will be seduced. Homosexuality has even been castigated as a 'disruptive factor in family life'. Yet this whole concept does not stand up to critical examination. For in adults seduction without coercion is rare, and at any rate, as already noted, homosexuals tend on average to be less violent than their heterosexual counterparts.

The populace believe that the entertainment world is riddled with homosexuals[32]. Whether this is true or not is still a matter for controversy. Green and Money[33] conducted longitudinal studies on 20 effeminate pre-pubertal boys. They found that a relatively high proportion of such individuals had a striking capacity for role-taking and stage acting. However, to equate such artistic talents with a propensity for homosex-uality is obviously a very dubious procedure. Certainly the entertainment world houses more flamboyant characters than does most other profes-sions, and homosexual attitudes in actors and actresses are more obvious to the public at large. Furthermore, liberal attitudes to sexual deviance are more prevalent and social norms less rigidly adhered to amongst enter-tainers. Hence, there is less reason for a homosexual to hide his natural proclivity.

The conventional wisdom of society throws up its hands in horror when marriage between homosexuals is mentioned. Yet why should this be so? For heterosexual marriages cannot be regarded as an advertisement for success as evidenced by the fact that at least 1 in 5 of them ends in divorce. The stability of homosexual unions has yet to be tested, but one would be doubtful if the overall record would be worse. A recent television programme presented by Alan Whicker (October 1973) discussed this question in some detail and showed considerable sympathy towards homosexuals. Indeed the mass media of communication have a vital role to play in destroying the shibboleths of the past and in disseminating progressive and liberal attitudes towards homosexuality.

## Concluding comment

The greatest of 20th century philosophers, Bertrand Russell[34], concluded the last volume of his autobiography with the following words:

'I have lived in the pursuit of a vision both personal and social. Personal, to care for what is noble, for what is beautiful, for what is gentle; to allow moments of insight to give wisdom at more mundane times. Social, to see in imagination the society which is to be created, where individuals grow freely and where hate and greed and envy die because there is nothing to nourish them'.

We should all strive to create the society so eloquently pictured by Bertrand Russell. For in such a society each of us — heterosexuals and homosexuals alike — will find a defree of tranquillity and fulfillment not vouchsafed to us in our present turbulent, prejudiced and bigoted universe.

## REFERENCES

1. Loraine, J.A. (1970). *Sex and the Population Crisis.* (London: Heinemann Medical Books)
2. Loraine, J.A. (1972). *The Death of Tomorrow.* Ch. 16. (London: Heinemann)
3. Ehrlich, P.R. and Ehrlich, A. (1972). *Population, Resources, Environment.* Second edition (San Francisco: W.H. Freeman and Co)
4. Population and Development (1974). The Role of Britain in World Population Year. Report of the Population Working Group of the United Kingdom Standing Conference on the Second United Nations Development Decade.
5. Population Reference Bureau (1973). World Population Data Sheet.
6. Population Reference Bureau (1974). February. The Demographic Express "World's 1974 Food Hopes Dim".
7. OXFAM Special Report (1974). Unemployment: the unnatural disaster.
8. World Development Movement (1974). Pamphlet on unemployment — *No jobs for the boys.*
9. Davis, Kingsley (1967). Science, **158,** 730
10. Davis, Kingsley (1973). Zero Population Growth: the goal and the means. *Daedalus,* Vol. 182 (Fall).
11. Guardian (1974). 30th March.
12. West, D.J. (1968). *Homosexuality.* Third edition. (London: Gerald Duckworth)

13. Terman, L. and Miles, C.C. (1936). *Sex and personality: studies in masculinity and femininity.* (New York: McGraw Hill)
14. Kinsey, A.C., Pomeroy, W.B. and Martin, C.E. (1948). *Sexual behaviour in the human male.* (Philadelphia: Saunders)
15. Kinsey, A.C., Pomeroy, W.B., Martin, C.E. and Gebhard, P.H. (1953). *Sexual behaviour in the human female.* (Philadelphia: Saunders)
16. Hoffman, M. (1968). *The gay world.* (New York: Basic Books)
17. Schur, T. (1972). Final report and background papers for the National Institute of Mental Health and Task Force on Homosexuality. (Livingquod, J.M., editor)
18. Ellis, H. (1928). *Studies in the psychology of sex.* Volume 1. (London: University Press)
19. Ellis, H. (1933). New introductory lectures on psychoanalysis. International Psychoanalytical Library, No. 24, London.
20. Freud, S. (1910). *Three contributions to the sexual theory.* New York.
21. Money, J. and Ehrhardt, A.A. (1972). *Man and woman, boy and girl.* (Baltimore and London: Johns Hopkins University Press)
22. Mead, M. (1935). *Sex and temperament in three primitive societies.* (London: Gollancz)
23. Mead, M. (1949). *Male and female.* (London: Gollancz)
24. Karlen, A. (1971). *Sexuality and homosexuality.* (Redwood Press)
25. Lambert, K. (1954). *Homosexuals.* Medical Press, No. 232.
26. Cory, D. (1960). *The homosexual in America.* (New York: Castle)
27. Cory, D. (1963). *The homosexual and his society, a view from within.* (New York: Citadel Press)
28. Loraine, J.A. (1972). *The Death of Tomorrow.* Ch.16 (London: Heinemann)
29. Toobert, S. (1959). *International Journal of Social Psychiatry,* **4,** 272
30. McGeorge, J. (1964). *Medicine, Science and Law,* **4,** 245
31. Gibbens, T.C.N. and Prince, J. (1963). *Child victims of sex offences.* Institute for the Study of Treatment of Delinquency, London.
32. Fenichel, O. (1946). *Psychoanalytical Quarterly,* **15.**
33. Green, R. and Money, J. (1966). *Archives of General Psychiatry,* **15.**
34. Russell, Bertrand(1969). *Autobiography,* Vol. 3, p. 223. (London: George Allen and Unwin.)

# Index

## ABOUT THE BOOK

The subject of homosexuality is both topical and complex. Its origins are multifactorial and its effects on social mores are becoming increasingly significant. Furthermore, society's attitudes to homosexuality are currently undergoing a rapid metamorphosis.

This book deals with both male and female homosexuality. It seeks to paint the canvas of the subject with a broad brush, and it has been fortunate in obtaining an outstanding series of contributions from a number of countries. There are chapters dealing with the aetiology of homosexuality in which psychological, biological and endocrinological factors receive consideration. Religious and legal aspects of homosexuality are reviewed and the current role of homophile organisations discussed. A chapter is included in which the relationship of homosexuality to the occurrence of venereal disease is described.

It is hoped that this book will interest individuals in a number of specialities and not merely members of the medical profession. The approach is intended to be interdisciplinary and the authors themselves are drawn from a wide spectrum of society.